Tense Future

Tense Future

MODERNISM, TOTAL WAR, ENCYCLOPEDIC FORM

Paul K. Saint-Amour

OXFORD

UNIVERSITY PRESS

OXFORD

UNIVERSITY PRESS

Oxford University Press is a department of the University of
Oxford. It furthers the University's objective of excellence in research,
scholarship, and education by publishing worldwide.

Oxford   New York
Auckland   Cape Town   Dar es Salaam   Hong Kong   Karachi
Kuala Lumpur   Madrid   Melbourne   Mexico City   Nairobi
New Delhi   Shanghai   Taipei   Toronto

With offices in
Argentina   Austria   Brazil   Chile   Czech Republic   France   Greece
Guatemala   Hungary   Italy   Japan   Poland   Portugal   Singapore
South Korea   Switzerland   Thailand   Turkey   Ukraine   Vietnam

Oxford is a registered trademark of Oxford University Press
in the UK and certain other countries.

Published in the United States of America by
Oxford University Press
198 Madison Avenue, New York, NY 10016

Library of Congress Cataloging-in-Publication Data
Saint-Amour, Paul K., author.
Tense future : modernism, total war, encyclopedic form / Paul K. Saint-Amour.
pages cm
Includes bibliographical references and index.
ISBN 978–0–19–020094–7 (cloth) — ISBN 978–0–19–020095–4 (pbk.) —
ISBN 978–0–19–020096–1 (updf)   1. Modernism (Literature)   2. War and literature.
3. War in literature.   I. Title.
PN56.M54S25 2015
809'.9112—dc23
2014024774

1 3 5 7 9 8 6 4 2
Printed in the United States of America
on acid-free paper

For my mother, Constance Saint-Amour
Never forgetting him that kept coming constantly so near

CONTENTS

Part Two

ACKNOWLEDGMENTS

When I started working on this book over a decade ago, I had no idea it would take up so much future. But then it started out, if you can believe it, as a cultural history of aerial perspective and took a long time to afflict me with a hunch about the traumatic uncanny, and longer still to become the place to which I trailed that frisson. That the intervening years were so much more absorbing than anxious I owe entirely to the family, friends, colleagues, and interlocutors who made the project a place worth staying in, to the point where it is oddly hard now to let it go.

I was supported at the earliest stages by fellowships from the American Council of Learned Societies and the Society for the Humanities at Cornell University. Dominick LaCapra was then director of the Society and introduced me to trauma studies. I was fortunate in the company and generosity of the other fellows, particularly Marlene Briggs, Joel Dinerstein, Neil Hertz, Simon Jarvis, Huda Mustafa, Gregory Shaya, and Mary Woods. We were all lucky that year to enjoy the administrative support and geniality of Mary Ahl, Linda Allen, and Lisa Patti.

Later on, fellowships from the Howard Foundation and the National Humanities Center enabled me to live with the project until it assumed something like its present shape. Exchanging chapters and ideas at the NHC with new friends Theresa Braunschneider, Peter Mallios, and Philip Rupprecht was one of that year's great pleasures. Another was the chance to discuss work with Scott Casper, Mark Fiege, and Mark Maslan. Catherine Gallagher ignited my interest in counterfactuals and has been a friend to the project and to me since then. My year in the Research Triangle would not have been the same without Mary Kinzie or Cara Robertson. Nor would it have been productive for any of us fellows without the Center's matchless librarians, Eliza Robertson, Betsy Dain, and Jean Houston. They were joined in their gift for generous provision by director Geoffrey Harpham, deputy director Kent Mullikin, and their colleagues Lois Whittington, Sarah Payne, Pat Schreiber, Bernice Patterson, Richard Schramm, Phillip Barron, Joel Elliott, and James Getkin. Thank goodness we caught the end of Corbett Capps's years in RTP, his pig pickin' and peach moonshine.

Work on this book has spanned two chapters of my institutional life. My colleagues in the Pomona College English Department—particularly Martha Andresen, Dan Birkholz, Ed Copeland, Kathleen Fitzpatrick, Rena Fraden,

Aaron Kunin, Paul Mann, Cris Miller, Sarah Raff, Arden Reed, Kyla Wazana Tompkins, Steve Young, and David Foster Wallace—were always ready with leads and readings and encouragement. Sam Yamashita told me, probably over monkfish liver, that he thought *bukimi* was important. And Gary Wilder convened a critical-theory reading group that sustained many of us. This book owes a great deal to his wide-ranging mind, and to his friendship.

I completed *Tense Future* at the University of Pennsylvania, with the support of a Weiler Fellowship. At Penn I've received input and feedback from many talented colleagues, including Rita Barnard, Karen Beckman, David Eng, Jim English, Michael Gamer, Amy Kaplan, Suvir Kaul, Ania Loomba, Heather Love, Josephine Park, Sharrona Pearl, Bob Perelman, and Chi-ming Yang. The members of my works-in-progress group—Barbara Fuchs, Kevin Platt, Emily Steiner, and Emily Wilson—were always incisive, unsparing only when I needed them to be. Participants in the Race and Empire group gave me helpful notes on chapter 1. The graduate students with whom I've had the privilege to work have afforded me all sorts of reasons to stay at the coal face, headlamp lit: my thanks to Beth Blum, Todd Carmody, Julia Dasbach, Scott Enderle, Nava EtShalom, Laura Finch, Devorah Fischler, Andy Gaedtke, Jess Hurley, Benjy Kahan, Jos Lavery, Cliff Mak, Melanie Micir, Daniel Morse, Kalyan Nadiminti, Václav Paris, Kelly Rich, Gabe Sessions, Sara Sligar, Philip Tsang, and Christine Woody. I'm particularly indebted to Beth, who, during a brief stint as my research assistant, gave the project an incommensurately big push.

I've been fortunate to be able to share and think through this work with colleagues at other institutions. I'm grateful for the friendship and hospitality of Marilyn Reizbaum and Aviva Briefel at Bowdoin; Jacques Khalip, Tamar Katz, Marc Redfield, and Ravit Reichman at Brown; Padma Rangarajan, Jane Garrity, Nan Goodman, Janice Ho, Laura Winkiel, and Sue Zemka at CU Boulder; Nico Israel at the CUNY Grad Center; Mary McGlynn and Darragh Martin at Columbia's Irish Studies Seminar; Ariela Freedman and Jason Camlot at Concordia; Jeremy Braddock, Aaron Rosenberg, and the other members of the Modernist Reading Group at Cornell; John Paul Riquelme, Matthew Wilson Smith, and participants in the Modernism Seminar at Harvard's Mahindra Humanities Center; Ann Fogarty and Luca Crispi at UCD's James Joyce Research Centre; Amanda Anderson, Frances Ferguson, and Daniel Stout, then at Johns Hopkins; Patrick Deer, Elaine Freedgood, and Catherine Robson at NYU; Tommy S. Davis, Murray Beja, Ellen Carol Jones, Stephen Kern, and Sebastian Knowles at OSU; Eric Hayot, Robert Caserio, Jonathan Eburne, and Janet Lyon at Penn State; Enda Duffy at UC Santa Barbara; Jane Elizabeth Dougherty and Ryan Netzley at SIU Carbondale; Erin Carlston, then at UNC, Chapel Hill; Hilary Schor at USC; Sean Latham and Carol Kealiher at Tulsa; Mark Wollaeger, Jennifer Fay, and Scott Juengel at Vanderbilt; and Sam Cross, Wai Chee Dimock, Amy Hungerford, Daniel Markovits, Justin Neuman, and Jessica Pressman at Yale's 20/21 Colloquium.

Each year I'm more aware how much I owe my undergraduate teachers, particularly Patricia Joplin, Langdon Hammer, Victor Luftig, and Mark Wollaeger. I hope they will recognize signs of their inspiration and good influence in these pages. Hilary Schor, whom I met only a little later, has kept me believing that this book would get finished—and that the time it took would be time it needed and deserved. One of the many ways she did this was by introducing me to Elaine Scarry, who inspires and challenges everyone who thinks about war and art. Two of the best Joyceans around, Bob Spoo and Margot Norris, befriended me early and have kindly supported my work ever since.

I feel lucky to share an academic generation with Doug Mao, Jesse Matz, Sarah Cole, Marian Eide, Victoria Rosner, Pericles Lewis, Rebecca Walkowitz, Priya Joshi, and Sharon Marcus; this book is better for the ongoing conversations I have with each of them and with their work. Genevieve Abravanel, Jessica Berman, Erin Carlston, Patrick Jagoda, and Jos Lavery all commented on chapters; so did the remarkable Kevin Dettmar, despite the wretched timing of my request. I'm grateful for their gifts of time and intelligence. Wendy Moffat shared her knowledge of British archives to help me confirm the sad absence of personal papers for L. E. O. Charlton, in whom we share an interest. I owe thanks to Michael Riordan at St. John's College, Oxford, and to my new colleague, J. C. Cloutier, for letting me geek out with them about Jenkinson's *Manual*, to which I was introduced by Connie Zhu back in 2007. Stacy Burton drew my attention to a remarkable passage in Rebecca West. Paul Statt shared his eleventh *Britannica*, and talked with me about Ford Madox Ford as we biked home from a string of near-wins at quizzo.

At Oxford University Press I've been favored to work with two editors who have advocated tirelessly for their authors, for academic freedom, and for scholarly access. Shannon McLachlan saw promise in this project when it was just starting to coalesce. With wit, bravura, and no-problemo assurance, Brendan O'Neill brought it home over all obstacles, including some of my making. At a crucial juncture, two anonymous readers for the Press offered detailed, constructive suggestions for the final phases of drafting and revision. Stephen Dodson, who keeps the wonderful Languagehat blog, copyedited with a keen and learned eye. And Jane Marsh Dieckmann tore herself away from late Brahms, gardening, and grandchildren to do one more matchless index.

Three friends have read and commented on virtually every word of this book, leaving deep imprints on it and on my thinking. Vincent Sherry read the whole manuscript for the Press in two installments and responded in reports that were humbling in their generous engagement with the project. That kind of response from so deep a thinker on war and modernism has been invaluable. Whether for dedicated summer writing weekends or in the middle of a semester, Eric Hayot bent his sensitive ear to my drafts, listening for energy, cadence, and argumentative gauge. In addition to helping me sharpen the book's claims and motivations, Eric helped me remember why we should love academic writing—largely through his infectious love of *thinking about* academic writing. If you know my colleague Jed Esty, you may also know what it's like to see, through his eyes, around the corners in your work to the prospects you didn't know were there. Half a dozen years of sharing work with Jed have only deepened my amazement at also getting to share a department with him.

Engagement with academic writing usually stops where family begins. But my father-in-law, Peter Buttenheim, started taking courses and clipping articles pertaining to this book long before I had chapters to give him, and when the latter finally came he actually *read* them. So, in at least two instances, did my mother-in-law and fellow Woolfian, Frances Buttenheim. When I was still thinking of the project in terms of verticality and optics, Toni O'Meara kindly translated an essay by Nadar for me. Jennifer Eremeeva inspired me by finishing her book first, and Renée Saint-Amour and Grant Coulter by living in the hugely openhearted way they do, and by giving us Ty and Quincy. My daughter Julia, like her little cousins, is too young to remember a time when I wasn't working on a book about dread, although her sister Claire isn't, and Francesca isn't. None of them knows how much, for me, their gaiety transfigures all that dread. But Alison knows, who knows so much, and is full of love.

Tense Future is dedicated to my mother. When she was two months old, she was held by *her* mother, Grace Lam Katsura, in a Honolulu bomb shelter during the attack on Pearl Harbor while my grandfather, Harry Katsura, participated in civil defense efforts outside. Like her parents, my mom has dedicated herself to the peaceful art of teaching, and to literature and music. She continues to show her students and her children—and now her grandchildren—not only *why* you always follow the frisson but *how*. And I write always remembering my father, David Saint-Amour, whose underage enlistment in the Marine Corps led him, happily, not to combat but to her.

Philadelphia
Summer 2014

The introduction draws on material published as "Bombing and the Symptom: Traumatic Earliness and the Nuclear Uncanny" in *diacritics* 30.4 (Winter 2000): 59–82 (published in 2002); "Queer Temporalities of the Nuclear Condition" in *Silence of Fallout: Nuclear Criticism in a Post-Cold War World*, edited by Michael Blouin, Morgan Shipley, and Jack Taylor (Newcastle-upon-Tyne, UK: Cambridge Scholars, 2013), 59–80; and "Air War Prophecy and Interwar Modernism," *Comparative Literature Studies* 42.2 (Spring 2005): 130–61, elements of which also appear in the first two chapters.

A shorter version of chapter 1 appeared as "On the Partiality of Total War" in *Critical Inquiry* 40.2 (Winter 2014): 420–49. Portions of chapter two appeared as "Gothic Temporality and Total War: Collins, Conrad, and Woolf" in *Gothic and Modernism: Essaying Dark Literary Modernity*, edited by John Paul Riquelme (Baltimore: Johns Hopkins University Press, 2008), 207–27. A section of chapter 4 appeared in "'The Imprevidibility of the Future': On Joycean Prophecy," *ReNascent Joyce*, edited by Sam Slote, Daniel Ferrer, and André Topia (Gainesville: University Press of Florida, 2013), 90–105. A partial version of the conclusion will appear as "Perpetual Interwar" in *Postmodern/ Postwar—And After*, edited by Jason Gladstone, Andrew Hoberek, and Daniel Worden (Iowa City: University of Iowa Press, 2015). I gratefully acknowledge permission to republish this material here.

Tense Future

Introduction

TRAUMATIC EARLINESS

The world has raised its whip; where will it descend?

—Virginia Woolf, *Mrs. Dalloway* (1925)

We also lack a history of the future tense.

—George Steiner, "The Great Ennui," *In Bluebeard's Castle* (1971)

anticipatory

Bukimi

Robert J. Lifton's pathbreaking work on the survivors of Hiroshima opens with a section called "Anticipation." A city leveled in a moment by a single, unknown weapon: anticipating such an experience is as hard to imagine as integrating it into the rest of one's life. In fact, the unassimilable nature of traumatic violence would seem to depend on the impossibility of its anticipation. Lifton implies as much: "Neither past experience nor immediate perceptions—the two sources of prior imagination—could encompass what was about to occur." Yet he also records an expectant, premonitory atmosphere in Hiroshima during the weeks before the bombing, a compound of past experience and immediate perceptions that, while it could not "encompass" the eventual experience of the bomb, cannot simply be dismissed as speculation that found an accidental correlate in the nuclear event.

Many used the Japanese word *bukimi*, meaning weird, ghastly, or unearthly, to describe Hiroshima's uneasy combination of continued good fortune and expectation of catastrophe. People remembered saying to one another, "Will it be tomorrow or the day after tomorrow?" One man described how, each night he was on air-raid watch, "I trembled with fear. . . . I would think, 'Tonight it will be Hiroshima.'" These "premonitions" were partly

japanese Book of short stories

attempts at psychic preparation, partly a form of "imagining the worst" as a magical way of warding off disaster.

While no one in Hiroshima knew ahead of time what would occur on August 6, 1945, many had noted the city's eerie exemption from conventional bombardment and speculated as to the reasons for it. During the summer of 1945, a series of rumors circulated in Hiroshima attributing the city's reprieve, variously, to its modest military and industrial significance; to the presence of prominent foreigners there, possibly including President Truman's mother; to important American prisoners-of-war supposedly held in the city; to the number of its citizens who had emigrated to the United States; to the large number of American spies supposedly living among its citizens; to its physical appeal in the eyes of Americans who had saved the city as a site for their postwar occupation villas; and, most wishfully, to the wartime miracle of a cartographic error: "We thought that perhaps the city of Hiroshima was not on the American maps."[1] Other inhabitants of the city feared that Hiroshima appeared all too prominently on U.S. maps, but had been reserved for "something unusually big"—perhaps the inundation of the city by floodwaters that could be released by the bombing of a massive upstream dam. Still others spoke of a "special bomb."[2] All these rumors responded to citizens' impression that their city had been in some way singled out, and the term *bukimi*—also meaning "ominous" or "uncanny"—spoke to the suspended question of whether Hiroshima and its inhabitants had been set aside for preservation or for annihilation.

The survivors who recollected their anticipatory *bukimi* years after the bombing may have retrospectively amplified their memories of weird expectation, perhaps as a way of attempting to master an incommensurable and singular event by installing it within a narrative of causality, continuity, even prophecy. Nonetheless, the *bukimi* experienced by inhabitants of Hiroshima should be understood neither as pure retrospection nor as groundless hunch, since it arose from a series of empirical observations later revealed to have had a single and coherent origin

---

[1] Robert J. Lifton, *Death in Life: Survivors of Hiroshima* (New York: Random House, 1967), 15–17. Many other accounts of the bombing mention both the eerie sense of expectation in Hiroshima before August 6 and the rumors that attempted to account for it. See John Hersey, *Hiroshima* (New York: Alfred A. Knopf, 1946), 4–5, 14; Toyofumi Ogura, *Letters from the End of the World: A Firsthand Account of the Bombing of Hiroshima*, trans. Kisaburo Murakami and Shigeru Fujii (Tokyo: Kodansha, 1997), 18; Fletcher Knebel and Charles W. Bailey, *No High Ground* (New York: Harper & Bros., 1960), 39–40; Joseph L. Marx, *Seven Hours to Zero* (New York: Putnam's, 1967), 158–59; The Pacific War Research Society, *The Day Man Lost: Hiroshima, 6 August 1945* (Tokyo: Kodansha, 1972), 220–23; Adrian Weale, ed., *Eye-Witness Hiroshima* (New York: Carroll & Graf, 1995), 147–48.

[2] Pacific War Research Society, *The Day Man Lost*, 220–22; Lifton, *Death in Life*, 17.

in U.S. strategy. By the summer of 1945, most Japanese cities whose size and military-industrial importance were similar to Hiroshima's had already been bombed with incendiaries; those who lived in Hiroshima had watched waves of American bombers fly past on their way to other targets, while the dozen or so bombs that had fallen accidentally on their own city had caused comparatively trivial damage.[3] Many assumed, of course, that the firebombing of Hiroshima was inevitable, and the military had already recruited a large civilian workforce to create firebreaks by demolishing tens of thousands of dwellings, preemptively destroying much more of the city than U.S. bombs had yet done. Strangely, though, when U.S. planes dropped leaflets listing the next twelve major cities destined for firebombing, Hiroshima—along with Kokura, Niigata, and Nagasaki—was absent from the list.[4] Together, those four cities made up the Allied list of reserved atomic targets.

The people of Hiroshima who experienced *bukimi* had detected the opening up of the conditional space of catastrophe—conditional because, despite the signs that informed its citizens' sense of uncanniness, Hiroshima might finally have been spared rather than razed if things had gone differently on the day of the drop.[5] In certain respects, the kind of conditional traumatic space that registered as *bukimi* was unique to human-made devastation, and particularly to early nuclear weapons. The careful sparing of atomic bomb target cities from conventional bombing bespoke U.S. military commanders' confidence in the destructive potential of the bomb and their desire to demonstrate that destructive power in the theater of relatively undamaged cities. Hiroshima's inhabitants strove to read the intention of the enemy in the signs that constituted their reprieve. Those signs, in a sense, had been returned from one of two futures: one culminating in the nonevent of preservation, the other in the limit event of catastrophe. When the limit event occurred, its survivors underwent a historically specific, unique traumatization. But in the period of eerie suspension before the explosion, those who registered the nuclear uncanny in Hiroshima were also the first to experience a condition that, in a more explicit form, would become familiar to everyone living in a targeted city under the Cold War doctrine of Mutual Assured Destruction: the sense that the present security and flourishing of the city were at once underwritten and radically threatened by its identity as a nuclear target.

---

[3] Knebel and Bailey, *No High Ground*, 39.

[4] Pacific War Research Society, *The Day Man Lost*, 215.

[5] This was actually the case with the second atomic bomb mission, whose primary target was the city of Kokura. When the plane carrying the bomb reached that city, smoke from a burning factory obscured the aiming point, and the crew opted instead to bomb the secondary target, Nagasaki.

The Precincts of Time

One didn't dare to inhale for fear of breathing it in. It was the sound of eighteen hundred airplanes approaching Hamburg from the south at an unimaginable height. We had already experienced two hundred or even more air raids, among them some very heavy ones, but this was something completely new. And yet there was an immediate recognition: this was what everyone had been waiting for, what had hung for months like a shadow over everything we did, making us weary. It was the end.[6]

Hans Erich Nossack's memoir, *The End: Hamburg 1943*, recalls the events of July 24 through August 3 of that year, an interval during which Allied bombers made six devastating air raids on the city in an operation code-named "Gomorrah." What would it mean, *The End* asks us, to recognize in "something completely new" the very thing one has spent months awaiting? How does a person come to expect the end, recognize it immediately when it arrives, and then live to write about it? In what relation to time does such a writer stand? Nossack and his wife, Misi, happened to be vacationing outside Hamburg when the raids began. On the night of the 24th, they woke to the sound of sirens, anti-aircraft fire, and engines; they watched from the porch of their rented cabin as the city was enveloped in smoke. Nossack's memoir describes what he saw during his return trips to the urban center between raids: charred victims of firestorms, crowds of bereaved and homeless citizens, the unrecognizable remains of the physical city. But even more than it is set in Hamburg's ruins, *The End* is set in the ruins of temporality. Refugees absorbed in the logistics of survival would suddenly abandon their chores to stand with other survivors and listen to their conjectures about how to get aid and restitution from the authorities. "To an uninvolved observer it must have looked as if we had a lot of time; but actually we were driven. We didn't have much time; indeed, we no longer had any time at all, we were outside of time. Everything we did immediately lost its meaning" (29). Too much time, too little, none at all: the familiar coordinates against which time's measure could be taken were gone. Even mourning, which had been possible after earlier, lighter raids, had become meaningless in the wake of Gomorrah: "What surrounded us did not remind us in any way of what was lost. It had nothing to do with it. It was something else, it was strangeness itself, it was the essentially not possible" (37).

---

[6] Hans Erich Nossack, *The End: Hamburg 1943*, trans. Joel Agee (Chicago: University of Chicago Press, 2004), 8. Further references are in the text. In "Air War and Literature," W. G. Sebald identifies Nossack as one of the few members of his generation to break the taboo on describing the firebombing of German cities, and *The End* as the only such account to eschew both epic conceits and Symbolist jargon in favor of "a steadfast gaze bent on reality." Sebald's essay is in his *On the Natural History of Destruction*, trans. Anthea Bell (New York: Random House, 2003), 11, 50–51.

Attempting to locate their home amid the ruins, Hans and Misi find "it was a detour": nothing survives but the dining-room radiator clinging to the one remaining wall (52). After offering a stunned *ubi sunt* over their lost belongings, however, *The End* records a more promising swerve from last things: "At the moment when we turn away from the ruins of our former home, there begins a path that leads beyond and away from the end" (59). Contrasting the survivors of Operation Gomorrah to "those that have been spared so far [and] are awaiting their hour with dread," Nossack writes, "For what we have gained and what has changed is this: We have become present. We have slipped away from the precincts of time." Yet if they have been released from the state of anticipation—of waiting to recognize the unprecedented should it arrive—still the present they have gained is not one of unbounded openness or hopefulness. In the final pages of his memoir, Nossack shifts into the mode of parable, personifying Time as a protective mother watching over her children. "Sometimes we fail to heed her call, because we were enriched by an object we had not previously recognized, and then she scolds us: How dreamy you all are." When the object that has become recognizable only amid the ruins shows itself to be a person, she instructs her children "not to keep going to that stranger. . . . He'll spoil you, and you won't amount to anything in life." One child replies, "Mother, you don't know him. He knows such beautiful games. He lives over there, where there are no more houses." After Mother Time returns to her chores, we learn the identity of the new playmate: the children who have slipped away from Time's precincts "have run back out on the street and are playing with Death. Now Time sits down sadly in a corner and feels useless" (61–63).

The worst raid's firestorms, on the night of July 27, killed many thousands of people, most of them women, children, and the elderly; altogether, the six raids left between 40,000 and 50,000 dead and leveled a third of the city's houses.[7] Nossack was unsure whether his status as survivor and spectator-at-a-distance was a privilege: "For me the city went to ruin as a whole, and my danger consisted in being overpowered by seeing and knowing the entirety of its fate." But privileged or not, he felt a mandate to set down what he had seen lest his mouth "remain closed forever": *The End* was written only three months after Operation Gomorrah (1–2). His memory of experiencing a sense of recognition that night of the first raid, then, would still have been fresh: "this was what everyone had been waiting for, what had hung for months like a shadow over everything we did, making us weary. It was the end." Yet one wonders: was his certainty that "the end" had come projected after the fact, as

[7] Death toll estimates for the raids on Hamburg in July 1943 vary widely. See Richard Overy, *The Bombers and the Bombed: Allied Air War Over Europe, 1940–1945* (New York: Viking, 2013), 260; Sven Lindqvist, *A History of Bombing*, trans. Linda Haverty Rugg (New York: New Press, 2001), 95; Robert A. Pape, *Bombing to Win: Air Power and Coercion in War* (Ithaca: Cornell University Press, 1996), 270.

a way of mastering an event without precedent or making sense of its bewildering aftermath? Even if Nossack did feel that sense of certain recognition at the time, was he assuming a worst-case scenario preventively, in the hopes he would be proved wrong? Or did he truly intuit, before the bombs began to fall on the first of six nights of raids, that the end had come? If so, hadn't he already slipped away from the precincts of time?

✢ 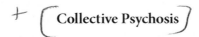 Collective Psychosis

> The sirens sound. Schoolchildren, factory hands, housewives, office workers, one and all don their gas masks. Whirring planes overhead lay down a blanket of protective smoke. Cellars open to receive their refugees. Red Cross stations to succor the stricken and the wounded are opened at improvised shelters: underground vaults yawn to receive the gold and securities of the banks: masked men in asbestos suits attempt to gather up the fallen incendiary bombs. Presently the anti-aircraft guns sputter. Fear vomits: poison crawls through the pores. Whether the attack is arranged or real, it produces similar psychological effects. Plainly, terrors more devastating and demoralizing than any known in the ancient jungle or cave have been re-introduced into modern urban existence. Panting, choking, spluttering, cringing, hating, the dweller in Megalopolis dies, by anticipation, a thousand deaths. Fear is thus fixed into routine: the constant anxiety over war produces by itself a collective psychosis comparable to that which active warfare might develop. Waves of fear and hatred rise in the metropolis and spread by means of the newspaper and the newsreel and the radio program to the most distant provinces.[8]

A year after the 1937 bombing of Guernica, five years before Operation Gomorrah, Lewis Mumford is describing a sequence of events in the war metropolis. An emergency, clearly, but for Mumford these events are more importantly a *routine*: the metropolis, in this account, is a space where the civil defense crisis has become ritualized, quotidian, a general rather than an exceptional case—the city as battlefield or trauma ward. Grimmer than this picture of emergency's routinization, more disturbing even than its primitivist take on urban terror, is Mumford's claim that "Whether the attack is arranged or real, it produces similar effects." The disaster that arrives and the disaster that might arrive have equal powers here to engender a "collective psychosis"; the real war and the rehearsal for war become psychotically indistinct, become nearly interchangeable backdrops before which the highly automated ritual of anticipation, dread, and mass traumatization unfolds. By refusing to identify the event he describes as real or as rehearsal, Mumford suspends his reader,

---

[8] Lewis Mumford, *The Culture of Cities* (New York: Harcourt Brace & Co., 1938), 275. Further references are in the text.

too, between the panic of the event and the panic of the drill that prepares for it, in the very space of future conditional anxiety inhabited by the war capital's citizens. There the reader experiences at the hands of Mumford's tightly regulated prose an attenuated version of what the citizen experiences in the air raid drill: "The materialization of a skillfully evoked nightmare" (275).

Entitled "A Brief Description of Hell," the section of *The Culture of Cities* that recounts the air raid alert does so in order to provide one example of a more general phenomenon: the assault on "all the higher activities of society" by what, masquerading as peacetime, is "equally a state of war: the passive war of propaganda, war-indoctrination, war-rehearsal: a preliminary maneuvering for position" (278, 275). This is a portrait of *total war*, an expression that indexes modern warfare's putative expansion beyond the battlefield to encompass a nation's every political, economic, and cultural domain. Despite being an urbanist, however, Mumford as he thinks about war and the city is less concerned with space than with time. Now even pre- and postwar periods will be belligerent; simulated and actual disasters will inflict equal psychic damage; and anticipation will be a condition in which one can "die a thousand deaths." For reasons he partly leaves us to infer, Mumford sees the air raid as typifying the war capital's violent temporality. Many of his contemporaries would single out the bomber's spatiality—its capacity to leap over conventional military fronts and strike the enemy's cities, the wild imprecision of its targeting—as its defining trait. But for Mumford, the violence most particular to the air raid arrives along the temporal vectors of preparation and expectation. What wounds is not expansion or extent but sequence: the series of protocols—sirens, searchlights, gas masks, scrambling, anti-aircraft guns, engines, bombs—whose terminus is the catastrophe. No longer a passive field within which violence unfolds, time—and anticipation in particular—has become a new medium for delivering injury. The concept of the front is implicitly transformed as well: not just enlarged spatially to include the city, but also redefined as a space that hosts a particular temporality. The front is anywhere futurity is attuned to imminent military force.

It is time to take seriously Mumford's suggestion that a collective syndrome might be instigated by expectation—that is, by the *eventuality* of a future-conditional war or attack as much as by the actual *event* of violence. Accordingly, this book is about the relationship between warfare and futurity. Delving into the prehistory of my three opening examples, it claims that early-twentieth-century military practices, particularly the aerial bombing of civilians and population centers, fundamentally altered the temporality of urban experience, turning cities and towns into spaces of rending anticipation. It goes on to argue that in the immediate wake of the First World War, the dread of another massive conflict saturated the Anglo-European imagination, amounting to a proleptic mass traumatization, a *pre*-traumatic stress syndrome whose symptoms arose in response to a potentially oncoming rather than an already realized catastrophe. Reading interwar fiction alongside contemporary works by air power theorists, international jurists, and civil defense writers, I show how the coercive psychodynamics of mass dread commonly associated with the Cold War emerged as a palpable threat during the 1920s, a decade we have long misrecognized as roaring only with postwar gaiety. During those years, I contend, the memory of one world war was already joined to the specter of a second, future one, framing the period in real time as an *interwar* era whose terminus in global conflict seemed, to many, foreordained. This apparent foreclosure of the future elicited dire responses: prophecies of social collapse, visions of the archive's effacement, and military theories that capitalized on both prospects. But it also produced kinds and intensities of critique that arise precisely when the future appears barred—radical defenses of childlessness and celibacy, for example, that took imminent war as the occasion for warding off the prospect of a politically and sexually retrograde peace. A *syndrome* is a complex of symptoms, etymologically a "running together" of signs. In describing an anticipatory syndrome between the wars, *Tense Future* attends to how doom and refusal run together, often within a single figure or work. It tells a story about concurrences: of the unthinkable with new ways and reasons to think; of writing's negation with its running riot.

The forms of conflict at issue here belong, in their scale and their transgression of limits, to the extreme category of total war. Modern war's apparent totality lay not just in the extent of its willingness to injure bodies and objects; it also targeted civilian workers' morale and psychic well-being through propaganda and, more engulfingly, through terror bombing campaigns. One of its chief means of causing psychological and emotional injury, this book suggests, was by weaponizing anticipation, making the future seem a predetermined site of catastrophic violence and therefore capable of inflicting damage in the present. Thus total war came to appear total in time, as it does in Mumford's portrait of the war capital.[9] Yet we will need to keep in

---

[9] In pursuing total war's complex address to futurity, I received an important early hint from Margot Norris's *Writing War in the Twentieth Century* (Charlottesville: University of Virginia Press, 2000). Norris observes that as the distinctions between soldier and civilian, front and home front, collapse in the Second World War, total war "takes on a temporal as well as an operational dimension, its effects perduring into the future, and into the lives of ensuing generations. In the case of nuclear war, the material and literal perdurance of injury—atomic weapons' effects on the intimate recesses of the body, on blood and genes, sexuality and reproduction, on the bodies and brains of children and grandchildren—symbolizes the ineradicable psychic and spiritual damage that survives all venues of total war" (32). Not *only* total war: the effects of "conventional" wars may also perdure into the future in a host of ways, not least through the far-reaching sequelae of combatants' physical, psychic, and spiritual damage. And even absent nuclear weapons, these sequelae may also be sexual, reproductive, and transgenerational. But Norris identifies a difference in scale and degree that begins to tilt toward a difference in kind.

mind that total war, for all that it was treated and experienced by millions of people as a fully realized phenomenon, was also massively influential as a complex of ideas and expressions in shifting fields of ideological force. So this book is equally about the emergence, limitations, and uses of the *discourse* of total war: about what that discourse excludes, what it occludes, and what kind of portrait it offers of which social totality. The dominant total war discourse during the twenties and thirties was exclusively metropolitan; by considering only conflicts between imperial nation-states to be "total," it rewrote the unlegislated violence those states were inflicting in colonial spaces as something else—as "small wars," "low-intensity conflicts," or "pacifications." A study of total war, then, must be a study of its partiality as an idea—of its prejudicial functions and its implications in an imperial world-system.

This book's second half is taken up with a particular genre of interwar modernist work that constitutes, by my reading, an indispensable counter-discourse to that of total war. This is a set of long, massively inclusive, formally striated fictions most commonly classified as "modern epics," a genre Franco Moretti associates with the period from 1800 to the present.[10] If we take epic to be the genre of organic national holism galvanized by war—a view shared, though with variations, by Hegel, Lukács, Benjamin, and Bakhtin—then, I maintain, we gravely misunderstand these long modernist works by considering them epics. To be sure, James Joyce's *Ulysses* (1922) and its most celebrated genre-mates—Ford Madox Ford's *Parade's End* tetralogy (1924–28) is my primary pairing with Joyce here[11]—are monumental works, seeking to capture a whole city or society within their pages. But the portraits they offer of their respective social totalities are neither as warlike nor as coherentist as epic's. In providing counter-portraits to the one offered by total war, I argue, these modernist works looked not to the epic but to the encyclopedia as a template. Substantiating this claim entails a long look at the eighteenth-century *Encyclopédie* of Diderot and d'Alembert, a project characterized by internal contradictions, deviant styles, a profound sense of arbitrariness and contingency, and an explicit dedication to warehousing Enlightenment knowledge against the possibility of its loss in war, revolution, or natural disaster. The *Encyclopédie* emerges in my account as an effaced but major precursor of these capacious interwar fictions, with their stylistic and technical polyphony, their complex orientation to time, and their provisioning against catastrophe.

---

[10] See Franco Moretti, *Modern Epic: The World System from Goethe to García Márquez*, trans. Quintin Hoare (London: Verso, 1996).

[11] One could add Marcel Proust's *À la recherche du temps perdu* (1913–27), Italo Svevo's *La coscienza di Zeno* (1923), Thomas Mann's *Der Zauberberg* (1924), Alfred Döblin's *Berlin Alexanderplatz* (1929), Robert Musil's *Der Mann ohne Eigenschaften* (1930–43), Hermann Broch's *Die Schlafwandler* (1931–32), and others.

By drawing them into a historically bounded genre, I aim neither to stabilize a canon of interwar encyclopedic novels nor to establish hard criteria for entry into such a canon. Instead, I offer a more focused alternative to the *longue-durée* genre of modern epic, which for Moretti is a creature of world economic systems and has nothing to say about world conflict systems. I understand epic as constellating war, form, and totality in a particular way— and encyclopedic fiction as departing most emphatically from epic in how it reconstellates the same terms. What emerges here is not a canon but a heuristic: a way of reading and studying works that exhibit different kinds and intensities of literary encyclopedism. At once symptoms of the anticipatory syndrome this book attempts to describe and powerful refusals of the totalizing war discourse that underlay it, the encyclopedic fictions of the twenties and thirties are ready to be placed among their century's most anxious, most arduous pacifisms.

Many of these works insist in various ways on their own singularity, as if they were the sole members of their literary species. I see this shared posture as part of what justifies their being read together here. Without conflating these highly idiosyncratic texts, I suggest we have a great deal to gain by reading them collectively back into an interwar moment traumatized by both a past conflagration and the prospect of a worse future one; marked by the rise of a totalizing war form that was inimical to internal contradiction, yet itself highly contradictory; and reflecting on the unprecedented proliferation and destruction of written records in modern war. Read together in this manner, the works in question respond to Leo Bersani's influential criticism of them for belittling both anxiety and historical trauma by claiming to offer aesthetic compensation for both. Such a criticism presumes that *Ulysses, Parade's End,* and the rest mean to pass themselves off as coherent surrogate worlds. *Tense Future* tells a different story: these works continue to fascinate us not because they offer a refuge from anxiety and history but because they are compounded of both, because their formal innovations bear the marks of past and possible wars as well as of perennial forms of violence, and because they are thoroughgoing vandals of their *own* totality-claims. In venturing the last of these, I hope to re-entangle two critiques of totalization that are currently wilting in isolation. One opposes baleful totalities (globalization, capitalism, and total war) with some more defensible counter-totality (*altermondialisme,* communism, and perpetual peace). The other opposes bad totalities through the partial, the local, and the fragmentary. My approach sees partiality and counter-totality not as discrete alternatives but as plaited into one another, dialectically enmeshed. A truly counter-totalizing work, I maintain, avows the partiality of its totality claims without renouncing them, taking up totalization under the sign of its impossibility. A truly partial work preserves a trace of the whole that it negates, thereby warning us not to misrecognize fragmentariness as a new and self-sufficient totality.

In reading encyclopedic modernism as intimately engaged with war, I am combining two columns of scholarship that have traditionally been kept separate. Partly owing to their scale, these sprawling fictions have produced criticism focused either on annotating them and mapping their composition or on developing their proximate contexts: metropolitan experience and media; gender, labor, and exchange; the history and politics of nation, colony, or empire. Major studies of literature and war in the period have meanwhile tended to dwell on writing "about" either the First or the Second World War, investigating how such writing (modernist and not) represents, commemorates, and formally registers the experience of war by individuals and collectivities, soldiers and civilians.[12] *Tense Future* builds on the growing body of work that breaks with these tendencies—scholarship that registers the ostensibly peacetime vibrations of war in the metropolis and expands our sense of what it means to write in a modernist temper "about" war. Among this latter group, Vincent Sherry's *The Great War and the Language of Modernism* has been especially important to me in reading wartime and interwar experimentalism not as representing the conflict in question but as a rejoinder to its enabling discourses—specifically, the British Liberal Party's bankrupt syllogisms about nation, war, and citizenship.[13] I have also benefited enormously from three titles outside modernist studies. Mary Favret's *War at a Distance* illuminates several continuities between the Napoleonic wars and the World Wars, even as it underscores the collapse of some of the distinctions between combatants and noncombatants in the latter conflicts. In a powerful chapter on "Duration," Kate McLoughlin's

---

[12] In lieu of a full survey of scholarship on literature and the First World War, I'll mention two revealing core samples. In its choice of foreground objects, Paul Fussell's *The Great War and Modern Memory* (New York: Oxford University Press, 1975) typifies the tightly constrained sense of what it means to write about the First World War, even as the book's peripheral vision is crammed with the kinds of oblique approaches that interest me. A more recent edited collection called *The Literature of the Great War Reconsidered: Beyond Modern Memory*, ed. Patrick J. Quinn and Steven Trout (New York: Palgrave, 2001), announces its intention to revise Fussell. It does this by usefully expanding the canon of Great War literature but sacrifices some of Fussell's peripheral sense of what it means to write about the Great War. In both cases, war writing crucially records or commemorates the event of war, reflecting only incidentally on what events or emerging conditions the past war portends.

For recent studies of modernism and the Second World War, see Marina MacKay, *Modernism and World War II* (Cambridge: Cambridge University Press, 2007); Patrick Deer, *Culture in Camouflage: War, Empire, and British Literature* (Cambridge: Cambridge University Press, 2009); and Leo Mellor, *Reading the Ruins: Modernism, Bombsites and British Culture* (Cambridge: Cambridge University Press, 2011). Mellor's book opens with a discussion of interwar depictions of a future war, but with a particular focus on the image of the ruined city rather than on the questions of temporality, totality, and literary form that draw me to the period. The center of gravity of all three of these studies is later than in mine; to the extent they associate late modernism with the "gathering storm" of the 1930s, *Tense Future* might be understood as an attempt to read the lateness of 1920s (conventionally "high") modernism.

[13] Vincent Sherry, *The Great War and the Language of Modernism* (New York: Oxford University Press, 2003).

Authoring War activates the varieties of temporality in war writing, particularly but not exclusively in the twentieth century. And Jan Mieszkowski's *Watching War* offers a deft analysis of how the concept of total war arises just as conflicts become so globally extensive as to be unwitnessable in their totality and are thus fully apprehensible only in fantasy.[14] I have been fortunate, too, to keep company with the likes of Sven Lindqvist, Roxanne Panchasi, Susan Grayzel, and Sarah Cole in attempting to make the interwar period's prophecy, foreboding, and anticipation safe for historicism.[15] I do not presume to speak for them when I add that such subjects should also, when given their full range and force of apprehension, make historicism unsafe to itself.

Returning to the three instances of uncanny trauma with which I began, I wish to note a few basic differences among them. Where most of the *hibakusha*—those who survived the atomic bombings of Hiroshima and Nagasaki—were physically injured victims of the nuclear event, Nossack describes the arrival of a disaster he witnessed from the sidelines, although his losses of property, domicile, and a sense of time's habitability may vex the distinction between witness and survivor. Whereas Nossack's sense of the unprecedented event's familiarity arrived with the event, the *bukimi* remembered by the survivors of Hiroshima responded to a specific absence or deferral of the disaster; it was a compound of fear and hope during a break in war's routine. Mumford, for his part, writes of "modern urban existence" in the abstract, although his portrait of the war metropolis attests to a familiarity with state-of-the-art civil defense practices while reactivating images of the bombed cities of the First World War and the Spanish Civil War. For all their differences, however, the *hibakusha* and Nossack and Mumford share a conviction that a total war catastrophe—either the catastrophe of the war itself or a catastrophic event during the war—is a foregone conclusion. Even in the *hibakusha* testimonies, the sense of relief at having been passed over on the nights before August 6 is overshadowed by the assumption that the unavoidable disaster has been simply and terribly delayed—that "tonight it will be Hiroshima." When the future appears foreclosed, anticipation loses its conditional relationship to that future: once seen as a fait accompli, a future event becomes a force in the

---

[14] Mary Favret, *War at a Distance: Romanticism and the Making of Modern Wartime* (Princeton: Princeton University Press, 2010); Kate McLoughlin, *Authoring War: The Literary Representation of War from the Iliad to Iraq* (Cambridge: Cambridge University Press, 2011); Jan Mieszkowski, *Watching War* (Stanford: Stanford University Press, 2012).

[15] Lindqvist, *A History of Bombing*; Roxanne Panchasi, *Future Tense: The Culture of Anticipation in France Between the Wars* (Ithaca: Cornell University Press, 2009), with whose notions of "pre-mourning" and "collective anticipation" (versus collective memory) my work is deeply sympathetic; Susan R. Grayzel, *At Home and Under Fire: Air Raids and Culture in Britain from the Great War to the Blitz* (Cambridge: Cambridge University Press, 2012), esp. chap. 4; and Sarah Cole, *At the Violet Hour: Modernism and Violence in England and Ireland* (New York: Oxford University Press, 2012).

present, producing effects in advance of its arrival. Thus the three instances share, too, a certain blurring of the line between anticipation and event, such that anticipation delivers some of the payload—in violence, or recognition, or both—of a still-future occurrence. The warning *is* the war; the drill and the raid are one.

To be clear: this evident foreclosure of the future was, to use Mumford's phrase, a "psychological effect" of total war as doctrine and practice, rather than a fact about futurity itself. This distinction between effect and fact is crucial. What I have called the anticipatory syndrome of the interwar period should be understood as a set of psychic and cultural responses to the First World War and its apparent legacy, not as proof that a second world war was inevitable. Nor should we misread the traumatic uncanny described by Nossack and the *hibakusha* as indicating that the bombings of Hamburg and Hiroshima were in any inescapable sense fated to occur. To make either of these mistakes would be to accept a determinist view of history, a move with profoundly troubling ethical and historiographic consequences. It would be, in essence, to contract a version of the syndrome this book attempts to describe. *Tense Future* is the story, then, of how metropolitan subjects under conditions of unbridled war, particularly of indiscriminate air war, *recognized* the future as foreclosed. Such a (mis)recognition—a sense that the self is futureless or the future worthless—is commonly listed by trauma theorists among post-traumatic symptoms. Without a doubt, the imminent raid or war can wound in advance the more deeply when it has past wounds to reopen. But to reduce these seeming foreclosures of the future to the remembered or repressed shocks of the past is to ignore what Mumford and Nossack and the *hibakusha* and numerous others we will encounter in this book are trying to tell us: that violence anticipated is violence already unleashed.

Facing Trauma

Tense Future: by now the meanings of my title should have begun to unfold, each word taking turns as noun and adjective. On the one hand, the grammatical future tense (the noun *tense* comes from the Latin *tempus*, "time"), a part of whose cultural history I will trace in relation to violence seen as oncoming. On the other hand, an anxious and even wounding sense of futurity, a tense future (the adjective *tense* comes from the Latin *tensus*, "stretched"). And pulled taut between the two, a sense of time stretched out of its usual modes, so that we must think historically about wounds preceding blows, about futures past, and about the tense prehistories of our own tense present.

As should also be apparent, this book is in dialogue with the field of trauma studies. Yet that dialogue is a tense one in both senses of the word, for according to the field's largely psychoanalytic chronology, the very notion

Freud

↓

of a *pre*-traumatic syndrome is practically nonsensical. According to Freud, one of trauma's foundational theorists, traumatic neuroses are initiated by experiences of shock or violence so extreme as to be unassimilable while they occur. Summing up the core paradigm of Freudian trauma studies, Geoffrey Hartman describes trauma as "registered rather than experienced. It seems to have bypassed perception and consciousness, and falls directly into the psyche," where its "exceptional presence" is bound up with the fact that it has not been fully or conventionally experienced.[16] Having arrived early—in advance of its capacity to be received and understood—the traumatic event makes its impact felt belatedly, often after a period of latency, via symptoms that can include the return of repressed memories and the compulsive repetition of behavior, gestures, dreams, and fantasies associated with the traumatic event. Those symptoms and the syndrome they constitute are thus emphatically and exclusively *post*-traumatic.[17]

What's more, this chronology works as both a recuperative and a normative standard in trauma studies. Freud noted that traumatic dreams and flashbacks differ from the norm in the literalness with which they replay the repressed event—in their seeming exemption from the distortive, encryptive operations of the psyche's dream-making faculties.[18] In part because of its insistently literal return, the traumatic past remains transgressively present as revenant, haunting, or possession, dominating the present rather than

---

[16] Geoffrey H. Hartman, "On Traumatic Knowledge and Literary Studies," *New Literary History* 26.3 (Summer 1995): 537.

[17] Clearly psychoanalysis, broadly understood, offers many instances of recursive, reverse, and proleptic temporalities. Slavoj Žižek's *The Sublime Object of Ideology* (London: Verso, 1989) has informed my thinking, particularly where Žižek elucidates Lacan's claim that the repressed returns, paradoxically, from the future. Symptoms, says Žižek, are "meaningless traces" whose meaning is "not . . . excavated from the hidden depths of the past, but constructed retroactively," such that the "effect" of the symptom precedes the "cause" of a traumatic framework subsequently symbolized through analysis (56–57). However, this itinerary is less preposterous than it sounds: Žižek's symptom is not precipitated by a future-conditional trauma; it simply awaits a moment of future analysis capable of installing it in a post-traumatic frame. Trauma studies tends to give even less quarter to preposterous traumatization than Žižek does. In her recent *Literature in the Ashes of History* (Baltimore: Johns Hopkins University Press, 2013), Cathy Caruth refers to "the question of futurity that lies not only at the heart of all trauma—as deferral and future repetition, as an attempted return that instead departs" (81). Such a futurity may host deferrals and repetitions of past traumas, but as a prospect it may not itself inflict trauma. Elsewhere Caruth suggests "the traumatic event *is* its future, is its repetition as something that returns but also returns to erase its past, returns as something other than what one could ever recognize" (87, original emphasis). This formulation comes nearer the traumatic recursivity of knowledge loss that we'll find in chapter 3, and nearer the return of the unprecedented that we encountered in the first pages of this introduction. Nonetheless, it persists in constructing the future as a container for the repetition of past traumas—one that holds "something missed, and about to return, a possibility, always, of a trauma *in* the future" (87, emphasis added)— rather than as a vector or agent of traumatization.

[18] See Sigmund Freud, *Beyond the Pleasure Principle*, trans. James Strachey (New York: Norton, 1961), 11, 37–38.

receding as it should into the past. According to the trauma studies model, the work of mourning, remembering, and working through should at least partially restore the pastness of the past and enable the survivor of trauma to reinvest in the present and the prospect of an unforeclosed future. For most trauma theorists, the stakes of this restored chronology are importantly ethical and political. Dominick LaCapra writes, "When the past becomes accessible to recall in memory, and when language functions to provide some measure of conscious control, critical distance, and perspective, one has begun the arduous process of working over and through the trauma in a fashion that . . . may enable processes of judgment and at least limited liability and ethically responsible agency." The critically tested historical narratives produced by collective memory-work, he adds, "contribut[e] to a cognitively and ethically responsible public sphere" and thereby help "make possible a legitimate democratic polity in the present and future."[19] For the individual and the collectivity alike, post-traumatic recovery and the capacity for ethical responsibility and political agency are measured by the degree of trauma's rechronologization—the reopening of the future via the past's resubordination to the present.

The basic psychoanalytic model I have sketched here has helped motivate important recuperative work, both for individuals suffering from post-traumatic stress disorder (PTSD) and for communities attempting to mourn, remember, and work through collective traumas—particularly, in the latter case, through restorative justice movements that engage the psychoanalytic model as an alternative to retributive forms of justice. For its part, trauma studies as an academic undertaking in the 1990s catalyzed new interdisciplinary alliances among the humanities, the humanistic social sciences, law, and medicine, while in its broader public manifestations it helped shape public discourses and cultural forms that addressed mass traumas, particularly the Nazi genocide. But since the turn of the millennium, trauma studies has been in a deepening shock of its own. It remains difficult to say conclusively why this is so. The early 2000s saw the publication of several influential critiques that, without entirely dismissing trauma theory, put skeptical pressure on some of its basic categories and ramifications.[20] Simultaneously, scholars in a range of fields—particularly queer theory, political theory, and postcolonial studies—were starting to explore more counterintuitive conceptions of time

---

[19] Dominick LaCapra, *Writing History, Writing Trauma* (Baltimore: Johns Hopkins University Press, 2001), 90, 91.

[20] I am thinking particularly of Ruth Leys's *Trauma: A Genealogy* (Chicago: University of Chicago Press, 2000), which traced trauma theory's historical oscillation between incompatible strains—what she calls *mimetic* and *diegetic* models—in Freud's work, and the collection *Loss: The Politics of Mourning*, ed. David L. Eng and David Kazanjian (Berkeley: University of California Press, 2003), which resisted trauma studies' central binarisms (melancholia vs. mourning, repetition vs. working through) and explored the politically generative potentials of loss and melancholia.

and ways of narrating history. By the light of these dissident temporalities, which I'll discuss in greater detail below, trauma theory's core chronology came to look conventional, even straitened—the more so given that many of these fields were arriving at their defamiliarized accounts of time through their own parallel engagements with psychoanalysis.

But perhaps even less assimilable by that field of study, at least in the United States, were the attacks of September 11, 2001, and their aftermath. In one sense, the attacks themselves—vast in scale, unanticipated, lacking a national precedent, afflicting their survivors with delayed symptoms— seemed to conform perfectly to the dominant model of trauma. This was the 9/11 that PTSD researchers in the hard sciences addressed through the massive studies of survivors they initiated five weeks after the attacks.[21] But the event played havoc with the premises of humanistic trauma studies. Far from overwhelming survivors and onlookers through its immediacy, it was ubiquitously mediated, most notably through images that seemed already to have appeared, everyone said, in dozens of Hollywood disaster and sci-fi films. This uncanny preemption—of an event by a mass culture that seemed, in retrospect, to have been rehearsing for it—was echoed in other registers, sometimes in preemptions of trauma studies itself. In President George W. Bush's declaration, just two months after the attacks, that "[T]he time for sympathy has now passed. The time for action has now arrived," the state seemed to usurp, even as it hastened, the calendrical understanding of collective mourning that trauma studies had labored hard to establish.[22] And in its color-coded terrorism threat advisory system, Homeland Security sought to do something for which a memory-oriented trauma studies paradigm had no receptor, but at which no First World War air raid warden would have blinked: ensure a citizenry's political docility during war by manipulating the expectation of violence. Partly because it had no way of reckoning with these uncanny loops, weird preemptions, and carefully administered threat levels, the humanistic wing of trauma studies went largely missing from the conversation about 9/11, the Patriot Act, Guantánamo, and the wars in Afghanistan and Iraq.[23] There is a dual need, I suggest, to take up the work trauma studies

---

[21] See, for example, H. Resnick, Sandro Galea, D. G. Kilpatrick, and D. Vlahov, "Epidemiology of Post-Traumatic Stress Disorder in the General Population after September 11 Attacks," *PTSD Research Quarterly* 15.1 (2004): 1–7, and R. Marshall and Sandro Galea, "Science for the Community: Mental Health after 9/11," *Journal of Clinical Psychiatry* 65 (2004, Supplement 1): 37–43.

[22] George W. Bush, Address to the United Nations General Assembly, November 10, 2001. The full paragraph reads: "After tragedy, there is a time for sympathy and condolence. And my country has been very grateful for both. The memorials and vigils around the world will not be forgotten, but the time for sympathy has now passed. The time for action has now arrived."

[23] A partial exception is Dominick LaCapra's "Toward a Critique of Violence," in *The Modernist Imagination: Intellectual History and Critical Theory Essays in Honor of Martin Jay*, ed. Warren Breckman, Peter E. Gordon, A. Dirk Moses, Samuel Moyn, and Elliott Neaman (New York: Berghahn, 2009), 210–41. LaCapra notes in passing that traumatization by 9/11 was almost compulsory if one was

left unfinished while at the same time subjecting it to an immanent critique, one that would consider what traits and biases left the field susceptible to being stymied in the post-9/11 world. *Tense Future* participates in that work by uncovering in both the interwar period and the Cold War something trauma studies conspicuously lacked at the turn of the millennium: an account of the traumatizing power of anticipation.

Among key interwar writings on trauma, Freud's *Beyond the Pleasure Principle* (1920) might have been just the one to link psychic wounding to anticipation. Ruminating there on the cases of shell shock or "war neurosis" that he had studied, Freud notes with puzzlement that symptoms sometimes appeared in the absence of physical injury—that the presence of an injury actually decreased the likelihood of traumatic neurosis, whose chief cause seemed to be fright. But he follows that observation with a taxonomy of responses to danger: *anxiety* is the expectation of or preparation for an unknown danger, *fear* the expectation of a known one, and *fright* what one experiences in the face of a danger one did not expect. "I do not believe anxiety can produce a traumatic neurosis," Freud then hazards. "There is something about anxiety that protects its subject against fright and so against fright-neuroses."[24] Later he elaborates: "preparation for anxiety" hypercathects (that is, libidinally hypercharges) the systems that receive the external shock, allowing them to bind and eventually dispose of the unwelcome stimulus that would otherwise have traumatized the subject.[25] His 1926 volume *Inhibitions, Symptoms, and Anxiety* goes the earlier text one better, insisting that traumatic neuroses, including war neuroses, result not from a fear of death but from a near-death event's reactivation of some "historical factor"

---

to be seen as "an American, or even a good person"—and that the event thus "brings out the way trauma may be both given a politicized and foundational, if not an apocalyptic, status and subjected to manipulation and self-interested use" (213). Significantly, two of the most discussed humanistic responses to 9/11 and its sequels, Judith Butler's *Precarious Life: The Powers of Mourning and Violence* (London: Verso, 2004) and *Frames of War: When Is Life Grievable* (London: Verso, 2009), used many of trauma studies' keywords without explicitly referring to the field. Butler's central question—how do particular kinds of lives get constructed as ungrievable?—is less interested in the psychodynamics of mourning than in mourning's ethico-political premises and ramifications.

[24] Freud, *Beyond the Pleasure Principle*, 11.

[25] This reading of anxiety as hypercharging the psyche's defensive shield produces in turn a revised understanding of dreams in patients suffering from traumatic neuroses. Rather than fulfilling unconscious wishes, dreams that repeat the scene of traumatization are attempting "to master the stimulus retrospectively, by developing the anxiety whose omission was the cause of the traumatic neurosis." In other words, the compulsively repetitive dreams of traumatized persons enact a kind of psychic revisionism, breaking into the archive of the past to plant a protective anxiety where originally there was only fright. That analeptic tampering lets the subject repeat the trauma but with a difference: *as if* with a protective shield charged by anxiety, and thus able to bind and eventually jettison the shock. Note the implicit play with moods and tenses. A repetition of the trauma in the subjunctive mood, *as if one were prepared*, leads to the disposal of the shock not in the simple future tense but in the future anterior—a future in which, thanks to those counterfactual dreams, one *will have been prepared* for the trauma.

in the subject's psychosexual past. Because "nothing resembling death can ever have been experienced," much less have left behind an intelligible trace, the psyche processes near-death experiences by analogy with earlier, more elementary object-losses: the fear of castration and, before that, the loss of the mother in birth, the site of the "earliest anxiety of all."[26] Even when confronting a scene of wartime violence in which the subject's annihilation seems imminent, Freud's metapsychology remains fixated on the subject's primordial past, recollected or repressed.

There is at least one interwar theory of the psyche whose gaze is fixed in the opposite direction. This is *Le temps vécu* [*Lived Time*], a study in phenomenology and psychopathology by the psychiatrist Eugène Minkowski. Born in Russia and educated in Munich, Minkowski was (like Freud's three sons) a First World War combatant, having enlisted in the French army in 1915. Although the earliest sketches toward *Lived Time* date from the war years (a chapter called "The Phenomenology of Death" was outlined during winter 1916–17, "in a calm sector of Aisne in a relatively comfortable shack"), the project gathered dust during the immediate postwar years for reasons about which Minkowski is movingly elliptical.[27] When the book finally appeared in 1933, that "long detour" had allowed it to both fully absorb and partly transcend its debts to the philosophy of Bergson and Husserl (8). *Lived Time* inverts the temporal priorities of "traditional psychology" (including Freud's work), which, Minkowski notes, "considers memory first of all. The future is thus considered to be only an image of the past projected in front of us." By contrast, his account of time as we live it demotes memory to a secondary place for the reason that it "remains necessarily *limited*, riveted to that which has actually been" (40). Because the vital force, *élan*, orients us in time, indeed pushes us, toward the future, *Lived Time* focuses its gaze on the future as well, asking in particular "How do we live the future?" (80). Lest this be mistaken for an attempt to foreknow or territorialize the future, Minkowski makes clear that foreknowledge, even if we could achieve it, would only impoverish the future by afflicting it with the condition of the past—that is, the condition of being subject to knowledge and memory because inert. "By nature, we are not prophets; and, if we were, if we could foresee everything, this could not

---

[26] Sigmund Freud, *Inhibitions, Symptoms, and Anxiety*, trans. Alix Strachey (New York: Norton, 1959), 57, 58, 66.

[27] In his introduction Minkowski writes, "During the war we were waiting for peace, hoping to take up again the life that we had abandoned. In reality, a new period began, a period of difficulties and deceptions, of setbacks and painful, often fruitless efforts to adapt oneself to new problems of existence. The calm propitious to philosophic thought was far from reborn. Long, arid, and somber years followed the war. My work lay dormant at the bottom of my drawer." After apologizing for the personal digression, he adds simply, "The war changed my life profoundly." Eugène Minkowski, *Lived Time: Phenomenological and Psychopathological Studies*, trans. Nancy Metzel (Evanston, IL: Northwestern University Press, 1970), 6–7; further references are in the text.

be omniscience, as we like to imagine. On the contrary, we would no longer experience the difference between the past and the future. Immobilized in our *élan*, we would find ourselves outside lived time" (41).

So far Minkowski's portrait of the future looks rosy, an open portal toward which the vector of *élan* points us, and through which progress and creativity enter. But *Lived Time*'s central chapter, "The Future," first sketched just after the Armistice, presents a more mixed account of futurity through its organizing typology of six phenomena: activity, expectation, desire, hope, prayer, and the ethical act. In activity we have the vital sense of traveling toward a future we are at every moment helping to create through our becoming. In expectation, activity's opposite, we are pinned in the high beams of a particular oncoming future; "we see the future come toward us and [we] wait for that (expected) future to become present."

> Expectation . . . englobes the whole living being, suspends his activity, and fixes him, anguished, in expectation. It contains a factor of brutal arrest and renders the individual breathless. One might say that the whole of becoming concentrated outside of the individual swoops down in a powerful and hostile mass, attempting to annihilate him; it is like an iceberg surging abruptly in front of the prow of a ship, which in an instant will smash fatally against it. Expectation penetrates the individual to his core, fills him with terror before this unknown and unexpected mass, which will engulf him in an instant. (87–88)

With its tableau of changeful forces massing above and rushing lethally down, Minkowski's description of expectation reads, says Stephen Kern, "like a phenomenology of life in the trenches" or (one might add) like a phenomenology of the air attack, at least until the passage invokes the prewar simile of iceberg and *Titanic*.[28] Despite expectation's many positive associations (with the coming of the Messiah; with good news, fortune, deliverance, transfiguration), in Minkowski's work it is always linked to unpleasure because it halts the open, vital movement of activity. He continues:

> Primary expectation is thus always connected to an intense anguish. It is always anxious expectation. This is not astonishing since it is a suspension of the activity which is life itself. Sometimes without any apparent reason the image of death, suspended in all its destructive power above us and approaching with giant steps, surges in us. Anguish and terror grip us. Powerless, we await the fatal annihilation close at hand, to which we

---

[28] Stephen Kern, *The Culture of Time and Space: 1880–1918* (Cambridge: Harvard University Press, 1983), 90. I came to Minkowski's book by way of Kern's, whose chapter "The Future" begins with a brief description of *Lived Time*. Panchasi also discusses *Lived Time* in *Future Tense*, 1–3.

Freud vs. Minkowski [margin annotation]

are condemned without mercy. In the presence of an imminent danger we wait, frozen in place as if paralyzed by terror. (88)

In Freud's work of the 1920s, anxious expectation in the face of danger protects one from traumatic neuroses. In *Lived Time*, such expectation *is* the traumatic site where the image of death outside us finds its counterpart in the death within us—where, as Caruth says of traumatic neurosis, "the outside has gone inside without mediation."[29] The heaving of that death-within pairs, for Minkowski, with the *future's* eclipse of the present ("the moment to come dominates the situation entirely" [89]). In Freud's account, traumatic neuroses manifest in the *past's* eclipse of the present and must be addressed through memory work that exposes the repressions of early psychosexual life. Facing in opposite temporal directions, the two psychopathologists stand back to back in the present, agreeing only that it is overshadowed by trauma.

Tense Future does not seek to apply Minkowski's work wholesale to the study of uncanny temporalities, total war discourse, or interwar modernism. But it does ask what a study of trauma might look like that could accommodate both Freudian and Minkowskian approaches; that could see in the experience of an apparently inescapable future, or of a wounding anticipation, something in addition to a symptom of past repression.[30] Such an approach to trauma would neither abjure the past nor abandon historicism, nor would it look to produce determinist anticipations of history. But it would take seriously the historicity of anticipation, specifically the mass-traumatic anticipation of violence, and insist that such anticipation be neither severed from nor reduced to the traumatic legacies of the past. Confronted with *bukimi*, it would frame that panic in relation to past chapters of the war while still attributing some of its elements to present-tense conditions of suspense in what would turn out to be a reserved target city. Faced with Mumford's claim of a "collective psychosis" of war anticipation, this approach would look to urban violence in the past, to the geopolitical suspense of Mumford's moment, and to the possibility that many of his contemporaries experienced that moment as eclipsed by the

---

[29] Cathy Caruth, *Unclaimed Experience: Trauma, Narrative, and History* (Baltimore: Johns Hopkins University Press, 1996), 59.

[30] As a small thought experiment in pairing these two approaches, imagine how Minkowski would reread Freud's account, in *Beyond the Pleasure Principle*, of *fort/da*. This was a game played by Freud's toddler grandson, who would toss a wooden reel out of his cot while saying "o-o-o-o" (which Freud understood as *fort*, "gone"), then joyfully retrieve the reel by its string while exclaiming, *da!* ("there!"). According to Freud, the child used the toy to restage his renunciation of instinctual attachment to his mother, mastering that unpleasurable past experience by repeating it in play. Rejecting this default to memory, Minkowski would read the child's game in a future-oriented manner—as, for instance, mastering *anxiety* through repetition, staging a prospective future loss in order to stage the ensuing recovery. Similarly, where Freud reads tragic drama as "artistic play" that turns unpleasure "into a subject to be recollected and worked over in the mind" (17), Minkowski would read tragedy by the light of the oncoming—as prayer, as warding off, as rehearsal.

violent future they saw looming. And, pondering a period *entre deux guerres*, it could imagine those who lived then apprehending themselves, without benefit of hindsight but not without neurosis, as dwelling in an interwar. Such an approach to trauma, which I attempt to model in the chapters that follow, would treat terms and phenomena such as prophecy, prolepsis, foresight, foreclosure, anticipation, and expectation in a fashion neither magical nor purely diagnostic: as modes, rather, of living *in* a particular present—and of living *toward* a future that seemed, for retraceable reasons, to be written in advance.

A moment ago I imagined Freud and Minkowski standing back-to-back in an interwar present, facing, respectively, the past and the future. The question of how one faces in time, and of how many times one may face, is a central one in this book. A central question, too, for one of *Tense Future*'s key interlocutors, the critical theorist Walter Benjamin. Having begun to describe my interest in how historical actors experienced the interwar period, in real time, *as* interwar, I'm mindful of Benjamin's critique of a historicism that aims to recognize the past "the way it really was." As Benjamin saw it, that approach often claims to sympathize with history's casualties but ends up sympathizing with the victors and with their counterparts in the present. For no sooner does such a historicism recover lost acts, experiences, and subjects than it reincorporates them into a progressive model of history, one that consecrates the violence of the rulers as law and forgets the barbarism involved in the production of their cultural treasures. Against this Whig historicism, Benjamin called for a historical materialism that would appropriate an image of the past "as it flashes up in a moment of danger" that "threatens both the content of the tradition and those who inherit it."[31] Rather than claim to retrieve the past "the way it really was" while actually serving ruling-class presentism, Benjamin's radical alternative "supplies a unique *experience with* the past" (396), constructing transtemporal encounters between the living historian and the historical actor—both of them historical subjects, and both endangered by power's conformism. Whence the question of how one faces in time. Conventional historicists, for Benjamin, may immerse themselves all they like in the past but always face that past's future—either their own present or the future that it self-flatteringly projects—and ratify its triumphalist view of history. The historical materialist, contrastingly, stays rooted in the precarious present but resolutely faces the past, refusing to countenance a future imagined by the rulers as consummating their aims, vindicating their acts, ratifying their laws.

---

[31] Walter Benjamin, "On the Concept of History," in *Selected Writings, Vol. 4: 1938–1940*, trans. Edmund Jephcott and others, ed. Howard Eiland and Michael W. Jennings (Cambridge, MA: Harvard University Press, 2003), 391.

Benjamin's meditations on the historian's temporal gaze produced one of the most haunting and most hotly debated passages in his work, the ninth thesis in "On the Concept of History," which he wrote less than a year after the start of the Second World War. The passage begins as a description of *Angelus Novus*, a 1920 drawing by the Swiss German artist Paul Klee:

> It shows an angel who seems about to move away from something he stares at. His eyes are wide, his mouth is open, his wings are spread. This is how the angel of history must look. His face is turned toward the past. Where a chain of events appears before *us*, *he* sees one single catastrophe, which keeps piling wreckage upon wreckage and hurls it at his feet. The angel would like to stay, awaken the dead, and make whole what has been smashed. But a storm is blowing from Paradise and has got caught in his wings; it is so strong that the angel can no longer close them. This storm drives him irresistibly into the future, to which his back is turned, while the pile of debris before him grows toward the sky. What we call progress is *this* storm. (392)

Benjamin's devastating allegory has provoked a vast range of questions in its readers. Is the angel an avatar of the historian, of the historian's divine other, or of history itself? In witnessing a catastrophe it cannot stay to redeem, does the angel figure a fruitlessly passive relationship to historical loss—or a vigilant refusal to let loss be chalked up to the cost of progress? Is the angel's helplessness in the storm of progress epitomized by its backwardness, or alleviated by it? Such questions have, in turn, prompted Benjamin's readers to imagine a variety of dissident historicisms—melancholic, backward, nonsynchronous, transtemporal, counterfactual—many of which belong to the "critical futurities" constellation I address in the next section.[32] Here, however, I wish to linger on the angel's face, turned, like the historical materialist's, toward the past. How does that one-way gaze unsettle a project like the present one—a project that constructs encounters between present and past moments of danger while also hoping to learn how historical actors experienced those past moments? And inasmuch as it locates part of history's catastrophe in futures past—that is, in past eras' assumptions and projections about futurity—how might such a project respond to Benjamin's tableau of the strictly backward gaze?

---

[32] Heather Love's *Feeling Backward: Loss and the Politics of Queer History* (Cambridge, MA: Harvard University Press, 2007) closes with a meditation on Benjamin's angel of history that traces some of its appearances in recent political theory and queer theory, particularly Wendy Brown's "Resisting Left Melancholy," in Eng and Kazanjian, eds., *Loss*, and Carla Freccero's *Queer/Early/Modern* (Durham, NC: Duke University Press, 2006). Love reads Benjamin's angel as standing apart from triumphalist histories, particularly post-Stonewall narratives of queer liberation—as a figure whose backwardness might be a prompt "to imagine and work toward an alternative form of politics that would make space for various forms of ruined subjectivity . . . a politics that allows for damage" (162).

If Benjamin's work could be said to offer a specific warning to a project like mine, it would be this: whatever anticipatory syndromes historical actors may have suffered are accessible to us only mediately, only discursively. To imagine otherwise is to risk assimilating their present to ours. If, however, we face the past's anxieties without the conceit of reliving them—if we try to touch its unique foreshudderings to those of our moment without forgetting that we construct the encounter between the two—we stand a chance of arriving at a future that is not just an extrapolation of present-day power. The temporal burden of Benjamin's angel-dialectics would be this: if the prospect of an unruined future can be reached at all, it is to be reached through an attempted retrogression, a return to ruins. But here the temporalities that guide this book's encounter with the past flash up in *their* uniqueness, posing questions of their own. What if, they ask, the debris left by the catastrophe of history were partly constituted of futures seen by the past as barred? What if certain retraceable structures of feeling in relation to futurity—*bukimi*, traumatic anxiety, collective psychoses of anticipation—were part of what injured history's casualties, part of their victimization? And what if some of the most trenchant critiques of violence we possess were mounted by those faced with a future they believed already lost to violence? In response, the angel of history would need, while facing the past, to bear witness to past apprehensions of the *future* as the disaster or the storm oncoming. This angel would be willing to look over the cold shoulder it gives to futurity, not to gaze in fealty at history's triumphant consummation but in the effort to catch dissident glimpses of the future—as otherwise, as retrograde, as null—that have since been consumed by progress. For Benjamin, the historical materialist's first task when faced with the barbarism inherent in cultural transmission is to dissociate herself from it as far as possible, "to brush history against the grain" (392). What I have described as a looking back from looking back—not at all the same as simply facing forward—uncovers a second task nested inside the first: to brush *futurity* against the grain.

Critical Futurities

Although dissident temporalities have yet to stir with much force in trauma studies, those winds have blown from other quarters in the humanities and social sciences. Together, they have begun ventilating the additive chronologism of which Benjamin was so critical, and to which the writing of history still defaults. This standard model favors linear, unidirectional narratives and divides history into periods that communicate minimally with one another, and then only with periods the model configures as "adjacent." It cleaves to what "did happen," indulging in counterfactual thinking only to underscore the decisive importance of some figure or event, not to cast lateral shadows on a given moment's contingencies. Because its notion of the past as fixed requires a concept of the future as contrastingly open, conventional historiography *analytically* ignores futurity, with the result that any *rhetorical* invocations of the future tend to replicate the ideologies embedded in that rhetoric. (President Bush, speaking in 2005 to the National Endowment for Democracy: "Because free peoples believe in the future, free peoples will own the future.")[33] A historiography uncritically premised on the future's openness pays scant attention to the shape of that opening, to the constraints on futurity's aperture. We need a loose rubric for work that applies skeptical pressure to reflexive invocations of the future. Call it *critical futurities*: scholarship that takes as its object past and present conscriptions of "the future," the rhetoric, poetics, and ideology of such conscriptions, and their ethical, political, and historiographic import. In its ambition to both describe and critique forestructured time, *Tense Future* has been shaped by many currents of thought in critical futurities. The three I discuss here have been indispensable: nuclear criticism, queer temporalities scholarship, and work that strives to reemplot or reactivate futures past.

Susan Sontag's 1965 essay "The Imagination of Disaster" offers a provocation: "Science fiction films are not about science. They are about disaster, which is one of the oldest subjects of art." In the course of discussing the "aesthetics of destruction" in Cold War science fiction films, Sontag ventures a traumatic referent for that aesthetics: "One gets the feeling, particularly in Japanese films but not only there, that a mass trauma exists over the use of nuclear weapons and the possibility of future nuclear wars. Most of the science fiction films bear witness to this trauma, and, in a way, attempt to exorcise it."[34] This formulation does not distinguish among the intense trauma of the *hibakusha*, the more attenuated national trauma experienced by non-*hibakusha* Japanese, and the worldwide response to the specter of nuclear war. One might observe, too, that the films in question likely did more to act out than to work through the trauma induced by the past nuclear bombing of cities or by the possibility of a future nuclear war. Still, Sontag's observation allows that certain traumatic responses to the use of nuclear weapons might not have been limited to the survivors of Hiroshima and Nagasaki, but rather shared by all who knew of nuclear weapons, their devastating effects, and the escalating likelihood of their use. In this, she seems to have been among the first to posit what we might call the hysteron proteron of the nuclear balance of terror: the sequentially inverted or *preposterous* phenomenon of traumatic symptoms—denial, dissociation, fragmentation, repression, the compulsive

---

[33] President George W. Bush, Speech at the National Endowment for Democracy, October 6, 2005.
[34] Susan Sontag, "The Imagination of Disaster" (1965), rpt. in *Against Interpretation* (New York: Farrar, Straus, and Giroux, 1966), 213, 219.

repetition of violence—that exist not in the wake of a past event, but in the shadow of a future one.

In the mid-1980s, a group of poststructuralist literary theorists attempted to grapple directly with the nuclear condition, including the preposterous temporality that Sontag had assigned to it. The nuclear criticism's inaugural statement was also its most compelling: Jacques Derrida's "No Apocalypse, Not Now (full speed ahead, seven missives, seven missiles)," written in 1984 for the group's founding colloquium at Cornell University and published that year in a special issue of *diacritics*. The seven missives in the essay's title refer to the prophetic and admonitory letters John sends to seven Christian churches in the Book of Revelation. Their doubling as "missiles" invokes another, faster kind of sending and occasions a series of claims about the speeds at which nuclear criticism must travel in relation to its object, and about the competence of scholars in the humanities to write about a form of conflict that has so far remained purely discursive. At the essay's core is a meditation on how literature, the archive, and mourning need to be rethought in relation to the nuclear condition. Individual deaths, says Derrida, "may always give rise to a symbolic work of mourning, with memory, compensation, internalization, idealization, displacement, and so on." This is not to diminish the catastrophe of every individual death, for which, he declares, "there is no common measure adequate to persuade me that a personal mourning is less serious than a nuclear war. But the burden of every death can be assumed symbolically by a culture and a social memory." What sets the nuclear condition apart, he continues, is not the number of individual deaths it threatens to bring about but the prospect of an irreversible annihilation of "the entire archive and all symbolic capacity," the "absolute effacement of any possible trace."[35] Were the symbolic order itself to be thus destroyed, mourning and commemoration could no longer meaningfully occur even if the nuclear catastrophe left survivors. The eerie implication: that by negating the possibility of a symbolic aftermath, the nuclear condition afflicts humanity with a case of anticipatory mourning, a mourning in advance of loss because the loss to come would nullify the very possibility of the trace. This is Sontag with an additional twist, a

---

[35] Jacques Derrida, "No Apocalypse, Not Now (full speed ahead, seven missiles, seven missives)," trans. Catherine Porter and Philip Lewis, *diacritics* 14.2 (Summer 1984): 28. Further references are in the text. Major statements in nuclear criticism since 1984 include J. Fisher Solomon, *Discourse and Reference in the Nuclear Age* (Norman, OK: University of Oklahoma Press, 1988); a dedicated issue of *Papers on Language & Literature* 26.1 (Winter 1990); Peter Schwenger, *Letter Bomb: Nuclear Holocaust and the Exploding Word* (Baltimore: Johns Hopkins University Press, 1992); Ken Ruthven, *Nuclear Criticism* (Melbourne University Press, 1993); *Silence of Fallout: Nuclear Criticism in a Post-Cold War World*, ed. Michael Blouin, Morgan Shipley, and Jack Taylor (Newcastle-upon-Tyne: Cambridge Scholars, 2013); and a special number of *diacritics* 41.3 (Fall 2013) marking the thirtieth anniversary of the inaugural conference and tracing links between the nuclear condition and climate change.

traumatizing expectation not just of disaster but also of a trackless aftermath in which there will be no mourning, no remembering, no working through.

"No Apocalypse" accompanies this notion of a mourning in advance of loss with a second upending of conventional sequence, one that has helped prompt my own reading of an interwar nuclear condition. I have in mind Derrida's claim that, at least since the Enlightenment, "literature has always belonged to the nuclear epoch" (27). The literature in question is neither all writing nor "the humanities" nor even the totality of so-called "imaginative literature." Derrida allows that certain discourses (sciences and nonliterary arts) and primordially oral literary modes (lyric and epic) whose archive is grounded in a "real referent" external to itself "might rightfully reconstitute themselves and thus, in some other fashion, survive" a nuclear disaster (26). But not so forms of literature whose chief referent is the archival "stockpile" of textual antecedents, legal precedents, and juridical systems that conditions those forms' internal meaning and social significance. Derrida thus gives the name of literature to "the body of texts whose existence, possibility, and significance are the most radically threatened, for the first and last time, by the nuclear catastrophe," adding that these writings have brooded on their fragility since they emerged in the Enlightenment—so much so that their total effaceability is also their transcendental referent (27). "The only referent that is absolutely real is thus of the scope or dimension of an absolute nuclear catastrophe that would irreversibly destroy the entire archive and all symbolic capacity, would destroy 'the movement of survival,' what I call '*survivance*,' at the very heart of life" (28).[36]

There are objections to raise here: to the implicitly Eurocentric claim about Enlightenment; to the assignment of a single transcendental referent to all literature since the seventeenth century; to the too-stark division of forms and discourses into those with self-referential archives and those without. But these problematic claims and moves do not impeach what I take to be the essay's central project of redefining the word *nuclear*. As long as it stays rooted in scientific, military, and foreign policy turf, the term can produce only belated, technologically determinist responses in humanistic study—a series of concentric circles rippling outward from the dropped stone of the Bomb. But to prize the word loose from the weapon, to call "nuclear" a writing that broods both after *and* before 1945 on the effaceable archive to which

---

[36] In standard French usage, *survivance* means "relic" or "leftover," but for Derrida it denotes something in excess of mere persistence—an active, resistant living-on in the face of prospective annihilation. The term has a related meaning in Native American studies, where Gerald Vizenor has influentially defined it as "an active repudiation of dominance, tragedy, and victimry"; see his *Fugitive Poses: Native American Scenes of Absence and Presence* (Lincoln: University of Nebraska Press, 1998), 15. The chief distinction between the two: where for Derrida *survivance* depends on the archive, for Vizenor it is closely tied to the "fugitive motion" of orality and its traces, as against the "sinecures of literature" (63).

it owes its existence—that shifts the balance of competence away from tech-nocratic elites, opens a broader range of works to nuclear readings, and rids those readings of the Bomb's chronological sponsorship.

> In what I am here calling in another sense an absolute epoch, literature comes to life and can only experience its own precariousness, its death menace and its essential finitude. The movement of its inscription is the very possibility of its effacement. Thus one cannot be satisfied with saying that, in order to become serious and interesting today, a literature and a literary criticism must refer to the nuclear issue, must even be obsessed by it. This has to be said, and it is true. But I believe also that, at least indirectly, they have always done this. Literature has always belonged to the nuclear epoch, even if it does not talk "seriously" about it. And in truth I believe that the nuclear epoch is dealt with more "seriously" in texts by Mallarmé, of Kafka, of Joyce, for example, than in present-day novels that would offer direct and realistic descriptions of a "real" nuclear catastrophe. (27–28)

Few nuclear critics subsequently took up Derrida's invitation to read pre-Trinity works as seriously engaged with the nuclear epoch. But the invitation stands and is accepted in the present book.[37] Although I resist equating the nuclear epoch with the general condition of (Western) literature since 1600, I am equally resistant to tearing history, literary or otherwise, at the perforation of 1945. It is not only after 1945 that the future looks likely to pro-hibit mourning by annulling the symbolic order. Previous futures, too, looked nuclear in that broader sense, and the pre-1945 works that attempted to con-jure or ward off those futures were often deeply conversant with their reliance on an archive whose effaceability could become, in a given moment, newly visible, newly possible.[38] The interwar works discussed here, for instance, bear

---

[37] Roland Végső accepts it too, although to different ends, in his *The Naked Communist: Cold War Modernism and the Politics of Popular Culture* (New York: Fordham University Press, 2013). In a chapter called "One World: Nuclear Holocausts," Végső argues that with the circumnavigation of the globe, modernity recognizes as the very condition of its emergence a catastrophic incom-mensurability between a spatially limited world and the limitless scope of human action released from divine teleology. Thus "the ultimate catastrophe is the birth of the modern itself . . . [which] simultaneously names the realization of the new as well as the principle of its self-cancellation" (112). Végső goes on to read Benjamin's angel of history as troping the split between modernity's content ("one single catastrophe") and its form (an infinite displacement of one trauma by the next where history is seen as a "chain of events"). This split, however, leads Végső to a strong theory of modern-ism as thematizing the limits of representation at the level of *form*, and of mass culture (e.g., atomic holocaust fiction) as thematizing the limits of representation at the level of *content*. Form emerges as the only register in which to "really speak" about catastrophe: modernist fragmentation is lauded for making "displaced catastrophic content" its transcendental signified, and mass culture dismissed for trying to "eliminate the problem of form" (117).

[38] I take this to have been the case before the First World War as well: as I indicate in chapter 4, even that quintessential Enlightenment project, the French *Encyclopédie* (1751–72), was to a large extent premised on the archive's effaceability. Conceiving of such a disaster as possible rather than foreordained, the *Encyclopédie* reads like a preemptive rebuke to both the confident optimism and

witness to the widening of the future-conditional space, not just of catastrophe in general, but of the erasure of cities, the destruction of archives in
bombing raids, and the alteration by emergency measures of the juridical
conditions that sustain literature's meaning. Even as I attend to how particular changes in war and its discourses contributed to that widening during the
1920s, "No Apocalypse" emboldens me to treat this book's two intervals—the
interwar and the Cold War—as having a nuclear denominator in common.

Derrida's essay differs in one other important way from most nuclear criticism and, for that matter, most late-twentieth-century nuclear disarmament
discourse. Both kinds of writing had frequent recourse to reproductivist
arguments in favor of purging nuclear weapons from the world. As I note in
chapter 3, Jonathan Schell's pro-disarmament classic, *The Fate of the Earth*
(1982), argued that nuclear arms posed such a threat to humanity's future that
people were losing interest in progenerative sex and consequently in marriage. "No Apocalypse," contrastingly, places *survivance*—a vital persistence
or afterlife through the symbolic order—"at the very heart of life," equating it
not with biological reproduction but with "the entire archive and all symbolic
capacity" (28). Derrida's essay in archival, as opposed to reproductive, futurism ends not by calling for the future to be made safe again for heteronormativity, but in a vision of God and the sons of Shem suspending their war
with one another in Babel because "they preferred to spend a little more time
together, the time of a long colloquy with warriors in love with life, busy writing in all languages in order to make the conversation last, even if they didn't
understand each other too well" (31). In attributing *survivance* to archives and
declining to advocate disarmament "in the name of our children" or "for the
sake of the unborn," "No Apocalypse" anticipates a body of more recent work
dedicated to tracing temporally normative conceptions of gender and sexuality—and, at the same time, to theorizing the relations between temporal and
sexual dissidence.

"Queer temporalities" as a theoretical rubric covers a broad array of scholarship by theorists and activists working, at least to date, predominantly in

---

the teleological nature of the Whig historiography that predominated during the nineteenth century. Yet that Victorian teleology of progress was variously shadowed and buttressed by a robust
nineteenth-century imagination of disaster whose chief nodes included famine and other global
climate events, the mounting evidence of past species extinctions, and late-century discourses of
degeneration. See Mike Davis, *Late Victorian Holocausts: El Niño Famines and the Making of the Third
World* (London: Verso, 2001); Patrick Brantlinger, *Dark Vanishings: Discourse on the Extinction of
Primitive Races, 1800–1930* (Ithaca, NY: Cornell University Press, 2003); and Gillen D'Arcy Wood,
Tambora: The Eruption That Changed the World (Princeton: Princeton University Press, 2014). The
First World War seems to intervene here in two ways: it makes the Whig teleology of progress much
harder to credit and it refocuses the imagination of disaster around modern warfare, which for
some—Cicely Hamilton, for instance, whom I discuss in chapter 3—replaced the Whig narrative
with an inverse teleology of civilizational collapse.

the United States.[39] More specific than a turn toward time as theme, this scholarship considers how heteronormative cultures perceive queer subjects in relation to history and futurity, how queer subjects experience and enact particular relations to history and futurity, and how queerness itself might be rethought as having less (or less exclusively) to do with sex and sexual typology than with dissident ways of being in relation to time. I have already referred to one of the chief temporalities from which queer subjects are variously excluded and dissenting: the "reproductive futurism" that conscripts the child as mascot for a heteronormative politics of hope—that is, for a future that can only be imagined in terms of biological reproduction and the modes of kinship, inheritance, and political succession it undergirds.[40] Such a conception of futurity and history militates against certain transgenerational ties, not least against the notion that the living could invest affectively in or form communities with the dead. In response, some scholars working on queer temporalities advocate just such a queer desire for history or "touch of the queer," the kind of unpunctual, affective approach that could permit one to ask, as Carolyn Dinshaw does, "How does it feel to be an anachronism?"[41] While acknowledging that the feeling of being out of step with one's contemporaries can be exploited to repressive ends, Dinshaw remains optimistic that transtemporal communities—living anachronisms in league with the dead—might produce politically salutary effects in a present whose dense multiplicity they help to restore.[42] Others, contrastingly, refuse a politics of hope they see as irreducibly heteronormative, urging queer subjects to embrace the negative position assigned them by reproductivism. Such an embrace can take many forms: an insistence on the destructive, anti-communitarian, at once selfish and self-shattering dimensions of sex and particularly homo-sex; an identification of the queer subject with the Freudian death drive, with its relentless opposition to a procreative understanding of libido; or a refusal of

---

[39] This rubric was consolidated in a special Queer Temporalities issue of *GLQ: A Journal of Lesbian and Gay Studies* 13.2–3 (2007), edited by Elizabeth Freeman. The issue's opener, "Theorizing Queer Temporalities: A Roundtable Discussion" (177–95), brought together nine of the critics most often associated with this area of study (Carolyn Dinshaw, Lee Edelman, Roderick A. Ferguson, Carla Freccero, Elizabeth Freeman, Judith Halberstam, Annamarie Jagose, Christopher Nealon, and Nguyen Tan Hoang).

[40] The concept of reproductive futurism is developed by Lee Edelman in *No Future: Queer Theory and the Death Drive* (Durham, NC: Duke University Press, 2004).

[41] Carolyn Dinshaw, *Getting Medieval: Sexualities and Communities, Pre- and Postmodern* (Durham, NC: Duke University Press, 1999), 151; Dinshaw et al., "Theorizing Queer Temporalities," 190.

[42] See also Ann Cvetkovich, *An Archive of Feelings: Trauma, Sexuality, and Lesbian Public Cultures* (Durham, NC: Duke University Press, 2003), and the work of Melanie Micir, particularly " 'Living in Two Tenses': The Intimate Archives of Sylvia Townsend Warner," *Journal of Modern Literature* 36.1 (Fall 2012): 119–31, and "Public Lives, Intimate Archives: Queer Biographical Practices in British Women's Writing, 1928–1978" (PhD diss., University of Pennsylvania, 2012).

queer triumphalism and a reclamation of the shame-laced backward look.[43] Still others look to fuse the negativity of these antisocial, arguably apolitical positions to a radical antiracist and anticapitalist stance, calling for a "punk negativity" whose oppositional politics declines the language of hope, redemption, and futurity and turns instead to vandalism, masochism, pessimism, and despair.[44] Real differences inhere among these approaches. But they share a root conviction: that temporality cannot be thought apart from the sexual norms through which it is figured, licensed, and imbued with or emptied of affect.

Owing to its semidormancy since the early 1990s, nuclear criticism has largely missed the chance to think through queer theory, whose formation as a field and main interventions have happened in the interim.[45] One occasionally sees comparisons between queer coming-out narratives and a nation's coming out as a nuclear power or a military person's coming out as an antinuclear activist. But the more suggestive commonalities between nuclear criticism and queer theoretical writing—most of them under the sign of temporality— remain unexplored. These include an intimate acquaintance with and even an embrace of the death drive and a related acquaintance with portraits of the future as negated or foreclosed. *Tense Future* takes up some of the questions that form at the conjuncture of the two approaches. Where nuclear criticism laments the way a seemingly foreclosed future projects trauma into the foretime of the disaster, a queer temporalities approach responds by asking what happens when the very terms in which the future is imagined *as open* foreclose a particular kind of subject or desire or being-toward-the-future. It also asks what gets created or fostered by the dissident temporality of the nuclear condition—what new forms of resistance, community, affiliation, or expression might be produced, like mineral allotropes, in the high pressures of the pre-traumatic. Are there situations, it asks, in which an evidently closed, apocalyptic futurity, far from draining our acts of responsibility or critical purchase, might be the only condition under which a certain kind of critique may be tendered, or a certain kind of kinship imagined; might be the catalyst for attending to negative affects instead of dismissing them as fatalism or quietism? Finally, confronted with the sexually normative arguments of much nuclear criticism, the analytic of queer temporality refuses to advocate for a

---

[43] See, respectively, Leo Bersani, "Is the Rectum a Grave?" *October* 43 (Winter 1987): 197–222 and *The Culture of Redemption* (Cambridge, MA: Harvard University Press, 1990); Edelman, *No Future*; and Love, *Feeling Backward*.

[44] See Judith Halberstam, "The Anti-Social Turn in Queer Studies," *Graduate Journal of Social Science* 5.2 (2008): 140–56.

[45] For a rare exception, see Peter Coviello, "Apocalypse from Now On," in *Queer Frontiers: Millennial Geographies, Genders, and Generations*, ed. Joseph A. Boone et al. (Madison: University of Wisconsin Press, 2000), 39–63.

future kept open on those narrow terms, demanding alternative lines along which the future's openness might be argued.

As I have indicated, one of these alternative lines is the archival conception of *survivance* we find in both Derrida's nuclear criticism essay and recent queer theory. Read by these dual lights, the archive can no longer be imagined exclusively as a repository of state, institutional, or corporate records, or as the historical basis of such entities' authority. It is also a repository for dissident temporalities, playing host to clashing portraits of the archivist as historiographic celibate and as ardent lover of the noncontemporary; of the past as variously benighted, authoritative, fragile, and desirable; and of the future as foreknown, or subject to probabilistic forecast, or radically unknowable.[46] This last stockpile—of what Reinhart Koselleck calls "futures past" or "superseded futures"—contains some of the archive's strangest, most important holdings, the traces of a past moment's orientation "to the not-yet, to the nonexperienced, to that which is to be revealed."[47] Concrete histories depend, says Koselleck, on the relationship in a given period between experience and expectation. Historical change will be legible not only in the shifting geometry between the two but also, writes David Scott in a gloss on Koselleck, in "the *reorganization* of the relation between their ideological contents," as happens, for example, in the shift "from a moment . . . when the future appears guaranteed by the present to one in which it seems undermined by it."[48] For Scott, our capacity to imagine more habitable political futures relies on how we narrate not just the past generally but futures-past specifically. The living, he argues, need to be able to renarrate futures-past so as not to be constrained by now-obsolete emplotments of those futures by earlier generations. Thus if an anticolonial program (his example is Frantz Fanon's *The Wretched of the Earth*) imagines its future in the terms of revolutionary, emancipatory romance, those living in the wake of what they see as that program's failure (Scott himself, for instance, growing up in postcolonial Jamaica) must be able to reemplot their antecedents' future as tragedy.[49] Such a renarration of the past superficially resembles the working-through modeled by trauma studies, but it differs in its etiology of historical blockage. What haunts, impedes, or overshadows the present in this instance is not an unassimilated past trauma

---

[46] On celibacy understood as a queer sexuality (rather than as stymied homosexuality or the negation of sexuality altogether), see Benjamin Kahan, *Celibacies: American Modernism and Sexual Life* (Durham, NC: Duke University Press, 2013). I discuss Hilary Jenkinson's interwar portrait of the archivist as celibate in chapter 3.

[47] Reinhart Koselleck, *Futures Past: On the Semantics of Historical Time*, trans. Keith Tribe (Cambridge, MA: MIT Press, 1985), 259.

[48] David Scott, *Conscripts of Modernity: The Tragedy of Colonial Enlightenment* (Durham, NC: Duke University Press, 2004), 44; emphasis in original.

[49] On the autobiographical subtexts of *Conscripts of Modernity*, see Stuart Hall, interview with David Scott, *BOMB* 90 (Winter 2005), http://bombsite.com/issues/90/articles/2711.

but a past *expectation*, subsequently displaced but not yet reemplotted to take account of supervening events. Scott gives us three reminders to be going on with. First, thwarted expectations can become encysted in our histories to the detriment of self-understanding and commitment in the present. Second, past narratives about the future are crucial historical artifacts. And third, those artifacts need not be permitted to dictate the conditions of their reception and interpretation.

One could place the emphasis differently, seeing the archive of futures-past not as confirming historical disappointment but as a storehouse of dormant possibilities that might be reactivated in the present.[50] Or one could recover a past moment's many possible futures to counter subsequent histories that treat its future as singular. The latter approach informs my final chapter, on Ford Madox Ford and (less centrally) Robert Musil, both of whom wrote against First World War historiography that presumed the war's inevitability. Where those histories *backshadowed* the war, imposing its later status as an accomplished fact on its foretime, Musil and Ford engaged in distinct practices of literary *sideshadowing* that emphasized the existence of historical alternatives, unrealized yet possible futures past. The italicized terms were coined by Michael André Bernstein and Gary Saul Morson, respectively, in their coordinated critique of "heavily forestructured" histories of mass trauma.[51] Treating a particular future-past as inevitable, they argue, is often the first step in chiding those who failed to heed the obvious portents of catastrophic futures and were thus, according to the backshadower, needlessly victimized by them. Such claims, which Bernstein shows a number of Holocaust historians have made about European Jewry in the 1930s, treat the future as a foregone conclusion and thereby deny the freedom of historical actors to have envisioned or helped produce a different outcome, effectively limiting their choice to acceptance or vain rejection of the foreordained. Against such apocalyptic histories, sideshadowing maps, or at least gestures toward, roads no less possible for having been untaken by events. The ethical stakes of such a project are not low for Morson and Bernstein: the foreclosure of futures past, they claim, may do nothing less than impede collective

---

[50] Gary Wilder offers just such a response to *Conscripts of Modernity*: "it is possible to accept [Scott's] critique of revolutionary anticolonialism without concluding, as he does, that all stories of colonial emancipation must be replaced with stories of impossible alternatives and tragic dilemmas." Wilder looks not at obsolete emplotments of the political future but at "futures that were once imagined but never came to be, alternative futures that might have been and whose not yet realized emancipatory possibilities may now be recognized and reawakened as durable and vital legacies." Gary Wilder, "Untimely Vision: Aimé Césaire, Decolonization, Utopia," *Public Culture* 21 (2009): 102, 103.

[51] See Michael André Bernstein's *Foregone Conclusions: Against Apocalyptic History* (Berkeley: University of California Press, 1994), and Gary Saul Morson, *Narrative and Freedom: The Shadows of Time* (New Haven: Yale University Press, 1994).

mourning, insofar as that mourning must be able to imagine viable alternative futures in which the victims survived and flourished if it is to begin taking the measure of their loss.

Together, the foregoing studies in critical futurity trace a cluster of problems *Tense Future* attempts to solve. How, in describing a traumatizing anticipation, do you balance its discursive and material components with its affective ones, its empirical dimensions with those that are radically internal? How do you write of pretrauma in a historicist key while replicating neither the narrow chronologism of conventional history writing nor the preposterous causality felt by your historical actors? How do you do justice to a widespread experience of the future as foreclosed without, on the one hand, just acceding to that view of the future or, on the other, condescending to those who held it? And how do you celebrate the uniqueness and dissidence of what is made in conditions of imminent disaster while deploring those conditions themselves? In each case, the answer would seem to entail a scrupulous adherence to different categories of evidence and analysis. Individual and collective experiences of imminent violence are real and consequential, but not in the same way that the material and discursive bases of violence-production are. Narrative is forestructured but history isn't. Expressions and arguments are distinct from their conditions of possibility.

Yet as I hope is already clear, the works, figures, problems, and phenomena this book draws together are partly absorbing because they weaken or overrun these categorical differences—because the riveter's affective response to the air raid siren had (and was meant to have) immediate material results on the war effort; because history's openness, no less than its putative foreclosure, gets flagged in the works I read here *as* a narrative; because I am attempting to write a chapter in the history of geopolitical suspense without being able to retreat fully from my own entanglement in it. My response to this difficulty has been to engage in a rotating series of thought experiments, inadmissible if performed all at once but lighting up, in sequence, the more uncanny or counterintuitive aspects of my subject. Hence *Tense Future*'s subjunctive approach to the interwar period, written of in one place as if it were long past, in another as if from its midst, and in yet another as if it extended to our own early-twenty-first-century moment—as if we remained lodged in a perpetual interwar.

Three Interwars

Given my sympathy with Morson and Bernstein's critique of historical backshadowing, the prominence I give to "the interwar period" as a historical formation may seem baffling. Surely a period can only be called interwar in hindsight, after a subsequent war ends it; to refer to moments between

November 11, 1918, and September 1, 1939, as interwar is to read the middle always by the black light of the terminus. One might respond, with Jürgen Habermas, that historical accounts must make use of narrative statements, many of which presuppose a retrospective vantage, and that it's entirely appropriate for a historian to write, "The Thirty Years War began in 1618" with the benefit of such hindsight.[52] In the course of twitting Habermas for holding a conventional view of narrative that allows middles to be subsumed by ends, Bernstein conjures an extreme case—"a contrary formulation in which we imagine a German burgher running through town shouting, 'The Thirty Years War has just begun!'"[53] Although I agree with Bernstein that we need flexible historical narratives less bent on closure and unity, my frequent past-perfect references to the interwar period resist the implication that we cannot invoke a historical period in retrospect without judging those who lived during it for failing to know what we know. But where I break most sharply from Bernstein, or at least from his use of the Thirty Years War example, is in my view of the interwar period as only partly a retrospective formation. It was also, I contend, understood by many from its midst, even from its inception, as an interval between the First World War and its likely sequel. Although no one in these pages says the words verbatim, I suggest that we badly misunderstand those years, and particularly the late teens and the twenties, until we can imagine a German burgher, a French factory worker, an English suffragist running through town shouting, "The interwar period has just begun!"

I say particularly the late teens and twenties because the 1930s are already understood as a time of mounting anxiety in regard to the apparent likelihood of another world war. Nazism's rise and Germany's rearmament had helped to saturate mass culture in England and on the Continent with premonitions of war; H. G. Wells's and Alexander Korda's film *Things to Come* (1936), with its opening scene of aerial bombardment, poison gas attacks, and mass death in "Everytown," offers only the best-known and least-encrypted example—and this was fully four years after Britain's de facto prime minister had warned Parliament, in a speech entitled "A Fear for the Future," that "The bomber will always get through."[54] Given this cultural climate, Mumford's 1938 reference to the "collective psychosis" of anticipation in the face of metropolitan air raids is of its season. But conventional wisdom would add that these lurid previsions are part of what sets the volatile, post-Crash thirties

---

[52] Jürgen Habermas, "A Review of Gadamer's Truth and Method," in Fred R. Dallymayr and Thomas A. McCarthy, eds., *Understanding and Social Inquiry* (Notre Dame, IN: University of Notre Dame Press, 1977), 346.

[53] Bernstein, *Foregone Conclusions*, 26.

[54] Stanley Baldwin, *Parliamentary Debates—Commons*, November 10, 1932, Vol. 270, cols. 631–32; rpt. as "Mr. Baldwin on Aerial Warfare—A Fear for the Future," *Times* (London), November 11, 1932: 7B. At the time, Baldwin was Lord President of the Council but increasingly covering for Prime Minister Ramsay MacDonald in the latter's senility.

apart from the insouciance of the twenties. For more than five decades, modernist studies has affirmed this splitting of the interwar period, disposing "high" and "late" modernism on either side of the 1929 crisis. Harry Levin may have been the first to dub 1922 modernism's annus mirabilis in "What Was Modernism?" (1960). One of that essay's projects is to situate the year 1922, and high modernism generally, in a "between-the-wars cosmopolitanism" unshadowed by past or possible world wars. In Levin's view, the interwar period—what E. M. Forster called "the long weekend"—"thought of itself in the present tense, separating modernity from history. The past was over; the present was happily more comfortable." The Great War had "settled history," and T. S. Eliot's formulation "History is now and England" was still to come.[55] Michael North's *Reading 1922*, a landmark renovation of that year, questions a range of narratives established by Levin's generation but concurs that the modernist wonder year had effectively emerged from the shadow of the war: as North records, the *Daily Mail* named 1922 England's "first real postwar year, when 'signs of, and restrictions connected with, the Great War were finally abolished,' a return to normalcy that seemed to be symbolized in the press by the wedding of Princess Mary."[56]

Accounts of the interwar period in the past perfect tense, as a completed interval, have difficulty transcending this rough emplotment: postwar relief and prosperity; financial crisis and Depression; rise of fascism and Axis militarism; gathering storm of war.[57] But if we approach it as if in the present tense, what we find is not (pace Levin) a comfortable modernity separated from history but, instead, a turbulent modernity jointly defined by the memory of a disastrous history and the prospect of an even more devastating futurity. In a move central to the subjunctive historicism I described above, *Tense Future* loops repeatedly back to the year 1922 while suspending, as it were, the rest of the interwar period's standard historical plot. I have chosen Levin's annus mirabilis not to consecrate it further as a year of elite- and mass-cultural wonders but in an effort to decenter those wonders, and to enable us to ask how they were variously supported, penetrated, eclipsed, and provoked by the memory and expectation of mass violence.[58] An approach

---

[55] Harry Levin, "What Was Modernism?" *The Massachusetts Review* 1.4 (August 1960): 619, 621.

[56] Michael North, *Reading 1922: A Return to the Scene of the Modern* (Oxford: Oxford University Press, 1999), 5.

[57] As the Hull poet and journalist Hubert Nicholson wrote in 1941, "The Twenties were post-war. The Thirties were pre-war." See his *Half My Days and Nights: Autobiography of a Reporter* (London: W. Heinemann, 1941), 100. Nicholson is quoted by Richard Overy, one of a handful of historians who shares my reading of the 1920s as deeply anxious about war and social collapse; see his *The Twilight Years: The Paradox of Britain Between the Wars* (New York: Penguin, 2009), 2.

[58] Levin's roster of masterworks ("What Was Modernism?" 618) includes Marcel Proust's *Sodome et Gomorrhe*, Joyce's *Ulysses*, Eliot's *The Waste Land*, D. H. Lawrence's *Aaron's Rod*, Virginia Woolf's *Jacob's Room*, Katherine Mansfield's *The Garden Party*, Thomas Hardy's *Late Lyrics and Earlier*, W. B. Yeats's *Later Poems*, and A. E. Housman's *Last Poems*. Michael North (in *Reading 1922*) adds a host of

meant less to enrich than to estrange, it shows us a differently postwar 1922, one not released from the aftermath of the Great War but still mired in it. Far more strangely, it gives us an anxious, prognostic, *pre*war year in which the legal, financial, political, and military groundwork for a prospective future conflict was being detectably laid: a year in which two international conferences failed to set up effective laws of warfare; in which new theories of air power's military future were being read alongside speculative fictions about a catastrophic next war; in which the Treaty of Versailles permitted Germany, to the consternation of its former adversaries, to begin rebuilding its fleet of commercial aircraft, even as the mark was reaching socially destabilizing levels of hyperinflation.[59]

1922 was also the inaugural year of Britain's experiment in the air control of Mesopotamia (now Iraq), an experiment centered around the use of bombing—both threatened and realized—as a tool for coercing noncombatants in Britain's new Middle Eastern mandate. As chapter 1 will show in greater detail, where *interwar* meant the cessation of hostilities for some, for others it meant the inception or continuation of hostilities stripped of the name and legal protections of war. For the inhabitants of many colonies, mandates, and protectorates during the 1920s and '30s, the underlying premise of an *entre deux guerres*—that wartime and peacetime are absolutely distinct—was negated by the routine experience of overflights, reprisal bombings, and other military performances of occupation. As much as we need to imagine a real-time account of the interwar period for the inhabitants of imperial and metropolitan nation states, we must also recognize how drastically the account changes when we zoom out from that core. A global portrait of the interwar displays a hugely varying distribution of conflict and the instabilities and scarcities that attend it: revolutionary and civil wars, proxy wars, and colonial "police actions" flaring through supposed peacetime decades that followed one paroxysmal war and throbbed to the prospect of another. If this sounds in some manner like the Cold War, then we've drawn alongside *Tense Future*'s third way of framing the interwar. Derrida's "No Apocalypse, Not Now" imagined

---

titles, including Claude McKay's *Harlem Shadows*, James Weldon Johnson's *Book of American Negro Poetry*, Willa Cather's *One of Ours*, and Ludwig Wittgenstein's *Tractatus Logico-Philosophicus*. North also discusses the year's mass-market literature and other broad cultural forms and events, including the Ancient Egypt craze kicked off by Howard Carter's rediscovery of Tutankhamun's tomb in November 1922.

[59] For 1920s writing on the threat inherent in German civil aviation, see Lt.-Col. Charles à Court Repington, *After the War: London-Paris-Rome-Athens-Prague-Vienna-Budapest-Bucharest-Berlin-Sofia-Coblenz-New York-Washington; A Diary* (Boston: Houghton Mifflin Company, 1922), 83; Unsigned, "Royal Air Force Notes," *Journal of the Royal United Service Institution* 67 (May 1922): 392–94; Rear-Admiral Murray F. Sueter, *Airmen or Noahs: Fair Play for our Airmen; the Great "Neon" Air Myth Exposed* (London: Sir Isaac Pitman & Sons, 1928), 318–20, 421; J. M. Kenworthy, *Peace or War?* (New York: Boni & Liveright, 1927), 155.

the nuclear condition as a *longue-durée* period that began around 1600. My book responds by asking what would happen if we were to transperiodize the interwar condition forward, conceiving of it as interrupted rather than ended by the beginning of the Second World War. Undoing some of the modularity of twentieth-century history in this way would make more visible a range of phenomena shared by the interwar and Cold War periods: the logic of deterrence, the deranging effects of geopolitical suspense, the underwriting of peace in spaces conceived as central by the persistence of war in spaces conceived as peripheral. By no longer reducing war to an event that either is or is not happening within a global frame, we could make the uneven distributions of conflict in both time and space the object of our pacifism. We could finally ask what it would mean to stop waging interwar.

Weak Modernism

The plural phenomenology of the interwar I have outlined informs *Tense Future*'s approach to its central literary texts. These must be seen as belonging neither to a period comfortably settled in a peacetime present, nor to one preoccupied only with the wartime past, nor even to one whose disquiet about the future has since been superseded. The interwar at issue here is the name we give to a wound that remains open in the present—both because we can reactivate the futures-past of the historical interwar and because we see them as still partly continuous with our own futurities. To thus reopen the closed case of a period—especially one as neatly emboxed as the interwar, and as ready to stand in for periodicity itself—is to raise questions about the instrumental relationship between that period and its cultural works. My claim is precisely *not* that the interwar period is important because it produced modernism's greatest achievements. It is closer to the reverse: that at least a certain range of the cultural spectrum we call modernist matters because it burned and shone during *interbellum* years whose peculiarity we can read more clearly by its light. But this formulation falls short in two ways. It implies that *modernism*, even trimmed within chronological, linguistic, and cultural limits, remains a strong, gatekeeping term in the project. And it reduces to symptoms and instruments of a period a set of texts that interest me as much for their still-unheeded warnings as for their use in renarrating the past.

When the word "modernism" appears in the subtitle of a literary studies book, it can trigger two reasonable expectations: that all the primary texts discussed within will be understood as modernist, and that the book will offer a definitional model of modernism to which its central works positively belong, and which as positively excludes some set of other works. Neither is the case here. *Tense Future* tarries with several literary texts—an apocalyptic "next war" novel from the 1920s, a boys' imperial adventure tale from the

1930s, a handful of Cold War speculative fictions about nuclear disasters—that almost nobody would call modernist and that don't become more illuminating if we do. The book does not advance a wholesale redefinition of modernism in relation to total war, traumatizing anticipation, or encyclopedic form. Even my discussion of encyclopedic modernist texts is confessedly partial: despite the existence of a number of long poems to which my analysis might be applied—

Eliot's *The Waste Land* (1922), Pound's *Cantos* through LXXI (1925–40), and David Jones's *In Parenthesis* (1937), to name just three—*Tense Future* is devoted exclusively to works whose encyclopedism collides with the history and conventions of the novel, at the scale and pace of long narrative. Preferring to epitomize rather than to anthologize interwar encyclopedic fiction, I enter no claim to an exhaustive overview. My uses of modernism here are associative instead of definitional, probabilistic instead of binary; to borrow a phrase, "connotative rather than denotative."[60] Instead of anchoring an all-or-nothing unified field theory, modernism functions in local and provisional ways, as an auxiliary term that supports other lines of argument not endogenous to its problem-space.

In chapter 2, for instance, modernism indexes Virginia Woolf's adaptation of the suspense-effects of nineteenth-century sensation fiction to modern wartime, culminating in the forms political commitment takes on the doorstep of a future that looks predetermined. The formally heterogeneous fictions I discuss in the book's second half I call modernist for their hybridizing of novel and encyclopedia as a pacifist riposte not just to conflict but to *total* war, a strong theory if ever there were one. The aim in part two, however, is not to meet a strong theory of war with an equally strong theory of modernism but instead to show how the local formal volatilities of the fictions I discuss interrupt the temptation to imagine a sovereign counter-totality to war. Thus the final chapter's discussion of *Parade's End* finds in that work's sporadic experimentalism—what others have read as its failed modernist gambits—a weak modernism whose ability to discredit forestructured historical narratives lies precisely in its tentativeness. There and elsewhere, the term "modernism" functions as nonexclusive shorthand for works that display, even speculatively or intermittently, an anticontemporary or counterconventional temper.[61] Among the works I discuss, this penchant for negation often

---

[60] David James and Urmila Seshagiri, "Metamodernism: Narratives of Continuity and Revolution," *PMLA* 129.1 (January 2014): 88. James and Seshagiri are characterizing the current status of the term *modernism* in modernist studies, not advocating that status. They call, in fact, for a return to a more denotative approach—to "a temporally bounded and formally precise understanding of what modernism does and means"—so that contemporary literature they designate as "metamodernist" may be read as responding to modernism rather than simply extending it.

[61] In my approach to the term, I have been informed by Eric Hayot's use of "Modernism" in *On Literary Worlds* (New York: Oxford University Press, 2012) to name "the mode of negation and refusal" in a work's orientation toward "the normative world-view of its era" (127, 132). (Hayot

pits formal strenuousness against normative ideas about war and futurity. But I propose no single geometry of negation, nor a muscular redefinition of modernism. Sometimes the term weakens to the point of near-tautology—*modernism*: that which exhibits traits that have been called modernist—as an artifact of its first descriptive uses, as a nod to the circular logic of all shorthand, and as preferable to doubling down on some untenable bright-line definition. And sometimes, as one might expect of a weakly theorized term, "modernism" fades out of my discourse altogether.

Strong theory, weak theory: this is not a distinction of my making but one that emerges from several sources that we can loosely bundle, and that bear on the current status of modernism as an analytical term within modernist studies. Writing in the 1960s, the psychologist Silvan Tomkins distinguished between strong affect theories, which attempt to unify a wide range of disparate objects, and weak affect theories, which "can account only for 'near' phenomena," venturing "little better than a description of the phenomena which [they purport] to explain."[62] Affect theories exist to maximize positive and minimize negative affect, says Tomkins; when they fail to do the latter, they tend to respond by becoming more extensive in the hope of warding off refutation and humiliation the next time around, of preempting bad surprises. The "reparative reading" that Eve Sedgwick advocated as a result of her reading of Tomkins finds the risk of bad surprises an acceptable price to pay for the prospect of good ones—for the hope "that the future may be different from the present," even if that opening of the future means entertaining "such profoundly painful, profoundly relieving, ethically crucial possibilities as that the past, in turn, could have happened differently from the way it actually did" (146). Reaching back to Morson and Bernstein, we might say that weak theory's abstention from absolute prediction makes it far more hospitable than strong theory to the counterfactual imagination. Along related lines, philosopher Gianni Vattimo has been a proponent of what he calls "weak thought" [*pensiero debole*] since the 1980s, arguing that the philosopher's duty is no longer to demonstrate but rather to edify; no longer to be "humanity's guide to understanding the Eternal" but to "redirect humanity toward history."[63] This in the wake of Nietzsche, who Vattimo says discredited the

---

capitalizes Modernism to distinguish it from its more familiar nonmodal senses.) The interwar works I call modernist here oppose normative (i.e., war-oriented) constructions of *totality*.

[62] Sylvan Tomkins, *Affect Imagery Consciousness: Volume II, The Negative Affects* (New York: Springer, 1963), 433; qtd. in Eve Sedgwick, *Touching Feeling: Affect, Pedagogy, Performativity* (Durham, NC: Duke University Press, 2003), 134.

[63] Santiago Zabala, quoting from Vattimo's *The Vocation and Responsibility of the Philosopher*, in Gianni Vattimo and Santiago Zabala, "'Weak Thought' and the Reduction of Violence: A Dialogue with Gianni Vattimo," trans. Yaakov Mascetti, *Common Knowledge* 8.3 (Fall 2002): 452. Vattimo's central statement on weak thought is *La fine della modernità* (1985), published in English as *The End of Modernity*, trans. Jon R. Snyder (Baltimore: Johns Hopkins University Press, 1988).

metanarratives—a unified, progressive notion of modernity; a foundational metaphysics; Hegelo-Marxian models of totality—on which strong thought relied. Most recently, Wai Chee Dimock has written about genre through a weak-theoretical approach that "does not aspire to full occupancy in the analytic field, that settles for a low threshold in plausibility and admissibility . . . that does not even try to clinch the case."[64] As against projects in which "there is a curious resemblance . . . between the totalizing zeal of the theorist and the totalizing claim being made on behalf of its object" (733), Dimock's weak theory

> cannot support a system of sovereign axioms. Instead, the frequency, diversity, and centrifugal nature of the spin-offs [i.e., threads in laterally propagated, associative networks] suggest not only that the points of contact will change from moment to moment but that the field itself might not even be governed by a single morphology, an ordering principle generalizable across the board and presetting its hierarchies. Local circumstances can do a lot to change the operating baseline and the various claims to primacy resting upon it. (737)

As in Sedgwick's and Vattimo's, weak theory in Dimock's account conceives of the future other than as the thing that will either refute or vindicate it. Where strong theory attempts to ride its sovereign axioms to "a future never for a moment in doubt," weak theory tries to see just a little way ahead, behind, and to the sides, conceiving even of its field in partial and provisional terms that will neither impede, nor yet shatter upon, the arrival of the unforeseen (733).

My reference to a weak theory of modernism may sound prescriptive, even polemical, but it is meant in a mostly descriptive spirit. As an aggregate, scholars in modernist studies have been weakening their central term for years now without anyone's having said as much. The field's early bent for gatekeeping criteria and canon building (see, again, Levin's "What Was Modernism?") remains a phantom reflex, but as a central project it began to ebb decades ago. In 1984, Michael Levenson's *A Genealogy of Modernism*, whose title seemed to promise a vivid, in-or-out account of modernism, instead described the term as "at once vague and unavoidable," a "blunt instrument" suited only to rough tasks but adequate "as a rough way of locating our attention."[65] Susan Stanford Friedman's recent essays have both captured and catalyzed further movement away from a strict, definitional approach based on aesthetic traits—away, too, from the old modernism's Eurocentrism and the strict periodization that

---

[64] Wai Chee Dimock, "Weak Theory: Henry James, Colm Tóibín, and W. B. Yeats," *Critical Inquiry* 39.4 (Summer 2013): 736. Further citations are in the text.

[65] Michael Levenson, *A Genealogy of Modernism: A Study of English Literary Doctrine 1908–1922* (Cambridge: Cambridge University Press, 1984), vii.

attended it.[66] Once a capitalized singular noun with a bounded referent, modernism in the hands of contemporary literary scholars has been pluralized, adjectivalized, decoupled from high culture, and rethought as a transnational and transhistorical phenomenon. Jessica Berman, for example, describes it as "a dynamic set of relationships, practices, problematics, and cultural engagements with modernity rather than a static canon of works, a given set of formal devices, or a specific range of beliefs." Eric Hayot theorizes Modernism as forming, with Realism and Romanticism, a system of literary world-making modes copresent throughout global modernity. And Tsitsi Jaji uses "modernism" and "modernity" in what she calls "intentionally flexible" ways, invoking the former "as a simple heuristic device for indexing aesthetic choices that reflect self-conscious performances of 'being modern.' "[67] Without suggesting that these approaches are compatible with one another, we can say that they all participate in a general weakening of the theory of modernism that structures the field of its study. That weakening is especially legible in the movement away from definitions of modernism in favor of uses, models, questions, temperaments, and possible typologies. None of the formulations I cite above is phrased in terms declarative enough to be susceptible of disproof; none of the theories of modernism they help constitute would allow one to say dispositively that a particular work is *not* modernist.

One might take the growth of a field centered around a single term as a sure sign of that term's theoretical strength; why else would so many scholars undertake to expand modernism's spatial, temporal, and cultural horizons along with the range of media, institutions, and cultural strata that can foster it? Here I would stress the difference between a strong theory and a strong field. Modernist studies has become a strong field—populous, varied, generative, self-reflexive—in proportion as its immanent theory of modernism has weakened and become less axiomatic, more conjectural, more conjunctural. In fact, we could say that modernist studies underwent a delay in emerging as a field partly because its immanent theory of modernism remained for several decades too strong to permit the kinds of horizontal frictions and attachments necessary for field-formation. A major index of the field's current strength is the enormous range of foreground terms we find moored to the field's weak central term. *Ethics* and *politics*,

---

[66] See Susan Stanford Friedman, "Definitional Excursions: The Meanings of Modern/ Modernity/Modernism," *Modernism/modernity* 8.3 (September 2001): 493–513; "Periodizing Modernism: Postcolonial Modernities and the Space/Time Borders of Modernist Studies," *Modernism/modernity* 13.3 (September 2006): 425–43; and "Planetarity: Musing Modernist Studies," *Modernism/modernity* 17.3 (September 2010): 471–99.

[67] Jessica Berman, *Modernist Commitments: Ethics, Politics, and Transnational Modernism* (New York: Columbia University Press, 2011), 7; Hayot, *On Literary Worlds*, esp. part II; and Tsitsi Jaji, *Africa in Stereo: Modernism, Music, and Pan-African Solidarity* (New York: Oxford University Press, 2014), 15.

worlds and *worlding, stereo* and *sound*: the topically and methodologically disparate books (Berman's, Hayot's, and Jaji's, respectively) that feature these terms remain intelligible within a single field because its key term has stopped playing bouncer and started playing host. Work in modernist studies can now be preoccupied with questions other than the old transcendental one: "But is it *really* modernist?" The present study hopes to offer a way of being *in* and even *for* modernist studies while continuing to soften our definitional gaze at its central term. Prominently featured in my subtitle, "modernism" should be understood there to index not a strong theory of modernism but the strong field made possible by that theory's waning.

With its investment in canonical fictions of the interwar metropole, *Tense Future* may appear to yearn for a bygone moment of strongly theorized modernism, even to attempt a reconsolidation of that strength. But where this book returns to cardinal works of a stronger modernism, it does so in order to pose questions that have only come to seem pertinent as the field's immanent theory of modernism has weakened. How do these works construct and critique the exceptional status of the metropole in a world system that unevenly distributes law and force? How is race configured in the covert memoranda and public spectacles of that distribution? In what ways do dissident models of history, temporality, sexuality, and gender interact with the interwar period's dominant models of totality? To which emergent phenomena does interwar modernism bear advance witness? And in congress with what earlier forms and figures is that witness borne?

Having brought such questions to the fore, a weak theory of modernism also informs this book's responses to them. But *Tense Future*'s interest in weakness finally exceeds modernism, taking us all the way back to total war. That exemplary strong theory aspires to fully occupy and unify its analytic field. It exempts no creature, structure, or act from the range of war and no degree of violence from war's prerogative. It produces strongly developmentalist histories, saying that all conflict evolves toward total war and all states toward the ability to wage it. And it both harbors and begets strong theories of the future as given, in advance, to belligerence without limit. In the chapters that follow, we will encounter many ways of dissenting from total war. Some invoke non-normative modes of narrative or historical time. Others re-imagine the state around something other than the sovereign right to violence. Still others model counter-totalities rooted not in war but in form, or in worry, or in archives. All these kinds of dissent are on intimate terms with weakness: with the fragility of lives, places, law, and writing; with partiality's way of preserving totality in a weakened state; and with the insurgent *minority* of certain major works.[68] Above all, the works and figures we will meet

---

[68] I have in mind here the minority described in Gilles Deleuze and Félix Guattari's *Kafka: Toward a Minor Literature*, trans. Dana Polan (Minneapolis: University of Minnesota Press, 1986), as

decline to view other times as warrants for the strong theories and strong tensions of the present. They attempt to see the future as other than the here and now—the more so when the moment oncoming looks just like the consummation of present violence. And they enact the possibility, at once painful and regenerative, that the past could have been other than it was.

---

affecting language with a "high coefficient of deterritorialization" (16) even as it connects individual narratives to political totalities, sees individual enunciations as perforce collective ones. Writing in a major language, writers of minor literature seek "to oppose the oppressed quality of this language to its oppressive quality," to be strangers within a major language rather than masters of it (26–27).

PART ONE

It appeared to me inevitable that war must follow . . . So I imagined myself widowed and childless, which was another instance of the archaic outlook of the unconscious, for I knew that in the next war we women would have scarcely any need to fear bereavement, since air raids unpreceded by declaration of war would send us and our loved ones to the next world in the breachless unity of scrambled eggs.

—Rebecca West, on learning in 1934 of King Alexander's assassination
Black Lamb and Grey Falcon: A Journey Through Yugoslavia (1941)

1

On the Partiality of Total War

A great war once joined is to-day a war of peoples. Not only armies in the field, but men, women, and even children at home, are concentrated on the single purpose of defeating the enemy, and armies, navies, and air forces are dependent upon the application to work, the output of war supplies, and, above all, the morale of the civilian population. Just as gas was used notwithstanding the Hague Convention, so air war, in spite of any and every international agreement to the contrary, will be carried into the enemy's country, his industries will be destroyed, his nerve centres shattered, his food supply disorganized, and the will power of the nation as a whole shaken.

—F. H. Sykes, *Aviation in Peace and War* (1922)

The most interesting thing which happened during this week was a performance by the R.A.F., a bombing demonstration. It was even more remarkable than the one we saw last year at the Air Force show because it was much more real. They had made an imaginary village about a quarter of a mile from where we sat on the Diala dyke and the two first bombs dropped from 3000 feet, went straight into the middle of it and set it alight. It was wonderful and horrible. Then they dropped bombs all round it, as if to catch the fugitives and finally fire bombs which even in the brightest sunlight made flares of bright flame in the desert. They burn through metal and water won't extinguish them. At the end armoured cars went out to round up the fugitives with machine guns. I was tremendously impressed. It's an amazingly relentless and terrible thing, war from the air . . .

—Gertrude Bell, Letter to H. B. (Baghdad, July 2, 1924)

Total war: in its standard definition, a conflict from which nothing and no one is exempt, "a war to which all resources and the whole population are committed."[1] Pitting both the productive and the belligerent energies of

---

[1] *OED*, under definition of "total." This standard definition of "total war" holds even in places where one might look for it to warp or splinter. While insisting on total war's connection with

whole populations against one another, it sees any member of an adversary's population as a legitimate target. This chapter disturbs the standard
definition by insisting on the spatial, temporal, and ideological partialities
of total war as a historically emergent concept. Not, I should emphasize,
as a historically emergent *phenomenon*: war that exempts no one from its
domain seems to have been the norm rather than the anomaly in human
history. But following the *concept* of total war back to its elaboration in
the early twentieth century prompts a series of more focused questions.
In contrast to what—and whose—concept of limited conflict is the new
expression "total war" intelligible in this period? What are the local effi-
cacies, and who the beneficiaries, of total war's totality-claims? Finally,
what subjects, collectivities, and forms of military violence fall outside the
bounds of limited war, total war, and the logic of their differentiation? To
pursue these questions, I argue, is to learn how the standard definition's
aggressive coherentism masks some of total war's other functions as a concept: its occlusions, its refigurings of space and time, and its discrimina-
tions in apportioning permissible violence.

Relying as it does on the protagonism of "whole populations," total war's
standard definition admits of no case studies, no exceptions, and no better
or worse exemplars. Such an approach needs no figure besides that of the
demographic mass pledged to all-out conflict. The counter-portrait I offer
begins by setting aside this protagonism of the whole and trailing a particular figure into the fractured problem-space of total war. That figure is
Lionel Evelyn Oswald Charlton (1879–1958), Royal Air Force officer, conscientious objector, and air war prophet. The chapter's opening section follows
Charlton through a series of sites and practices too seldom linked in the
historiography of total war. These include the European and U.S. capital cities where interwar congresses tried unsuccessfully to create binding international laws of war; the violently policed mandate in "peacetime," which
gave the lie to the very categories on which international laws of war were to
be based; and an array of places where world war was both remembered and
anticipated. Trafficking among these sites, Charlton is exemplary in at least
two senses: he *stands out* from his contemporaries in having objected strenu-
ously to the bombing of colonial civilians outside the context of declared
war and he *typifies* the view of interwar military elites that declared wars
from now on would require the indiscriminate killing of civilians. Neither
his exceptionality nor the rule it proved was a mere function of the other.

---

capitalist investment, Deleuze and Guattari keep to what I am calling a "coherentist" view of
population and economy within the steady frame of the nation-state: "Total war is not only a war
of annihilation but arises when annihilation takes as its 'center' not only the enemy army, or the
enemy State, but the entire population and its economy." Gilles Deleuze and Félix Guattari, *A
Thousand Plateaus: Capitalism and Schizophrenia*, trans. Brian Massumi (Minneapolis: University of
Minnesota Press, 1987), 421.

Their co-presence underscores how interwar military theory consecrated differences of time (wartime versus peacetime) and space (metropole versus colony) in licensing state violence and, more surprisingly, how adamantly the concept of total war disavowed those differences. Charlton's double exemplarity opens onto a broader discussion of total war as a concept less concerned to describe a new form or degree of violence than to establish a pretext for violence intensified.

The Case of L. E. O. Charlton

When Charlton (Fig. 1.1) left London for the Persian Gulf in late 1922, his bags were laden with books. He would save Marcel Proust's *À la recherche du temps perdu*, along with volumes of poetry and philosophy, for the months ahead in Baghdad. But on the P & O liner to Karachi, and then on a smaller ship to Basra, he passed many hours reading, as he later put it, "official handbooks on the country of his future sojourn—James Joyce's *Ulysses*, and *The Decay of Capitalist Civilization*, by Sidney and Beatrice Webb."[2] The flight from Basra to Baghdad enchanted him: he could see the Tigris and Euphrates in a single panoramic view, and the ruins of ancient cities reminded him of a child's sand drawings by the sea. The shipboard leisure, the engrossing desert over-view, the warm greeting he received from his superior officer, John Salmond, whom he had known since flying school—all these seemed to augur well for his assignment as RAF Senior Air Staff Officer in the new British mandate of Iraq. His career was flourishing. Having served with distinction as an Army officer in the Boer War and flown combat and reconnaissance missions for the Royal Flying Corps during the First World War, he had spent three years in Washington, D.C., with the British Embassy. Although he had watched with dismay as the 1921–22 Disarmament Conference foundered, he had been a success at his work as air attaché. By exempting himself from social rounds, he had left himself plenty of time to read American poetry and his-tory, William James, and Freud; his readings in political theory had also con-tributed to his becoming a socialist, although he concealed his politics while he was in the RAF. And he had settled down with a lover, a young man with the Swiss Legation who had accompanied him back to London as his secre-tary and personal assistant and was now enrolled at the Polytechnic Institute while Charlton was in the Gulf.

The RAF had taken on sole military responsibility for the mandate in October 1922, having persuaded the Cabinet that air control would be cheaper, more effective, more humane, and less controversial than ground occupation. Charlton's experience with two armed services in European and colonial

---

[2] L. E. O. Charlton, *Charlton* (London: Faber & Faber, 1931), 269. Further references cited in the text.

FIG. 1.1. *Air Commodore L. E. O. Charlton, date unknown.*

conflicts seemed to suit him ideally to the project of colonial air policing in Iraq. But early on in his posting, while touring a hospital in the central Iraqi town of Diwaniya as part of a visit to a local chieftain, he experienced "something of a shock": among the patients were victims of a recent punitive bombardment by the RAF. He recorded his reaction in his 1931 memoir *Charlton*, which he wrote, after the example of *The Education of Henry Adams*, in the third person:

> It seemed to him a most cold-blooded proceeding and a grave reflection on the ends of justice, that at one moment people were so harmful as to deserve sudden and terrifying death, and the next so harmless that no expense was spared in patching up their injuries. He was aghast to learn on further inquiry that an air bomb in Iraq was, more or less, the equivalent of a police truncheon at home. It was a horrible idea and, in his private opinion, work in which no one with a moral standard should be asked to engage. In declared war or in the case of open rebellion no objection could possibly be advanced, but the indiscriminate bombing of a populace without power of selecting the real culprits, and with the liability of killing women and children, was the nearest thing to wanton slaughter which he

had come across since the massacre at Dijon in 1914. But he was careful not
to express himself too forcefully on the subject. (271)

Eventually Charlton did express himself to Salmond. Objecting to a planned
air strike against an uncooperative sheik, he warned that "direct action by
aeroplanes on indirect information by unreliable informants . . . was a species of oppression which tended to render infamous the British name for fair
dealing throughout the world." But Salmond was unyielding, and after the
raids killed a large number of civilians, Charlton asked to be relieved of his
duties: "on grounds of conscience, he could no longer subscribe to the bombing policy so constantly in force" (277–78). Under the pretence of official business, he was sent back to London, where the Chief of the Air Staff, Hugh
"Boom" Trenchard, informed him that there would be no inquiry into his
request to leave Iraq, and that while he would never be reassigned to an overseas mandate, his future with the Air Force would be otherwise unimpaired.
After a furlough at half pay, Charlton spent several years preparing an Air
Ministry report on how to expand the RAF to wartime strength; in 1928 a
letter from the Air Ministry informed him he would no longer be promoted
or reappointed.

    Other RAF officers expressed misgivings to their superiors about the eth-
ics of the bombing policy in Iraq, but Charlton was the only one of his generation to resign in protest, the only one to publish his criticism in an interwar
memoir.[3] His name has become synonymous with conscientious objection
within military elites; air power observers during the second Gulf War were
still debating which dissenting figure within the Coalition forces could be
considered that conflict's "21st-century Charlton."[4] Yet for all that his reflections about Diwaniya express his outrage at the use of the bomb as a truncheon, they are also remarkable in what they accept: that "in declared war or
in the case of open rebellion no objection could possibly be advanced" to the
bombing of civilians. What seems to repel him morally is not the practice of
bombing "with the liability of killing women and children" but the fact that
the RAF employs it outside the legitimate context of declared war or open
rebellion—that his fellow airmen have been terror-bombing the innocent
during peacetime in order to discipline a resistant minority. Because Charlton

---

[3] See David E. Omissi, *Air Power and Colonial Control: The Royal Air Force 1919–1939*
(Manchester: Manchester University Press, 1990), 176. This chapter, particularly its second half,
is generally indebted to Omissi's enthralling book. I have also benefited enormously from Sven
Lindqvist's *A History of Bombing*, trans. Linda Haverty Rugg (New York: The New Press, 2001),
whose unique way of organizing theme and chronology reimplicates total war and colonial violence.

[4] Bret Holman, December 2, 2005 posting, "21st century Charlton?" on the website "Airminded: Air
Power and British Society," http://airminded.org/2005/12/02/21st-century-charlton/. In 2006, Mike
Marqusee deplored the fact that a statue of Arthur Harris, who masterminded Britain's area bomb-
ing of German cities, still stood on London's Fleet Street but that there was no memorial in Britain to
Charlton's conscientious objection; see "Imperial Whitewash," *Guardian*, July 31, 2006: http://www.
guardian.co.uk/commentisfree/2006/jul/31/whitewashingtheempire.

is elliptical here—because he does not say exactly what is unobjectionable during declared war or open rebellion—we might read him as accepting the bombing of military but not civilian targets. Nonetheless, in several airpower books he wrote after completing *Charlton*, the projected mass death of civilians by bombardment is axiomatic. These works of the thirties describe the next war between the great powers as an "eliminating race" in which "the mechanical employment of using enemy cities as bomb dumps" will be central. In a 1938 volume, we find Charlton agreeing with former Prime Minister Stanley Baldwin that "the only possible rejoinder if enemy aircraft [kill] our women and children, [is] for us to kill theirs, preferably in greater quantity." But he adds, with chilling instrumentalism, that "it must be the right sort of women and children whom we kill"—that "small-town folk are no good at all, because they are not of much account in any case, and the vocal efforts of the insignificant can be disregarded," as against the greater tactical advantage of killing "more important sections of the community." Even his proposals for an international peacekeeping air force recommended endowing that agency with the deterrent power to make a devastating first strike against the cities of uncooperative powers. In peacetime, the threat of bombing would serve as a truncheon in the policing of nations.[5]

Charlton's air power books bear remarkably little trace of the conscientious objection that ended his RAF career. It is as if, having left the Iraqi mandate behind, he had become an advocate and prophet of the very practices over which he had resigned his post there. A biographer might describe Charlton's air power writings as attempts to recoup the military credibility his conscience had cost him, or as evidence of his powers of emotional and ethical compartmentalization. But there is a third possibility: Charlton's conscientious objection and his air power advocacy in fact twine around one another, and tracing their entanglement might help us to see the broader lattices of thought on which they both depend. His crucial caveat again: whereas the bombing of civilians was morally objectionable in peacetime police actions, "in declared war or in the case of open rebellion no objection could possibly be advanced." This formulation contains several articles of faith: colonial policing is emphatically not a state of war; a state of war can only be entered through a nation's declaration or through a subject people's "open rebellion" against imperial rule; and wartime and peacetime are absolutely distinct when it comes to civilian lives, which are to be gently policed in peace but forfeit in war. Without doubt, Charlton's insistence on a gentler policing than bombardment set him apart from many of his RAF contemporaries. But with this exception, his conscientious objection left intact, and even relied on, a matrix of distinctions that was typical not only of RAF doctrine but also of

---

[5] L. E. O. Charlton, "The New Factor in Warfare," in L. E. O. Charlton, G. T. Garratt, and R. Fletcher, *The Air Defence of Great Britain* (Harmondsworth, UK: Penguin Books, 1938), 76, 105–10.

military theory, imperial policy, and international law during the interwar years. This conceptual grid reserved the status of war for declared conflicts between nation-states, consigning state violence against colonial, mandate, and protectorate populations to the unlegislated status of "low-intensity conflicts." By denying these same populations the right to declare war on the imperial nation-states that controlled them, it also denied them access to the protections accorded to states by international rules of warfare. The legal meaning of state violence in the colony was thus dissevered from the legal meaning of state-on-state violence in the metropole.

The rest of this chapter traces the political, institutional, and cultural formations by which a conscientious objector to violent colonial policing could also, and without especial psychosis, be a prophet of unbridled air war and an advocate of preemptively muscular air power. Although we will make forays into other interwar locales and national cultures, our focus will be Britain and its empire during the 1920s and early 1930s. The period's metropolitan obsession with the "next war" and its energetic prosecution of "small wars" in the periphery have both been underexamined, as has the intimate connection between the two—between the future bombing of the metropolis and the present bombing of the hutment, kraal, and hinterland. Our terminus will be the moment when the interdependence of these bombings became a more public matter: the Geneva Disarmament Conference of 1932–33, where the British delegation proposed abolishing all military air forces except those needed "for police purposes in certain outlying regions."[6] This was a move designed to preserve London from air raids in the future while maintaining the economies of peripheral bombing now. It said, Let us wage provident air war abroad in the present while being safeguarded at home from the bombs of a future adversary; in bombing, let us not be bombed. Note how space and time lace up here, with the colony knotted into an active violence of the continuous present, the metropolis into a future or future-conditional violence, an absent or latent or imminent one.[7] Because questions of extent are central to both imperialism and the concept of total war, we will need to consider how space is imagined in interwar military debates and practices, how air power advocacy was based on a putative shift from wars of fronts to wars of areas, how the lexicons and theories of total war imagined empire in terms of concentric circles of licensed violence, and how law and imperial policy helped legitimize these concentrisms. But in addressing the relationships among total war, air power, and anticipation, and in linking total war with colonial policing, we will also be surveying temporalities in their capacity to give meaning to space. Some of these temporalities would partition space: to

---

[6] See CAB 23/75; Draft Disarmament Convention Submitted to Conference, March 16, 1933, C.P. 74(33); CAB 24/239.

[7] This chapter's epigraphs exhibit just such a set of distinctions.

the metropolitan subject, home is the space of the total war *to come*; abroad, the space of *ongoing* small wars. Others brought news of unlooked-for proximities: the colony now, insofar as it is the testing ground for techniques of state terror, is the future of the metropolis.

Charlton, the mandarin who recoiled at what he saw in the colonial proving-ground, might have brought such news, but the ideological *cordons sanitaires* between police action and declared war, between the options of present imperial defense and the necessities of total war in the future, held firm in nearly all of his work. Surprisingly, though, where his dissent accepted and even reinforced these firewalls, the most zealous advocates of air power walked through them in the course of their careers. Several key figures in colonial air policing during the interwar period went on to leadership positions in Bomber Command during the Second World War, presiding over the devastating area bombing of German cities. Data flows within the RAF, too, trace continuities that Charlton refused or failed to recognize. During the 1920s, statistical evaluations of the psychological effects of Great War city bombing were adduced in favor of "morale-bombing" in the Middle East, and the putative success of colonial air control was, in its turn, invoked in support of the "morale-effects" of a bomber offensive against Germany. Thus if we want to understand the partiality of total war doctrine, we need to attend not only to dissenting voices but also to the language of air power advocacy and to the disjunction between that language and the interwar forces deployed in its name. Although Charlton now cedes the foreground to other figures, we will continue to visit his ports of call: the experience and legacy of the Great War, the prophetic interwar doctrines of total war and air power, the evolving practices of colonial policing, and debates about international rules of warfare. And modernism: having completed this itinerary, we will be able in a later chapter to take up the question of how Charlton could have understood *Ulysses* as "an official handbook on the country of his future sojourn"—that is, as a book that might speak to questions about the legality, ethics, and cultural ramifications of Britain's policing of Iraq. Surveying these developments will allow us, too, to apprehend the 1920s as a postwar civil edifice marbled with two kinds of darker material: the prospect of a disastrous unrestrained war to come and the present-tense practice, in colonial spaces, of cognate "forms of frightfulness."

Of course this is only a partial account of European policies and attitudes with respect to conflict during the first interwar decade. The twenties also saw postwar military budget cuts and disarmament, developments in pacifist thought and action, and a series of international treaties whose signatories guaranteed existing borders, committed to arbitration, and appeared to relinquish war as a policy instrument. However, rather than attempt a panoramic portrait of Europe in the 1920s, this chapter takes a sustained look at total war's conceptual emergence and its legal and political elaborations.

By ascribing *partiality* to the concept of total war, I mean to call attention both to the constraints it imposed on what "counts" as war and to the ideological biases that informed and were enforced by those constraints—biases that denied colonial civilians even the fragile legal protections available to their European counterparts in declared war. Total war discourse, I suggest, was partial toward Eurocentric imperialist distinctions between center and periphery, peacetime and wartime. By cementing the latter distinction, it covered for the fact that forms of violence forbidden in the metropole during peacetime were practiced in the colony, mandate, and protectorate—that the distinction between peace and war was a luxury of the center. At the same time, by predicting that civilians in the metropole would have no immunity in future wars, it contributed to the erosion of the very imperial geography (center versus periphery) that it seemed to shore up. My concern, then, is to describe an imperial military discourse that misrecognizes and misrepresents its view of totality as exhaustive even as it contains intimations of that view's partiality.[8]

Intimations of Totality

Total war has become a widespread, even an indispensable concept for military historians, students of war culture, and theorists of peace, conflict, and sovereignty. Yet notwithstanding what I have called its standard definition, the expression has come to have a bewildering array of meanings. For some scholars, total war denotes a conflict in which the distinction between civilians and combatants is dissolved—the kind of conflict that negates civilian immunity through destructive technologies such as aerial bombing, poison gas, submarines, blockades, and nuclear and biological weapons. For others, total war means the industrial and ideological mobilization of entire populations by wartime governments; here the emphasis is not on how war is waged militarily but on the massive productive forces required to wage it and on their management through state bureaucracies, propaganda, and censorship. Other writers focus on total war's extreme goal—not just the defeat of an adversary but the unconditional surrender, collapse, or even extermination

---

[8] I have attempted to understand these dynamics predominantly from the inside, as it were, rather than by tracing the individuals, movements, or discourses that opposed them, in part because the latter approach has been undertaken by other scholars (see, especially, Omissi's chapter "Indigenous Responses to Air Policing" in *Air Power and Colonial Control*, 107–32). One result of this immanent critique is that my own archive is decidedly partial, favoring the British case and, within it, the published and unpublished writings of military theorists, practitioners, and propagandists. Because my thesis is, in essence, that what gets coded as "total" in respect to total war is in fact a special case of the partial, I have embraced the necessary partiality of my examples and the attendant circumscription of my claims rather than attempting to project from them an insupportably total account of my subject.

of an enemy civilization—and on the discourse of intolerable fundamental difference (e.g., liberalism versus militarism, fascism versus communism) that underpins such extreme goals. And still others understand total war as entailing particular kinds and degrees of subordination: of the individual to the state, or of civilian officials to a military dictatorship.

Some of these distinct definitions can be seen to interlock in powerful ways. Rule by military dictatorships may abet the mobilization of populations, for example, and qualms about targeting enemy civilians might be assuaged by official war cultures that depict the enemy as subhuman. At the same time, the range of meanings clustered under the expression "total war" can be profoundly at odds with one another. It makes a great difference whether you ascribe the targeting of civilians to the rise of certain weapons technologies, to an exterminatory war of ideas, or to the emergence of a certain kind of state or military-industrial complex. Scholars who write of total war must choose between incompatible options—between viewing it, for instance, as an expanded conflict (e.g., from fronts to areas) versus an intensified one (e.g., from defeating to eliminating an enemy). Or they must content themselves with all-of-the-above arguments. As a concept, total war has become at once so comprehensive and so self-contradictory that even those who remain committed to it must repeatedly justify their use of the term.[9]

If its truck with totality makes the concept of total war rhetorically omnivorous, its retroactive historical appetite has been equally keen. Although the expression itself dates from the middle of the First World War, historians have dubbed several earlier wars—the U.S. Civil War and the wars following the French Revolution, to name only the most prominent examples—"the first total war."[10] That we now debate whether a given conflict was or was not a total war illustrates the positivist drift of the concept, a drift that seems to have been quickened rather than hindered by the concept's increasing vagueness, as if historians were rushing to plant a flag on melting ice. In what follows, I will refrain both from joining the argument about historical priority and from hewing to one definition over the rest. Instead, I want to return the doctrine of total war to the period and, even more importantly, the temporality or time-attitude of its emergence. For although the discourse of total war has links to nineteenth-century war theory and to the First World War, it is at

---

[9]See, for instance, Roger Chickering, "Total War: The Use and Abuse of a Concept," in *Anticipating Total War: The German and American Experiences, 1871–1914*, ed. Manfred F. Boemeke, Roger Chickering, and Stig Förster (Cambridge: Cambridge University Press, 1999), 13–28; and David A. Bell, *The First Total War: Napoleon's Europe and the Birth of Warfare as We Know It* (Boston and New York: Houghton Mifflin, 2007), 8–9.

[10]T. Harry Williams's *Lincoln and His Generals* (New York: Knopf, 1952) opens with the claim that "The Civil War was the first of the modern total wars, and the American democracy was almost totally unready to fight it" (3); and David Bell's *The First Total War* attributes "the fusion of politics and war that distinguishes modern 'total war'" after 1792 to "the intellectual transformations of the Enlightenment, followed by the political fermentation of 1789–92" (8–9).

heart an *interwar* phenomenon, and in two ways: chronologically because the idea of total war was elaborated and canonized between the world wars, and temporally because it results from that period's thoroughgoing sense of itself as an interval between two wars. As a concept, we might say, total war precipitates out of the front between two massive pressure systems: the memory of the Great War and the anticipation of the next war, whose occurrence and greater severity were widely regarded, during the 1920s and 1930s, as unavoidable. Although that next war in whose shadow total war was first theorized is now many decades behind us, we are jerked back inside the interwar logic of total war's emergence every time we invoke the concept. For total war always designates a war to come, an asymptote that the *next* next war—which is often imagined now as the *final* next war—will approach more nearly.[11] Even the drive to identify the *first* total war might be understood as a historiographic symptom of total war doctrine's interwar formation: to locate the first total war in the past, decades or centuries before the concept's emergence, is to cancel a limit by claiming it was reached long ago, effectively warding off total war's defining imminence.

Although total war would appear to be a static designation, its function in the writing of history is a narrative one, and not just in contortionist claims that war is becoming "increasingly more total" during a given period.[12] As Roger Chickering has argued, total war now belongs to a stock historical script according to which war grows in extent and intensity until it "culminates in the self-transcendence of war in Auschwitz and Hiroshima—in a destructive achievement so consummate that it defies historical representation—whereupon the narrative falls into foreboding silence." Chickering

---

[11] It is tempting to argue that the asymptotic nature of total war—its role as an unreachable ideal type—is the concept's primary inheritance from the Prussian strategist Carl von Clausewitz, with whose notion of absolute war it is often conflated. For Clausewitz, however, absolute war was not a limit that real wars would approach in the future but a thought experiment, a hypothetical war that was unobstructed by chance, probability, political exigency, or moral restraint. Because Clausewitz viewed war in the real world as "the continuation of politics by different means," an absolute war that served no political rationale was by definition an abstraction. Even in the case of Napoleonic warfare, which Clausewitz identified as the closest thing to absolute war in his own time, "We must allow for natural inertia, for all the friction of its parts, for all the inconsistency, imprecision, and timidity of man." See Carl von Clausewitz, *On War*, ed. and trans. Michael Howard and Peter Paret (Princeton: Princeton University Press, 1976), 580. Nor, for all that Clausewitz envisioned the total mobilization of the state's destructive power in the service of its political aims, does he seem to have imagined absolute war as entailing the slaughter of civilians. However, the frictions and inconsistencies in Clausewitz's exposition made it possible for late-nineteenth- and early-twentieth-century readers of his work to understand absolute war as an imminent, rather than a purely abstract, form of conflict. On the reception and interpretation of Clausewitz's work, see *Clausewitz in the Twenty-First Century*, ed. Hew Strachan and Andreas Herberg-Rothe (Oxford: Oxford University Press, 2007), especially Hew Strachan, "Clausewitz and the Dialectics of War" and Jan Willem Honig, "Clausewitz's *On War*: Problems of Text and Translation."

[12] This is Ian F. W. Beckett's description of warfare during the nineteenth century in "Total War," in *War, Peace and Social Change in Twentieth-Century Europe*, ed. Clive Emsley et al. (Milton Keynes: Open University Press, 1989), 31.

dubs this narrative "romantic" in its self-transcendence; one might characterize it, alternately, as a kind of *Bildung* or maturation story in which warfare
comes of age along pre-established lines.[13] Either way, this (teleological, often
determinist) emplotment of a nation's growing capacity and willingness to
wage total war tends to correspond additionally to the plot of national development, as if the emergence of total war were a kind of shadow modernization narrative. A shadow Enlightenment narrative, too, insofar as civilian
immunity in war is seen as an index of civilization, progress, and reason's triumph over barbarism.[14] These stories have acquired so much momentum and
familiarity that they are difficult to see as stories, much less to intervene in.
And they efface and exclude a great deal. Even if we accept the premise that
total wars have taken place in fact, we often find that the *less* modernized sides
are the *more* fully mobilized, as in the case of the South in the U.S. Civil War.
The masterplot of total war deals badly with instances of restrained warfare
in supposedly total theatres and shears off examples of extreme mobilization
and civilian-killing in eras it considers too early. Its portrait of a national life
completely subordinated to a war effort misses the persistence of the everyday
during even the most unrestrained conflicts. In liquidating the distinction
between soldier and civilian, it fails to recognize how those crucially gendered figures and the labor they perform remain segregated even in putatively
total wars.[15] And most saliently for the present chapter, the narrative of total
war has clung since its interwar elaboration to the fiction that war between
imperial nation states has nothing to do with colonial violence—and that colonies and protectorates, no matter how fully and coercively mobilized they
are, cannot by definition declare or participate in total war because they are
not yet nations, not yet autonomous, not yet modernized.

The expression "total war" appears to have been coined by the right-wing
French editor Léon Daudet in March 1916, during the early weeks of the Battle
of Verdun. That month, Daudet's journal *Action Française* carried his article
"Une guerre totale: eux ou nous" ["A Total War: Them or Us"], which argued
that the war now involved—and must involve—every element of national
life and character. At the time, Daudet was less interested in theorizing an
emergent form of warfare than in providing a rationale for extreme suspicion

---

[13] Chickering, "Total War: The Use and Abuse of a Concept," 15.

[14] See, for example, Igor Primoratz's gloss on Hobsbawm: "The idea of limited war in general, and
of immunity of civilians (non-combatants) in war in particular, was seen as an outcome of a process
of civilization and humanization of warfare that had its roots in ancient philosophical and religious
thought, had evolved as a major tradition in philosophy and moral theology in the Middle Ages,
and had been systematically developed by philosophers and political and legal thinkers of the modern age until it came to be recognized as one of the most important achievements of moral progress." Igor Primoratz, "Introduction," *Civilian Immunity in War*, ed. Igor Primoratz (Oxford: Oxford
University Press, 2007), 2.

[15] Here I am summing up the more expansive historiographic critique of total war in Chickering's
invaluable "Total War: The Use and Abuse of a Concept," 18–23.

toward naturalized Germans: "every German living in France is necessarily a spy," he wrote.[16] Daudet's follow-up book, *La guerre totale* (1918), was driven by a similar animus against Louis Malvy, Joseph Caillaux, and other radical French advocates of a negotiated peace. But this time Daudet took the trouble to define his title phrase as "the extension of war . . . to political, economic, commercial, industrial, intellectual, juridical, and financial realms. It is no longer just armies that fight, it is also traditions, institutions, customs, laws, spirits, and above all banks."[17] For Daudet, with his blood-and-soil organicist view of the nation, modern warfare had become total partly in intensity, demanding that one extinguish rather than merely defeat the enemy. But it was the metaphorics of extent—the claim that war must encompass every space, every civil system, every aspect of national life—that was uppermost in his definition of total war, and would preoccupy military theorists for most of the interwar period.

Perhaps owing to its origin in French wartime political maneuvering, the expression "total war" would go virtually dormant for years.[18] This dormancy during the 1920s and early 1930s allowed what became the doctrine of total war to lose most of its originary association with the integralist royalism and xenophobic nationalism of Daudet's *Action Française*. But the concept of a totally mobilized and therefore totally targetable nation was widely adopted by military theorists after 1918. This was particularly true among the first theorists of air power, whose writings became the main proxy-space where competing narratives about total war were debated and elaborated, under other aliases, during the interwar years. Among the reasons for total war doctrine's displacement into air power theory is their shared portrait of totality: the bomber's limitless target seemed to correspond perfectly, albeit from

---

[16] Léon Daudet, "Une guerre totale: eux ou nous," *Action Française*, March 11, 1916.

[17] The French original reads: "Qu'est-ce que la guerre *totale*? C'est l'extension de la lutte . . . aux domaines politique, économique, commercial, industriel, intellectuel, juridique et financier. Ce ne sont pas seulement les armées qui se battent, ce sont aussi les traditions, les institutions, les coutumes, les codes, les esprits et surtout les banques." Léon Daudet, *La guerre totale* (Paris: Nouvelle Librairie Nationale, 1918), 8; my translation above.

Speaking before the French legislature in November 1917, the new prime minister Georges Clemenceau called for "la guerre intégrale" ["integrated war"], a war in which citizens would share the privations of the soldiery and in which both the German adversary and left-wing French "appeasers" would be targeted with equal ferocity. Clemenceau's "guerre intégrale" is sometimes translated as "total war" but seems to have a more constrained meaning, serving the same political ends as Daudet's "guerre totale" without making the same hyperbolic claims about war's compass.

[18] The expression's best-known interwar revival took place in German general Erich Ludendorff's *Der totale Krieg* (Munich: Ludendorffs Verlag, 1935), which argued, contra Clausewitz, that the total mobilization of a nation's resources in war required a military dictatorship. But total war had become safe, as it were, for air power theory by 1931, when the French Douhetian strategist Camille Rougeron published "La guerre totale et l'aviation" in *L'Illustration* 4619 (September 12, 1931): 30–32. Carl Schmitt's writings take up the concept of total war explicitly in 1937, with his "Total Enemy, Total War, and Total State," rpt. in *Four Articles, 1931–1938*, trans. Simona Draghici (Washington, DC: Plutarch Press, 1999).

the other side of the bombsight, to the limitless mobilization advocated by Daudet. As proponents of an expensive, underfunded new military technology during a period of postwar disarmament, early air power theorists also needed a hyperbolic promotional story, one that could conjure funding by making independent air forces sound synonymous with the future of warfare and national defense. Total war doctrine could supply both the hyperbole and the futurity. Despite having been coined to serve Daudet's immediate political agenda, the bald hyperbole of total war could only refer to a future in which the inarguably partial phenomena of the present moment—partial extent and intensity, partial mobilization, partial targeting—reached the limit of the total. Total war's futurity was inseparable, in other words, from its conceptual power: it was rhetorically inexhaustible in proportion as it never quite arrived, something to be interminably called for or warded off rather than pointed to.[19] What's more, this inherent futurity aligned total war's temporality with that of aerial bombardment, a rapidly developing technique whose power to terrorize during the First World War had seemed to offer foreglimpses of a far more terrible future, and whose psychological power, as we saw in the Introduction, lay principally in its coercive, panic-laden structure of anticipation.

Interwar Air Power Theory

30,000 deaths in a single night (Hamburg, July 27–28, 1943); 40,000 deaths in a single night (Dresden, February 13–14, 1945); 90,000 deaths in a single night (Tokyo, March 9–10, 1945); 100,000 deaths from a single bomb (Hiroshima, August 6, 1945).[20] The estimated death tolls from Second World War bombing make it difficult, now, to read in the corresponding numbers from the First World War either the shattering memories or the grave portents those numbers held for survivors and interpreters of that war. But both the dread and the theory of future aerial bombardment during the interwar years were anchored firmly in those Great War statistics and the experiences to which they referred. Between 1914 and 1918, bombs dropped from airplanes and airships by both sides killed more than 2,000 people and injured nearly 5,000. German Zeppelin and bomber raids on London between May 1915

---

[19] Even Joseph Goebbels's famous shriek *"Wollt ihr den totalen Krieg?"* ["Do you want total war?"] at the Berlin Sportpalast rally in 1943 acknowledges the futurity of total war.

[20] Because of the extreme conditions in all four of these cases, death toll estimates vary widely. Here I have consulted Sven Lindqvist, *A History of Bombing*; A. C. Grayling, *Among the Dead Cities: The History and Moral Legacy of the WWII Bombing of Civilians in Germany and Japan* (New York: Walker & Co., 2006); Jörg Friedrich, *The Fire: The Bombing of Germany, 1940–1945*, trans. Allison Brown (New York: Columbia University Press, 2006); and Richard Overy, *The Bombers and the Bombed: Allied Air War Over Europe 1940–1945* (New York: Viking, 2013).

and May 1918 set 224 fires, destroyed 174 buildings, seriously damaged 619 more, and caused damage in excess of £2,000,000.[21] The raids forced over 300,000 Londoners from their homes and disrupted the war industry by causing worker fatigue and absenteeism. Along with the loss of life, property, and productivity, air raids caused significant psychological trauma. Civilians in severely bombarded towns reported suffering from weeks-long anxiety states.[22] In London, indications of an incoming raid could induce panic fatalities even when the alarm turned out to be false: H. A. Jones describes, for instance, how fourteen Londoners were trampled to death and as many injured when a crowd mistook an alert-mortar as a bombing raid and stampeded for two underground stations.[23] Suspicion flourished under the airships, too, as Londoners accused one another of signaling the Zeppelins and looted shops with German-sounding names.[24]

During the war, official narratives about British home-front determination and stoicism in the face of the raids prevailed. But the early twenties saw key moments in the gathering and interpretation of Great War data—key moments in the war's reception, if you will—and these underscored the psychological effects of bombardment on both sides. In 1920 the British Air Ministry issued the results of a bombing survey designed to assess wartime damage in order to inform air services' future bombing plans. The report found that the material damage caused by bombs had been outweighed by their "indirect effects," which included the disruption of factories and railways by raids and alerts, drops in production owing to worker evacuation and absenteeism, and morale damage to workers in target areas. A section on German chemical and munitions factories showed that frequent *false* alarms had in some cases affected productivity more than had the damage inflicted by actual bombing raids. Output deficits had been further increased by the fact that "constant alarms and raids ruined [workers'] nerves, in some cases for life."[25] Other findings contested the degree to which bombing alerts and raids had weakened the morale of the bombed. But whatever the actual experience of those on the ground had been, these surveys (another appeared in

---

[21] Basil Henry Liddell Hart, *Paris, or The Future of War* (New York: E. P. Dutton, 1925), 38.

[22] E. Wittkower and J. P. Spillane, "A Survey of the Literature of Neurosis in War," in *The Neuroses in War*, ed. E. Miller (New York: Macmillan, 1940), 3–4.

[23] Sir Walter Alexander Raleigh and H. A. Jones, *The War in the Air: Being the Story of the Part Played in the Great War by the Royal Air Force* (6 vols.; Oxford: The Clarendon Press, 1922–1937), vol. 5, 114.

[24] See "Zeppelins Kill Four in London; Riots Renewed," *New York Times*, June 2, 1915; see also Douglas H. Robinson, *The Zeppelin in Combat: A History of the German Naval Airship Division, 1912–1918* (London: G. T. Foulis, 1962).

[25] "Results of Air Raids on Germany Carried out by the 8th Brigade and Independent Force," Air Publication (A.P.) 1225, 3rd ed., Air Ministry, London, January 1920; qtd. in Tami Davis Biddle, *Rhetoric and Reality in Air Warfare: The Evolution of British and American Ideas About Strategic Bombing, 1914–1945* (Princeton: Princeton University Press, 2002), 57–59.

1925) pointed to two emerging strategies in modern warfare: the targeting of the enemy's whole industrial matrix, including worker housing, and the targeting of civilian morale by bombs and by the dread of bombs. The routinized anxiety later described by Lewis Mumford had been recognized by military strategists as a potent psychological weapon. Regardless of whether bombs actually fell, the air raid siren, with its power to create a climate of dreadful and disruptive expectation, had been weaponized.[26]

Even as the Great War receded into the past, its casualty statistics were continually invoked as a benchmark against which to measure the payloads of developing weapons technologies. In 1922, a highly publicized Committee on Imperial Defense report calculated that "an enemy air force could drop 150 tons of bombs on London during the first day of hostilities (or half the total dropped by Germany in the First World War), 110 tons on the second day, and 75 tons daily thereafter."[27] As dire as these postwar prognoses may have sounded to civil defense officials, they seemed to ratify the claims of early air power theorists, most of them Great War veterans who were beginning to make the case for strong, independent air forces. The first of these to emerge after the Armistice was an Italian, Giulio Douhet, who in 1922 became Mussolini's first subsecretary of aeronautics. A friend of D'Annunzio's and an admirer of the Futurist Marinetti, Douhet was an amateur novelist, painter, and poet in addition to being a professional soldier. During the First World War, he had been court-martialed and jailed for criticizing the Italian general staff's air strategy and making dire predictions about how it would affect the outcome of the war; his commission was eventually restored when his forecasts were borne out in the Italian army's defeat by the Austrian Air Force at Caporetto. Douhet was promoted to brigadier general in 1921, the year his *Il dominio dell'aria* [*The Command of the Air*] was published by the Italian Ministry of War. The book eventually became its generation's definitive work of air power advocacy, and its influence and reputation extended well beyond Italy. Though no German translation appeared until 1935 and no official English one until 1942, unpublished translations were circulating in the RAF and the U.S. Army Air Corps during the late 1920s, by which point Douhet's name and theories were also frequently mentioned in the pages of *Militär-Wochenblatt*, a semi-official journal of the German army.[28] By the outbreak of the Second World War, the basic

---

[26] The famous Klaxon air raid siren did not make its appearance in England until 1917, as a result of the failure of other devices to sound the alarm audibly and unambiguously to an entire city. I mean "air raid siren" here as a synecdoche for the air raid alert generally and for the industrial and psychological disruptions it caused.

[27] Josef W. Konvitz, "Cities as Targets: Conceptions of Strategic Bombing, 1914–1945," Working Paper No. 85, International Security Studies Program, Woodrow Wilson International Center for Scholars (1987), 41; citing Terence O'Brien, *Civil Defense*, History of the Second World War, United Kingdom Civil Series (London: HMSO, 1955), 12.

[28] Azar Gat, *A History of Military Thought from the Enlightenment to the Cold War* (Oxford: Oxford University Press, 2001), 588, 592n62.

position articulated in *The Command of the Air* had become, whether by direct influence or parallel development, standard air power doctrine, particularly in the writings of William Mitchell and Alexander de Seversky in the United States and Jan Christian Smuts and Hugh Trenchard in the United Kingdom.

Along with Douhet, these theorists became known by their contemporaries as the "prophets" of classical air power. In Douhet's case, the name recalled the vindication of his Great War forecasts, beginning with his 1909 insistence that "the sky too is about to become a battlefield."[29] It also evoked his conviction that when dealing with a technology as young as aviation, the analysis of past wars was next to useless in theorizing future ones. "In the name of charity, let us forget the last war!" he wrote, and many pages of *The Command of the Air* and its sequels are written in a clairvoyant future tense, about a coming war that will take place in aviation's maturity rather than in its bygone infancy:

> By virtue of this new weapon, the repercussions of war are no longer limited by the farthest artillery range of surface guns, but can be felt directly for hundreds and hundreds of miles over all the lands and seas of nations at war. No longer can areas exist in which life can be lived in safety and tranquility, nor can the battlefield any longer be limited to actual combatants. On the contrary, the battlefield will be limited only by the boundaries of the nations at war, and all of their citizens will become combatants, since all of them will be exposed to the aerial offensives of the enemy. There will be no distinction any longer between soldiers and civilians . . . .
>
> The brutal but inescapable conclusion we must draw is this: in face of the technical development of aviation today, in case of war the strongest army we can deploy in the Alps and the strongest navy we can dispose on our seas will prove no effective defense against determined efforts of the enemy to bomb our cities.[30]

While international jurists labored to reestablish the distinction between soldiers and civilians in the international laws of war, Douhet simultaneously predicted and promoted the final liquidation of that distinction, collapsing

---

[29] Qtd. in Eugene M. Emme, *The Impact of Air Power: National Security and World Politics* (Princeton, NJ: D. Van Nostrand, 1959), 161. Douhet's mantle of prophecy remained in place after his death in 1930; his lectures and essays were collected posthumously in *Le profezie di Cassandra* [*The Prophecies of Cassandra*] (Genoa: Lang & Pagano, 1931).

[30] Giulio Douhet, *The Command of the Air*, trans. Dino Ferrari (New York: Coward-McCann, 1942), 9–10. Further references cited in the text. Ferrari tends to remove some of the regional particulars of the original, rendering Douhet's "Roma, Milano, Venezia, od una qualunque delle nostre cento città" as "our cities" at the end of the passage I cite above; see Giulio Douhet, *Il dominio dell'aria: saggio sull'arte della guerra aerea, con una appendice contenente nozioni elementari di aeronautica* (Rome: Stabilimento Poligrafico per l'Amministrazione della Guerra, 1921), 8. However, I use the Ferrari translation here owing to its importance in the international reception of *Il dominio dell'aria*.

the distance between military fronts and home fronts. For him, and for other air war prophets, the city would be the space of the decision in war—the kind of decision that had been catastrophically deferred in the last war by the impasse of the trenches. As British air power advocate J. M. Spaight put it, "the attacks on the towns will be the war."[31]

The Command of the Air advises beginning a war with such devastating air strikes and poison gas attacks that the adversary's citizenry revolts against the state, demanding capitulation before land and sea forces have had time to engage one another.[32] A paroxysmal slaughter of civilians in the first days of a conflict, that is, would preempt both mobilization and the attendant loss of combatants' lives. Rather than conflate civilian and soldier, Douhet goes so far as to mobilize the former in defense of the latter in a spectacular inversion of conventional views of war. Almost as unsettling as this exchange is the anecdote with which Douhet punctuates it, one that captures both the pre-traumatic syndrome of the bombed and the doubly haunted temporality of the interwar years, linking them at the interface between traumatic memory and catastrophic anticipation. Douhet writes:

> A complete breakdown of the social structure cannot but take place in a country subjected to this kind of merciless pounding from the air. The time would soon come when, to put an end to horror and suffering, the people themselves, driven by the instinct of self-preservation, would rise up and demand an end to the war—this before their army and navy had time to mobilize at all! The reader who thinks I have overcolored the picture has only to recall the panic created at Brescia when, during funeral services for the victims of an earlier bombing—a negligible one compared with the one I have pictured here—one of the mourners mistook a bird for an enemy plane. (58–59)

It is bad enough that the experience of being bombed should make every bird look like the next bomber. But for that apparition to arrive during the commemoration and interment of bombing victims, for it to turn mourning into an occasion for mass panic, suggests the power of aerial bombardment, as both a practice and a sustained threat, to rend chronology itself. The temporality of mourning—a looking backward in order that one may come to live forward again—is split open and made to accommodate a more violent

---

[31] J. M. Spaight, *Air Power and War Rights* (London: Longmans, Green and Co., 1924), 12.

[32] Douhet's claim that bombing would demoralize the bombed to the point of provoking their political revolt is one instance where his prophecies proved famously wrong: if bombing civilians in the Second World War did not always strengthen their resolve, it never resulted in their rising against the state and demanding a surrender. As Robert Pape points out, "in the more than thirty major strategic air campaigns that have thus far been waged, air power has never driven the masses into the streets to demand anything." Robert A. Pape, *Bombing to Win: Air Power and Coercion in War* (Ithaca, NY: Cornell University Press, 1996), 68.

futurity: the dread in which the next catastrophe declares its imminence. This collision of mourning and anticipatory panic—this interruption of grief by a panic that returns the mourner forcibly to the originary scene of loss—characterizes not only the experience of the victims of repeated aerial bombardments but the historical uncanniness of the interwar period: a waiting for the unprecedented to return.

The verb tenses in which the prophets of air power thought and wrote, then, bound them weirdly to the victims of the bombings they predicted—to those who awaited the inevitable raid or could be coerced by the threat of one. Though Douhet's work imperfectly grasps it, this new strain of urban dread was not just epiphenomenal to air power; it was air power's essence. That coercion might be more effectively brought about through expected than through realized devastation, a notion only latent in Douhet, would become a rudiment of Cold War air power strategy thanks to key formulations by the likes of nuclear game-theorist Thomas C. Schelling in *Arms and Influence* (1966): "To be coercive, violence has to be anticipated. . . . It is the expectation of *more* violence that gets the wanted behavior, if the power to hurt can get it at all."[33] This is nuclear deterrence strategy in a nutshell, and as such is concerned with the coercion of states; but the civilian bodies against whom that expected violence threatens to discharge itself cannot register coercion in the way a state can, by altering its alliances, its foreign policy, or its military posture; they register it, instead, in something like the "collective psychosis" described by Lewis Mumford—in a permanent and somatized version of the panic felt by the mourners at Brescia.

Rival Preemptions of Law and War

One way to disarm a weaponized anticipation would be to out-anticipate it. As Douhet's ideas began to influence military elites in the early 1920s, international jurists were attempting to make the deliberate bombardment of civilians a war crime by reformulating the laws of war, pitting the futurity of the law—its bid to preempt future actions by proleptically banning them—against the prospect of devastating air strikes against population centers.

---

[33] Thomas C. Schelling, *Arms and Influence* (New Haven: Yale University Press, 1966), 2–3; emphasis in original. Jan Mieszkowski detects a related antecedent to Cold War temporality in the war machine's capacity, after 1918, to "generate fictional visions of wars not yet waged. . . . The real legacy of the Great War lies not in its status as the standard of pure destructiveness against which all subsequent clashes must be compared, but in the way it alters the judging of military achievements such that future triumphs or defeats have to be assessed with reference to a hypothetical 'super conflict' that may never come to pass. This shift in the evaluation of military ventures comes to fruition in the Cold War, where visions of apocalyptic scenarios become the medium of combat itself." Jan Mieszkowski, "Great War, Cold War, Total War," *Modernism/modernity* 16 (2009): 212.

Although Daudet's expression had not yet been resurrected, these were, at root, attempts to outlaw total war. But while the conferences in question took up law in the hope of preventing unrestrained warfare, they were also lessons in the strange congruence between law and what it seeks to interdict, a congruence made all the tighter by air war's attempt to jump law's claim on futurity. Because they all but presuppose a "next war," conferences on the laws of war bestow an official status on that dread eventuality. Like the writings of war theorists, they provide stages for imagining the war to come, and nowhere more so than in their urgent attempts to shape that war's legal practicability. Even more striking, in the case of the early 1920s, is the isometry between the Douhetian scenario and that shared by the conferees. Although they approached it from different normative perspectives, the prophets of unrestrained air war and those who hoped to criminalize it were working with nearly identical depictions of the war to come. These portrayed belligerent nations in a still-emergent way: neither as impregnable allegorical figures nor as entities metonymically "headed" by a particular sovereign, caste, or generation, but as national totalities that were finite, vulnerable, and integrated by war.[34]

International modernism's *Wunderjahr* was bookended by conferences on the laws governing warfare. L. E. O. Charlton attended the 1921–22 Conference on the Limitation of Armament at Washington, D.C., in his capacity as air attaché to the British embassy; the 1922–23 Hague Commission on the Rules of Warfare would meet as he was settling into his new post in Iraq. In Washington the main group consisted of governmental representatives from Great Britain, France, Italy, Japan, and the United States, with envoys from China, Belgium, the Netherlands, and Portugal attending a subset of meetings on Pacific and Far Eastern questions. Of the meeting's failure to produce multilateral commitments to disarmament, Charlton wrote ominously that "A noble ship of peace had suffered shipwreck, and the sea overhead was again calm" (*Charlton*, 266). But the talks were not entirely fruitless: on the last day, the major participants signed a treaty prohibiting "the use of submarines as

---

[34] Owing partly to the title of his 1936 publication *La Guerra integrale*, Douhet is often misrecognized by English-speaking scholars as an early adopter of the expression "total war." The confusion has been amplified by semantic backshadowing in the English translation of this passage from *Il dominio dell'aria*: "Le attuali forme sociali hanno portato alle guerre di carattere nazionale, ossia alle guerre che coinvolgono nella mischia popoli interi: e, poiché l'evoluzione dell'assetto sociale si mantiene decisamente su questa via, è da prevedersi—nei limiti entro i quali debbono contenersi le previsioni umane—che il carattere degli eventuali futuri conflitti si manterrà nettamente nazionale" (3). Ferrari's 1942 translation renders "di carattere nazionale" as "a character of national *totality*" and "il carattere degli eventuali futuri conflitti si manterrà nettamente nazionale" as "future wars will be *total* in character and scope" (5; emphasis added). For Douhet in 1921, the expression "national wars" was sufficient to denote a new degree of mobilization and vulnerability, whereas by 1942 the national extent of war was so taken for granted that it required the intensification of "total."

commerce destroyers, as well as the use in war of asphyxiating, poisonous, or other gases, and all analogous liquids, materials or devices" between the contracting parties, who also agreed to encourage other nations' signing on to the prohibitions.[35] Still, it was clear that the conferees did not entertain such radical steps as decommissioning national militaries or subordinating them to an international Association of Nations; this was an occasion for divining the shape of ongoing war-provisioning by sovereign imperial nation-states still trembling from a world war. "At present the chief powers of the world show no signs of the collective action demanded," wrote one observer on the left. "They are still obsessed by old-fashioned ideas of national sovereignty and national competition, and though all verge on bankruptcy, they maintain and develop fresh armies and fleets. That is to say, they are in the preparatory stage of another war."[36]

That observer, H. G. Wells, attended the Washington conference as a reporter. In his opening article, Wells dismissed the notion that the Great War had, in any meaningful sense, ended. "The catastrophe of 1914 is still going on," he wrote, citing famine and social collapse in Russia, the instability of the world monetary system, the failure of Versailles, and the continual arming of major powers. "Since 1919 this world has not so much healed its wounds as realized its injuries" (2–3). He added that his friend Charlie Chaplin, visiting London recently for the first time in a decade, had said, "People are not laughing and careless here as they used to be. It isn't the London I remember. They are anxious. Something overhangs them." Wells's kakangelism arose out of his vision of "the world's economic life, its civilization, embodied in its great towns, [as] disintegrating and collapsing through the strains of the modern war threat and of the disunited control of modern affairs" (5–6). The anxiety Chaplin noted among Londoners responded, in his friend's view, to the Great War's general legacy of political and economic precariousness, but it also registered changes the war had wrought specifically on the sensoria of city-dwellers. "The hum of the Gotha and the long crescendo of the barrage as the thing gets near," sounds unfamiliar to most of Wells's American readers, still echoed in the ears of Londoners who, like the mourners at Brescia, were still traumatically attuned to the skies. "There was much mental trouble; London possesses now a considerable number of air raid lunatics and air raid defective children, and these are only the extreme instances of a widespread overstrain" (223–24). But the lingering mental trouble produced by Great War "air stress," as he called it, would be dwarfed by the physical destructiveness of bombing raids in a future war.

---

[35] John Bassett Moore, *International Law and Some Current Illusions and Other Essays* (New York: Macmillan, 1924), 184.

[36] H. G. Wells, *Washington and the Riddle of Peace* (New York: Macmillan, 1922), 16. This volume collects Wells's 1921–22 articles from the Washington Conference. Further references cited in the text.

The powers we have considered will . . . push their air equipment on a quite different scale; they will be bound to deliver their chief blows with it; we may certainly reckon on the biggest long-range airplanes possible, on the largest bombs and the deadliest contents for them. We may certainly reckon that, within three or four hours of a declaration of war between France and England, huge bombs of high explosive, or poison gas, or incendiary stuff, will have got through the always ineffectual barrage and be livening up the streets of Paris and London. Because it is the peculiarity of air warfare that there are no *fronts* and no effectual parries. You bomb the other fellow anywhere, and similarly he bombs you. (221–22)

The conference's prohibitions on the use of submarines and chemical warfare reflected principles of warfare that had been, in the words of one participant, "accepted by the civilized world for more than one hundred years": namely, "that unnecessary suffering in the destruction of combatants should be avoided" and "that innocent non-combatants should not be destroyed.[37] An aeronautical subcommittee had met to discuss limitations on the use of aircraft, but no regulations could be agreed on; these would be taken up, according to a resolution of the Washington conferees, at The Hague in December 1922. That the discussion of air war had to be set aside by a conference whose "very action and foundation" were the preservation of noncombatant immunity underscored the special challenges air war posed to that immunity— challenges legible in Wells's vision of a frontless war taken to the streets of capital cities.[38]

In fulfillment of the resolution passed in Washington, a Commission of Jurists convened in December 1922 in The Hague to consider amending the international laws of warfare to incorporate two "new agencies of warfare," the radio and the airplane. There was a sense among jurists that the Commission addressed public concern more than legal or technical necessity.[39] That public concern, as the Commission's president, U.S. Judge John Bassett Moore, noted, was concentrated around "the preservation of the distinction between

---

[37] Report of the General Board of the Navy, presented by Rear Admiral W. L. Rodgers, Chairman: *Proceedings of the Conference on the Limitation of Armament, 1921–1922* (Washington, DC: Government Printing Office, 1923), 734–36; qtd. in Moore, *International Law*, ix.

[38] Moore, *International Law*, ix. On the likelihood that Wells's writing, particularly the prewar speculative fiction *The War in the Air* (1908), influenced Douhet's early thinking about strategic bombing, see Frank J. Cappelluti, "The Life and Thought of Giulio Douhet" (PhD diss., Rutgers University, 1967), 105–6.

[39] William L. Rodgers, now acting as a technical advisor to The Hague's Committee of Jurists on the Laws of War, wrote: "It is doubtful if this demand for a code of rules for these two new agencies was felt by combatants so much as by the public. Technical representatives at The Hague of at least one Power said informally in conversation that to them personally the last war had not emphasized the need of any formal addition to the laws of war for the purpose of dealing with aviation and radio." See his "The Laws of War Concerning Aviation and Radio," *American Journal of International Law* 17.4 (October 1923): 630.

combatants and non-combatants, especially as affected by aerial bombardment. . . . The Commission is now face to face with the question of preserving this great principle, for the benefit of the present generation and of future generations."[40] Although several delegations had lobbied for more comprehensive prohibitions, the Commission finally reached unanimity on 62 Articles, to be taken home by the delegates and ratified by their nations. The pivotal Articles on aerial bombardment prohibited it "for the purposes of terrorizing the civilian population, of destroying or damaging private property not of military character, or of injuring non-combatants," permitting it only "when directed at a military objective." Such objectives consisted of "military forces; military works; military establishments or depots; factories constituting important and well-known centers engaged in the manufacture of arms, ammunition or distinctively military supplies; lines of communication or transportation used for military purposes."[41] When such objectives could not be targeted without indiscriminate bombardment of the civilian population, belligerents were to abstain from attacking them. These provisions would replace those in the 1907 Hague Convention IV forbidding "The attack or bombardment, by any means whatsoever, of undefended towns, villages, dwellings, or buildings." Critics of the 1907 Convention pointed out that the criterion of "defense" did not fairly or rationally correspond with a city's military industrial importance—that it made "undefended" manufacturing centers immune to bombardment while leaving trivially "defended" cities that lacked war industry plants open to bombing. Moreover, the projected growth of air power would change the very nature of "defense"; as Paul Whitcomb Williams put it, "a vastly augmented and almost ubiquitous air force . . . in a sense confers upon every town the distinction of being defended, and consequently of being destroyed."[42]

But Williams went on to complain in 1929 that the 1923 draft convention had introduced fatal ambiguities of its own. "Who can say what are 'distinctively military supplies' in wartime," he asked, "when so much of the output of almost every factory producing anything from jam to steel goes to assist the conduct of military operations? No doubt this provision was designed to exclude jam factories and include woolen mills making army clothing, for example, but who shall say that meat is less important to an army in the field than raiment, and why should aircraft be permitted to bomb one and not the other?" Under emerging warfare trends, Williams argued, in which combatants "regard the industrial sinews of a state as vital and sufficiently related to the military arm as to be properly subject to

---

[40] Moore, *International Law*, 200–201.

[41] From 1922–23 draft Hague Rules, Articles, 22 & 24, qtd. in Moore, *International Law*, 241–43.

[42] Paul Whitcomb Williams, "Legitimate Targets in Aërial Bombardment," *American Journal of International Law* 23.3 (July 1929): 573.

attack . . . it is no longer possible to distinguish at all times and as sharply between the men at the front and the workers in the factories."[43] With the whole productive power of industrial nations feeding in some manner into their war efforts, no product or factory or worker could be detached from the military-industrial complex and thereby exempted from bombing. Now that jam had been militarized, jam should be targetable. So should jam works, jam makers, and the homes of the latter. It was no wonder, Williams added, that rather than surrender their rights to bomb an enemy's "industrial sinews" up and down their full length, the prospective signatories had so far, as of 1929, left the Hague Commission's rules unratified. By the outbreak of war in 1939, the rules were still only a draft. Although voluntarily observed during the first months of the war, they were quickly forgotten in the escalations of area bombings that became common practice during most of the Second World War.

In their unratified state, the 1923 Hague rules demonstrated that the Commission's "great principle" of noncombatant immunity had been weakened rather than strengthened by the terror bombings of the First World War—that prospective signatories were unwilling to rule out targeting the urban factories, war-industry workers, and civilian morale of their adversaries in a future conflict. Some military elites maintained that international laws were not worth the trouble because they would be as ineffectual in the next full-scale war as they had been in the last one. But the prospect of effectively prohibiting air strikes against civilian centers had foundered against an even more unsettling assumption: that air war would arrive before law. As we have seen in Douhet's work, air power theorists argued that the next war would begin with an attempted "knockout blow": a surprise air strike by the aggressor against the capital cities of the adversary in the hopes of provoking surrender before a full-scale war had begun. Delivered before war was formally declared, such a knockout blow would be struck, in effect, while the law was asleep.[44] We are at some limit of the law here—a speed limit. It is not the rough seam between national sovereignty and international accords familiarly traced by international law; nor is it the challenge of trying to limit forms of violence that tend to intensify over time. Air war would devastate not by stamina but by velocity, by earliness, overtaking law at the gate. Even if they were ratified, legal guarantees of civilian immunity would hold only until the moment before they were needed.

---

[43] Williams, "Legitimate Targets," 576–77; 560.

[44] F. H. Sykes's claim typifies this view: "But while the speed of mobilisation is of vast consequence to the older services, it is vital for air forces: for the first aerial blow may be struck *before* the actual declaration of war, and on its result the very possibility of naval and military mobilization may depend." Sykes, *Aviation in Peace and War* (London: Edward Arnold, 1922), 210; emphasis in original.

National Totality and Colonial Air Control

As the proxy-space for total war doctrine, air power theory provided limitless occasions for representing the national totality. The most common trope envisioned nations as integrated bodies whose vulnerable points—brain, nerves, heart, Whitcomb Williams's "industrial sinews"—were correspondingly physical. Writing to the London *Times* in 1922, air power theorist Brigadier General P. R. C. Groves predicted that in future air wars, "Each side will at once strike at the heart and nerve centres of its opponent: at his dockyards, arsenals, munition factories, mobilization centres, and at those nerve ganglia of national *morale*—the great cities."[45] Even absent the trope of the national body, belligerent nations were described in terms that fused totality, unity, and fragility. Here is another British air war prophet, Basil Liddell Hart, in his influential *Paris, or the Future of War* (1925):

> A modern state is such a complex and interdependent fabric that it offers a target highly sensitive to a sudden and overwhelming blow from the air. We all know how great an upset in the daily life of the country is caused at the outset of a railway strike even. Business is disorganized by the delay of the mails and the tardy arrival of the staff, the shops are at a standstill without fresh supplies, the people feel lost without newspapers—rumours multiply, and the signs of panic and demoralization make their appearance. . . . Imagine for a moment London, Manchester, Birmingham, and half a dozen other great centres simultaneously attacked, the business localities and Fleet Street wrecked, Whitehall a heap of ruins, the slum districts maddened into the impulse to break loose and maraud, the railways cut, factories destroyed. Would not the general will to resist vanish, and what use would be the still determined fractions of the nation, without organization and central direction?[46]

---

[45] P. R. C. Groves, "The New Warfare," *Times* (London), March 21, 1922; rpt. in P. R. C. Groves, *Our Future in the Air: A Survey of the Vital Question of British Air Power* (London: Hutchinson & Co., 1922), 11. See Konvitz, "The City as Target," 40, for a partial list of biological metaphors in interwar air power writing. Charlton, whose experience in Iraq might have equipped him to see the limitations of the national "body" metaphor, wrote: "If Paris was the heart of France, these two selected areas—Lille, Lyon–Valence—were the right and left brain-lobes which directed her activities and co-ordinated her bodily control. That night they were paralysed, so that the heart of France went dead within her and the rest of her body lay numb." See L. E. O. Charlton, *War over England* (London: Longmans, Green and Co., 1936), 229.

[46] Liddell Hart, *Paris, or the Future of War*, 41–42. Hugh Trenchard placed Liddell Hart's book on the RAF's list of recommended reading; see Biddle, *Rhetoric and Reality in Air Warfare*, 105. Liddell Hart's vision is, in fact, keyed to the bodily projection of the national totality: his "Paris" is the adversary who aims for a nation's Achilles' heel—its citizens' morale, where "a nation's nerve system, no longer covered by the flesh of its troops, is now laid bare to attack" (36–37).

Liddell Hart's fantasia of the diorama conjures an England whose complexity, interdependence, and total visibility are also the conditions of its vulnerability. Unsurprisingly, given his far-right political sympathies, the wartime state's "organization and central direction" are the things most imperiled by air war and the civil unrest it would unleash. In fact, Liddell Hart cannot imagine the national totality without invoking internal revolt, either as a peacetime railway strike or as an orgy of looting in the maddened slum districts on the heels of massive air strikes. It is as if the passage half remembered the origins of the phrase "total war" in Daudet's wartime campaign against French radicals, illustrating the fact that portraits of totality and interdependence are produced as much through the threat of internal resistance and dissent as by the prospect of attack from outside.

Whether it was constructed under the imaginative pressure of external attack, internal revolt, or some combination of the two, the national totality portrayed by Groves, Liddell Hart, and other air war prophets invariably ended at the borders of the state; concomitantly, the next war invoked by those writers referred exclusively to conflicts among sovereign nation-states.[47] Because the violence wrought by those same powers in their colonies took place outside the boundaries of the national body, such violence went virtually unacknowledged by classical air power theory and other forms of next-war discourse, including international law. When colonial campaigns were spoken of in other sectors of military theory and policy, they were either belittled as small wars or covered in a slew of euphemisms—*police actions, low-intensity conflicts, constabulary missions, pacification, colonial policing*—that denied them the status of war altogether. International law, for its part, would not allow anti-colonial or national liberation movements the benefits of the laws of war until 1977.[48] But as historians of interwar British imperialism have begun to show, a number of classical air power theorists were also architects and practitioners of colonial violence. While the likes of Hugh Trenchard, John Salmond,

---

[47] One respondent to Groves's 1922 *Times* articles argued that the ruin of European cities was in some way contingent on imperialism. Imperial nation-states, said the writer, were most likely to attack one another in order to obtain their adversary's imperial holdings; relinquishing rule over "black and dusky races" would do away with risk of another European war, making London and Paris as safe as Berne and Geneva. *The Nation and the Athenaeum*, April 1, 1922; rpt. in Groves, *Our Future in the Air*, 105. Yet even this exceptional response can imagine the colonies only as stakes in a total war between European states, not as spaces where unrestrained violence cognate with total war is already being waged. The connection adduced by the writer, in other words, was still symptomatic of the occlusive work performed by the concept of total war in respect to empire.

[48] The first Protocol Additional to the 1954 Geneva Convention, adopted on June 8, 1977, classifies "armed conflicts in which peoples are fighting against colonial domination and alien occupation and against racist regimes in the exercise of their right of self-determination" as international conflicts, stipulating that the victims of such conflicts are eligible for the Convention's legal protections for the victims of war. See Geneva Convention, Protocol I, article 1, § 4.

and Winston Churchill debated the probable course of air war in Europe's future, they were at the same time using the imperial periphery as a testing range for the bomber's efficiency, destructive power, and psychic coerciveness. A truly total conception of war would have insisted openly on the legal, ethical, political, and technological connections between European conflagration and colonial air control. But instead, the ideologically partial concept of total war doubly effaced such connections—first by setting them beyond the national limits of its totality-claims, and second by inviting this useful occlusion to be misrecognized as comprehensive portraiture. In turning now to 1920s colonial air control, we will be looking at a larger, transnational economy of injury, coercion, and administration through whose occultation the national totality was producible as a discrete body, integrated in both vulnerability and sovereignty.

Whatever its other distinctions, 1922 was a pivotal year in the survival and consolidation of the RAF. For most of the Great War, British military aviation had taken shape as two structures ancillary to the army and navy, respectively: the Royal Flying Corps and the Royal Naval Air Service. After the Zeppelin and Gotha raids on London in early 1917, widespread concern about England's ineffective air defense led to the creation of a single air force overseen by the new Air Ministry. Two months after the Armistice, Churchill was appointed Secretary of State for War and Air with the expectation that he would repartition the RAF into its army and navy subsidiaries. Growing public demand for disarmament and military spending cuts made the elimination of an expensive third agency seem attractive. But Churchill was a stubborn proponent of an independent air force, and in 1919 and 1920, he and Trenchard, his new Chief of Air Staff, began to step up RAF operations in the colonies, hoping to demonstrate that air power could efficiently and affordably contribute to "imperial defense." During those years, air raids were carried out against Dacca, Jalalabad, and Kabul in the Third Afghan War; against Enzeli in Iran; against demonstrators in the Punjab and an uprising in the Transjordan; against Mahsud and Wazir tribes along India's North West Frontier; and against the Dervish followers of the "Mad Mullah" Mohammed bin Abdulla Hassan in Somaliland (Somalia). The RAF claimed success in these operations, although many of its reports exaggerated the accuracy of air strikes, suppressed or failed to collect civilian casualty numbers, and underrepresented the extent to which tribal adversaries adapted to strafing and bombardment. By 1922 Churchill and Trenchard resolved that the RAF be put entirely in charge of military operations in Mesopotamia (Iraq), which Britain had acquired in 1920 by League of Nations mandate after the dissolution of the Ottoman Empire. According to their proposed scheme of "air substitution," the costly and politically controversial prospect of an occupation could be replaced by a vastly cheaper "control-without-occupation" from the air: fifty-one battalions of British and Indian ground troops would be replaced by eight or nine squadrons and a vastly reduced garrison, both under RAF control.

The prospect of air substitution in Iraq intensified the rivalry between the RAF and the Army as the two services competed for diminished postwar military funds. This competition took some strange shapes, including the War Office's assault on the RAF for the inhumanity of air policing. But the strangest interservice melee was routed through competing theories about whether bombing's effectiveness depended on the race and development of the bombed. In July 1922, shortly before Churchill took the air control scheme to the Cabinet for approval, the Army's Staff College in Quetta, India, hosted a conference on the future of colonial air policing. The presence of both Army and RAF personnel inflated the rhetorical stakes of the occasion, making it appear nothing less than a duel for the future of imperial defense. In his attempts to discredit the new doctrine of air substitution, the Army's Staff College Commandant, Major-General Louis Vaughan, argued that whereas the sensitive nervous systems of Europeans made them keenly vulnerable to prolonged aerial bombardment, the "little sensitive psychology" of nonwhite tribesmen would permit them to adapt to bombing.[49] Against this view, John Salmond—Charlton's old flight-school classmate—insisted that "humanity was the same the world over," and that the population of Kabul would react to bombing just as the population of London had during the Great War. Vaughan had effectively declared the lessons of that war's strategic bombing irrelevant to the question of colonial policing, but Salmond's invocation of an undifferentiated humanity drew air control techniques explicitly under the aegis of total war. He went on to delineate three universal phases of response to bombardment: first, panic, especially if it were an adversary's first experience of bombardment; next, indifference or contempt in the face of continued air attacks; and finally, after sustained bombing, weariness and a longing for peace that would produce compliance with the bomber's demands.[50]

The proponents of colonial air control were perfectly capable of adducing racialist pseudo-ethnographic arguments in favor of their policies. They claimed, for instance, that tribal adversaries were more susceptible to the spectacle of technologically advanced weapons, either because such adversaries feared what they could not understand or because "the more primitive the race is, the more it respects sheer power."[51] They argued, too, that

---

[49] Vaughan to CGS India, July 15, 1922, Salmond Papers B2598, qtd. in Omissi, *Air Power*, 110.

[50] Conference held at Quetta on July 2, 1922, Salmond Papers B2592; qtd. in Omissi, *Air Power*, 110. Salmond's three-stage schema seems to have become RAF doctrine. In December 1923, Wing-Commander Charles Edmonds told an audience at the Royal United Services Institution, "The shocks and interruptions, the inconvenience and indignity of it all, will tell in the end. The civilized nation will go through the same three phases as did the semi-civilized tribe: alarm, indifference, weariness; followed ultimately by compliance with our will." See C. H. K. Edmonds, "Air Strategy," *Journal of the Royal United Services Institution* 70 (1925): 198.

[51] Lecture to the Boys at Marlborough by W/Co. N. H. Bottomley, Bottomley Papers B2240; qtd. in Omissi, *Air Power*, 110.

the very notion of noncombatant immunity had to be rethought in respect to Iraq, whose masculine warrior culture turned all males into combatants while devaluing women and children to the point where their deaths in raids should not much vex the British conscience.[52] But Salmond's position at Quetta was not an eccentric one. In its fundamentals it accorded with an internal Air Staff position paper on imperial defense that had been circulated the previous year:

> It may be thought better, in view of the allegations of the "barbarity" of air attacks, to preserve appearances by formulating milder rules and by still nominally confining bombardment to targets which are strictly military in character . . . to avoid emphasizing the truth that air warfare has made such restrictions obsolete and impossible. It may be some time until another war occurs and meanwhile the public may become educated as to the meaning of air power.[53]

The 1921 memo implies what Salmond avowed openly: the salient difference is not between how different populations ("European" versus "Arab," "civilized" versus "semi-civilized") react to air war but between air war and all previous forms of war.[54] Notice how this recognition ramifies differently for the two populations in question, however. The British public will need to be fed reassuring fictions about the nature of the air attacks its government is ordering in Iraq and to be incrementally "educated as to the meaning of air power"—an education that will be completed by the next, presumptively unbridled war. The tribal subjects of air policing, in contrast, will receive a shorter, sharper education in unrestricted air war, undergoing in policing operations what their British counterparts will have to wait for the next total war to experience. The emphasis on universality in Salmond's theory of aerial bombing masked the particularity of its application to the subjects of air policing. The more like us the tribes are, the theory said, the better argument we have for bombing them in peacetime as we have just got through bombing Europeans in war.

The RAF's arguments prevailed when, in October 1922, the service commenced sole military control over Iraq with Salmond as Air Officer Commanding. The ensuing ten years of air control over Iraq (whose mandate status ended when the country joined the League of Nations in 1932) provided

---

[52] Priya Satia, *Spies in Arabia: The Great War and the Cultural Foundations of Britain's Covert Empire in the Middle East* (New York: Oxford University Press, 2008), 249–50.

[53] S. 12847, AIR 5 192; qtd. in Charles Townshend, "Civilization and 'Frightfulness': Air Control in the Middle East Between the Wars," in *Warfare, Diplomacy, and Politics: Essays in Honour of A. J. P. Taylor*, ed. Chris Wrigley (London: Hamish Hamilton, 1986), 159.

[54] Here I am elaborating on Omissi's observation that Salmond's three-stage schema "radically reconstructed both the 'native' and 'European,' eliminated their differences and gave maximum weight to the power of 'aerial attack.'" See Omissi, *Air Power*, 111.

an alternative to ground occupation at a fraction of the cost in soldiers' lives and pounds sterling, and later in the century U.S. military theorists would invoke that decade when advocating the use of air power in "small wars" and evolving the doctrine of "global reach—global power."[55] Recognizing the controversial nature of police bombing, the RAF took great care to "preserve appearances" by limiting the release of details about its operations in Iraq. Trenchard ordered Salmond to withhold specifics about casualties and bomb tonnage because the news "that two tons of bombs have been dropped on some little village daily" might give "a wrong sense of proportion at home."[56] The decision to forgo a formal inquiry into Charlton's resignation was part of the same strategy for preserving appearances.

Bombing Display I

But secrecy was in fact only half a strategy; the RAF also preserved appearances by spectacle. Once a year, the service's semicovert operations in the colonies and mandates were marketed to the British public through an overt op at home: the RAF pageant at the Hendon Aerodrome in North London. This event aimed to make the public more "air minded" by displaying the latest ordnance and techniques of the RAF, whose status as an independent agency was uncertain in 1920 when the first Hendon pageant took place. That one was watched by 40,000 people. By 1927, *Flight* magazine was claiming that the pageant had eclipsed Ascot in social glamour; in 1932, some 170,000 paying spectators crowded inside the airfield enclosures for what had been rechristened Empire Air Day, with several hundred thousand others watching for free outside.[57] Charlton described the event as "a truly representative concourse, a veritable section of the totality of class," adding that with so many heads of state, diplomats, church dignitaries, and members of the military elite present, Hendon was like "a large slice of cherry cake with all the fruit collected at the top."[58]

---

[55] See George C. Morris, "The Other Side of the COIN: Low-Technology Aircraft and Little Wars," *Airpower Journal* 5.1 (Spring 1991): 60; David J. Dean, *Air Power in Small Wars: The British Air Control Experience* (Maxwell Air Force Base, AL: Air University Press, 1985); Kenneth J. Alnwick, "Perspectives on Air Power at the Low End of the Conflict Spectrum," *Air University Review* 35.3 (March–April 1984): 17–28. For a critical view of British air control's applicability to contemporary low-intensity areas (specifically, the Clinton administration's proposal to apply air power in Bosnia), see David Willard Parsons, "British Air Control: A Model for the Application of Air Power in Low-Intensity Conflict?" *Airpower Journal* 8.2 (Summer 1994): 28–39.

[56] Trenchard to Salmond, July 27, 1922, and February 13, 1923, Trenchard Papers MFC 76/1/138; qtd. in Omissi, *Air Power*, 163.

[57] Omissi, *Air Power*, 171.

[58] Charlton, *War over England*, 158.

The pageants of 1920 and 1921 culminated in staged attacks that echoed Great War scenarios, but the 1922 pageant marked the advent of colonial air control by introducing a new climactic set piece: an "Eastern Drama" in which a British squadron destroyed a desert stronghold (Fig. 1.2). This was a hundred-foot tower constructed of the wings of obsolete planes and defended by a group of airmen in tribal dress and blackened faces, described in the pageant program as "Wottnotts" (a portmanteau of *Hottentot* and *whatnot*, a racial "etcetera"). After showing off forced landings and emergency repairs, the RAF planes destroyed the tower with incendiary bombs to the wild applause of the spectators[59] (Fig. 1.3). (Hold this surreal event in your mind— the mocked-up desert stronghold built out of scrapped Great War planes on the outskirts of the imperial metropolis; the costumed blackface pilots; the spectacularizing of imperial violence before a domestic audience—and ask yourself later on, when we are considering the "Circe" episode of *Ulysses*, whether even Joyce's imagination could generate anything as arresting, repellent, and hallucinatory as the 1922 Hendon pageant finale.) As unabashed as the "Eastern Drama" was in its imperial propagandizing, it stopped short of showing what planes and bombs could do to noncombatants. That was left until the 1927 pageant, in which the RAF bombed the inhabitants of "the Eastern village of Hunyadi Janos, in Irquestine" after rescuing a group of "white women and children" captives from their "pretty-coloured natives" in what was clearly a fantasy recuperation of the Sepoy Rebellion of 1857.[60]

Given that internal RAF doctrine saw all people as one under bombardment, why did the service's public spectacles during the 1920s insist so outlandishly on the whiteness of the bomber, the blackness of the bombed? As we have seen, Salmond's conviction that "humanity was the same the world over" tacitly recognized that total air war, not race or culture or development, was the difference that mattered now; by the light of that recognition, the dividing line between colonial air control and unrestrained war was purely rhetorical. But while RAF officers acknowledged internally that their airmen in Iraq and other mandates and colonies were in training for the next total war, such an

---

[59] [Unsigned], "The R.A.F. Aerial Pageant," *Flight International* 14 (June 1922): 368–73. The 1922 finale, Omissi notes, did provoke some objections in the House of Commons for its inflammatory depiction of an Eastern adversary. Even the editor of *The Aeroplane*, a conservative pro-air-power magazine not generally given to racial and ethnic sensitivity, warned that the finale "[P]erhaps cut to the heart of our Moplah and Gandhist compatriots. It is a terrible thought. It is worse than the insult offered to the Jews by that insensate fellow who dared to win a race with a horse called 'Pogrom.'" See David Omissi, "The Hendon Air Pageant, 1920–37," in *Popular Imperialism and the Military, 1850–1950*, ed. John M. MacKenzie (Manchester: Manchester University Press, 1992), 203–4.

[60] [Unsigned], "The Eighth R.A.F. Display," *Flight International* 19 (Summer 1927): 460. Hunyadi János (known as John Hunyadi in English) was a fifteenth-century military strategist who united Christian armies against Ottoman Muslims; his name was also borne by a laxative mineral water bottled at springs near Budapest. "Irquestine" is evidently a portmanteau of Iraq and Palestine.

FIG. 1.2. *Poster for the RAF's 1922 Hendon air pageant. Original caption: "Bombing a desert stronghold."*

AN EASTERN DRAMA AT THE R.A.F. PAGEANT : 1. The "Wottnott" stronghold before the raid. 2. The enemy anti-aircraft battery. 3. A trio of "Wottnott" defenders potting at an attacking bomber. 4. Massed "Wottnotts" defending the stronghold from an aerial attack. 5. The stronghold in flames.

FIG. 1.3. *Photo collage of the Hendon air pageant's "Eastern Drama,"* Flight International, June 29, 1922.

understanding could not be part of the service's public self-portrait at home. It would have exposed a postwar public to two profoundly disquieting possibilities: that British aviators overseas were routinely committing crimes of (undeclared) war abroad; and that the forms of airborne terror Britons had experienced only a few years before might be deployed against them by their own government in domestic policing.[61] As much as the Hendon pageants sought to awe and excite their audiences through displays of British air power, they were also exercises in mass-reassurance, and the difference that underwrote that reassurance was race. 1920s air masquerades that marked bombing victims as Eastern, tribal, primitive, and colored—and therefore as both more deserving of and less disturbed by bombardment—permitted white spectators to believe they were safe from both peacetime air policing at home and complicity in true atrocities abroad. And by racially sorting bomber from bombed, the pageants asserted an absolute difference between the service's colonial operations and the white-on-white bombardments of the Great War. Under cover of these extrovert dramas the RAF held to its unutterable brief: *hone the techniques of total war in colonial air control.*

Such performances were not limited to Hendon or even to England. In 1924, the Iraq specialist Gertrude Bell, one of Churchill's chief advisors in the region, wrote of her amazement at witnessing an RAF bombing demonstration—not her first—at Hinaidi (see this chapter's second epigraph). Complete with machine guns, armored cars, an artificial village, and stage fugitives, the display Bell describes sounds like an etude for Hendon, although its mixed audience of British military forces, Iraqi leaders, European expatriates, and locals would have been differently interpellated by the spectacle. In a sense, though, displays like these were redundant in the mandates and colonies; air control was itself a careful staging of force for the sake of impressing spectators with a sense of their vulnerability and visibility from the air. For control-without-occupation to work, the RAF needed to show Iraqis via actual, devastating air strikes (also known as bombing demonstrations) the dire consequences of rebellion or tax evasion. Once potential insurgents had witnessed or heard of these force displays, the theory went, they would become self-policing and pacified in response. Their quiescent state would then be maintained by a second kind of aerial theater. If, as an Air Staff paper put it, "the speed and range of aircraft makes [sic] it practicable to

---

[61] Omissi reports that in May 1920, Churchill approved an Air Staff paper stipulating that airborne weapons not be used in Britain except in a state of declared war or if domestic rioters were using aircraft weapons. In a draft version of the paper, however, Trenchard had countenanced "a limited amount of bombing and machine gun fire" in order to quell violent workers' uprisings in British population centers. See Air Staff Memo, May 1920; memo by Trenchard, ca. April 1920; qtd. in Omissi, *Air Power*, 41.

keep a whole country under more or less constant surveillance," the crucial disciplinary effect of such patrols required that the planes be *seen* surveying: "from the ground every inhabitant of a village is under the impression that the occupant of an aeroplane is actually looking at *him*. . . establishing the impression that all their movements are being watched and reported."[62] In essence, air substitution sought to turn the bombing demonstration and the reconnaissance overflight from discrete events into an architecture of social control.[63] Under RAF command, the Iraqi mandate was an armed and perennial Hendon pageant whose indigenous spectators were simply less insulated (whether by fake ordnance or by the reassurances of racial masquerade) than their British counterparts from the violent ramifications of what they were being shown.

Air war would henceforth be total for the bombed, but it would be total first for those on what military policy constructed as the periphery, and with neither the publicity nor the scanty protections of declared war. The RAF's superficially nonracist argument that "humanity is the same the world over" underwrote the use of "forms of frightfulness"—diabolical weapons and terror techniques—against racially marked bodies in colonial spaces remote from the metropole.[64] Looking at the deployment of air power during the twenties, we can see permissible violence moving outward, like centrifuged molecules through a gel, in concentric rings from the imperial metropole. Over London there were civilian aircraft; skywriters promoting laundry detergent, motor oil, and newspapers; and the occasional

---

[62] Air Staff, "On the Power of the Air Force," March 1920, qtd. in Satia, *Spies in Arabia*, 245. Satia's gloss on this passage concludes that air control "was intended to work like the classic panopticon."

[63] Parsons implicitly makes interwar colonial air control an antecedent of nuclear strategy by referring to the former as "colonial administration based on the deterrent effect of rapid worldwide force projection"; see "British Air Control," n.p. Even more surprising is the embrace by Parsons, a USAF captain, of a Foucauldian distinction between force and power, which enters his discussion through citations of historian Anthony Clayton. "Power, then, with the minimum actual use of force, was to be the keynote [of colonial rule]," writes Clayton. "Such power would by charisma produce the correct response from colonial peoples, who would choose to obey the orders of the system rather than be forced into so doing." Another way of putting this: a policy of threats and ultimata, buttressed by a few illustrative deployments of violent air power, could produce coercion without massive and expensive use of force. What Clayton calls "choos[ing] to obey," one notes, is really being forced through a weaponized anticipation. See Anthony Clayton, *The British Empire as a Superpower, 1919–1939* (Athens: University of Georgia Press, 1986), 11; qtd. in Parsons, n.p.

[64] A December 1922 Air Staff memo on "Forms of Frightfulness" inventoried the RAF's means of "making life a burden" for Iraqi tribals. These means included delayed-action bombs to prevent villagers from going home under cover of darkness, phosphorous bombs, "crow's feet" for laming livestock, fear-inducing fireworks and whistling aerial darts, crude oil to poison water supplies, and an antecedent of napalm called "liquid fire." Townshend observes of the memo, "There was no sign of discomfort at the adoption of an approach to warfare which had so recently caused the Germans to be branded as barbarians"; see his "Civilization and 'Frightfulness,'" 150–51, quoting DDOI, Memorandum for DCAS [Draft], December 16, 1922, and Encl.2(a), "Forms of Frightfulness." PRO. AIR 5 264.

mock dogfight exhibiting the RAF's capacity to defend the realm. Above England's northern industrial cities during the general strike of 1926, heavy bombers dropped government leaflets and state-approved newspapers by the ton.[65] In Ireland during the Troubles, air attacks against the Irish Republican Army were allowed, but only in rural areas and against combatants.[66] And in the remoter colonies, protectorates, and mandates, official protocols about advance warnings of bombardment were put in place tardily and often ignored, warning leaflets were dropped on largely nonliterate communities, and enemy and accidental casualties were reported vaguely when they were reported at all.

Bombing Display II

We have seen how the colonial policing displays at Hendon disavowed the continuity between those "forms of frightfulness" and the prospect of total air war in Europe. It was not until the early 1930s that this continuity would find its way into public discourse. A decade after Charlton's arrival in Baghdad and the failure of the Hague Convention, the Geneva Disarmament Conference met with the aim of outlawing aerial bombardment and possibly abolishing military air forces altogether. The British delegates seem to have had a dual objective: to protect British cities, and particularly London, from bombing in a future world war while reserving the right to continue bombing their own colonies, mandates, and protectorates. After failing to achieve this through technicalities of sovereignty, the delegation proposed "the complete abolition of bombing from the air (except for police purposes in certain outlying regions)."[67] This double standard looked like a byproduct of economics: colonial air control was cheaper than garrisons on the ground; aerial disarmament at home was cheaper than maintaining large air forces to defend Europe's cities. But the budgetary rationale only thinly concealed the intimate causal link between bombed colonies and bomb-free capitals: remote zones served as training-grounds and laboratories for the total air war that many military planners assumed would come to Europe regardless of the laws of war. When that war came, Britain would be prepared to treat its adversaries as it had long treated its colonies; by this logic, the colonial state of exception *was* the salvation of the

---

[65] Omissi, *Air Power*, 41.

[66] On how RAF policies varied from one colony or mandate to another, see Roger A. Beaumont, "A New Lease on Empire: Air Policing, 1919–1939," *Aerospace Historian* 26 (Summer/June 1979): 84–90. On the RAF policy toward air strikes in Ireland, see AIR 6/806–1919, n.d., "Use of Aeroplanes Against Rebels," qtd. in Beaumont, 90n49.

[67] Cmd. Miscellaneous No. 2, 1933; qtd. in Uri Bialer, *The Shadow of the Bomber: The Fear of Air Attack and British Politics 1932–1939* (London: Royal Historical Society, 1980), 38.

capital. But the British insistence on the colonial loophole opened them to wide-spread criticism and was an important factor in the Conference's failure to produce multilateral accords.[68]

L. E. O. Charlton's conscientious objection and his air power advocacy, together, shared the geography of the British delegates' concern but with inverted attitudes: instead of promoting in the colonies what he dreaded in the metropole, he objected to the practice in peacetime colonial policing operations of what he thought inevitable in the war metropolis.[69] (He would even, in 1936, imagine German bombers starting the next war by surprise-attacking that spectacle of imperial reassurance, the Hendon pageant.[70]) But where *Charlton* gave its author's objection and resignation dramatic pride of place, his subsequent writings on air war bear fading traces of that apostasy, consigning it, for example, to a feeble dependent clause in *War from the Air: Past Present Future* (1935): "The lesson was also learnt of air control in mandated territories, and extended to include the disciplining of tribesmen on the North-West Frontier of India, though the humanity or inhumanity of such a policy remains a highly debatable

---

[68] P. R. C. Groves, who was Chairman of the Air Committee for part of the Geneva Conference, quotes the following July 21, 1933, letter to the *Times*, "signed by the secretaries of thirteen women's leagues and similar organizations," as a typical criticism of the British delegation's position: "The nations are at last realizing the danger (of aerial bombardment) and are disposed to agree to its abolition; but the British Government, rather than be deprived of the right to use air bombing against a few predatory tribes, would appear to be willing to risk the destruction of civilization. The proposition seems scarcely believable, for whatever may be the technical advantages of such a procedure, they cannot surely be allowed to weigh against the good of humanity as a whole." (Note how even in this letter of protest, the barrier between colonial bombing ["against a few predatory tribes"] and world war ["the destruction of civilization"] remains in place. Far from being objects of concern, the bombed tribes are deemed unworthy of risking the good of "humanity as a whole," which is a byword for modernized Europe.)

In response, Groves insisted that police bombing was not only cost-effective but also "far and away the most humane method yet discovered of maintaining peace in the regions where it is exercised," adding that it would be pointless for Britain to forgo air control in the interest of a worthless and unenforceable ban on aerial bombardment. Rather than abandon air control, Groves favored globalizing its principles: an International Air Force would have a monopoly on military aviation and would use it to ensure that nations maintained only unarmed commercial air fleets. See P. R. C. Groves, *Behind the Smoke Screen* (London: Faber and Faber, 1934), 322–23; 317.

[69] *Charlton* induced at least one reader to rethink colonial air control. A reviewer for *Flight International*, the magazine of the RAF, wrote: "The use of air bombs in Iraq has been discussed in Parliament, and the ordinary citizen quite satisfied by the answers given by the Air Minister, which were to the effect that this method of keeping the country in order was not only the most economical and efficient, but also the most merciful way of dealing with law-breakers. Air Commodore Charlton, writing with personal experience, challenges this comfortable view and arouses in us serious misgivings. Not unfrequently the ordinary Briton is inclined to think that a man who late in life becomes a Socialist and an opponent of 'blood sports' must have developed into what is popularly known as a 'crank.' The passages in this book which deal with bombing in Iraq are not, however, written in the strain which one usually associates with the outpourings of a 'crank.' They make one feel that a further examination of the facts is desirable." [Unsigned], "A Psycho-Analytical Autobiography" (review of *Charlton*), *Flight International* 23 (Autumn 1931): 1116.

[70] See Charlton, *War over England*, 158–64.

point to this day."[71] Even that little equivocation would disappear with the onset of the Second World War: his triumphalist *Deeds That Held the Empire: By Air* (1940) would describe military aviation as "the cement of Empire, whereby the edifice is stayed" and the RAF's bombing of tribal people as "a last resource, not with the avowed object of slaughtering the nomads, but to make them see the error of their ways by destroying their encampments after due notice has been given that aircraft will soon be on their heels." The onetime critic of colonial air policing had become its apologist and propagandist:

> From time to time small paragraphs appear in the papers that such action has been taken. But such are bald accounts indeed of an incessant watch and guard kept by the Royal Air Force, which intermingles disciplinary measures with friendly visits afterwards to the scenes of the disturbance, and so contrives to exercise a magisterial function rather than that of an avenging fate. A full history of the R.A.F. in that region of the globe would provide exciting reading, and be, at the same time, an object lesson in the art of governing.[72]

This is the RAF, absurdly, as loving parent: reluctant to discipline, and then only with fair warnings and warm follow-ups. Charlton makes no mention of the fact that his own friendly visit to the civilian victims of the RAF's disciplinary measures had caused him to resign his command in Iraq.

Yet just a few years before *Deeds That Held the Empire*, the retired Air Commodore had wrung "exciting reading" out of colonial air policing to extremely different effect. *Near East Adventure* (1934) was one of several boys' adventure novels Charlton wrote during the 1930s as a respite from his writings on air power.[73] Ostensibly an imperial runaway tale, *Near East Adventure* follows the escapades of two fifteen-year-olds, Robert Hilton and Leonard McIntosh, who flee their charmless Brighton lives only to blunder, one night, on a makeshift landing strip and fall into the clutches of a circle of international drug traffickers. Because the boys have seen too much to be let go, they are abducted first to a Belgian chateau and later, by way of a chartered plane along the northern rim of the Mediterranean, to Damascus. There, the

---

[71] L. E. O. Charlton, *War from the Air: Past Present Future* (London: Thomas Nelson and Sons, 1935), 76. Published seven years before the first English translation of *Il dominio dell'aria*, *War from the Air* discussed Douhet explicitly, helping introduce the Italian air power theorist's ideas to a broader English-speaking audience.

[72] L. E. O. Charlton, *Deeds That Held the Empire: By Air* (London: John Murray, 1940), 2, 275.

[73] On the genre and history of imperial romance, predominantly in the high imperial period, see Martin Green, *Dreams of Adventure, Deeds of Empire* (New York: Basic Books, 1979); Patrick Brantlinger, *Rule of Darkness: British Literature and Imperialism, 1830–1914* (Ithaca, NY: Cornell University Press, 1988); Nicholas Daly, *Modernism, Romance, and the Fin de Siècle: Popular Fiction and British Culture, 1880–1914* (Cambridge: Cambridge University Press, 1999); and Robert L. Caserio, "Imperial Romance," in *The Cambridge History of the Novel*, ed. Robert L. Caserio and Clement Hawes (Cambridge: Cambridge University Press, 2012), 517–32.

merciful Director of the cartel has arranged to apprentice them to a Christian silk merchant until they can be safely repatriated. But the Director's implacable henchmen have other ideas: pocketing the apprenticeship deposit, they fly the boys up over the Palestinian desert and push them (in their parachutes) out of the plane with no provisions. Just as they are about to die of thirst and exposure, lucky Bob and Len are found by a tribe of Bedouins. These are the same allegedly dangerous Beni Sokhr who, the boys learned in Damascus, had recently been bombed during Ramadan by the French Air Force. ("To me it sounded rather sickening," Bob narrates, "a little like murder on a wholesale scale, and I wondered what these unfortunate people, these Beni Sokhr, had done to deserve being slaughtered by government order").[74] Their nomad rescuers, however, are models of hospitality, nursing the runaways back to health, teaching them their language and customs, and giving them the same privileges as their own youths. Already clad in regional garb since Damascus, the boys become wiry and sun-browned and adapted to the ways of the Bedouin. But finally the sheik decides that the boys must be returned to the British authorities in exchange for guns and ammunition, or money, that will help the Beni Sokhr recover from the recent French bombing and defend themselves against a marauding rival tribe. The sheik, his sons, and the two Brighton boys set off across the desert to make the exchange.

Up to this point, *Near East Adventure* is a boilerplate imperial boys' tale: a story in which junior T. E. Lawrences come of age by going native, their mastery of Eastern languages and customs implicitly recuperable to imperial governance. That the real T. E. Lawrence had joined the RAF in 1922 to participate in the service's colonial air control project made the sympathetic infiltration narrative of "going native" seem compatible with the distance technology of air power; the notion that air control required a combination of distant, punitive displays and intimate bedside manner had become RAF doctrine by the time *Near East Adventure* was published.[75] Ernest Ratcliff's frontispiece to the novel (Fig. 1.4), which depicts

---

[74] L. E. O. Charlton, *Near East Adventure* (London: Thomas Nelson and Sons, [1934]), 101–2. Further references cited in the text. In the second volume of his autobiography, Charlton refers dismissively to his "boys' books" and "books of juvenile adventure" adding (as usual in the third person), "His attempt was to be strictly realistic on the bare side of credibility, and never to get his heroes into a fix unless they could be extricated without recourse to extravaganza." See L. E. O. Charlton, *More Charlton* (London: Longmans, Green and Co., 1940), 116–17.

[75] Patrick Deer writes fascinatingly about Lawrence's nomadological view of desert warfare, of his renunciation of the "Lawrence of Arabia" persona after the 1921 Cairo Conference, and of his 1922 enlistment in the RAF under the name of John Hume Ross, Aircraftsman 2nd Class; see Patrick Deer, *Culture and Camouflage: War, Empire, and Modern British Literature* (Oxford: Oxford University Press, 2009), 64–73. See also Satia, *Spies in Arabia*, 241–51, on Lawrence's advocacy for colonial air control, his characterizing the airplane's distributed force as the desert nomad's secret sharer, and his claims about Arabs' particular susceptibilities to aerial bombing as "not punishment, but a misfortune from heaven striking the community" (251).

FIG. 1.4. *Ernest Ratcliff, frontispiece to L. E. O. Charlton,* Near East Adventure, *[1934].*
Original caption: "There was a deafening explosion."

two turbaned, camel-mounted English youths overflown by RAF planes,
could almost be propaganda for the air control doctrine of "disciplinary
measures with friendly visits," in Charlton's later phrase. But the caption
jars—"There was a deafening explosion"—as do the looks of terror and surprise on the boys' faces. This is an image of imperial omnicompetence gone
wrong, and the scene it portrays undoes the reassurances of the genre in
ways the novel later disfigures itself by attempting to undo. As they cross
the desert, Bob, Len, and their Beni Sokhr escorts hear engines and make
out a wedge of RAF planes, getting closer. "Gosh! It's good, isn't it, to know
how near at hand we are to the protection of the British flag?" Bob, the narrator, remarks. "We could pretend that those five aeroplanes were sent to
meet us and escort us in. It makes me feel quite weepy" (172–73). Although
their hosts are unnerved, the boys halt their camel as the planes break formation and begin to circle; they crane their necks "to look up and admire
the skill of the pilots, thrilled to think we were having a little 'Display' all
to ourselves." Expecting their own private Hendon, they watch the lead
plane level off and approach: "Something fell from it. There was a deafening

explosion" (173–74). When the boys regain consciousness, they find they are both wounded, their Beni Sokhr hosts are all dead, and the carrion birds are gathering.

> Len broke the silence by saying with startling suddenness, "It's no good, Bob. We must discuss it. Why did they do this?"
>
> "There isn't any answer," I replied, "at least, none that I can think out! A party of Bedouins on eight camels are riding westwards, when they are overtaken by British aeroplanes and bombed out of existence. How can there be an answer to that?"
>
> "But we don't do things like that," he argued.
>
> "We do, apparently," I observed, with bitterness, and neither spoke for some time. (178)

The rest of *Near East Adventure* attempts to paint out the scene's vandalism of the "scared safe" contract typically offered by the adventure tale. Bob and Len are discovered by British soldiers in an armored car and brought back to an RAF base, where their wounds are tended; their story exposes the bombing as an error by a young pilot who mistook their party for a group of bandits; the real bandits are killed and the Beni Sokhr amply recompensed for their losses; the drug traffickers are captured and brought to trial thanks to details provided by Bob under mild hypnosis; and the boys return to England with enough reward money to save them from having to return to their unfit parents and guardians. What's more, they are given King's cadetships by the Air Ministry and will be tutored at RAF charge until they are old enough to take their exams and enter the service's academy. "After all," jokes their airman benefactor, Group Captain Wadham, "you were all but done in by the RAF, so the least it can do now is to see you out" (225).[76]

By likening RAF police bombing to the "massacre at Dijon in 1914," *Charlton* had brought colonial air control alongside unrestrained war only to raise the firewall of "declared war" between them. Although at once more coded and more self-divided than either his memoirs or his air power writing, *Near East Adventure* may be Charlton's most subversive statement about the relationship between peacetime colonial policing and total war. Like the Hendon pageants, imperial adventure was a genre of reassurance, displacing danger geographically

---

[76] We are reminded what friendship has cost the Beni Sokhr only in the novel's final lines, where Len expresses his hope of being stationed in Palestine or Iraq so the boys can "keep up acquaintance" with the nomads. Bob's reply—"And I said he could bet we would" (232)—impersonates the jauntiness of imperial romance while inviting a more sober or foreboding reading, something that gestures toward the final "No, not yet... No, not there..." of E. M. Forster's *A Passage to India* (1924; rpt. San Diego: Harcourt, 1984), 362. Charlton, as it happens, was a member of Forster's circle; see Wendy Moffat, *A Great Unrecorded History: A New Life of E. M. Forster* (New York: Farrar, Straus and Giroux, 2011), 205.

into colonies and other peripheries and ontologically into staged and bounded fictions. But *Near East Adventure* uses these displacements not to reassure but to disquiet, putting two underage Britons in the crosshairs of their own air force. Costuming them like Hendon Wottnotts, it says that going native in the age of air policing no longer means slipping unseen and swiftly from encounter to encounter. The privileged access it affords is to state atrocities committed in security's name, witnessed from the subject-position of the bombed. Even the novel's concluding swerve from conscientious objection to recruiting propaganda, for all that it retraces Charlton's own more gradual retreat into RAF orthodoxy, lands us in an ambiguous place. Bob and Len are financially independent heroes, free from their families and poised on the brink of a patriotic—indeed, a homonationalist—manhood that will commence with their initiation into the same eroto-military fraternity that had ejected Charlton. But they are also mobilized child-civilians, recruited before they are technically old enough to serve, and the schooling they must undergo before accepting their commissions will be entirely instrumental to their passing the RAF's entrance exams. And as white civilians who have been at the receiving end of an imperial nation state's bombs despite the supposed guarantees of race, genre, and geography, they call to mind the air raids of the Great War even as they portend or invite some sequel by dedicating their futures to air power. When the boys behold the corpses of their hosts, their epiphany speaks not just to colonial air control but to a whole system of disavowed continuities and uneven distributions of law and violence, the world system of total war's partiality. *But we don't do things like that / Apparently, we do.*

In placing Charlton's memoirs and air power writings beside his genre fiction, we've begun to see how literary representation can inflect the discourse of total war, materializing its abstractions in particular bodies, events, and narratives. *Near East Adventure* has also shown us a novel setting out to resolve contradictions in its writer's experience—between conscientious objection and air power advocacy, between the RAF as male homosocial fellowship and as practitioner of state terror—only to transpose those same contradictions into seemingly inevitable features of its virtual reality. And in the curdled imperial romance of Bob, Len, and the Beni Sokhr, we've seen expectations aroused by literary genre violated to shocking effect. In the next chapter, Virginia Woolf's writings will lead us through the landscape of war and gender along a path very different from Charlton's. When it came to war, Woolf's dissident energies were directed against the same fraternal militarism for which Charlton prized the RAF, and which he saw as endangered by the agency's dishonorable colonial bombing practices. Woolf's primary perspective is the civilian's. While air war prophets, including Charlton, were trying to annul the distinction between combatant and noncombatant in the context of declared war, Woolf was lodging her most radical critiques of sexism and militarism inside that distinction, even as she was acutely aware of how modern warfare was altering it. Amid these differences, however, there are common elements in Charlton's genre fiction and Woolf's more experimental writings on war, gender, and futurity. Chapter two begins with the unlikeliest of these commonalities: a central engagement with *suspense*. In different registers, of course; what for Charlton is a desirable effect of well-plotted fictional events is for Woolf a deplorable trait of everyday life, intensifying with the imminence of mass violence and requiring new ways to motivate fiction and regulate textual time. But the two kinds of suspense share at least one incarnation in these writers' work: the ambiguous figure of the plane, leveling off over London or the Negev Desert, picking up speed, nearly *here*.

2

Perpetual Suspense

VIRGINIA WOOLF'S WARTIME GOTHIC

Am I trifling, here, with the necessities of my task? Am I looking forward to the happier time which my narrative has not yet reached? Yes. Back again—back to the days of doubt and dread, when the spirit within me struggled hard for its life, in the icy stillness of *perpetual suspense*. I have paused and rested for a while on my forward course. It is not, perhaps, time wasted, if the friends who read these pages have paused and rested too.

—Wilkie Collins, *The Woman in White* (1860)

. . . and the comparison of arrowheads necessitates cross-country journeys to the country towns, an agreeable necessity both to them and to their elderly wives, who wish to make plum jam or to clean out the study, and have every reason for keeping that great question of the camp or the tomb in *perpetual suspension*, while the Colonel himself feels agreeably philosophic in accumulating evidence on both sides of the question.

—Virginia Woolf, "The Mark on the Wall" (1917)

Could anything short of war compel us to speak of suspense in Virginia Woolf's fiction? In a 1937 letter to Stephen Spender, Woolf described narrative's forward impetus as "the horror to me of the novel."[1] A dozen years earlier she had argued in "Modern Fiction" that as long as the writer lay down in the procrustean bed of the conventional novel (three volumes, thirty-two chapters), he would be stretched and broken by "some powerful and unscrupulous tyrant who has him in thrall to provide a plot, to provide comedy,

---

[1] Virginia Woolf, *The Letters of Virginia Woolf*, 6 vols., ed. Nigel Nicolson and Joanne Trautmann (New York: Harcourt Brace Jovanovich, 1975–80), vol. 6, 123. Further references to Woolf's letters are cited in the text as *L* followed by the volume number.

[Handwritten note at top: Quote from Modern Fiction]

[Handwritten notes in right margin: Stream of-consciousness / structure / time]

tragedy, love, interest, and an air of probability embalming the whole." In place of such imperatives, Woolf called for a form sensitive and flexible enough to record "myriad impressions" as they "fall upon the mind in the order in which they fall, [letting] us trace the pattern, however disconnected and incoherent in appearance, which each sight or incident scores upon the consciousness"; that could, in her often-quoted formulation, conceive life not as "a series of gig lamps symmetrically arranged [but as] a luminous halo, a semi-transparent envelope surrounding us from the beginning of consciousness to the end." Free of plot's compulsory symmetries, such a form would let the novelist show how "the accent falls differently from of old; the moment of importance came not here but there." Not "this" but "that" would interest modern novelists and must be their exclusive material. And "for the moderns," she added, "'that,' the point of interest, lies very likely in the dark places of psychology."[2]

"Modern Fiction" (1925) gives many names to what Woolf yearned to capture: life, truth, reality, spirit, character, "luminous halo," "the moment of importance," "the essential thing." All of these suggest tableaux in which plot's headlong propulsiveness is arrested, even overwritten, by a radiant presence that the modern novel will seek new ways to apprehend. This halo of presence is nowhere more dazzling than in Woolf's use, throughout her work, of deixis—linguistic shifters such as "now," "here," and "this" whose reference is entirely specific to the scene of their utterance, and whose utterance makes referent and reader linguistically copresent in that scene. Think, for instance, of how often the moments of importance in *Mrs. Dalloway* (1925) turn on deixis: "This moment in June." "What she loved was this, here, now, in front of her; the fat lady in the cab." "Here is my Elizabeth." "[T]his voice . . . this vow; this van; this life; this procession." "What is this terror? what is this ecstasy?" "For there she was."[3] Woolf scholars have tended to see such moments as disclosing some lustrous and essential property of the object in question. Robert Alter, for instance, reads *Mrs. Dalloway*'s deictic moments-of-being as incarnating London's capacity to "entranc[e] the beholder as a constant kinetic revelation of presences," enriching the mind with its variety.[4] But deixis has other functions as well in Woolf. Note how the deictic moments in "Modern Fiction" differ from *Mrs. Dalloway*'s "this, here, now": the moment of importance comes

[Handwritten heart symbol in right margin]

---

[2] Virginia Woolf, "Modern Fiction," in *The Essays of Virginia Woolf, Vol. 4: 1925–1928*, ed. Andrew McNeillie (London: Hogarth Press, 1994), 160–62. An earlier version of the essay was published as "Modern Novels" in the *TLS* in 1919; the revised version appeared in *The Common Reader* in 1925. Further references to Woolf's essays are cited in the text as *E* followed by the volume number; publication details for the six-volume set can be found in the bibliography.

[3] Virginia Woolf, *Mrs. Dalloway* (Orlando, FL: Harcourt, 2005), 4, 9, 47, 135, 190. Further references are cited in the text.

[4] Robert Alter, *Imagined Cities: Urban Experience and the Language of the Novel* (New Haven & London: Yale University Press, 2005), 106–7.

her sometimes vague time signifiers create uncertainty + suggest unspoken traumas —me

not here but *there*; not this but *that* will interest the modern novelist, whose flourishing will occur not now but in some future-conditional *then*. Here a linguistic mode that can fuse us luminously with the time and place of its utterance has been used to put what matters at a distance, in the darkness, "very likely in the dark places of psychology." Across this distance, we are reminded that even "this ecstasy" in *Mrs. Dalloway* is centrifugal, a "standing outside" (*ekstasis*), and that "this terror" is somehow entailed in it. For there is terror in all that deixis fails to specify—a terror that what looks like a luminous blank will either engulf the viewer or fill with unendurable detail; that the coordinates Clarissa Dalloway calls "this, here, now" may place us not in the corona of the moment but in its crosshairs; that another name for "the moment of importance" is the disaster.

Two kinds of moment, then: the radiant moment of presence, the rending moment of disaster. They index, in turn, discrete phases in the feminist reception of Woolf's writing. The first phase read the luminous moment approvingly, as an interruption of bourgeois values and the linear forced march of masculinist historiography. The second phase, practically the photonegative of the first, has objected to trauma studies' fixation with rupture, reading that fixation as a masculinist view of history that deprivileges and implicitly feminizes the everyday.[5] In both approaches, interruption and flow are exclusively gendered. And the moment in question, whether luminous or annihilating, is distinguished by its intense *presence*—it is crucially *here* and *now*, even if its import must wait until some later time to be understood. But what if Woolf's writing were concerned not only with present luminosity and present disaster but also with structures of expectation; not only with *immanence* but also with *imminence*? What if flow, instead of being opposed to interruption, were understood as suffused with the *prospect* of interruption, and were even constituted of that prospect? What if the "dark places in psychology" toward which Woolf canted her fiction had less to do with the disaster in and of itself than with the unbearable imminence of everyday life?

Woolf's best-known manifestos chronicle the failures of her predecessors to "catch life" alongside her own frustrations at "let[ting] my Mrs. Brown"— her figure for the modern novelist's living quarry—"slip through my fingers" (*E3*, 432). The fiction she hoped would remediate these fumblings might be described as a writing of *apprehension* in which the mind understands, grasps, or literally "reaches toward" what it beholds, arresting it through an act of

---

[5] An example of the first approach is Lucio Ruotolo's *The Interrupted Moment: A View of Virginia Woolf's Novels* (Stanford: Stanford University Press, 1986), which reads Woolf's "moment" as interrupting patriarchy and possessive individualism. Liesl Olson's *Modernism and the Ordinary* (New York: Oxford University Press, 2009) exemplifies the second in centering its feminist attention on the very "cotton wool of daily life" that figures, for Ruotolo, all the conventions that the moment would disrupt.

fine, empathic formulation. This chapter takes a different tack, portraying Woolf as one of our central anatomists of the *other* apprehension: the sense that something terrible, even annihilating, is at hand. This is a different kind of grasping: in a state of apprehension or apprehensiveness, <u>what appears to reach out before itself is not the anxious subject but the menacing object.</u> <u>Apprehensiveness is the uncanny condition in which some still-forming</u> thing appears to take hold of us, as if from a future that has itself become prehensile. No longer that which seizes, the mind becomes a thing seized; if it grasps anything it is its own bewildering loss of the power to apprehend. Such a state may resemble the post-traumatic, which also results from a disparity between experience and cognition. According to the dominant trauma studies model, a disaster that cannot be registered in real time and falls into the unconscious has in a sense "not yet" happened to the subject, making itself known only through encrypted symptoms; historically in the past, it remains psychically imminent. But although the "not yet" in Woolf has a power to shock, its imminence is not only psychic but also historical in that the event has not yet, in fact, happened. It is not only individual but also, at least potentially, collective in that the event, if it happens, will happen to others too. And its symptoms appear to lead both backward and forward in time—back to past shocks that help set one on edge, and forward to the disaster that may be about to arrive. Like the reader of sensation fiction, the apprehensive subject is caught in a split or paradoxical relation to the imminent. She is prepared to be taken unawares.

In Woolf's writing, this apprehensive subject, once taken hold of, often recovers and reaches back, arriving at a forceful if belated kind of recognition.[6] We might even say that, <u>for Woolf, anxiety about some imminent blow or shock is the necessary prologue to recognition; that there is no apprehending without apprehension.</u>[7] In a different kind of writer—one concerned to allay

---

[6] In 1939, Woolf would hypothesize that "the shock-receiving capacity is what makes me a writer" insofar as it provoked a desire in her to explain, organize, and verbalize the shock. Every "blow from an enemy hidden behind the cotton wool of daily life" was or would become "the revelation of some order." Virginia Woolf, "A Sketch of the Past," in *Moments of Being*, 2nd ed., ed. Jeanne Schulkind (San Diego, CA: Harcourt Brace Jovanovich, 1985), 72.

[7] The phenomena <u>I am describing</u> share certain <u>traits associated with the sublime</u>, including a <u>mixture of terror and fascination, a sense of scale ruptured and limits transgressed</u>, and the prospect of some cognitive recovery. For several reasons, however, I wish to stop short of describing this strain in Woolf as some new or refurbished subcategory of the sublime (the "wartime sublime," say, or the "geopolitical sublime"). First, the experience of terror is only sometimes followed by a cognitive recuperation in Woolf's writing; apprehensiveness does not reliably lead to apprehension. Second, <u>terror in Woolf</u> often leads to an awareness that one belongs to a traumatized collectivity, whereas the sublime more typically confirms the reason or cognition of the individual. Finally, I am wary of replicating a rather strong tendency in trauma studies to conflate historically situated traumatic experiences with transhistorical categories such as the sublime, the sacred, or the Lacanian real. On this tendency, see Dominick LaCapra, "<u>Trauma Studies: Its Critics and Vicissitudes</u>," in *History in Transit: Experience, Identity, Critical Theory* (Ithaca, NY: Cornell University Press, 2004).

suspense—this late-breaking recognition would allow the subject to surmount anxiety by comprehending its source. But increasingly in Woolf's fiction after the First World War, anxiety leads to a recognition not of the dreadful object but of anxious others, and of the communal life for which, as Ravit Reichman has argued, apprehensiveness might be a channel.[8] Consider for the moment a single brief example from *Mrs. Dalloway*:

> Septimus Warren Smith, aged about thirty, pale-faced, beak-nosed, wear-ing brown shoes and a shabby overcoat, with hazel eyes which had that look of apprehension in them which makes complete strangers apprehen-sive too. The world has raised its whip; where will it descend? (14)

At issue here is not the raised whip of the world—its identity or nature, the likely time and place of its descent—but the communicability of apprehen-sion from stranger to stranger and even, through the device of free indirect discourse, from character to narrator. The sense that some shock is immi-nent travels outward from Septimus until it affects the novel's whole social fabric. Having begun as a narratorial ventriloquism of a single traumatized veteran's thoughts, the split assertion/question "The world has raised its whip; where will it descend?" comes to index a condition of unquenchable fore-boding that both afflicts and conjoins the novel's characters. If this presages what Lewis Mumford would call in 1938 the "collective psychosis" of the war metropolis, it puts equal emphasis on both terms: without minimizing either the psychic costs of dread or the varieties of hurt it may augur, Woolf's writ-ing understands anxiety less as a solitary pathology than as a form, however lamentable, of being and thinking and feeling in common. It would find some rapprochement between the active and passive attitudes toward futurity that Eugène Minkowski sketched in his psychopathology of anticipation: a recog-nition that people living in the shadow of the raised whip of the world might discover new forms of responsibility and connection to one another and, per-haps, new forms of collective action.

The anxiety-in-common that now appears as one of Woolf's great themes is not, of course, reducible to the civilian's experience in putatively total war. Neither modern warfare nor any of its manifestations should be mistaken as the transcendental referent of her writing. Yet from 1917 on, the air raid—perhaps the paradigmatic form of civilian suspense in twentieth-century warfare—becomes a major node in Woolf's thinking and writing about col-lective anxiety, one to which she returned obsessively in her diaries, letters,

---

[8] Reichman's marvelous *The Affective Life of Law: Legal Modernism and the Literary Imagination* (Stanford: Stanford University Press, 2009) makes a strong case for reading Woolf along normative and reparative lines. I am especially persuaded by Reichman's understanding of the public nature of suspense and the collectively binding power of grief (see her second chapter, "The Strange Character of Law").

second-hand trauma/
proximity to pain/
Woolf's death

essays, and fiction. Without wanting to reduce those writings to the
the war to the raid, I wish to make several immodest claims about
raid's significance in Woolf's writing. The first is that it will not do to
of the raids *in the writing*, as if they were discrete mimetic objects ⌣. par
with flowers, gloves, pears, or parties. In the raid, the radical asymmetry of
forces reduces thought to raw counting, alters the experience of space and
time for those on the ground, and warps sociality's forms; at the same time,
this once-unthinkable event becomes routinized, expected, almost ordinary.
For Woolf, the air raid was at once an awful singularity and a metonym for
the more broadly volatile conditions of everyday peril she felt had intensified
as of August 1914, and by which she felt compelled to some response.[9] It would
be better, then, to speak of her writing, beginning around 1917, as intensively
in the raids (and *despite* and *against* them). The raids pressed her First World
War diaries to so dire a pitch that the dipping of the house lights, even in
a false alarm, seemed full of some darker portent: "finally the lights went
out, & standing on the kitchen stairs I was deluged with certain knowledge
that the extinction of light is in future our warning."[10] Twenty years later, a
raid scene quarried from those same diaries would serve in *The Years* (1937)
as a quasi-Platonic parable for a crouching, furtive modernity in which we
live "like cripples in a cave," a condition that would have to be surmounted
before people could "live adventurously, wholly" in a "New World."[11] And less
than a year before Woolf's death, the air raid would again provide the setting for invoking and addressing a New World—"America," this time, where
her extraordinary "Thoughts on Peace in an Air Raid" (1940) was published,
and where she aimed her plea to give young men an alternative to what Lady
Astor called their "subconscious Hitlerism." If for Woolf the air raid was the
cardinal instance of barbarism, precluded futurity, and the interruption of
continuous thought, it was also the thing in whose face the Blakean "mental

air
raids

---

[9] This view is most clearly crystallized in Woolf's 1940 essay "The Leaning Tower," which turns
on the contrast between the pre-1914 writers' towers of stucco and gold (middle-class birth and
expensive education) and the leaning towers inhabited by the Auden generation. Of Jane Austen and
Sir Walter Scott, Woolf claimed "their model, their vision of human life, was not disturbed or agi-
tated or changed by war. Nor were they themselves. It is easy to see why that was so. Wars were then
remote; wars were carried on by soldiers and sailors, not by private people. . . . That immunity from
war lasted all through the nineteenth century." After the commencement of the Great War, "even in
England towers that were built of gold and stucco were no longer steady towers. They were leaning
towers. The books were written under the influence of change, under the threat of war" (*E6*, 261, 267).

[10] Virginia Woolf, *The Diary of Virginia Woolf*, 5 vols., ed. Anne Olivier Bell with Andrew
McNeillie (New York: Harcourt Brace Jovanovich, 1977–84), vol. 1, 70. Further references to Woolf's
diaries are cited in the text as *D* followed by the volume number.

[11] Virginia Woolf, *The Years* (San Diego, CA: Harcourt Brace Jovanovich, 1937), 297. *Three Guineas*
extends the generalization of the air raid shelter-seeker by using the image "a cripple in a cave" to
designate those whose professional success has resulted in the loss of their health, humanity, sense
of proportion, and sensory keenness. Virginia Woolf, *Three Guineas* (San Diego. CA: Harcourt Brace
Jovanovich, 1938), 72. Further references to both works are cited in the text.

fight" of critical deliberation must be most doggedly sustained in wartime and peacetime alike (*E6*, 243–44).[12] The thinking in question, moreover, was not to be a solitary endeavor but an ongoing exercise in extending the reach of one's critical and ethical imagination, whether to other shelter-seekers, to the enemy airmen above one, or to faraway readers who seemed likelier to survive. And given the alternative of a future reopened under regressive terms, it was to prefer both the skeptical pressures and the tenuous new obligations that could arise in the penumbra of disaster.

By forgoing the discharge of suspense offered by conventional plotting, Woolf's writing entered into an intimate relationship, at once critical and imitative, with what she and many of her contemporaries would understand as the interminable geopolitical suspense particular to modern warfare. Her fiction set up a narrative energetics—and, as I will suggest, an ethics—of perpetual suspense, a phrase whose lineage and import I will explore in a moment. A slight variation on that phrase, "perpetual suspension," occurs in "The Mark on the Wall" (1917), a wartime short story Woolf wrote in a lull after the last Zeppelin attacks on London, and which she typeset amid the more destructive Gotha raids that began in late May 1917. Often read as her breakthrough into experimental stream-of-consciousness writing, "The Mark on the Wall" was also Woolf's first experiment in writing of war through an extravagantly uncanceled suspense, an experiment she would continue, with important modifications, for the rest of her career. As we will see, both the phrase "perpetual suspension" and the technique it describes connect Woolf's story to several unlikely antecedents. Chief among these is one to which I have already gestured, the mid-nineteenth-century sensation novel, which took gothic out of the elite precincts of church, castle, and manor and grafted it into contemporary bourgeois interiors, fusing trauma with the quotidian. In a similar vein, "The Mark on the Wall" makes one of gothic's core questions ("What *is that*?"—a question that returns us to the deixis of terror) the font of its drawing-room meditations, finally invoking the war to drain that question's answer of its adequacy even as it assimilates the suspensefulness

---

[12] The line "I will not cease from mental fight," from Blake's *Milton*, was popularly associated with Hubert Parry's setting of it in the Anglican hymn "Jerusalem." In her excellent discussion of war and late Woolf, Marina MacKay points out that the hymn was adopted not only by suffragists and the Labour Party but also by the Women's Institute, a community-based organization that aimed to involve women from rural communities in wartime food production, and for which Woolf volunteered in 1940. Her allusion to the hymn, MacKay writes, "illustrates how the same cultural property can be used to motivate both patriotic sentiment and progressive good deeds"; Marina MacKay, *Modernism and World War II* (Cambridge: Cambridge University Press, 2007), 26. Whereas for MacKay "Thoughts on Peace in an Air Raid" is thus closer to the politically centrist ruralism of *Between the Acts* than to the radical pacifism of *Three Guineas*, I read the 1940 essay as departing from both positions, manifesting a radical feminism that rejects a patriarchal peace no less vehemently than it does war.

of wartime to everyday domestic spaces, temporalities, and media. A kind of second-generation sensation fiction, Woolf's story adapts late gothic to the civilian's experience of world war.

A moment ago I described Woolf's relationship to the perpetual suspense of total war as intimately critical *and imitative*. I mean the latter half of that claim to challenge a widespread account of her pacifism, an account whose crispest articulation is still Alex Zwerdling's in *Virginia Woolf and the Real World*: "While others were carefully distinguishing between 'just' and 'unjust' wars, war and revolution, combatant and noncombatant service, all she could feel was an involuntary revulsion for the whole business."[13] This is a reactive, instinctive, undifferentiated pacifism that wants nothing to do even with the discourses of war, finding any attempt to theorize war as abhorrent as war itself. Where such pacifism does stoop to make distinctions, they are along essentialist gender lines: "For though many instincts are held more or less in common by both sexes, to fight has always been man's instinct, not woman's" (6). These are Woolf's own words in *Three Guineas* (1938), one of whose working titles was "The Next War"; they testify to her having tarried long enough, at least, with the combatant/noncombatant distinction to chart its gendered divisions. According to this mapping, both instinct and law (in the latter case, conscription) compel men to be combatants; both instinct and law (here, the interdiction of a female soldiery) compel women to be noncombatants. Even the exceptions to these distinctions prove the rule. Her claim that "We were all C.O.'s in the Great War" draws attention to women's compulsory status as noncombatants, even as it tacitly feminizes those men who assimilated themselves to the noncombatant position through conscientious objection.[14]

This gendered metaphysics is undoubtedly present in Woolf's writing, supplying nothing less than *Three Guineas'* core architecture. But while its key formulations in her work were prompted by the rise of fascism and the run-up to the Second World War, the emphatic gendering of combatant and noncombatant is, we should note, more applicable to a nineteenth-century view of limited war than to the discourse of total war that had emerged since 1916. To see Woolf's pacifism as in essence a critique of limited war, or as nothing more than an "involuntary revulsion" to war, full stop, is to miss the depth of her engagement with total war doctrine, its activation in conflicts such as the Spanish Civil War, and her own experience of air raids in both world wars. These war forms greatly altered the gendered metaphysics of limited war by openly targeting noncombatants and by conscripting women to projects of

---

[13] Alex Zwerdling, *Virginia Woolf and the Real World* (Berkeley: University of California Press, 1986), 272.

[14] Virginia Woolf, "Reminiscences of Julian," Monk's House Papers A 8:9, University of Sussex Library, qtd. in Zwerdling, *Virginia Woolf and the Real World*, 274.

total economic mobilization. To be a woman was no longer perforce to be a conscientious objector, to be exempt from economies of injury. Rather than shrink from these developments, Woolf asked what could be seen anew from inside the logic of total war. Hers was a pacifism that took war's structure and lexicon as indispensable tools for thinking past war; it claimed war as a promontory from which to see how conflict's natal conditions might be undermined, and from which to develop a critical relationship not just to conflict but also to terms such as "peace" and "civilian."[15] What Woolf most crucially derived from total war, I suggest, was a critique of the same gendered metaphysics with which her pacifism is still most commonly associated. This critique saw the male soldier and the female civilian not as opposed by nature and law but as intimately connected through social webs, structures of feeling, and their shared legitimation by a reproductive view of a national future. From the systemic bent of total war doctrine, Woolf gleaned an understanding of a war–gender system wherein militarism secured its future by exempting its key propagative figures from present conflict. "Civilian," in such a system, is the name under which future combatants and their primary caretakers ("children" and "women") are held in reserve for a conflict-to-come; "noncombatant" is a rhetorical time-release capsule containing the soldier of the future and the figures of his succor and tutelage.

Total war doctrine prescribed outrages. And it was adept at camouflaging behind claims of indiscriminate targeting and total mobilization its own continuing investments in gendered divisions of labor, affect, and injury. But it could also provide a critical view of the categories of limited war. Insofar as the limit of totality is never reached, only fitfully approached—insofar as some distinction between combatant and noncombatant persisted—such a critique still mattered in the epoch total war doctrine claimed as its own. If that epoch's perpetual suspense and evidently barred futurity were among its most oppressive features, they also suspended the ideological tendency of the future to go without saying, leaving a breach across which alternative futures, however improbable, could be glimpsed with a special vividness and urgency. In *Three Guineas*, the words "Air Raid Precaution" writ large on blank walls are a dreadful pedal point atop which the essay's fugal argument develops. To a woman reader, they signal the state's failure to protect her despite all the tolls it has exacted of her freedom and resources in the name of

---

[15] My claim that Woolf's work manifests a pacifist curiosity about war discourse aligns with Karen L. Levenback's account of the novelist as a war-theorist in *Virginia Woolf and the Great War* (Syracuse, NY: Syracuse University Press, 1999) and with Sarah Cole's *At the Violet Hour: Modernism and Violence in England and Ireland* (New York: Oxford University Press, 2012), whose climactic chapter is devoted to Woolf. The author of *Three Guineas*, writes Cole, "was not content with merely repudiating or reversing concepts like action [a fascist buzzword during the interwar years]. Instead, she engages critically with her culture's central formulations around violence" (201).

that protection; they announce that "the security of her person in the future is highly dubious" (108; also 88). My point is that these words, along with the raids they both foretell and recall and the war form they encode, have a grounding function as well as a foreboding or foreclosing one in Woolf's work. To think of peace in an air raid is not just an act of desperation, duty, or rash hope; it may be precisely in relation to an air raid, whether *here* and *now* or *then* and *there*, that one may think about peace without accepting its conventional terms. There may be no more radical—or suspenseful—act of pacifism, when confronting an occluded wartime future, than to resist both unlimited war and the wrong kind of peace.

Morphologies of Suspense

What would it mean to undergo a perpetual suspense? In what infernal place would we endure a limbo-without-end? Are we able to experience an interminable middle *as* a middle? The terms *suspend, suspense,* and *suspension* cover a large semantic range, from cessation to debarring to delay to withholding to uncertainty. All these senses share two elements: a status as *pending*—as letting hang or being left hanging—and the implicit *temporariness* of that status. They imply that whatever has been interrupted will resume, whatever has been revoked will be restored. In this chapter's first epigraph, Walter Hartright, the redactor-protagonist of Wilkie Collins's *The Woman in White* (1860), affirms the temporariness of suspense even in the act of invoking its perpetuity. Accompanying him on his "forward course," readers can expect to enjoy periodic rests—a suspension of suspense in which to ask, "when will the suspense resume?" But they can also expect to be delivered to that "happier time" in which the condition of suspense, and with it the chief motive for reading, will finally stand revealed as unperpetual.[16] In contrast to this terminal suspense, a suspense truly perpetual would cancel any expectation of release or resumption. It would seem to negate the temporariness suspense requires; it would be no suspense at all.

Sensation fiction, which flourished in the 1860s and 1870s, is strung tight between a nervous posture and a nerve-wracking event. In the first of these, the reader's state of keyed-up expectation is modeled by characters who await, variously, an end that is held conspicuously and forebodingly in store, a fate to whose obscure logic they are conscripted, or an inscrutable, often spatialized future that casts its shadow over the present. The following passages

---

[16] Wilkie Collins, *The Woman in White* (Harmondsworth, UK: Penguin, 1999), 479–80. Further references are cited in the text.

from Collins's novel illustrate the force exerted by an undisclosed "End" or "Design" the text invokes with compulsive frequency:

> The foreboding of some undiscoverable danger lying hid from us all in the darkness of the future, was strong on me. The doubt whether I was not linked already to a chain of events which even my approaching departure from Cumberland would be powerless to snap asunder—the doubt whether we any of us saw the end as the end would really be—gathered more and more darkly over my mind. Poignant as it was, the sense of suffering caused by the miserable end of my brief, presumptuous love, seemed to be blunted and deadened by the still stronger sense of something obscurely impending, something invisibly threatening, that Time was holding over our heads. (77–78)

> I felt the ominous Future, coming close; chilling me, with an unutterable awe; forcing on me the conviction of an unseen Design in the long series of complications which had now fastened round us. I thought of Hartright—as I saw him, in the body, when he said farewell; as I saw him, in the spirit, in my dream—and I, too, began to doubt now whether we were not advancing, blindfold, to an appointed and an inevitable End. (283)

The future, in such passages, is less a hypothetical time-to-come than an engulfing and already materialized environment. Both the characters and the events in sensation fiction are deep-sea organisms kept from explosive decompression by the downward pressure of the future, a liquid mass in which they also move. Yet in making foreboding the narrative's enabling medium, these passages also promise a final decompression in which the ominous will become patent. However protracted, the state of apprehensiveness alone does nothing to deny—in fact, does everything to affirm—the temporariness of suspense.

Paradoxically, it is when sudden events interrupt this state of expectation—that is, when just the kind of unheralded thing we expect to occur in sensation fiction *does* occur—that suspense takes a step toward perpetuity. That an atmosphere of foreboding could amplify the effects of suddenness may already seem counterintuitive: wouldn't the arrival of the sudden affect us more if we were *not* waiting for something to happen, if the sudden event ambushed our nerves while they idled? But for the sensation novel, the central feature of suddenness is that it at once exceeds and falls short of apprehensiveness: anticipation has indeed failed to prepare us for the event (or we wouldn't perceive it *as* sudden), yet the same event always fails, in its turn, to discharge the suspense that was unequal to it all along. The sudden no sooner arrives than it points beyond itself to some still-unrevealed event or end, much as, in Collins's novel, the woman in white herself points "toward the dark cloud over London" seconds after appearing on the scene. Before this, the woman's touch has indeed caught Hartright unprepared, "idly wondering . . . what the Cumberland young ladies would look like—when, in one moment, every drop of blood in my body was brought to a stop by the touch of a hand laid lightly and suddenly on my shoulder from behind me" (23–24). Although Hartright may have been lost in reverie just before the electrifying touch, the reader, cued by the setting (deserted crossroads, full moon, starless sky), is in a state of neural readiness the scene does nothing to diminish. Hartright, for his part, remains in nervous thrall to the encounter long after the plot it initiates has concluded, and even from the safety of the later scene of writing, he continues to react to the memory with unabated intensity: "I tremble now, when I write it," he tells us of his promise to help the strange woman, and "I trace these lines, self-distrustfully, with the shadows of after-events darkening the very paper I write on" (26). Having overwritten the expectant scene into which it erupts, the sudden encounter is immediately overshadowed by its aftermath, both as the reader forecasts it and as the writing Hartright recollects it. What we are encountering here cannot adequately be described as a *temporal perspective* that simply looks forward or backward in time; it is, rather, a *temporality*—a tendency toward a particular relation to time, in this case toward a foreboding that is neither fulfilled nor defused. Never commensurate with its objects, suspense in the sensation novel can neither prepare us for what will come nor release us from what has come already.

I have described the effects of suspense in terms of equivalence or proportion, as an ongoing negation of adequacy, but the sensation novel also demands that we think of suspense in terms of velocity and timeliness. Sensation fiction is a speed technology; the trouble is in specifying the speed or speeds at which it travels. In the scene I have just considered, the strange woman's touch occurs in a sense too soon, overtaking both the reader's and the protagonist's readiness, yet the state of nervous expectancy it interrupts outlasts it, is prolonged beyond the terminus of the narrative into its aftermath: "I tremble now, when I write it." This puzzling coincidence of fast and slow leaves legible traces in scholarship on sensation fiction, where the stakes of the genre's velocity are not only phenomenological but also philosophical and political. D. A. Miller has read *The Woman in White* and its genre-mates as inciting (partly by representing) racing hearts, trembling bodies, adrenalized subjects. The reader of these texts experiences a quickening not just of pulse and respiration but also of hermeneutic pace, "repeatedly jumping to unproven conclusions, often literally jumping at them."[17] For Miller the sensation novel interferes with readers' reflective calm and thus with their ability to weigh evidence, but Caroline Levine argues that the genre attempts to teach

---

[17] D. A. Miller, *The Novel and the Police* (Berkeley: University of California Press, 1988), 158.

readers to suspend judgment, fostering "energetic skepticism and uncertainty rather than closure and complacency."[18] Where Miller's reader is subject to incarceration and predisposed to political docility, the reader of sensation fiction in Levine's account might undergo a "rigorous political and epistemological training" and be thereby released from the prison of habit. However much we credit Miller's and Levine's arguments on their own, together they register the fact that the genre produces both accelerative and decelerative effects in respect to cognitive and political processes. I would add that sensation fiction's two speeds should not be treated in isolation from one another and that what is particular to the genre is precisely its fusion of two untimely temporalities, the too-soon and the ever-deferred. The modernisms (including but not limited to Woolf's) that descend from the work of Collins and others will be less exclusively reliant on the revelatory throb of plot because they recognize structures of imminence that always exceed what plot can discharge. But what they put in place of the suspense plot also comes from sensation fiction: an energy-system based on the copresence of instantaneity and prolonged apprehensiveness.

A perennialized suspense that neither readies us sufficiently for imminent trauma nor releases us from traumas past: such suspense is not easily distinguished from the everyday. Much as it amalgamated the codes and pulsions of gothic with those of bourgeois realism, the sensation novel let these genres' default modes—the traumatic and the quotidian—bleed into one another. This is not to say that sensation fiction completely stopped distinguishing among degrees of trauma, or between crisis and daily life. But it allowed that some kinds of stress, anxiety, and foreboding were not temporary states but ineliminable features of quotidian experience. It made the everyday safe for crisis, which is to say that it registered the everyday's unsafeness; as Woolf would put it in *Mrs. Dalloway*, it is "very, very dangerous to live even one day" (8). As I mentioned above, scholars of modernism have lately reclaimed everyday life as a central category of analysis, exposing the tendency of crisis-oriented thinking to privilege certain subjects, narratives, and ethico-political stances over others.[19] Yet this corrective position has

---

[18] Caroline Levine, *The Serious Pleasures of Suspense: Victorian Realism and Narrative Doubt* (London and Charlottesville: University of Virginia Press, 2003), 2.

[19] See, for example, Bryony Randall, *Modernism, Daily Time, and Everyday Life* (Cambridge: Cambridge University Press, 2007); Siobhan Phillips, *Poetics of the Everyday: Creative Repetition in Modern American Verse* (New York: Columbia University Press, 2009); Sara Crangle, *Prosaic Desires: Modernist Knowledge, Boredom, Laughter, and Anticipation* (Edinburgh: Edinburgh University Press, 2010); Liesl Olson, *Modernism and the Ordinary*; and Olson's "Everyday Life Studies: A Review," *Modernism/modernity* 18.1 (January 2011): 175–80. Thomas S. Davis's *The Extinct Scene: Late Modernism and Everyday Life* (New York: Columbia University Press, forthcoming) traverses the opposition between crisis and the quotidian by arguing that late modernism's aesthetic forms, particularly those preoccupied with everydayness, mediate the world-systemic distress of the 1930s and 1940s. See also Rita Felski, "The Invention of Everyday Life," in *Doing Time: Feminist*

focusing primarily on war time / trauma — real war

made some brittle claims of its own—for instance, that the everyday in some manner "trumps" trauma. Like its antecedents in late-Victorian gothic, <u>much of Woolf's writing negotiates subtler, more productive détentes between the traumatic and the everyday than its readers have yet done</u>, and may at times be primarily motivated by the possibility or necessity of such détentes. These recognize that both past and imminent traumas are structuring elements of the quotidian; that total war affords both the worst and the most instructive case of trauma's assimilation to the everyday; and that the pressure of imminence, particularly the extreme case of a barred futurity, should move us in the direction of intersubjective experience and action.

+

Mark Time

But of course Woolf's writing didn't arrive at such negotiations all at once. In returning to it now, I will trace the working out of a cluster of positions longitudinally, across a series of texts. On the map of her work, an air raid archipelago: a chain of scenes that address, obliquely and directly, the experience of the metropolitan civilian in the early decades of air power, and the putative loss of civilian immunity as both an obstacle to and an aperture for thought. By the time Woolf started publishing fiction, total war no longer registered as a vague eventuality but rather as an emergent reality for fiction to meet more obliquely the closer war came to home. In "Before Midnight," a review published a few months before "The Mark on the Wall," Woolf confessed to "two, perhaps unreasonable, prejudices: we do not like the war in fiction, and we do not like the supernatural. We can account for the first of these prejudices by the feeling that the vast events now shaping across the Channel are towering over us too closely and too tremendously to be worked into fiction without a painful jolt in the perspective." When it came to the war, a sense of looming danger blocked the distance-optics that representation demanded; as for gothic, its reflexive turn to the supernatural weakened its ability to address natural but nevertheless "uncharted territories of the mind"—territories, the coupling implies, that included the mind overtowered by war (E2, 87).[20] Woolf was still confessing her prejudice against contemporary gothic in a 1921 review of Henry James's ghost stories, where she

---

Theory and Postmodern Culture (New York: New York University Press, 2000), and "Everyday Life," *New Literary History* 33.4 (Autumn 2002): 607–22.

[20] Woolf's description ("vast events now shaping across the Channel") strangely diminishes and distances a war that not only was fully shaped by 1917 but also routinely crossed the Channel in the form of German air raids; these are at most half-acknowledged in the ensuing references to the war's "towering over us too closely" and the "painful jolt" such an imminent force delivers to fictional perspective.

proposed that the original readers of gothic romance were terrified by the genre in proportion as they were not *her* contemporaries, had not seen what her generation had seen. "Mrs. Radcliffe amused our ancestors because they were our ancestors," she wrote, going on to describe the leisurely pace of life and information in eighteenth-century villages. In contrast, "Nowadays we breakfast upon a richer feast of horror than served them for a twelvemonth. We are tired of violence; we suspect mystery . . . Moreover, we are impervious to fear" (*E3*, 321).

In another review of the same year, this time of Edith Birkhead's *The Tale of Terror: A Study of the Gothic Romance*, Woolf allowed that modern nerves might not be immune to terror after all but added that writers hoping to evoke that response would have to abandon the supernatural for new methods and pathways, "subtler means" such as the "use of psychoanalysis to startle and dismay":

> It is at the ghosts within us that we shudder, and not at the decaying bodies of barons or the subterranean activities of ghouls. Yet the desire to widen our boundaries, to feel excitement without danger, and to escape as far as possible from the facts of life drives us perpetually to trifle with the risky ingredients of the mysterious and the unknown. Science, as Miss Birkhead suggests, will modify the Gothic romance of the future with the aeroplane and the telephone. (*E3*, 307)

This is a deeply divided statement. While ostensibly defending gothic's vitality and adaptability, the passage works even harder to deny the contemporaneity of gothic. As a fundamentally escapist and anti-realist mode, gothic as described here can have no interest in grappling with the present. The benign excitement it conveys explicitly avoids a sense of danger, stimulating the reader without reference to the sort of imperiled present over which vast events loom closely. And if the scientifically modified gothic romance of the future does one day take up the airplane and the telephone, Woolf implies, it will do so only because their native epoch has long since lapsed; future gothic will escape to the historically remote twentieth century much as eighteenth-century gothic escaped to the Middle Ages.

In proclaiming the obsolescence of traditional gothic romance, Woolf repeatedly tapped James's *The Turn of the Screw* (1898) as the avatar of a living gothic, one whose horror lay in showing us "the power that our minds possess for such excursions into the darkness" where "the ghosts of the mind, untracked desires, indistinct intimations" were legion (*E2*, 219). But both Woolf's insistence on eighteenth-century gothic's noncontemporaneity and the exception she appeared to make for James downplayed her own serious investments, as a fiction writer, in gothic. By 1918, when Woolf wrote this account of *The Turn of the Screw*, she had already begun to rehabilitate gothic for the new velocities of the airplane and telephone, taking on contemporary speed technologies in communications, transportation, and war without belittling terror as an exotic escape from present danger.[21] She was, in essence, writing what she called "the Gothic romance of the future" in and about the present. This was a proleptic and untimely gothic that refused to wait until the early twentieth century had become a mossy ruin, preferring to grapple *now* with the condition of impending ruination that was emerging as one of the century's defining features. It first appears in "The Mark on the Wall," her earliest published story, composed (again, during a suspension of air raids) "in a flash, as if flying" and paired with a story by Leonard Woolf in the inaugural Hogarth Press release (*L4*, 231). Written at speed, "The Mark on the Wall" and its companion took the Woolfs, at that point novice printers, two and a half months to typeset, print, and bind (during a period of resumed raids).[22] The contrast between these two speeds of literary production is almost a symptom of the story, whose dilatory general tempo is punctuated by images of high-speed urban transit and, even more notably, by the insistent question of what the mark on the wall, in fact, *is*.

This question may sound both trivial and easily answered, but in its articulation by Woolf's narrator and in her mystifying refusal to get up and end the speculation, it is obscurely menacing, soaked with a somehow awful potential. No opening of a Woolf story is more Poe-like in describing the origin of an uncanny fixation that still seems to possess the narrator. "Perhaps it was the middle of January in the present year that I first looked up and saw the mark on the wall. In order to fix a date it is necessary to remember what one saw. So now I think of the fire; the steady film of yellow light upon the page of my book . . . "[23] The question of the date, the language of deduction and deposition, the narrator's claim that seeing the mark relieves her from the "automatic fancy" that her cigarette coals are "a cavalcade of red knights riding up a black rock"—all these elements try to minimize the unaccountable fascination exerted by the "small round mark, black upon the white wall, about six or seven inches above the mantelpiece." Yet for all the febrile handling of the mark, and for all the narrator's apparent wish to fix the date when she *first*

---

[21] See, for example, the high-speed geostrategic decision-making network that appears in Woolf's fiction of the 1920s, as in this passage from *Jacob's Room* (1922): "The wires of the Admiralty shivered with some far-away communication. A voice kept remarking that Prime ministers and Viceroys spoke in the Reichstag; entered Lahore; said that the Emperor traveled; in Milan they rioted; said there were rumours in Vienna; said that the Ambassador at Constantinople had audience with the Sultan; the fleet was at Gibraltar." These voices are fed to the bald mandarins who "decreed that the course of history should shape itself this way or that way," which means that young men like Jacob Flanders will die in droves. Virginia Woolf, *Jacob's Room* (Orlando, FL: Harcourt, 2008), 181–82.

[22] Hermione Lee, *Virginia Woolf* (New York: Knopf, 1997), 359. The story was published in July 1917, along with Leonard's story "Three Jews," as the Hogarth Press's *Publication No. 1*.

[23] Virginia Woolf, "The Mark on the Wall," rpt. in *The Complete Shorter Fiction of Virginia Woolf*, 2nd ed., ed. Susan Dick (San Diego, CA: Harcourt Brace Jovanovich, 1989), 83. Further references are cited in the text.

saw it, the story is exactly coextensive with the mark's status as unidentified, as if only the unfixed and vaguely threatening thing were narratable. In asserting the compatibility of dread with the drawing room and in pinning narratability to a mystery that seems solvable, the story's opening paragraph declares its allegiance to Collins et al., although its brevity suggests a rescaling of their efforts to an era in which one is "blown through the Tube at fifty miles an hour" (83–84).

As the story proceeds, it sets up a second, pastoral mode in opposition to its gothic opening. "I want to think quietly, calmly, spaciously, never to be interrupted, never to have to rise from my chair," the narrator tell us, "to slip easily from one thing to another, without any sense of hostility or obstacle" (84–85). To the pastoral belong the narrator's horticultural fantasies about an experience "after life" and her invocations of "a world which one could slice with one's thought as a fish slices the water with his fin, grazing the stems of the water-lilies, hanging suspended over nests of white sea eggs" (84, 87). In contrast to these peaceful depths, gothic is "the surface, with its hard separate facts," a world encompassing everything from tablecloths to Whitaker's Table of Precedency, all the putatively "real things" that mass under the banner of the mark (85, 86). We begin to see what a dramatic transvaluation of gothic "The Mark on the Wall" produces: a mode that once tended toward antirealism has been linked here to a demystified social stage cluttered with realism's favored props, as if to insist that the world has caught up with and even overtaken the horrifying sense of untimeliness once captured by gothic. Suspense has become so generalized that the resumption of the suspense plot can function, at the story's end, as a reassertion of the everyday—even if it is, as we learn there, a pointedly wartime everyday whose suspense has at least one undeniable referent.[24]

Just at the moment the narrator struggles to harmonize the natural world with the human order, her increasingly labored meditations are blocked and then closed down by a final interruption:

> [. . .] but something is getting in the way . . . Where was I? What has it all been about? [. . .] I can't remember a thing. Everything's moving, falling, slipping, vanishing . . . There is a vast upheaval of matter. Someone is standing over me and saying—
>
> "I'm going out to buy a newspaper."

---

[24] In the prelude to her superb *War at a Distance: Romanticism and the Making of Modern Wartime* (Princeton: Princeton University Press, 2010), Mary A. Favret assembles a series of fireside poems by civilians meditating on distant wars, including works by Cowper, Coleridge, Frost, and C. K. Williams. "The Mark on the Wall" belongs among these as well, and may be in close dialogue with "The Winter Evening" section of Cowper's *The Task* (1785), with its red cinders, its foreboding, and its way of figuring inwardness as pastoral.

The Mark on the Wall

"Yes?"

"Though it's no good buying newspapers . . . Nothing ever happens. Curse this war; God damn this war! . . . All the same, I don't see why we should have a snail on our wall."

Ah, the mark on the wall! It was a snail. (89; unbracketed ellipses in original)

I want to note a few things about this last exchange. First, the question with which the story opens—the question of the date on which the narrator first saw the mark—is *not* the one whose answer brings the story to a close. The newspaper may stand in a metonymic relation to the prospect of dating an event, but its public chronology seems orthogonal to the finally dateless private one implied by the story. What's more, the newspaper's ability to chronicle even public events is thrown into question by "Someone's" remark that "it's no good buying newspapers. . . . Nothing ever happens." The ensuing curse implies that the news is boring because the war is uneventful. A war, presumably, of attrition, an ongoing condition rather than a string of discrete events; war as what stays news, stays *in* the news, without ever being newsworthy. And last, as if to ratify the claim that war is antithetical to news, there is the narrator's final line, which registers the news of the mark's identity but contains no trace of the war: "Ah, the mark on the wall! It was a snail."

This line's refusal to absorb either the newspaper or the war, terms shockingly dropped into the story by the other speaker, seems a stubborn enactment of the narrator's earlier prophecy that "the novelists of the future" will "explore the depths" of the individual mind's relationship to itself, "leaving the description of reality more and more out of their stories, taking a knowledge of it for granted" (85–86). For the narrator, then, mention of the war and the newspaper at the story's end affords the perfect chance to demonstrate fiction's imperviousness to "reality" by keeping focused on the interior question of the mark. But the story's preceding pages have readied us for a different conclusion: namely, that the question of the mark in some sense *is* the question of the war. Noticing that the mark on the wall seems to cast a shadow, the narrator envisions it as a tiny tumulus and thinks of barrows on the South Downs, which are either tombs or camps. These sites are trawled, she imagines, by retired colonels who will cross the country to compare arrowheads with one another and who "feel agreeably philosophic in accumulating evidence on both sides of the [tomb vs. camp] question." Their wives, meanwhile, "have every reason for keeping that great question of the camp or the tomb in perpetual suspension" in order to keep the old duffers out of the house during spring cleaning (86–87). The domestic cast of this "perpetual suspension" resonates with the narrator's desire "never to have to rise from my chair, to slip easily from one thing to another, without any sense of hostility, or obstacle." Yet in both cases the project of a peaceful domestic interlude comes to grief against the "hostility" and decisive identification it attempts to ward off: perpetual suspension (with an echo, perhaps, of the phrase "suspension of hostilities") leads to the camp that may be a tomb and the ancient warhead in the hands of the living ex-colonel; and the narrator rejects her own "generalizations" about interiority because the word itself reminds her of generals, cabinet ministers, things martial. In the end, the open question of the mark's identity, having stimulated the narrator's pastoral imagination, is slammed shut by the simultaneous arrival of war and snail. Yet inasmuch as both terms compete to close the copula "the mark was," the story asserts rather than reaches closure. For when we read "Ah, the mark on the wall! It was a *snail*" we half-hear "Ah the mark on the wall! It was the *war*." This ghost audio is produced partly by the sound-chain of *mark/war/wall/snail*, and partly by the way the unheralded and, for the first-time reader, shocking reference to "*this* war" destroys the possibility that a snail could be sufficient to dispel the anxiety massed around the question of the mark.

As gothic terminus to the pastoral "train of thought," the mark "puts a full-stop" to that train when it leads unexpectedly to generals or cabinet ministers or arrowheads or even to the image of a tree with "nothing tender exposed to the iron bullets of the moon"; the mark is what Nature bids you think of if "you must shatter this hour of peace" (88, 89).[25] But if that gothic mark re-steadies the narrator's thoughts in the face of the pastoral's repeated militarization, it does so thanks to the suspension of its identity, a quality it shares with war.[26] One runs away from the image of violence into a "perpetual suspension" the

---

[25] For those who had lived through the First World War near London, "exposed to the iron bullets of the moon" would have evoked memories of the Gotha raids of 1917–18, which were heaviest during the full moon. Fifteen months after "The Mark on the Wall" was published, during the German retreat a few weeks before the Armistice, Woolf would write in her diary: "one went to bed fairly positive that never again in all our lives need we dread the moonlight" (*D1*, 205–6).

[26] Among Woolf's later works, the text that descends most directly from "The Mark on the Wall" is the "Time Passes" section of *To the Lighthouse* (1927), which stages in the Ramsays' untenanted summer home a deep-time pastoral punctuated by shockingly terse reports of the main characters' life and death events, many of which have to do with the war. However, two earlier drafts of "Time Passes"—the holograph version and a 1926 typescript revision from which a French translation was prepared for standalone publication in the journal *Commerce*—not only figure or refer to the war more frequently but also contain two conventionally gothic elements. These are 1) a series of passages about "ghostly confidantes," "spirits," or "sharers" who leave the bodies of the sleeping Ramsays to haunt the house and its environs in search of some unspecified communion, only to be stymied by signs of the war; and 2) two apocalyptic passages about night "musing and mourning as if she lamented the doom which drowned the earth and extinguished its lights and of all ships and towns left nothing," lamenting, too, the dreamers "who only spin this clothing from terror, weave this garment for nothingness." James M. Haule, Virginia Woolf, and Charles Mauron, "'Le Temps passe' and the Original Typescript: An Early Version of the 'Time Passes' Section of *To the Lighthouse*," *Twentieth Century Literature* 29.3 (Autumn 1983): 279, 290, 280. In finally deleting these paranormal and eschatological elements from the published novel and replacing them with the famous square-bracketed reports of characters' marriages and deaths, Woolf again bent gothic away from its conventional content and toward the sorts of rending discursive and scalar shifts experienced by civilians in wartime. On the prepublication drafts of "Time Passes," see James M. Haule, "*To the Lighthouse* and the Great War: The Evidence of Virginia Woolf's Revisions of

war has resignified as the moment that is always just about to be rent by violence, the moment in which that dark shape in the sky is always already a Zeppelin, that explosion a bomb. One runs away from war straight into the arms of war. Thus in the act of disavowing reality and description, "The Mark on the Wall" describes the reality of the wartime civilian's psychomachia, her failed attempts to reconvert the condition of perpetual suspension into a quiet, pastoral experience without prospect of hostility. As a sign, the mark is fittingly split: it points to both the urgency and the seeming impossibility of unthinking the world-become-target—the world in which all tender things seem exposed to the iron bullets of the moon, all vectors are potential targeting vectors, and all space is a potential space of marksmanship.[27]

In a visual sense, the supersession of pastoral by gothic provides a way to think about how trench warfare transformed the European countryside. But "The Mark on the Wall" couples gothic with total war through spatiotemporal codes more than visual ones. As we have seen, gothic can be adapted to this end for several reasons, foremost among them being its tradition of addressing imminent but still-absent threats. The sense of dread that pervades the sensation novel, for instance, is generally incommensurate with immediately present danger. Violence is always oncoming in late gothic and not less so at the moment when violence is also being inflicted: Dracula might be in the room, but seems governable compared with what he might unleash on the world in the near future. Even in the midst of violence we are in dread. Yet the contract of gothic, as a literature of suspense, is that some cause or object of dread will eventually arrive, even if it is incommensurate with the text's dreadful affect. Mixed with the teleological elements of gothic, the "perpetual suspension" of pastoral will always curdle. Finally, late gothic is, in England at least, a literature in which what is strange and threatening returns from the periphery to the metropole, from East to West, from abroad home. This, as we saw in the previous chapter, is the itinerary of total war both in the early-twentieth-century metropolitan imaginary, in which so-called "savage" practices of injury are brought to the capitals of Europe, and in the history of

---

'Time Passes,'" in *Virginia Woolf and War: Fiction, Reality, and Myth*, ed. Mark Hussey (Syracuse, NY: Syracuse University Press, 1991), 164–79. For a full-scale discussion of war and form in "Time Passes," see Cole, *At the Violet Hour*, 241–47.

[27] Rebecca Walkowitz reads the indirection of "The Mark on the Wall" as deliberately refusing to pay war the kind of attention that patriotism and propaganda would make reflexive. Responding to readers who indict "The Mark" for preferring speculation to action in a time of catastrophe, Walkowitz compellingly argues that the story "resists the passive experience of war by making thought happen" and by entwining great events with the shaping operations of "daily sociability." See Rebecca L. Walkowitz, *Cosmopolitan Style: Modernism Beyond the Nation* (New York: Columbia University Press, 2006), 89. My reading of the story is not incompatible with Walkowitz's but places greater emphasis on the nature of the catastrophe in question, as a way to connect the story's particular strategies for "making thought happen" to the rising pitch of war's imminence and instantaneity.

Empire, where we find that the "savageries" incubated in the colonies tended to be practiced by the colonizer upon subjects who were seldom protected by strong or consistently enforced distinctions between combatants and non-combatants. The colonizing practices both masked by and entailed in the discourse of total war leave no explicit trace in "The Mark on the Wall," but the imminent "return" of colonial violence to the metropole would have been, for Woolf's contemporaries, part of the story's geopolitical suspense.

Mrs. Dalloway and the Gaze of Total War

"Nothing ever happens . . . Curse this war; God damn this war!" "The Mark on the Wall" makes wartime an uneventful backdrop before which the eventfulness of thought may be staged, even as thought is laden with displaced recognitions that the war may become eventful at any moment. Among those displacements is the mark itself, whose resistance to identification allies it with the paradigmatic early-twentieth-century object in whose ambiguity terror and ecstasy met:

> "That's where I saw my first aeroplane—there between those chimneys . . . I was standing here, looking out . . . It must have been just after I'd got into the flat, a summer's day, and I saw a black spot in the sky, and . . . I said to Miriam, 'Is it a bird? No, I don't think it can be a bird. It's too big. And yet it moves.' And suddenly it came over me, that's an aeroplane! And it was! You know they'd flown the Channel not so long before. I was staying with you in Dorset at the time: and I remember reading it out in the paper, and someone—your father, I think—said: 'The world will never be the same again!'" (328–29; ellipses added)

This is Eleanor Pargiter in Woolf's *The Years* (1937), speaking during the mid-1930s of a moment in 1909 or 1910 and in terms as direct as "The Mark" is oblique, almost as if the later novel were annotating the earlier story in retrospect. There is more ecstasy than terror in Eleanor's memory, although the remark by "someone"—again the eternal "someone" in proximity to the eternal newspaper—that "the world will never be the same again" has already, in *The Years*, been vividly borne out by the 1917 air raid scene that precedes the above passage by forty pages. I will return later to that scene but want to linger on a few moments of anxious identification in Woolf's First World War diaries. For it is these moments, along with the fictional scenes for which she mined them, that expose the kind of immediate consequentiality of recognition that "The Mark on the Wall" needs to suppress in order to maintain its meditative solitude. By the time that story was published, the airplane had made wartime eventful again for Londoners, foregrounding collective acts of speculation, interpretation, and identification over solitary ones like those detailed in "The Mark." Woolf's first fictive meditation on the civilian's relationship to emergent war forms is also her last to confine itself rigorously to a consciousness defending its solitude. Henceforth, she would adapt both the predicament and the techniques of "The Mark" to communal suspense, public trauma, and the persistence of ethical reciprocity in war.

I suggested in chapter 1 that the air raid siren had, as a result of the bombing assessments following the First World War, been recognized as a weapon whose power rivaled that of the airborne bomb. This power lay not in the alert's ability to inflict physical damage but in its capacity to disrupt industrial war efforts and shatter a citizenry's peace of mind. The same assessments implied that the panic induced by false alarms was in some ways more disruptive than that caused by actual raids. Unlike the realized physical violence of a raid, a false alarm provides no discharge for the sense of endangerment it produces; it mobilizes anxiety without providing it with a kinetic outlet. Thus the very falsity of the alarm emphasizes a condition of hideously prolonged expectation, a state of emergency that is both perennial, in having been detached from the arrival of violence in a singular event, and horribly deferred—the advance symptom of a disaster still to come. In her diary entry for February 1, 1915, Woolf recorded how the mere threat of Zeppelin raids, four months before bombs actually fell on London, had produced a continuous state of apprehensiveness and frayed nerves among Londoners:

> In St James Street there was a terrific explosion; people came running out of Clubs; stopped still & gazed about them. But there was no Zeppelin or aeroplane—only, I suppose, a very large tyre burst. But it is really an instinct with me, & most people, I suppose, to turn any sudden noise, or dark object in the sky into an explosion, or a German aeroplane. And it always seems utterly impossible that one should be hurt. (*D1*, 32)[28]

Nearly three years later, in March 1918, Woolf records a mirror-image event:

> I'd taken my third & final roll in bed, when there was an explosion. For half a minute a raid seemed so improbable that we made out it was one of the inexplicable outbursts of motor omnibuses. However, next minute the guns went off all round us & we heard the whistles. There was no denying it. (*D1*, 124)

In the first entry, the everyday urban sounds of a large tire bursting or a car backfiring have been rewritten as signs of bombardment, occasions for scanning the sky even as the writer's sense of her own immunity ("it always seems utterly impossible that one should be hurt") comes to her aid. In the

---

[28] The first Zeppelin raids against England occurred in January 1915, but no bombs fell on London until the night of May 31–June 1, 1915.

second, months of raids have inverted the earlier responses: after being warded off as a mere backfire, the raid is recognized through a now-routine sequence of sounds, producing a denial of denial ("there was no denying it"). Both incidents can be heard echoing in an early scene in *Mrs. Dalloway*, when "a pistol shot in the street outside," a "violent explosion" coming from a royal car in Bond Street, causes Clarissa to jump and draws the attention of passersby to the car and its exalted passenger (13). That the events recorded in the diary have been shorn of their air raid referent in the novel, or rather split into an explosion and the subsequent appearance of a sky-writing plane, attests not only to the postwar moment of *Mrs. Dalloway* but also to the fact that the raw material—and the raw nerve—of that postwar moment is still the war itself.

Set in 1923, *Mrs. Dalloway* reminds us early on that "The War was over, except for some one like Mrs. Foxcroft at the Embassy last night eating her heart out because that nice boy was killed and now the old Manor House must go to a cousin; or Lady Bexborough who opened a bazaar, they said, with the telegram in her hand, John her favourite, killed; but it was over; thank Heaven—over" (4–5). Four and a half years have elapsed since the war's end, yet the credibility of the pronouncement that "The War was over" is nearly breached by the exceptions the narrator makes for those bereaved civilians whose grief recognizes no Armistice. Mediating Clarissa's thoughts through free indirect discourse, the narrator's "but it was over; thank Heaven—over" asserts closure as an ongoing psychic performance rather than testifying to it as an accomplished historical fact. If "the high singing of some aeroplane overhead" joins brass bands and barrel organs among the sounds Clarissa loves in "this moment of June" (4), it may do so thanks to a similarly forced and uneasy assertion of closure: the war machine is now, thank Heaven, a singer of benign peacetime songs—isn't it? The wartime translation of a burst tire into a bombing raid seems at last to have been reversed, but the demilitarized song of the plane still sounds some overtone of threat in the text, triggering, with all its nervous qualifications, the narrator's insistence in the next paragraph that "The War was over." Though the hostilities have ceased, the funeral for the war dead is clearly still underway—those lost are still mourned as if their loss were fresh, the present is still defined as the aftermath of a war nearly five years gone—and as a consequence any winged objects overhead retain their potential for deadly transformation. It is this sense of future-conditional violence rather than any direct representation of wartime panic that makes *Mrs. Dalloway* the closest analogue in interwar fiction to Douhet's vignette about the bird above the Brescia cemetery. Douhet's point, remember, was less the mourners' terror than the fact that bombardment had reorganized their perceptual reflexes: they were now predisposed to misread an airborne object by the light of past violence or to take on faith the misperceptions of others. Even the interval between raids, or between wars, trembles with the question: is this the return of violence, or just a false alarm? Again, this drawn-out suspension between false and true alarm is not, as Lewis Mumford recognized, just a legacy of violence, but a new incarnation of violence, an uncertainty so dire and so prolonged that the psychic harm it does can outlast a war by many years.

Having sung overhead during Clarissa's morning walk through Westminster, the plane reappears shortly after the "pistol shot" of the motor-car, summoned by that false alarm to a second scene of suspenseful reading. This time the reading is literal: the plane performs a cryptic skywriting that the crowds in Bond Street and Regent's Park attempt, uneasily and inconclusively, to parse.

> Suddenly Mrs. Coates looked up into the sky. The sound of an aeroplane bored ominously into the ears of the crowd. There it was coming over the trees, letting out white smoke from behind, which curled and twisted, actually writing something! making letters in the sky! Every one looked up.
>
> Dropping dead down the aeroplane soared straight up, curved in a loop, raced, sank, rose, and whatever it did, wherever it went, out fluttered behind it a thick ruffled bar of white smoke which curled and wreathed upon the sky in letters. But what letters?
>
> . . . All down the Mall people were standing and looking up into the sky. As they looked the whole world became perfectly silent, and a flight of gulls crossed the sky, first one gull leading, then another, and in this extraordinary silence and peace, in this pallor, in this purity, bells struck eleven times, the sound fading up there among the gulls.
>
> The aeroplane turned and raced and swooped exactly where it liked, swiftly, freely, like a skater. (19–20)

In the hefty amount of commentary it has provoked, the motorcar/skywriting sequence in Woolf's novel has been read as signaling everything from the unseating of human by technological authority to the new ascendancy of commercial over royal spectacle in the national imaginary. For Gillian Beer the skywriting functions as "an image of equalizing as opposed to hierarchy, of freedom and play . . . [t]he aeroplane figures as the free spirit of the modern age returning the eye to the purity of a sky which has 'escaped registration.'" Beer adds that "the aeroplane in *Mrs. Dalloway* is no war-machine. Its frivolity is part of postwar relief."[29] Jennifer Wicke, too, cautions against conflating the skywriter and the warplane: "Precisely what is not meant, it seems to me, is that this airplane is the mere replica of that other engine of destruction. Here the airplane, for good or ill, is an ineluctable feature of modernity capable

---

[29] Gillian Beer, "The Island and the Aeroplane: The Case of Virginia Woolf" in *Nation and Narration*, ed. Homi K. Bhabha (London: Routledge, 1990), 275–76.

of hieroglyphic play, of hierophantic writing . . . emblematic of all writing under the sign of mass culture."[30] Vincent Sherry, by contrast, underscores the "ominous" sound of the plane, its "dropping dead down," and the connections between skywriting and the Air Ministry, which saw the practice as a commercially funded way to keep combat pilots in training. Sherry adds that the numerology of the eleventh hour, which strikes as the onlookers strive to read the skywriting, would have had a particular significance for the novel's postwar readership: "The recent war, which ended officially on the eleventh hour of the eleventh day of the eleventh month, still owns this number by rights of association as heavy as those ritualized, already annually ceremonialized memories [i.e., the two minutes of "Great Silence" that yearly commemorate the Armistice]".[31] The bells that break the silence of aerial writing and reading signal, in Sherry's account, mourning and memorialization more than postwar relief.

Given the military origins and potential of skywriting, one might argue that the airplane's significance in *Mrs. Dalloway* is not exclusively commercial or military but a new alloy of the two; the power of the scene would emanate, then, not just from the confluence of consumer culture with gigantic scale and hierophantic mystery, but from the cohering of all three phenomena around a wartime technology that had all too recently terrorized civilians.[32] But the tendency in the novel's critics to assign the airplane either a

---

[30] Jennifer Wicke, "Coterie Consumption: Bloomsbury, Keynes, and Modernism as Marketing," in *Marketing Modernisms: Self-Promotion, Canonization, Rereading*, ed. Kevin J. H. Dettmar and Stephen Watts (Ann Arbor: University of Michigan Press, 1996), 122.

[31] Vincent Sherry, *The Great War and the Language of Modernism* (Oxford: Oxford University Press, 2003), 265.

[32] Skywriting was developed during the First World War by the British flying ace J. C. Savage, who patented the technology; his company, Savage Skywriting, was the first to deploy it commercially, writing "Castrol," "Daily Mail," and "Persil" over Derby in May 1922. As for the military potential of skywriting, here is the Aeronautical Correspondent to the London *Times*, responding on August 18, 1922, to Savage's first skywriting over London: "Vast as the possibilities of advertising by sky-writing are, that is only one of the many purposes to which it may be put, and there can be no doubt that in the near future, generously developed, it might easily rival the tape-machine and wireless telegraphy for the dissemination of news. If one machine can write one or two words at an altitude of ten thousand feet, to be read by millions of people simultaneously, there is no reason why sentences should not be produced rapidly by a fleet of these machines. . . . Obviously the uses of the highly developed sky writing in peace and war are manifold. From the spelling out of a single word, or a single sentence, it is easy to foresee the stage when long messages will be written by cooperating machines. Already several experiments have been made with the Morse code, and the purposes to which, over sea or land in wartime, such a system of communication might be put are clearly apparent. One can imagine, too, the new sort of aerial conflict that would arise when, if the operating machines were not successfully attacked, efforts would be made to blot out their messages with heavy smoke clouds. The writing of misleading orders would offer a fascinating occupation to the imaginative, and the possibilities of the use of smoke writing for propaganda purposes over the enemy's lines would be considerable." Unsigned, "Sky-Writing by Aircraft: Wide Scope in War and Peace," *Times* (London), August 18, 1922: 5d.

military or a commercial significance confirms the scene's power to transmit the characters' dire uncertainty to its readers, delegating to them the anxious work of assigning a value to a dangerously ambiguous object—the work, that is, of distinguishing between a true and a false alarm. Having depicted the skittishness of the interwar urban civilian, *Mrs. Dalloway* also inflicts that skittishness on its readers by placing them among war survivors in a scene of high-stakes reading: standing on the ground amid the onlookers, the reader struggles alongside them not only to parse the gnomic skywritten message but also to ascertain the intentions of the writing machine. And if, as the London *Times* reported in 1922, skywriting "obviously thrills and fascinates everybody who sees it," it did not succeed in totally overwriting the wartime association of planes over cities with bombardment.[33] As late as 1932, the Air Defenses of Great Britain exercises were moved away from London to allay civilians' anxieties; not only was the Geneva disarmament conference taking place concurrently but, as Tami Davis Biddle notes, "bombers over London seemed to have the effect of underscoring the concerns given voice in the popular fiction of the day."[34] Unlike those popular fictions, one of which I discuss at length in the next chapter, *Mrs. Dalloway* neither describes bombing raids nor imagines the dystopian future of a bombed-out world. Both its memory and its anticipation of the civilian-as-target are more attenuated, etched not in descriptions of realized violence but in scenes of imperiled aerial reading and in the alertness of its war-survivor characters, whose nerves have not yet heard the All Clear.

If the airplane in Woolf's novel is an object of fearful ambiguity, even an embodiment of illegible alterity, what are we to make of the fact that *Mrs. Dalloway*'s narrator seems to sit in its cockpit? One function of the skywriting scene is to tell the story of its readers, the crowd of Londoners and London visitors whose attention is first arrested by the appearance of the royal motor-car and then drawn away by the airplane. Coming from heterogeneous class backgrounds, the members of this crowd briefly constitute an audience thanks to the two spectacles they witness, yet the narrative emphasizes the disunity and variety of their responses to both car and plane. The skywriting, in particular, attracts a collectivized attention without succeeding in total-izing or dominating the collective through a coherent, authoritative message. Through the agency of the narrator, however, the onlookers' unspoken reac-tions to the spectacles of car and plane are given voice, salted with details about those characters' pasts and class identities and itineraries, and assem-bled in an image of the social totality; they are the first large-scale illustration

[33] Ibid.

[34] Tami Davis Biddle, *Rhetoric and Reality in Air Warfare: The Evolution of British and American Ideas About Strategic Bombing, 1914–1945* (Princeton: Princeton University Press, 2002), 107.

of the gossamer social web in which the novel is so interested, and of which the central illustration will be the connection between Clarissa Dalloway and Septimus Smith—between an MP's upper-class wife and a petty-bourgeois Great War veteran she will never meet. *Mrs. Dalloway's* narrator achieves these radiant portraits of the social matrix by way of extraordinary powers of mobility, penetration, observation, and juxtaposition—by, in effect, turning and racing and swooping exactly where she likes, swiftly, freely, like a skater. Small wonder, then, that the descriptions of the plane over London engage in so much narratorial stunt-pilotry:

> Ah, but that aeroplane! Hadn't Mrs. Dempster always longed to see foreign parts? She had a nephew, a missionary. It soared and shot. She always went on the sea at Margate, not out o'sight of land, but she had no patience with women who were afraid of water. It swept and fell. Her stomach was in her mouth. Up again. There's a fine young feller aboard of it, Mrs. Dempster wagered, and away and away it went, fast and fading, away and away the aeroplane shot; soaring over Greenwich and all the masts; over the little island of grey churches, St. Paul's and the rest till, on either side of London, fields spread out and dark brown woods where adventurous thrushes hopping boldly, glancing quickly, snatched the snail and tapped him on a stone, once, twice, thrice. (27)

Only a narrator who can move effortlessly from Mrs. Dempster's disappointments to a panoramic overview of London airspace to a thrush's tapping a snail on a stone, the passage suggests, is capable of tracing the filaments of feeling, information, and fellow-suffering across the metropolis to connect Clarissa with Septimus.[35] Affiliated with the airplane's mobility and capacity for penetrating overview, the narrator admits the machine into her own airspace in order either to imitate it or to outperform it in the registers of sympathetic and high-resolution seeing.[36]

---

[35] Karen Piper makes a similar point: "[I]ndeed, as a kind of roaming omniscient narrator, the airplane appears to determine the logic of the narrative itself. . . . [It] is a means of getting perspective, of getting beyond one's house and body and escaping into pure thought." Piper observes that the narrator of Woolf's short story "Kew Gardens" (1919) also "mimics an aerial perspective—with sudden shifts in altitude and visual resolution"; see Karen Piper, *Cartographic Fictions: Maps, Race, and Identity* (New Brunswick, NJ: Rutgers University Press, 2002), 66. See also Woolf's posthumously published essay "Flying Over London" (1928/1950) and discussions of it in my "Over Assemblage: *Ulysses* and the *Boîte-en-valise* from Above" in *Cultural Studies of James Joyce: European Joyce Studies* 15, ed. R. Brandon Kershner (Amsterdam: Rodopi, 2003), and in Leo Mellor, *Reading the Ruins: Modernism, Bombsites and British Culture* (Cambridge: Cambridge University Press, 2013), 33–34.

[36] It would clearly be an error to read the mobile, omniscient narrator in Woolf's work—to say nothing of fiction generally—as a simple emanation or phenomenalization of heavier-than-air flight. But we do, I think, need to attend to those rare moments when the typically disembodied convention of the omniscient narrator is linked to a specific figure or conceit within the diegesis, as when Dickens invokes, in *Dombey and Son*, "a good spirit who would take the housetops off, with

To the extent the narrator finds an avatar in the airplane's mobile point of view, the onlooker's anxious questions of the plane must also be asked of the narrator: what are the intentions behind this narratorial reconnaissance? Of what sorts of violent conflations might this narrator be capable—and to what end? In October 1922, Woolf recorded in her diary that her short story "Mrs. Dalloway in Bond Street" had "branched into a book," adding "I adumbrate here a study of insanity & suicide: the world seen by the sane & the insane side by side" (*D*2, 207). Whether or not Clarissa and Septimus are exhaustively described as "the sane & the insane," there is no denying that *Mrs. Dalloway* juxtaposes them. Much work on the novel during the last two decades has focused on a pairing different from "the sane & the insane": that of the civilian and the soldier. The early pages of the novel appear to establish the discreteness of these categories: if for Clarissa the war is "over; thank Heaven—over," for the shell-shocked Septimus "the world wavered and quivered and threatened to burst into flames" (15). He is still visited by the apparition of his commanding officer Evans, killed in Italy just before the Armistice; he still sees himself as a "giant mourner" with "legions of men prostrate behind him" (68–69). For the combatant, the traumatic aftereffects of the war overwhelm the present, whereas noncombatants like Clarissa seem free to buy flowers, mend a dress, meditate on aging, plan a party. Yet, as we have seen, *Mrs. Dalloway* numbers civilians, too, among those for whom the war has not fully ended. Clarissa's aunt, old Miss Parry, is "an indomitable Englishwoman, fretful if disturbed by the War, say, which dropped a bomb at her very door, from her deep meditation over orchids and her own figure journeying in the 'sixties in India" (174). In the late war the bombs came calling like houseguests, and the domestic threshold, formerly a space for welcoming or warding off social calls, was made to receive more disastrous visitations. Whereas the "indomitable Englishwoman" in mid-Victorian India was at least theoretically protected from military violence by the "figure" she cut—by her gender and by her racial and social consecration as a memsahib—the same woman at home in England during the First World War enjoyed no such protection. With its aftershocks still being felt, the bomb at Miss Parry's door signals the remaking of the civilian as target, and as a bearer of postwar stress.

---

a more potent and benignant hand than the lame demon in the tale, and show a Christian people what dark shapes issue from amidst their homes." *Mrs. Dalloway*'s brief projection of omniscient narration upon the airplane, I suggest, repurposes the panoramic gaze of total war for countervailing ends. See Charles Dickens, *Dombey and Son* (London: Penguin, 2002), 702. On the convention of the Asmodeus flight (as exemplified in Dickens's "good spirit"), see Jonathan Arac, *Commissioned Spirits: The Shaping of Social Motion in Dickens, Carlyle, Melville, and Hawthorne* (New York: Columbia University Press, 1989); Audrey Jaffe, *Vanishing Points: Dickens, Narrative, and the Subject of Omniscience* (Berkeley: University of California Press, 1991); and David L. Pike, *Metropolis on the Styx: The Underworlds of Modern Urban Culture, 1800–2001* (Ithaca, NY: Cornell University Press, 2007).

It would be going too far to say that the novel connects Clarissa and Septimus solely to collapse the distinction between civilian and soldier or to endorse that collapse, although toward the end of her life Woolf would explore the critical possibilities latent in just such a collapse. *Mrs. Dalloway* links its protagonists mostly through their similarities of temperament and experience: they share a history of illness and a dread of doctors who worship the sister goddesses, Proportion and Conversion; they have both witnessed the motorcar in Bond Street and the airplane above it; they can apprehend the coalescence of chatter and accident, occasionally, in a moment of radiant presence that is seldom fully dissociable from a sense of dread. Though they belong to disparate classes, they are brought closer by the vertical relation of patient to physician: at her party, Clarissa learns from the wife of Septimus's doctor that "a young man . . . had killed himself. He had been in the army" (179), and this news precipitates Clarissa's feeling "somehow very like him—the young man who had killed himself. She felt glad that he had done it; thrown it away. . . . He made her feel the beauty; made her feel the fun" (182).[37] Even more intimate is the link forged between Clarissa and Septimus by narratorial echoes in scenes a hundred pages apart. Mending her dress for the party after she has completed her errands, Clarissa recalls a passage ("Fear no more the heat o' the sun") she read earlier that morning in an edition of *Cymbeline* propped open in the window of Hatchards bookshop. The narrator describes Clarissa's calm: "Fear no more, says the heart. Fear no more, says the heart, committing its burden to some sea, which sighs collectively for all sorrows, and renews, begins, collects, lets fall. And the body alone listens to the passing bee; the wave breaking; the dog barking, far away barking and barking" (39). In a later scene, Septimus experiences a similar moment of peace while his wife decorates a hat: "his hand lay there on the back of the sofa, as he had seen his hand lie when he was bathing, floating, on the top of the waves, while far away on shore he heard dogs barking and barking far away. Fear no more, says the heart in the body; fear no more" (136). We know that Septimus reveres Shakespeare and may, like Clarissa, have been reminded of the phrase that morning by the same copy of *Cymbeline* in the same Piccadilly shop window; the quotation will sound again in Clarissa's thoughts during the novel's final pages, just as she allows herself to be gladdened by the news of Septimus's death (182). But in the hat-decorating scene it is not only the phrase itself but also the heart's articulation of the phrase, the oceanic language, and the far away bark of the dog that echo Clarissa's meditations.

---

[37] The final sentence in this quotation ("He made her feel the beauty; made her feel the fun") appears in Woolf's American proofs and in all U.S. editions of the novel but *not* in any British ones. For a detailed discussion of this and other variants, see Anne E. Fernald, "Introduction," in Virginia Woolf, *Mrs. Dalloway* (Cambridge: Cambridge University Press, 2014), esp. lxxxiv–xc.

One might take these echoes to ratify Clarissa's feeling "very like" Septimus by demonstrating that the states of mind, the interior tableaux, even the mental diction of socially disparate people can be nearly identical. But a more disquieting reading emerges when we return to the narrator through whose agency the momentary fusion of Clarissa and Septimus occurs—a narrator who is conspicuously mobile, surveillant, penetrating, sometimes totalizing, and possessed of an archivist's retentive and cross-referencing powers. This is a narrator, after all, who not only keeps track of individual bodies, phrases, commodities, and thoughts as they circulate in the metropolis but also maps the complex transactions among them in space and time. This narrator traces a Shakespeare quotation that sounds nonsimultaneously in two minds back to a single shop window and forward to their mystical but indirect communion during a party, tracks the ambulance carrying the dying Septimus past Clarissa's old suitor Peter Walsh, in whom, as he stands by the pillar box opposite the British Museum, it triggers "a moment, in which things came together; this ambulance; and life and death" (148). The *Mrs. Dalloway* narrator ravels the web that joins Shakespeare to shell shock, jam to the war machine, because hers is the gaze of total war. In keeping with an airborne vantage that observes the linkages among discrete things in order to deem them equally legitimate as targets, the narrator's command of particularities leads, chillingly, not to the fortification of discreteness but to its erosion. The sensitive apparatus through which Septimus and Clarissa are observed ends up fusing even the interior language of combatant and noncombatant, threatening to violate the very "privacy of the soul" on which the novel appears to insist (124).

This is not to claim that *Mrs. Dalloway* adopts the gaze of total war for warlike purposes. If the novel's narratorial gaze is the massively interconnective one of a Douhet, it is also, paradoxically, the opposite—a gaze that wants to "travel the spider's thread of attachment" (112) between people, places, things, beliefs, and affects in order to point up the fragility of their interdependence, the susceptibility of the whole social matrix to trauma if even a small part of it is assaulted or destroyed. Woolf's novel, one might say, attempts to capture the logic of total war for redeployment in a deeply pacificist agenda.[38] Yet this is not the same thing as exempting the novel

---

[38] My tight focus on Woolf leaves to one side the pacifisms of the rest of the Bloomsbury circle, a subject Christine Froula addresses comprehensively in *Virginia Woolf and the Bloomsbury Avant-Garde: War, Civilization, Modernity* (New York: Columbia University Press, 2005). Froula shows (5–6) how prescient John Maynard Keynes and Clive Bell were in arguing that a humiliating peace would increase the likelihood of another war—the central argument not only of Keynes's *The Economic Consequences of the Peace* (1919) but also of Bell's *Peace at Once* (1915). Yet for Froula, these next-war prophecies did not predispose Woolf to a sense of the future's foreclosure, even when, during the final years of the novelist's life, they seemed to have been terribly fulfilled. Of Woolf's suicide, Froula writes, "perhaps it was not that she had ceased to believe in civilization's future but that

from that logic or the gaze it produces. To protest total war on the grounds that social, cultural, industrial, and military systems are crucially inter-penetrative is not to step outside the logic of total war; it is simply to resist one application of that logic. By the same token, the novel's replication of a certain Douhetian gaze does not necessarily weaken its pacifism; it simply attests to the central sorrow of the pacifist in the era of total war: that the architecture of total war proceeds from assumptions few pacifists would reject. These assumptions—e.g., that the war machine is funded and built by civilian workers whose safety, morale, peace of mind, and consent are vulnerable and therefore effective targets—do not, of course, lead inevita-bly to an endorsement of total war; but to replicate such assumptions, even while deploring the end to which they are put, can seem like a concession of defeat, even an endorsement of that end. Clausewitz argued that whereas the purpose of war is to serve a political end, the nature of war is to serve only itself.[39] War subjects the self-understanding of all things—ambu-lances, Bartlett pears, skywriting, Shakespeare, this moment of June—to a military-industrial undertow. As the limit approached by war's centripetal force, the doctrine of total war is susceptible to rejection but not to disproof. The replication of its logic and its gaze in *Mrs. Dalloway*, despite the clearly pacifist vectors along which these are mobilized, may be both the text's pri-mary symptom and its most strategic pacifism: the self-inflicted violence exhibited by the text acts out, at once neurotically and instructively, the brute circularity of war, conspicuously refusing to fabricate some fictive escape from total war's inexorable logic. At the same time, it stages, amid the effects of recent trauma, the persistence of collective but nontotalized reading, thinking, and feeling—which is to say, the persistence of commu-nity. As a de facto reading of Douhet, it says that the mourners at Brescia may have had their rite shattered, but they were joined in both the rite and its shattering.

The Years: Immunities Lost and Found

"To freshen my memory of the war, I read some old diaries. How close the tears come, again & again. . . . The sense of all that floating away for ever down the stream, unknown for ever: queer sense of the past swallowing so much of oneself" (*D4*, 193). This is Woolf in mid-December 1933, preparing to write the First World War section of the book she was calling "Here & Now." By late

---

she could fight no more," adding of *Between the Acts*, "neither the madness to which she attributed her suicide nor her death negate[s] the future that pageant and novel leave open" (324).

[39] The elegant paraphrase of Clausewitz is John Keegan's, in *A History of Warfare* (New York: Alfred A. Knopf, 1993), 21.

January, her memory refreshed, she was drafting an air raid scene, her first; when the book was published three years later as *The Years*, a much-rewritten version of the raid would form the centerpiece of the "1917" chapter. Woolf's diary mining is legible in the date-stamped, chronological arrangement of *The Years*. But in other respects, the private notations of the diaries have been revised out of recognition into an account of aggregate experiences focalized through the members of the Pargiter family. Her novels of the 1920s had given voice to the "privacy of the soul" through fluent, highly interior language. *The Years* refocuses on public time and collective experience; no longer the key nodes of articulateness, its protagonists are practically aphasic compared with, say, the six logorrheics who intone most of *The Waves* (1930). This shift to an impersonal, exteriorized, public register—one supposedly antithetical to Woolf's stylistic gifts—is often cited as a principle reason for *The Years'* failure as a novel. But what *The Years* forgoes in lyrical intensification it looks to gain in staging the formation of unconventional social ties in times of crisis. Whereas *The Waves* enacted intersubjectivity by lapping the soliloquies of its six speakers in a uniform style, *The Years* retreats to the more jagged territory of half-completed gestures and utterances, intermittent bursts of fellow-feeling, and fleeting or grudging alliances. If *The Years* moves more haltingly than "The Mark" or *The Waves*, it may be because it refuses the consolation of solipsism or intersubjectivity for chancier, more uneven modes of social being.

The Years opens in 1880 with a panoramic reconnaissance that recalls the bird's-eye narrations of *Mrs. Dalloway*, relating the movements "of shoppers in the West end, of business men in the East" while also singling out small acts: the posting of a letter, the amorous song of a thrush. Where the *Mrs. Dalloway* narrator had followed the skywriting plane out over forests on the city's outskirts where a thrush tapped a snail on a stone "once, twice, thrice" (27), here "virgins and spinsters with hands that had staunched the sores of Bermondsey and Hoxton carefully measured out one, two, three, four spoonfuls of tea" (4). Whether it belongs to a scene of predation or social ritual, counting grounds the distances and agglomerating sweep of overflight in the scarce, the specific. The chapter architecture of *The Years* participates in this logic, using the sequential procession of years—1880, 1891, 1907, 1908, 1910, 1911, 1913, 1914, 1917, 1918, and "Present Day"—to steady its gaze upon a period of volatile change. In *Mrs. Dalloway*, the phrase "the leaden circles dissolved in the air" indexed the unified clock-time of the metropolis, its verbatim repetition troping the homogenizing effects of mass-synchronization. Counting in *The Years* belongs initially to the world of private ritual in which time is measured out in teaspoons and sugar lumps. "And he hung his cap on the bust of our grandfather. And I poured out the tea. 'How many lumps of sugar does a lieutenant in the Royal Rat-catchers require?' I asked. 'One. Two. Three. Four . . .'" (285). This is Sara Pargiter relating a scene in which she has made tea for North, her first cousin once removed. But the book's procession of years affects these minute enumerations: it is 1917, and North will leave tonight for the Front.

Five pages later, the act of counting is wholly resignified, alongside the concept of clock-time, with the onset of a Gotha raid. In response to the warning siren, Sara, her sister Maggie and Maggie's French husband Renny, their cousin Eleanor, and Renny's Polish friend Nicholas descend to the cellar of Maggie's Westminster home, dinner plates in hand. In the ensuing scene, Eleanor's heightened awareness of her immediate surroundings is juxtaposed with the terse, flatly declarative language of suspense ("a gun boomed"; "the silence was profound"; "it was on top of them"; "nothing happened") and with Nicholas's use of sound and second hand to map the course of the bombers over London:

> "They've got through the defences," said Nicholas.
>
> They began to eat their pudding.
>
> A gun boomed again. This time there was a bark in its boom.
>
> "Hampstead," said Nicholas. He took out his watch. The silence was profound. Nothing happened. Eleanor looked at the blocks of stone arched over their heads. She noticed a spider's web in one corner. Another gun boomed. A sigh of air rushed up with it. It was right on top of them this time.
>
> "The Embankment," said Nicholas. Maggie put down her plate and went into the kitchen.
>
> There was profound silence. Nothing happened. Nicholas looked at his watch as if he were timing the guns. There was something queer about him, Eleanor thought; medical, priestly? He wore a seal that hung down from his watch-chain. The number on the box opposite was 1397. She noticed everything. The Germans must be overhead now. She felt a curious heaviness on top of her head. One, two, three, four, she counted, looking up at the greenish-grey stone. Then there was a violent crack of sound, like the split of lightning in the sky. The spider's web oscillated.
>
> "On top of us," said Nicholas, looking up. They all looked up. At any moment a bomb might fall. There was dead silence . . .
>
> One, two, three, four, Eleanor counted. The spider's web was swaying. That stone may fall, she thought, fixing a certain stone with her eyes. Then a gun boomed again. It was fainter—further away.
>
> "That's over," said Nicholas. He shut his watch with a click. And they all turned and shifted on their chairs as if they had been cramped. (290–91; ellipses added)

As in Woolf's diary accounts of the 1917–18 Gotha raids on London, a darkened city that is doubly invisible from a dark cellar can nonetheless be mapped as the sounds of its defense and injury register in the activated distance around the listener.[40] This is a different kind of leaden circle dissolving in the air: the telltale sounds of threat plotted in concentric proximity to oneself, coming closer—Hampstead, the Embankment—sitting atop one, and finally receding.[41] But if the raids underscored a given listener's particular coordinates, they also played a role in public chronometry, the more so because the leaden circles of Big Ben's chimes were stilled and its face darkened between 1916 and 1918 to deny the raiders a prominent aiming point; as the narrator tells us, the post-raid quiet is all the deeper because "The clocks that used to boom out the hour in Westminster were silent" (294). Although the German raiders did not arrive as punctually during the First World War as they would during the Blitz, the Gothas were nonetheless a kind of surrogate clock chime, their aural signature synchronizing the experience of Londoners separated from one another by blocks or miles. In marking the end of raid-time, the click with which Nicholas's watch closes also marks the end of an integrated, citywide experience of time and the resumption of private time without the unifying peal of public clocks.

The 1917 chapter of *The Years* acts, I suggest, as a prequel to *Mrs. Dalloway*, inviting us to read the earlier novel anew by its light. Big Ben's chimes, it reminds us, would still, in 1923, have been an affirmatively peacetime sound whose absence in the recent war remained lodged in Londoners' collective memory. Clarissa thinks of "an indescribable pause; a suspense (but that might be her heart, affected, they said, by influenza) before Big Ben strikes. There! Out it boomed. First a warning, musical; then the hour, irrevocable. The leaden circles dissolved in the air" (4). That "suspense" arises partly out of Clarissa's love of life and sense of awe; but it also commemorates a time when the listener would have waited in vain for a sound suspended in war, and when an audible "warning" would have heralded a different kind of strike. (That Clarissa attributes her sense of suspense to a heart weakened by post-war influenza calls attention to the strange manner in which her illness displaces any personal memory of London at war akin to Eleanor Pargiter's or Virginia Woolf's.) *Mrs. Dalloway's* emphasis on noninjurious public forms

---

[40] Here, for example, is Woolf's description of an early morning Gotha raid on December 6, 1917: "They fired very quickly, apparently towards Barnes. Slowly the sounds got more distant, & finally ceased; we unwrapped ourselves & went back to bed. In ten minutes there could be no question of staying there: guns apparently at Kew. Up we jumped, more hastily this time, since I remember leaving my watch, & trailing cloak & stockings behind me. . . . Guns at one point so loud that the whistle of the shell going up followed the explosion. One window did, I think, rattle. Then silence. Cocoa was brewed for us, & off we went again. Having trained one's ears to listen one can't get them not to for a time; & as it was after 6, carts were rolling out of stables, motor cars throbbing, & then prolonged ghostly whistlings which mean, I suppose, Belgian work people recalled to the munitions factory. At last in the distance I heard bugles" (*D1*, 85).

[41] In this respect, Nicholas's audio mapping of the German bombers provides a spatial analogue to the chronological procession of *The Years*, whose chapters come steadily closer to an unnumbered "Present Day" that the reader, through yet another vertiginous deixis, is invited to adopt as her own.

of time and on a visible, readily traversable London look different, too—look more like the reparative exercise of freedoms curtailed during the war—when read by the light of *The Years*.

But the later novel does not just backlight the earlier; it also extends its thinking about the reciprocal ties and alliances that may form among those who endure the charged futurity of modern warfare. *Mrs. Dalloway* strung filaments of memory, responsibility, and fellow feeling between civilian and combatant but stopped short of bringing them face-to-face in life; that Clarissa can receive a dead veteran's encouragement from beyond the grave is at once the novel's transcendence and its limit. *The Years*, for its part, shows more interest in new coalitions of the living: through Eleanor's sense that the war "remov[es] barriers" and blurs "the edges of things," freeing them "from some surface hardness"; through her experiencing a "sharp shiver of repugnance" at the news that Nicholas is a homosexual, only to realize that that sharpness had "touched nothing of importance," had in fact left in its wake "one feeling, one whole—liking" (284, 287, 297–98).[42] To be sure, the raid has been a "complete break" not just in the flow of conversation but also in memory and continuous thought (292). But even as it drives home the absence of civilian immunity in war, the raid leaves Eleanor feeling beneficially "robbed by the presence of death of something personal," feeling in some other sense "immune." This immunity seems to entail a greater receptivity to others: not just a sense that what is "queer" in them cannot cut her but a desire to "live adventurously, wholly" in some still-unimagined and collective freedom (297). As Nicholas puts it, "The soul—the whole being . . . It wishes to expand; to adventure; to form—new combinations?" (296). That some of these new combinations are purely hypothetical, purely counterfactual—as with Eleanor's realization that her cousin's husband Renny, despite being twenty years her junior, "is the man . . . that I should like to have married" (299)—only expands the sense of the soul's opening to others.

The "single spider's thread" that attached *Mrs. Dalloway*'s Lady Bruton to her outbound lunch guests "became hazy with the sound of bells," stretched as the dowager grew drowsy, and finally snapped as she nodded off (109–10). But where the bells and repleteness of peacetime produce broken or attenuated threads in the earlier novel, the spider's web Eleanor Pargiter watches during the raid survives, "swaying." There is an unnerving suggestion here: that the lattice of resilient social ties necessary to transcend war can only be formed in war, when sexual mores and partitions of nation, class, and generation lose

---

[42] While drafting the scene, Woolf wrote to Quentin Bell, "I am writing about sodomy at the moment and wish I could discuss the matter with you; how far can one say openly what is the relation of a woman and a sod? In French, yes; but in Mr. Galsworthys [*sic*] English, no" (*D*5, 273).

their "surface hardness" enough to permit new combinations to form. It is as if the loss of civilian immunity were the necessary prelude to acquiring something like Eleanor's immunity, the displacement of personal fearfulness by the sense that others' strangeness contributes to "one feeling, one whole." Whether we accept this suggestion on its face or construe it as a desperate attempt to make a virtue of necessity—to wring *something* generative out of the war—we should note that it does not trade on the portrait or promise of a suspenseless world. Much as characters in the final chapter of *The Years* think their way repeatedly back to the raid, Woolf's work in general cycles back to the war even in the midst of peace, yet without adopting an energetics of relief that would conjure the experience of war only to take pleasure in its cessation. Instead, her writing pitches the memory and prospect of the disaster as a danger-gradient that thought must continue to scale. The immunity that matters here—the kind in which Eleanor finds "not only a new space of time, but new powers, something unknown within her" (297)—can only arise in the presence of death, against the threat of thought's extinction. To think at all is to think in a raid.

"Thoughts on Peace in an Air Raid"

"It's all damned rot!" exclaims Renny, throwing down the newspaper he had picked up after the raid, and his outburst cuts short Eleanor's and Nicholas's deliberations about the soul's wish to expand and form new combinations (296). As in "The Mark on the Wall," thought is broken off by a bystander's anger at the distortions of wartime journalism, with the difference that here the interrupted thinking is dialogic, a face-to-face conversation between two strangers born in different countries and still wary of one another. In both *Three Guineas* and *Between the Acts* (1941), Woolf would continue to engage the question of how to form, represent, and give voice to dissident communities in the shadow of escalating conflicts that openly dispensed with civilian immunity. In recent years, these major late works have received ample attention from scholars interested in Woolf's attempts to think gender, war, and politics together.[43] Rather than discuss either of them at length, I turn now to her most radical rewriting of "The Mark on the Wall," and perhaps the "latest"

---

[43] On *Between the Acts* in this context, see Jed Esty, *A Shrinking Island: Modernism and National Culture in England* (Princeton: Princeton University Press, 2004); MacKay, *Modernism and World War II*; and Mellor, *Reading the Ruins*. On *Three Guineas*, see Jessica Berman, *Modernist Commitments: Ethics, Politics, and Transnational Modernism* (New York: Columbia University Press, 2011) and Gayle Rogers, *Modernism and the New Spain: Britain, Cosmopolitan Europe, and Literary History* (New York: Oxford University Press, 2012). On both works, see Froula, *Virginia Woolf and the Bloomsbury Avant-Garde*, and Patrick Deer, *Culture in Camouflage: War, Empire, and Modern British Literature* (Oxford: Oxford University Press, 2009).

of her late works in its implacable rendezvous with barred futurity. This is the short essay "Thoughts on Peace in an Air Raid," a meditation on militarism, gender, and critical thinking narrated as if it were coextensive with a bombing attack being endured by the speaker.[44] Commissioned by an American women's symposium and published in October 1940 in the *New Republic*, the essay was incubated during the final weeks of the Battle of Britain and written in late August and early September, on the eve of the London Blitz. It opens by enchaining its present-tense account of a raid in a series of prior raids, prior wars, and (by implication) Woolf's earlier writings on war: "The Germans were over this house last night and the night before that. Here they are again" (*E6*, 242). The diurnal quality of the raids also links them to her diary from the period, which from midsummer 1940 onward makes nearly daily mention of them; "Weeping Willie" the air raid siren, she notes on August 28, "is as punctual as the vespers" (*D5*, 313).[45] And like both the diary and Woolf's earlier published writings on war, "Thoughts" leans heavily on the deixis of present danger, which both emphasizes and collapses the distance between the embattled here-and-now of the essay ("*Here* they are again"; "The drone of the planes is *now* like the sawing of a branch overhead") and the still-sleeping American readers to whom its "fragmentary notes" will be sent (*E6*, 242–43).

This split between raid and reading is matched, in the essay, by a weird rift at the heart of its argument and core temporality. In an early invocation to the unborn, "Thoughts on Peace in an Air Raid" appears to declare allegiance to a reproductive conception of the future: "Unless we can think peace into existence we—not this one body in this one bed but millions of bodies yet to be born—will lie in the same darkness and hear the same death rattle overhead." Thinking peace—"the only efficient air raid shelter"—into being is the only way to prevent an eternal repetition of the raid and its attendant terrors. Most of the ensuing meditations seem to proceed, accordingly, in the name of the unborn: for the sake of those future generations, the English woman must use the "weapon" of "private thinking, tea-table thinking," a "thinking against the current" that can generate alternatives to the militarized portrait of masculinity that lures one generation of young men after another into war. In order to emancipate men from the tyranny of their "subconscious Hitlerism,"

---

[44] I refer to the "speaker" of the essay as distinct from "Woolf" because "Thoughts on Peace in an Air Raid" so aggressively foregrounds its form (i.e., a brightly burnished meditation *as if* in the real time of a raid) as a conceit or construction that its first-person voice is closer in nature to the narrator of "The Mark on the Wall" than to the less enframed, less embodied, less endangered "I" of the conventional essay.

[45] The description of the raid that frames "Thoughts on Peace" is essentially quarried from Woolf's August 1940 diary entries. For example: "The sound was like someone sawing the air just above us . . . Hum & saw & buzz all round us" (*D5*, 311); "The drone of the planes is now like the sawing of a branch overhead. Round and round it goes, sawing and sawing at a branch directly over the house" (*E6*, 245).

the essay argues in a seeming reprise of *Three Guineas*, women first must free themselves from the commoditized femininity of the shop window and the cosmetics counter. Because "Hitlers are bred by slaves," the breeders must become free if the dynasty of tyrants is to end (*E6*, 242–43).

Yet having established this story about a reproductive future unbarred by women's self-emancipation, the essay engages in a brief thought experiment that upends that story and marks a departure even from a work as recent as *Three Guineas* in its take on war, gender, and reproduction. Against the claim that instincts, tradition, and tutelage combine to make male militarism unalterable, the reader is asked to think in parallel about the malleability of women's maternal instincts.

> Suppose that imperative among the peace terms was: "Child-bearing is to be restricted to a very small class of specially selected women," would we submit? Should we not say, "The maternal instinct is a woman's glory. It was for this that my whole life has been dedicated, my education, training, everything . . ." But if it were necessary, for the sake of humanity, for the peace of the world, that childbearing should be restricted, the maternal instinct subdued, women would attempt it. Men would help them. They would honour them for their refusal to bear children. They would give them other openings for their creative power. (*E6*, 244)

Although the essay goes on to close the loop of analogy by calling for a reengineered masculinity, the strangeness of the thought experiment exceeds its analogical function, exceeds even the essay's concluding return to the idiom of fertility ("The emotion of fear and of hate is therefore sterile, unfertile"; "The seed [of a de-mechanized, post-nationalist civility] may be fertile" [*E6*, 244–45]). As a rhetorical gambit, this swerve into speculative fiction can seem deeply baffling. For many of the essay's readers, the maternal instinct would have seemed even less changeable than the martial one. And a peace dependent on elite, state-regulated fertility and eugenic selection hardly makes a stable, self-evident platform for arguing by analogy. If the essay seeks greater reproductive freedoms for women, including the freedom from ideologically compulsory child-bearing, one wonders why it camouflages as a far-fetched speculative sacrifice what is in fact its desideratum—unless it is to ask, offhandedly, why women alone should have to curb their instincts in the name of humanity.

But through the portal of analogy, something else enters "Thoughts on Peace in an Air Raid"—a radical, causal rethinking of the symbiosis between militarism and reproductivism. While appearing to draw war and maternity alongside one another, Woolf in fact joins them end to end—"Hitlers are bred by slaves"—implying that if peace hangs on the problem of what to do with our young men, one solution may be to encourage women to bear fewer of them and fewer female "slaves" to perpetuate the cycle. Until we learn to produce peaceable male children and emancipated female ones, it suggests, we will only replicate war's generative conditions. One way to interrupt that cycle would be to reduce the war machine's procreative inputs and shift women's energy from reproduction and childrearing to other, perhaps more critical, forms of creativity. (Note that *fatherhood* is never proposed as a male alternative to warfare in the essay, which wants to imagine alternatives to reproduction for both men and women.) It is here that "Thoughts on Peace" ceases to be a mere pendant to *Three Guineas*. Despite its radical demand that the state pay a wage "to those whose profession is marriage and motherhood," *Three Guineas* conceives of this wage as a means "to recruit the child-bearing force" just as military pay raises might induce enlistment. Even the Lysistrata scenario in its endnotes imagines women going on a reproductive strike in order to end war—in order, that is, to hasten a peace in which children could again be made for some other destiny than "the supply of 'cannon-fodder'" (110–11, 147). But "Thoughts on Peace" imagines a curb on reproduction not just as a condition of a future peace but also as an emancipatory feature of that peace, a means by which women might develop other openings for their creative power.

One cumulative result of these moves is to expose the logic of reproductive futurism (in Lee Edelman's phrase) that permeates the figure of the civilian— paradigmatically, the woman or child to be exempted from wartime targeting in the name of a peaceful human future that her survival will help to guarantee.[46] Where that conventional understanding of the civilian places women and children outside the war machine, "Thoughts on Peace in an Air Raid" puts them at its heart, insinuating that war perpetuates itself by camouflaging its deadliest assets—present "slaves" and their offspring, the bondswomen and tyrants of the future—as noncombatants. In effect, the essay renews and extends *Mrs. Dalloway*'s bid to appropriate the doctrine of total war to critical and pacifist ends. Limited war, it says, preserves the lie about human reproduction through which war reproduces itself; total war, in liquidating civilian immunity, at least tacitly recognizes the mutually reinforcing connections among patriarchy, heteronormativity, reproductive futurism, and the war machine. Pacifism must learn to see with the cold eye of total war, tracing

---

[46] For Edelman, "reproductive futurism" names the limits of political discourse as such, insofar as the future in whose name both the Left and the Right claim to act is incarnated in the figure of the Child. As against this compulsory heteronormativity, "the queer comes to figure the bar to every realization of futurity, the resistance, internal to the social, to every social structure or form." Lee Edelman, *No Future: Queer Theory and the Death Drive* (Durham: Duke University Press, 2004), 4. Although "Thoughts on Peace in an Air Raid" does not accede to the position of radical negation with anything like Edelman's ferocity, the ramifications of its reproductive thought experiment and its refusals to unbar the future by invoking the figure of the Child seem largely congruent with his position.

conflicts beyond their proximate conditions to the war-and-gender system where their enabling conditions are made.

The essay's critique of reproductive futurism, we should note, is undertaken not on behalf of the nonprocreative (the queer, the celibate, the childless) but rather on behalf of those whose procreative lives might have been led otherwise, or might be so in the future. As much as it seeks to spare the "millions of bodies yet to be born" the experience of an air raid, "Thoughts on Peace" is at least as interested in delivering the unborn from compulsory or unreflective reproductive acts, which it thinks into a progenitive relation with the raid. One might expect Woolf's essay to devote its final paragraphs, then, to some nonreproductive portrait of the future, if only to establish that its critique of reproductive futurism is not just a symptom or traumatic accessory to a general sense of futurelessness. But that the speaker refrains from such a portrait—that she appears to belittle, even to vandalize a work whose afterlife she can only half imagine—suggests that her thoughts on peace may not be quite distinct from the wartime sense of annulled futurity; that critique may not be fully separable from syndrome in this case.[47] "Let us send these fragmentary notes to . . . the [American] men and women whose sleep has not yet been broken by machine-gun fire," she says, "in the belief that they will rethink them generously and charitably, perhaps shape them into something serviceable. And now, in the shadowed half of the world, to sleep" (*E6*, 245; ellipses added). What was framed as critical thinking weaponized against what *The Years* called the "complete break" of the raid threatens to dissolve into fragments or disappear in the gulf between the somnolent speaker and her still-sleeping readers.

We do not have to read back through Woolf's suicide to understand the speaker's imminent sleep "in the shadowed half of the world" as a figurative death, and the essay itself as a petition from the doomed to the living. A last reinvention of gothic, it takes the convention of speech from beyond the grave and bends it to the matter of war. As brave as we may find the essay's "thinking" in the raid "against the grain," its most compelling traits may after all be its willingness to exhibit traumatized affect, its desolate pause on the threshold of the future, and its making visible a new community even as the speaker prepares to travel beyond the pale of all communities. An all but posthumous epistle to living strangers, it reprises Septimus's appeal to Clarissa. But unlike that appeal, it does not entreat the living to feel, in the language of

---

[47] Woolf's wartime diary dwells often on how war, in barring the future, also dissevers her from a sense of her readers and from their contributions to her sense of both security and location. Her entry for June 27, 1940, is a powerful instance of this: "Further, the war—our waiting while the knives sharpen for the operation—has taken away the outer wall of security. No echo comes back. I have no surroundings. I have so little sense of a public that I forget about Roger coming out or not coming out. . . . We pour to the edge of a precipice . . . & then? I can't conceive that there will be a 27th June 1941" (*D5*, 299). Woolf is referring to her biography of Roger Fry, which would be published in July 1940.

Clarissa's thoughts, the beauty or the fun. "Thoughts on Peace in an Air Raid" is Eurydice's envoi to Orpheus. It says, be blown backward into the future with your gaze fixed on past wars and past writing, as well as on peacetimes past. If it offers any tonic to wartime nationalism beyond the weak entreaty to "make happiness," it is a European cosmopolitanism located explicitly in the past; if it offers anything "positive, reviving, healing," it is not futurity but the persistence of memory in the presence of death:

> The sound of sawing overhead has increased. All the searchlights are erect. They point at a spot directly above this roof. At any moment a bomb may fall on this very room. One, two, three, four, five, six . . . the seconds pass. The bomb did not fall. But during those seconds of suspense all thinking stopped. All feeling, save one dull dread, ceased. A nail fixed the whole being to one hard board. The emotion of fear and of hate is therefore sterile, unfertile. Directly that fear passes, the mind reaches out and instinctively revives itself by trying to create. Since the room is dark it can create only from memory. It reaches out to the memory of other Augusts—in Bayreuth, listening to Wagner; in Rome, walking over the Campagna; in London. Friends' voices come back. Scraps of poetry return. Each of those thoughts, even in memory, was far more positive, reviving, healing the creative than the dull dread made of fear and hate. Therefore if we are to compensate the young man for the loss of his glory and of his gun, we must give him access to the creative feelings. We must make happiness. We must free him from the machine. We must bring him out of his prison into the open air. But what is the use of freeing the young Englishman if the young German and the young Italian remain slaves? (E6, 244–45)

Between the suspension of thought and its resumption is the memory of friends' voices—voices from earlier iterations of a scene Woolf has been writing and rewriting across the span of her career. We are back with Eleanor, Sara, Renny, Maggie, and Nicholas in the 1917 section from *The Years*, counting out seconds, feeling thought stop in the suspense, struggling to reconstitute it in creative, reparative acts or in a sense of immunity rooted elsewhere ("Immune, she repeated. It was a picture of a hill and a village perhaps in the South of France, perhaps in Italy" [294]). We are by the fire, once more, with the narrator of "The Mark on the Wall," for whom a nail or snail, in effect, "fixed the whole being to one hard board." And we are again with Clarissa, the civilian woman trying to fathom the drives, decisions, and experiences of the young male combatant, only this time he is German and Italian as well as English, and he is thousands of feet directly above her in space. Even on the verge of the dark—where else if not *there*? when else if not *then*?—Woolf is conjuring interlocutors from the past, from abroad, from above. Conjuring, too, the irreducible particularity of her own work in the course of bidding it, under pressure of this unmasterable moment, farewell.

For all her concern with attenuated or barred futurity, Woolf left one prospect of futurelessness virtually unexplored: that the archive of human knowledge and expression, or the conditions of that archive's legibility, might be destroyed in war.[48] Even *Mrs. Dalloway's* archaeological sublime imagines London in ruins only as a backdrop to persistent historical and political knowledge: "the enduring symbol of the state . . . will be known to curious antiquaries, sifting the ruins of time, when London is a grass-grown path and all those hurrying along the pavement this Wednesday morning are but bones with a few wedding rings mixed up in their dust and the gold stoppings of innumerable decayed teeth. The face in the motor car will then be known" (16). The next chapter is about the limit-scenario of the archive's destruction. It revolves around two of Woolf's contemporaries for whom the archive's radical fragility was a matter not of hyperbole but of imminent concern. These are Hilary Jenkinson (1882–1961), the prominent theorist of archive administration; and the writer and suffragist Cicely Mary Hamilton (1872–1952). When in 1931 Woolf delivered the lecture that would precipitate both *The Years* and *Three Guineas*, Hamilton was in the audience but by that time had lost the political optimism that suffused her feminist treatise, *Marriage as a Trade* (1909). Her experiences during the First World War had left her convinced that the future—not just her individual future or her generation's, but humanity's—was foreclosed by an inexorable bent toward conflict and eventual social

---

[48] In only one late work, and there only in superseded drafts, did Woolf toy with the prospect of catastrophic knowledge loss in war. This was "The Searchlight," a posthumously published short story that she began in 1929 and worked on at several points between January 1939 and her death in 1941. The published version takes place in a London mansion-turned-club one summer night before a war that has subsequently begun. "It was peace then; the air force was practicing; searching for enemy aircraft in the sky." A searchlight beam wheeling "like the wings of a windmill, or again like the antennae of some prodigious insect" flashes across the balcony where Mrs. Ivimey and her party are gathered before going to the theater. It prompts her to retell a family story about the romance of seeing at a distance. But the same searchlight that catalyzed the story interrupts it, trapping the storyteller for a moment in the gaze of a more ominous distance-vision: "A shaft of light fell upon Mrs. Ivimey as if someone had focused the lens of a telescope upon her. (It was the air force, looking for enemy air craft.)" The story ends with the Ivimey party ready to decamp for the theater and the RAF's searchlight beams focusing, in a mixture of threat and glorification, "on the plain expanse of Buckingham Palace" (279, 270, 272).

An earlier draft of the story, set on Freshwater Down, ends by shattering both the tale's verifiability and the pastoral scene of its retelling: "But since Hitlers [sic] bombs the other day destroyed a copy of the DNB it has been impossible to verify these facts." Later drafts expand this sentence to a coda: "If anyone should complain, birds never sang so loud; hollyhocks never [grew so] high, it is impossible to contradict them, for the book in which the whole story is told in plain English was destroyed the other day 'by enemy action.'" The loss of a single volume gestures at the loss of verification, the loss of empiricism, the loss of literacy itself. See Virginia Woolf, drafts of story titled "Scene from the Past," Sussex, Monks House Papers, B 10e: 24–25; qtd. in J. W. Graham, "The Drafts of Virginia Woolf's 'The Searchlight,'" *Twentieth-Century Literature* 22.4 (December 1976): 386. See also Laura Marcus, "'In the Circle of the Lens': Woolf's 'Telescope' Story, Scene-Making, and Memory," *Journal of the Short Story in English* 50 (Spring 2008): n.p.

collapse, the latter effacing any political, technical, and cultural gains a society made while it flourished. Yet like Woolf, Hamilton saw the future's apparent foreclosure as reason not for quietism but for intensified dissent. Hilary Jenkinson's vigilance took different forms: in a 1922 theory of archive administration precipitated by modern warfare's capacity to produce and destroy documents at an unprecedented rate, and later—and more pragmatically—in his bucket-wielding on the roof of the Public Records Office as the bombs of the Blitz were falling. Although Jenkinson's undercelebrated archival ethics cut a path distinct from Hamilton's, it cut it through the same space, insisting that those charged with safeguarding archives from war and other discontinuities neither instrumentalize written records nor presume to represent the future in whose name they must be preserved. Jenkinson's and Hamilton's discrete ways of connecting survival and the archive link them, in turn, to two scenarios we now more commonly associate with post-Hiroshima science fiction: one in which humanity survives the loss of the archive, the other in which the archive persists after the extinction of humanity. Hence the two nuclear fantasias with which I begin.

Fantasias of the Archive

HAMILTON'S *SAVAGE* AND JENKINSON'S *MANUAL*

Wasn't it noticeable at the end of the war that men who returned from the battle-field had grown silent—not richer but poorer in communicable experience? What poured out in the flood of war books ten years later was anything but experience that can be shared orally. And there was nothing remarkable about that.... A generation that had gone to school on horse-drawn streetcars now stood under the open sky in a landscape where nothing remained unchanged but the clouds and, beneath those clouds, in a force field of destructive torrents and explosions, the tiny, fragile human body.

> —Walter Benjamin, "The Storyteller: Observations on the Works of
> Nikolai Leskov" (1936)

The fact is that the enormous stock of fresh experience which has been accumulated during the War and which will be material for the work of the future historian, not to mention students in other branches of learning, is hidden in a mass of documents so colossal that the question of their housing alone (apart from those of their handling, sifting and use) presents quite novel features.

> —Hilary Jenkinson, *A Manual of Archive Administration* (1922)

Nuclear Fantasia, First Type. Fourteen generations after the Hellfire ravaged earth, mantling its surface in perennial dust clouds, the prentice Ganil is initiated into the Lodge of the Machine. Naked, holding a lit torch ("the Light of Human Reason") over his head, he must walk forward on faith and plunge into the Grave of Knowledge, where "lie [his] forefathers forever beneath the ashes of the fires of Hell."[1] Having led him, like his ancestors, to this fatal

---

[1] Ursula K. Le Guin, "The Masters," *Fantastic* 12 (February 1963), rpt. in *The Wind's Twelve Quarters* (New York: Harper & Row, 1975), 34.

precipice, the Light of Human Reason must be renounced in favor of the Light of Common Day: Ganil will spend the rest of his life fixing crude steam engines and drilling his students in addition tables they are forbidden, on pain of death, to grasp computationally. Advanced scientific knowledge, we infer, caused the Hellfire. So Invention and Computation are now heresies in a society governed by severe priests. Yet Ganil's curiosity has not been extinguished with the torch; along with his coworker Mede Fairman and several others, he works in secret to revive mathematical knowledge: to reinvent zero, fathom the duodecimal system, and calculate the speed and trajectories of falling bodies. When Mede Fairman is discovered trying to measure the distance to the sun on a rare cloudless day, he and his associates are accused of heresy. Ganil is exonerated when Mede, to protect him, lies about his aptitude. After being forced to watch his convicted friend burn at the stake, Ganil leaves the only town he has ever known for a self-imposed exile of mathematical discovery, renouncing the Light of Common Day. He takes with him Mede's treatises on momentum and ballistics, documents that testify to the unquenchable human thirst for knowledge and that may—for nothing in this fable reassures us to the contrary—play a role in reinventing weapons capable of devastating the world anew.

Nuclear Fantasia, Second Type. Robert Ashton is pretending to read Plato's *Dialogues* when the woman gives him the accelerator bracelet and asks him to rob the British Museum. The bracelet slows time to a crawl: outside the seven-foot radius of its effect, a minute passes for every year within, so Ashton will be able to steal every item on his client's long wish list before the museum guard blinks. On his way into the Reading Room, he cheekily flashes his reading card at a frozen attendant, noticing that the motionless readers under the dome look no different than usual. After stealing every book on the list, he helps himself to the manuscript of Carroll's *Alice*—a bonus atop the million pounds his mysterious client has promised him on the completion of the job. Later, having removed a pile of antiquities from the Museum, he rejoins her and asks for the accelerator in lieu of the cash payment, so that he may help himself to the remaining treasures of the world's libraries, vaults, and galleries. She assents, but only after informing him that she is a visitor from the future who has traveled by way of a singularity in time created by the release of a massive amount of energy. A nearby newspaper headline reveals the source of the temporal singularity: "super-bomb test today." The visitor explains that the explosion, which her presence proves has already begun, will destabilize the earth's core, causing oceans and continents to fly into space. The shattered earth will become a second asteroid belt. Ashton learns that his client and her fellows are not thieves but alien conservationists who hope to archive a doomed civilization. She leaves Ashton with the bracelet and a terrible choice: to live out the rest of his life in utter isolation or to switch off the device and end with the world.[2]

---

[2] Arthur C. Clarke, "All the Time in the World" (*Startling Stories*, July 1952); rpt. in Arthur

Cold War speculative fictions about nuclear disaster break down into two types. The first envisions human beings surviving a nuclear war but undergoing a profound loss of "civilization" emblematized by the end of literacy and numeracy and thus of access to mathematics, science, and written records. These stories—the example above is Ursula Le Guin's "The Masters" (1963), but Walter M. Miller, Jr.'s *A Canticle for Leibowitz* (1961) and Russell Hoban's *Riddley Walker* (1980) would do just as well—are all aftermath. Bombed back to the Stone Age, the survivors live among the physical and linguistic ruins of a high-technological society, misinterpreting those ruins but nonetheless rediscovering the semiotic and technological means of inflicting mass death. The second type of nuclear parable, represented here by Arthur C. Clarke's "All the Time in the World" (1952) imagines a catastrophe *without* a survivable aftermath.[3] An "apocalypse without revelation," in Jacques Derrida's phrase, requires that any human response, whether panicked or reflective, take place in advance of the nuclear extinction event. If, as Derrida claimed, nuclear war partly defines itself by threatening the "irreversible destruction, leaving no traces, of the juridico-literary archive," then an archive that can remain legible after such a disaster will do so thanks to some paradox, some reversal.[4] "All the Time in the World" solves the problem by imagining a nonhuman reader abducting books and artifacts to a safe and future scene of study; the human symbolic order will outlive its originary species. Clarke's "The Star" (1955) reverses the scenario: its figure of impossible reading is a Jesuit astronaut who discovers the buried culture-ark of a nonhuman civilization, inhabitants of a planet destroyed by a supernova that turns out, in a twist that shakes the astronaut-priest's faith, to have been the star of Bethlehem. In both situations, an archive that should not have survived is read by the absolute other, an alien inhabitant of a future inaccessible to the extinguished species. The nuclear condition, with its warped temporality, has required such contortions in the scene and chronology of reading its remains.

Two narrative types: one imagining the persistence of the species and the extinction of the symbolic order, the other the persistence of the symbolic order and the extinction of the species. Notice that neither type can envision the extinction of both the species *and* the symbolic order, a double nullity that

---

C. Clarke, *From the Ocean, From the Stars: An Omnibus Containing the Novels "The Deep Range" and "The City and the Stars" and Twenty-Four Short Stories* (New York: Harcourt, Brace & World, Inc., 1961), 259–69.

[3] Unlike other post-apocalyptic time-travel narratives of the Cold War, such as Chris Marker's film *La Jetée* (1962), Clarke's explicitly connects its preposterous chronology to the disastrous event itself: time travel is not just necessary but possible because of the super-bomb. By making the disaster rupture standard chronology, the story recognizes the nuclear condition's peculiar temporality, whereby mourning precedes, or at least appears to precede, loss.

[4] Jacques Derrida, "No Apocalypse, Not Now (full speed ahead, seven missiles, seven missives)," trans. Catherine Porter and Philip Lewis, *diacritics* 14.2 (Summer 1984): 27, 26.

would bar narrative altogether. For even tales of species-extinction obliquely hail the reader as human survivor, or else as alien archivist; to be legible and narratable, even extinction stories must construct or at least imply the survival of a reader. Alongside the survival that reading entails, both narrative types centrally involve stalled or cyclical temporalities and thus bar the way to an open future. Type One foredooms humanity to endless cycles of development and collapse, cycles driven by the fact that each disaster, by extinguishing literacy and numeracy, denies later epochs the ability to understand and be fully warned by their ancestors' downfall. Type Two condemns those living in the shadow of an extinction event to mourn in advance what they will not survive to mourn later on. In both cases, the linear unfolding of time has been bent into an unyielding cul-de-sac from whose vantage the future appears to be either an eternal repetition of the past or the blinding flash of the eschaton. The reader of such stories is both abandoned and protected by their conceit of futurelessness: abandoned because diegesis breaks off at the very moment when the loop or impasse becomes apprehensible; protected because the narrative interval, while it lasts, turns out to have afforded a shelter in advance of the coming tempest. If as readers we are always walking through the walls between actual and fictional worlds, the nuclear fable makes us doubly spectral. Because the story and the story-world are coterminous—because the story ends as its world ends (or prepares to end again)—our act of reading is absolutely contained by the diegetic frame. Yet because we are reading at all in the wake of reading's collapse, or on the brink of a narrated extinction event, we are also emphatically outside the nonliterate or posthuman diegesis.[5] We occupy the position of the utterly other, exempt from the disastrous loop or dead end of the story, natives of a futurity closed off to those inside the fictional world.

Speculative fiction about a catastrophic high-tech war has been around a lot longer than nuclear weapons. Decades before heavier-than-air flight, William Delisle Hay's *Three Hundred Years Hence* (1881) imagined air fleets as engines of racial genocide—in this case the extermination of nonwhite communities by white ones. Superweapon narratives featuring radioactive waves, electrobombs, weaponized bacilli, sterilizing rays, and even atom bombs flourished during the early years of the twentieth century.[6] Yet I. F. Clarke notes

---

[5] Outside it, too, because, in the case of Type One stories, we belong to the literate, high-technological Golden Age whose collapse is mourned in the fictional world of the story, and whose signs the denizens of that world read badly if at all. Works such as *Riddley Walker* invite us to observe the possible consequences of our folly in the present, chief among which is the radical discontinuity by which, having been stripped of literacy, our remote descendants might lack the ability to comprehend or recognize us.

[6] Sven Lindqvist mentions Roy Norton's *The Vanishing Fleets* (1908), Hollis Godfrey's *The Man Who Ended War* (1908), J. Hamilton Sedberry's *Under the Flag of the Cross* (1908), Jack London's "The Unparalleled Invasion" (1910), Rudyard Kipling's "As Easy as A.B.C." (1912), and H. G. Wells's *The World Set Free* (1914). Most of these stories conclude with eternal world peace, though often not until

a discontinuity between pre- and post-First World War examples of the two types of story. In contrast to the "nationalistic ready-for-anything" pieties of the earlier texts, he writes, "from 1918 to 1939, the mood shaping most of these tales of the war-to-come was a profound sense of anxiety and doubt about the future, which came out in many stories describing the end of civilization and in frightening visions of the terrible disasters that awaited mankind. . . . for the first time since the eighteenth century, when the earliest tales of the future began to appear, there was a succession of stories devoted to a single theme: the coming destruction of civilization."[7] This apocalyptic turn was sufficiently recognized at the time to inspire the minting of new generic terms, such as the German *Weltuntergangsroman* ("world's-end novel"), and to give even more broad-based terms an eschatological tinge.[8] In his preface to a 1921 reprint of *The War in the Air*, H. G. Wells defined the genre "fantasias of possibility" as works that "take some developing possibility in human affairs and . . . develop the broad consequences of that possibility." Although Wells offered the phrase as an alternative to the genres of "scientific romance" and "futurist romance," its coinage in relation to a novel about calamitous aerial bombardment is not incidental. The prospect—and, by 1921, the metropolitan experience—of air war braided together social and technological strands that were considered paradigmatically modern or near-futuristic: the airplane, the incendiary bomb, poison gas, the metropolis, the military-industrial complex, the factory workers who powered it, and the possibility of their mass panic and revolt against the state in wartime. Air war became, in fact, the quintessential scenario for interwar fantasias of possibility, even as it tended to make *possibility* a byword for cataclysm.

The air war fantasias of the twenties and thirties afforded their writers the chance to register both the physical damage and the weaponized anticipation of First World War air attacks and to extrapolate from these to the erasures of cities, the collapse of the social order, the annihilation of cultural legacies, the killing off of whole races, and the extinction of humanity. Even a partial roll call of the genre makes plain its prophetic, often eschatological bent:

Edward Shanks, *People of the Ruins* (1920)
William Le Queux, *The Terror of the Air* (1920)

---

the destructive power of the weapon in question has been proven against enemy forces or populations. See Sven Lindqvist, *A History of Bombing*, trans. Linda Haverty Rugg (New York: New Press, 2001).

[7] I. F. Clarke, *Voices Prophecying War: Future Wars 1763–3749* (Oxford: Oxford University Press, 1992), 5, 7, 54–56, 131, 142–44.

[8] Clarke notes that the term *Weltuntergangsroman* was coined to describe texts such as Curt Abel-Musgrave's *Der Bacillenkrieg* (1922), Ludwig Hofbauer's *Der Pestkrieg* (1927), and Pagill (Paul Gille)'s *Gletscher über Europa* (1940); see Clarke, *Voices*, 145.

Cicely Mary Hamilton, *Theodore Savage, A Story of the Past or the Future* (1922)

P. Anderson Graham, *The Collapse of Homo Sapiens* (1923)

Reginald Glossop, *The Orphan of Space: A Tale of Downfall* (1926)

Shaw Desmond, *Ragnarok* (1926)

Philip Frances Nowlan, *Armageddon 2419 A.D.* (1927)

Carl W. Spohr, "The Final War" (1932)

Ladbroke Black, *The Poison War* (1933)

Hans Gobsch, *Europe at the Abyss* (1933)

H. G. Wells, *The Shape of Things to Come* (1933)

Neil Bell, *Valiant Clay* (1934)

Moray Dalton, *The Black Death* (1934)

Frank McIlraith and Roy Connolly, *Invasion from the Air: A Prophetic Novel* (1934)

Leslie Polland, *Menace: A Novel of the Near Future* (1935)

Simpson Stokes (pseud. of Frank Fawcett), *Air-Gods' Parade* (1935)

Joseph O'Neill, *Day of Wrath* (1936)[9]

These texts share much besides their premonitions of a war in which civilians will be massively targeted. They tend to begin in the city and end in the country, or in the strangely repastoralized rubble fields where cities once stood. They are animated by a mass-psychology that sees crowds as violent, retrogressive, and incapable of intellection. At the level of form they share a propensity for catalogue, particularly in relation to the lost world; these texts teem with *ubi sunt* inventories. And as Sven Lindqvist has shown, many of these speculative fictions extend the pre-1914 coupling of air war and race-based genocide, but with a difference: interwar fantasias typically summon Asian or African air fleets to rain destruction down on European capitals, which are reinscribed through their annihilation as metonyms of civilization itself.[10]

By this point, we should not be surprised to discover forerunners of the nuclear fable in the first half of the twentieth century, or even to find these earlier speculative fictions grappling with genocide and extinction scenarios. What remains startling is that well in advance of 1945, and even before

---

[9] This roster reflects works discussed or mentioned by Clark and Lindqvist. For additional surveys of "next war" fiction of the twenties and thirties, see Martin Ceadal, "Popular Fiction and the Next War, 1918–1939," in *Class Culture and Social Change: A New View of the 1930s*, ed. Frank Gloversmith (Brighton: Harvester Wheatsheaf, 1980), 161–84; Ian Patterson, *Guernica and Total War* (Cambridge: Harvard University Press, 2007), chap. 2; Leo Mellor, *Reading the Ruins: Modernism, Bombsites and British Culture* (Cambridge: Cambridge University Press, 2011), 16–22; and Susan R. Grayzel, *At Home and Under Fire: Air Raids and Culture in Britain from the Great War to the Blitz* (Cambridge: Cambridge University Press, 2012), chap. 4.

[10] See Lindqvist, *History of Bombing*, esp. the "Bombing the Savages" thread.

1914, future-war fiction exhibits a growing preoccupation with the efface-ability of literacy, numeracy, and the archive—a specific preoccupation that scholars have tended to associate with Cold War speculative fiction and with the nuclear criticism of the 1980s. One of the founding texts of pre-nuclear archive fever is Wells's aforementioned *The War in the Air*, which was serial-ized in *Pall Mall Magazine* in 1908. It features Wells in his self-styled role as prophet, one he had explicitly cultivated in his *Anticipations of the Reaction of Mechanical and Scientific Progress upon Human Life and Thought* (1901). *Anticipations* predicts that the twentieth-century state, being "organized pri-marily for war . . . will have triumphantly asserted the universal duty of its citizens" in a way that invalidates the distinction between combatants and noncombatants. Although it imagines that heavier-than-air flying machines may not appear until 1950, it accurately envisages the psychological effects of air dominance: "Everybody everywhere will be perpetually and constantly looking up, with a sense of loss and insecurity, with a vague stress of pain-ful anticipations."[11] *The War in the Air* could serve as a template for post-1918 future-war fiction in part because it had applied the political premonitions of *Anticipations* to a world in which, by 1908, airplanes already had a five-year history. Its visions of dogfighting aircraft and major cities bombed by German Zeppelins would have seemed prophetic to those looking back at the Great War from the 1920s; its characterization of war as an affair of areas rather than of fronts would have spoken to their sense of what air power augured for the next war.

But even more influential was *The War in the Air*'s depiction of political and social collapse in the wake of total war. After New York, London, Paris, and Berlin are bombed, the international credit system goes under; political crises are followed by martial law, famine, pestilence, guerrilla air raids by Asiatic and African air-pirates, technological collapse, and cultural degeneration. In the novel's epilogue, the protagonist's elderly brother tells his young nephew about the world before the War in the Air, the Famine, and the Purple Death. Fittingly sheltered by the "splintered pinnacles of the Crystal Palace," the old man offers an inventory of technologies and luxuries worthy of some bygone Great Exhibition but now lost in the disaster: bicycles, airships, monorails, plate-glass windows, baskets of imported fruit. Pride of place in this mourn-er's catalogue, however, is given to books. Old Tom Smallways relates how he and a friend once explored a town full of intact houses whose inhabitants had died in the plague:

> ". . . I went into one—me and old Higgins las' year—and there was a room with books, Teddy—you know what I mean by books, Teddy?"

---

[11] H. G. Wells, *Anticipations of the Reaction of Mechanical and Scientific Progress upon Human Life and Thought* (serialized in *Fortnightly Review* in 1901; rpt. Mineola, NY: Dover, 1999), 106, 111.

"I seen 'em. I seen 'em with pictures."

"Well, books all round, Teddy, 'undreds of books, beyond rhyme or rea-son, as the saying goes, green-mouldy and dry. I was for leavin' 'em alone—I was never much for reading—but ole Higgins he must touch 'em. 'I believe I could read one of 'em *now*,' 'e says."

" 'Not I,' I says.

" 'I could,' 'e says, laughing, and takes one out and opens it.

"I looked and there, Teddy, was a cullud picture, oh, so lovely! It was a picture of women and serpents in a garden. I never see anything like it.

" 'This suits me,' said old Higgins, 'to rights.'

"And then kind of friendly he gave the book a pat—"

Old Tom Smallways paused impressively.

"And then?" said Teddy.

"It all fell to dus'. White dus'!' . . . He became still more impressive. "We didn't touch no more of them books that day. Not after that."[12]

The books have survived as objects, but no longer as an archive: decompos-ing at a touch, they cannot both exist and be read. Even worse, their spon-taneous disintegration is so eerie that the men who have witnessed it will avoid books from now on and refrain from teaching the next generation to read; their glimpse of a "cullud picture" of the original fall marks human-ity's last encounter with the costlier kinds of knowledge. The scene implies that if the bomb is the nemesis of the book, theirs is a familial enmity: the bomb is not an absolute stranger to the book but the parricidal offspring of a scientific tradition emblematized by the library. No wonder the book explodes.

As Peter Schwenger and other exponents of nuclear criticism showed dur-ing the 1980s and 1990s, Cold War speculative fictions frequently linked the Bomb and the archive by emphasizing what Derrida called the "fabulously textual" nature of both. Not yet having occurred, a full-scale nuclear war exists only in discourse—it is an affair of textuality. Literature is fabulously textual as well, existing, as Schwenger puts it, "without any referent out-side of the words by which it constitutes itself. Consequently, there would be nothing by which it could reconstruct its past if the bomb that is hypo-thetically constructed in textuality explodes in reality."[13] Intimately similar, the archive and the Bomb are also mutually exclusive: as long as the Bomb remains only textual, texts can persist; if the Bomb is activated, the archive will be lost, along with the material and social conditions that permit it to

---

[12] H. G. Wells, *The War in the Air* (Lincoln and London: University of Nebraska Press, 2002), 246, 251.

[13] Peter Schwenger, *Letter Bomb: Nuclear Holocaust and the Exploding Word* (Baltimore: Johns Hopkins University Press, 1992), xvi.

produce meaning. In Hoban's *Riddley Walker*, for instance, the radical discontinuity of nuclear apocalypse initiates a break in literacy; two thousand years later, a primarily oral tribal culture is just beginning to rediscover literacy and to reinvent gunpowder, reprising the mingled genesis of the weapon and the word, of science and the sign. That *Riddley Walker* could not be written or read by the illiterate majority of its protagonists places its ontology as a book in a conspicuous tension with its subject: the textual artifact we hold in our hands is either forecasting the moment of its illegibility or insisting on the fictive quality of its premise. But again, these attributes bridge the seventy-plus years that separate Hoban's Thatcher-era novel from Wells's Edwardian one. As a book whose last pages herald the end of reading, *The War in the Air* shares with *Riddley Walker* a certain metafictional energy, one that calls attention to the textuality of the text, to the literate culture required for its meaning-making, and to the fragility of that culture with respect to unbridled modern war.

Whether we find them in future-war fiction before or after 1945, such reflexivities are powerfully self-authorizing. They make writing's fragility and its admonitory power functions of each other: as the medium most endangered by total war, the book is also ideally equipped to ward off such wars; by the same token, literature's power to warn by conjuring a future social collapse is the very thing you will lose by permitting such a future to arrive. Does anything, then, differentiate interwar fantasias of the archive from their nuclear-era counterparts? How do we link those interwar texts to the post-1914 intensification of dread and anticipation that Clarke mentions, and that we have observed in discourses as various as urban planning, civil defense, and military theory? Libraries, museums, and archives were *not* hit hard by air attacks in the First World War. How, then, do we understand the subsequent ratcheting up of the effacement-of-the-archive scenario?

I ground my responses to these questions in two historical observations. The first is that the immense bureaucratic scale of the First World War produced so massive a surge in administrative documents as to create new problems of storage, selection, and custodianship. The result was a rapid development of the archivist profession accompanied by the emergence of a so-called "modernist" archive theory for which the war archive was the defining challenge of the day, an anomalous case that was beginning to look like a new paradigm.[14] Far from being menaced by the war, written records

[14] Scholars refer to the archive theories of Hilary Jenkinson (see below) as "modernist" in contrast to the "postmodern" archive theories of the Cold War and beyond. Where Jenkinson stressed a non-appraising, objective custodianship model, later theorists such as Theodore R. Schellenberg insisted that archivists should take an active role in appraising and, where pragmatically necessary, destroying records. Still more recent archive theorists have described the archivist's work as performative and identity-related. Although the terms "modernist" and "postmodern" in archive theory do not map neatly to the corresponding terms in literary and cultural studies, we might see a rough

proliferated in wartime as never before. Yet for many, the First World War presaged future conflicts that *would* threaten not only the written record itself but also the conditions of its legibility and transmission. This leads to my second observation: that the penumbra of historical foreclosure created by the war manifested itself specifically as an impending threat to the material archive and to the very presumption of unbroken legibility that allowed the archive to stand in for futurity itself.

The rest of this chapter posits something like a covalent bond—a mixture of attraction and repulsion stabilized by shared components—between 1920s next-war fiction and archive theory. Its paired nuclei are two texts from the year 1922: Cicely Hamilton's now little-known apocalyptic novel *Theodore Savage: A Story of the Past or the Future* and Hilary Jenkinson's *Manual of Archive Administration, Including the Problems of War Archives and Archive Making*, its generation's most celebrated English-language work of archive theory. In their premises, aims, and eminence, the two books could not be more different, yet they share certain key attributes in their orientation to war, writing, and futurity. Both Hamilton and Jenkinson had returned from war years spent at or near the Western Front. From professionally and culturally distant sites, the two writers were articulating, and in surprisingly complementary terms, the ramifications of what they had experienced during the war.[15] These ramifications centered on the power and fragility of the written record and on the ease with which the contexts required for its interpretation could be effaced or lost. Futurity itself, for Hamilton and Jenkinson, is embodied in transmissible texts rather than in biological descent; both writers' emphasis on an archival futurism, whether open, endangered, or altogether barred, is also a refusal to default to a reproductive view of the future—particularly in the case of Hamilton, an avowed feminist and spinster. But I have mainly brought *Theodore Savage* and Jenkinson's *Manual* together here because of the reciprocal haunting they perform, the one a fable of apocalyptic discontinuity haunted by the uncanny notion of recurrent social collapse, the other a practical meditation on continuity as a

---

homology in Jenkinson's advocacy of an impersonal theory of the archivist versus the tendency of Schellenberg and others to endow the archivist with a non-neutral and uncancelable, if also performative and/or multiple, self.

[15] I address Hamilton's First World War experiences below. Jenkinson's, which do not feature in my discussion of the *Manual*, can be read about in his *War Service of a Siege Battery, 1916–1918* (Privately printed, 1919). Jenkinson fought in the latter part of Battle of the Somme as well as at Arras, Messine, Nieuport, Ypres, and Cambrai, and he participated in the retreat and advance of 1918. After the Armistice he was posted to the War Office as captain, General Staff, Army Education Corps; there, he created the library system that was later absorbed by the War Office. After his discharge, he returned in 1922 to work at the British Library's Round Room, where he was in charge of Literary Search. See also the unsigned "Memoir of Sir Hilary Jenkinson" that opens *Studies Presented to Sir Hilary Jenkinson*, ed. J. Conway Davies (London: Oxford University Press, 1957).

professional duty, visited in its turn by the radical discontinuities of war and ethics. Lifted out of their usual generic silos and juxtaposed, the two works act as foils for one another, the extreme traits and formulations of one standing out the more vividly against the other's discourse world. Taken together, they contribute as well to a heterodox portrait of 1922, Anglo-European modernism's wonder year, as a decisively interwar moment saturated with traumatic memory and anxious prevision; with the proleptic making of arrangements; and with the prospect that modern war's anomalies would emerge as a new, deplorable norm.

A Promise of Terror to Come

Cicely Mary Hamilton (Fig. 3.1), the British actor, writer, and suffragist, spent the second half of the First World War in the French town of Abbeville organizing theatrical and musical events for an organization called Concerts at the Front. A base for military support operations, Abbeville was also home or home base to thousands of civilians, many of whom were displaced and threatened by nightly German air raids that only perfunctorily targeted military infrastructure. A recollection Hamilton wrote at the time and later included in her 1935 memoir *Life Errant* depicts the able-bodied civilians of Abbeville (the aged and infirm stayed behind with the military personnel) pouring out of the town every night in anticipation of the raids, seeking cover in the countryside.

> I remember thinking, as I passed the blank houses, that here was a phenomenon unknown to the wars whereof history tells us. In the old wars men sheltered behind walls and found safety in numbers; our states and social systems are what they are because safety was in numbers and in walls. But in our wars, the wars of the air and the laboratory, the wall, like enough, is a trap that you fly from to the open, and there is danger, not safety, in numbers—the crowd is a target to the terror that strikes from above. All the country, nightly, was alive with men and women who, in obedience to the principles of the new warfare, had fled from the neighborhood of the target—the town—and scattered in small groups that they might be ignored and invisible. They crowded into barns or lay out on the hillside while the Gothas swooped down on their homes in the town and the batteries spat fire in defense of them; they watched the wheeling of the searchlight and wondered, as they listened to the roar of high explosive, what a coming day and journey home would reveal. And this, one realized, was only the beginning of air-power and the need for invisibility that air-power imposes; what we saw was but a promise of terror to come, a foreshadowing of full-grown achievement. Lying on the hillside one glimpsed

FIG. 3.1. *Cicely Mary Hamilton. Photo by Lena Connell (later Beatrice Cundy), 1910s. National Portrait Gallery, London.*

something, at least, of the chaos of full-grown achievement. The chaos of a people, an industrial people, driven out of its towns and kept out of them; not returning, as we did, in the comparative safety of daylight but—by gas or continuous raiding—kept out of them. And not only kept out of them, but kept on the run; driven hither and thither, reduced to starvation and savagery.[16]

A mass is mobilized and fragmented all at once. Time fractures too: this is a reminiscence of a trauma whose moment-by-moment violence lies partly in what it augurs for a future beyond the present panic. Looking through the

---

[16] Cicely Hamilton, *Life Errant* (London: J. M. Dent & Sons, 1935), 148–49. Further references are cited in the text. Hamilton's description of the raid at Abbeville first appeared, with minor differences, in her foreword to *Lest Ye Die: A Story from the Past or of the Future*, a revised version of *Theodore Savage* that was published in the United States in 1928. During the war's final months, Hamilton had published an article containing elements of these later accounts, though without speculating about air war's ramifications for the future or its illuminations of past collapses; see Cicely Hamilton, "Bombarded," *North American Review 208* (Oct. 1918): 574–80.

chaos before her as if it were a scrim, Hamilton sees beyond it a future in which the terror of a mature air power would, she imagined, turn town-dwelling civilians into starving, barbarous nomads.

Yet having dubbed air war "a phenomenon *unknown* to the wars whereof history tells us," Hamilton suddenly cancels that claim of absolute novelty, or rather insists on the limits of history's ability to know about past wars. On the most intense night of the air raids, Hamilton records, the Gothas scored a hit on an ammunition dump in the Somme valley, and as she watched the glare from the explosion, the world was suddenly changed for her. "Above and beyond my personal fear was fear and horror of the future. For on that night there was born an idea which, however I thrust it to the back of my mind, I have never been able to get rid of; the idea—there are times when I call it conviction—that if Science destroy our civilization, it will not be for the first time." She reads the stories of Adam and Eve, Icarus, and Prometheus as testifying to past disasters resulting from "the presumptuous powers that knowledge bestows upon humanity . . . How else, but by such myths, would a people reduced to ignorance and barbarism . . . explain the malignant power of the chemist, the aviator, the engineer?" That night, beneath the waves of planes, Hamilton loses nothing less than her "old beliefs in progress, and the onward march of humanity" (149–51). That loss of the Enlightenment narrative appears to happen, in part, because the terror of air power annihilates the continuity of past, present, and future on which such a narrative depends. Here, a present trauma triggers a horror of the future, a horror whose content is, surprisingly, an epiphany about the past: namely, that technologies such as those that intersect in aerial bombardment have already caused radical historical breaks. For Hamilton, the terror is certain to come because it has happened before, and the proof of this lies paradoxically in the absence of proof—in past wars' having left behind no record but the myths of "a people reduced to ignorance and barbarism." The seemingly unprecedented disaster will, uncannily, be a repetition, and our apprehension of it *as* a repetition will partly constitute its terrible strangeness.

Something else changed for her that night, writes Hamilton. Now that air war had altered the meaning of walls, she could no longer see houses and streets as permanent or even solid. "They are, so to speak, the shadows of old houses and streets." Returning to Abbeville the morning after the raid, she realized "not only that walls and roofs looked different, but that they always would look different." Again, the present has been diminished to a bit of gauze through which both past and future may be seen. The effect, moreover, is a lasting one. A year later, Hamilton is in Cologne looking at the Hohenzollern Bridge, trying to see it as solid, failing. That failure leads her to consider whether the trauma of the bombing has left some enduring mark: "As to whether that is an illusion, resulting from a species of mental shock, or whether one's conception of an object as solid or fragile has an actual effect on one's vision, I express no opinion, because I have none to express." The ramifications of her "mental shock," as she provisionally calls it, go far beyond the solidity of buildings, touching her faith in a habitable future, her political agency, her investment in her life:

> When you have once accepted the more than possibility that your civiliza-
> tion is heading for destruction, it is almost inevitable that you will slip into
> indifference towards many ideas and interests and activities that would
> otherwise have seemed to you important. That at least has been the case
> with me; I find it impossible to take any real interest in long-distance politi-
> cal "planning" of any sort or kind, and as for the erection of outsize build-
> ings, however I admire them (as I often do), I never get over the feeling of
> wonderment that any one should think it worth while. (It is a good thing,
> no doubt, that everybody doesn't feel like that, or the world would lapse
> into inertia.) Unless we can master the air-menace, the city, as we know
> it, is bound to go; on the day the first aeroplane rose from the ground the
> foundations of every city in the world were shaken. . . . Curious to reflect
> that when I was young no one would have dared to suggest that indiscrimi-
> nate massacre was permissible as a weapon of war, whereas now we take
> such massacre for granted. (151–52; ellipses in original)

Indifference, numbing, a conviction that effort and achievement are worth-less: these we now recognize as classic symptoms of post-traumatic stress dis-order. *Life Errant* bears out Hamilton's self-diagnosis of "mental shock" in its symptomatic accounts of even pre-1914 events, which it retroactively empties of significance in comparison to the coming violence. Hamilton had spent the years before the war in a flurry of activism. She had cofounded the Women Writers' Suffrage League, acted in fund-raising shows for the movement, gone on speaking tours, written pro-suffrage plays, pamphlets, and a novel. But *Life Errant* makes the extraordinary claim that women's suffrage was finally granted in 1918 "because of its supreme unimportance at that juncture to our national life. What use was the vote as a weapon against German guns, submarines, and Gothas?" Although most of the meetings from Hamilton's days of political agitation have "left not a wrack of memory behind," she does recall being notified of her registration on the Chelsea electorate. She was in Abbeville watching a battery of guns fire at an enemy reconnaissance plane overhead—a plane likely taking pictures to assess recent bombing raids and direct future ones: "Now, at this moment of achieved enfranchisement, what really interested me was not the thought of voting at the next election, but the puffs of smoke that the Archies sent after the escaping plane" (67, 85, 67–68).

That so politically committed a person as Hamilton might so wildly dis-count her work in the wake of a "mental shock" shows us how post-traumatic stress, on top of its psychic, somatic, and emotional effects, can impair a suf-ferer's political will. Yet Hamilton's shock did not pose a complete obstacle to her activism or her literary work; after the war, she remained involved in international women's suffrage efforts and wrote several books, among them *Theodore Savage*, a speculative fiction whose description of a future air war followed by societal collapse realizes Hamilton's premonitions and epiphanies under the German bombs at Abbeville. The novel begins with a gesture at once retrospective and counterfactual, with the narrator looking back through some dark but as yet unspecified later moment upon a vanished world where records could be made, kept, and read by others. "If it had been possible for Theodore Savage to place on record for those who came after him the story of his life and experiences, he would have been the first to admit that the interest of the record lay in circumstance and not in himself."[17] That unremarkable and unrecordable self, the young Savage, is a clerk in the Distribution Office and a producer of the administrative records and memoranda whose disappearance the book's first sentence laments. *Theodore Savage* opens, that is, in a mode of nostalgia for its implied reader's bureaucratic present. At the same time, it positions itself as a record of the world's subsequent becoming recordless, and thus as a transcendent or impossible object—as precisely the sort of memo that cannot, by its own account, pass through the cusp of civilizational ruin. Part document and part fable, it forms the missing link between a literate, technological society and the nonliterate, brutal one that it insists will succeed it.

Savage Foreclosures

Much as Hamilton could perceive the "terror to come" through the veil of her experience at Abbeville, visions of the post-collapse Savage, "a toiler with his hands in the company of men who lived brutishly," repeatedly intrude on the introduction of his younger self (9). But the pre-collapse Savage eventually takes shape as the ultimate white-collar drone: "the product of a public school, Wadham and the Civil Service," a collector of Hepplewhite furniture, color prints, and English glass. He has "gained a minor reputation on the golf-links" and within a few pages becomes engaged to his boss's daughter, Phillida, a "porcelain girl" he looks forward to adding to his collection (9–10, 18). Yet all of this takes place, disquietingly, against the backdrop of the Karthanian imbroglio, in which a "half-civilized little democracy" refuses the verdict of an international Court of Arbitration and triggers a cascade of secessions, often along racial lines, from the League. The inevitability of

---

[17] Cicely Hamilton, *Theodore Savage: A Story of the Past or the Future* (London: Leonard Parsons, 1922), 9. Further references are cited in the text. The 1922 edition of the novel is available as a public domain reprint. HiLo's Radium Age Science Fiction Series released a repaginated edition of the novel in 2013.

war is debated, with a scientist named Markham expounding what would seem to be the novel's position: that despite human beings' individual capacities for learning and reason, their collective lives incline them far more powerfully toward destruction and self-sacrifice; that scientific discovery would always be warped by bloodlust toward military applications; that scientists were therefore better "strangled at birth" for humanity's sake (56). When the world vindicates Markham by exploding into war, Theodore Savage is dispatched to York after saying what will be his final farewell to Phillida. For a few weeks he endures the tedium of his work. But if the young Savage finds "something aesthetically wrong about a fussy process of docketing and checking while nations were at death grips and the fate of a world [hung] in the balance"—if the bureaucratic world elegized by the novel fails to engage him—he will get to test the aesthetic rightness of modern warfare when the devastation reaches England (63).

The subsequent chapters of *Theodore Savage* could almost be excerpts from that inaugural work of air power theory, Douhet's *Il dominio dell'aria*, published a year before Hamilton's novel. As both works envision it, the next war will no longer feature clashing armies; instead, adversaries will bombard one another's civilian populations not just to weaken their contributions to the war effort but to turn them into "an auxiliary destructive force." Where Douhet advocates provoking enemy civilians to overthrow the state, however, Hamilton imagines them "hunted out of cities by chemical warfare and the terror from above," with strategists angling for "the exhaustion of the enemy by burdening him with a starving and nomadic population" (65–66). It is Abbeville again—the abandoned town, the populace scattered in flight through the countryside—but on a civilizational scale, with the import of air war run speculatively forward. The cities of Europe lie in ruins, their displaced populations "a horde of human rats driven out of their holes by terror, by fire and by gas" (75). Scarcity and desperation lead to resource hoarding by the military, informal food and sex economies, and looting; lynch law arises, in place of the defunct justice system, to punish thieves; informational and distributional networks disintegrate; total societal collapse ensues. For the clerk Savage, though, the end of civilization is signaled not by some spectacular conflagration but by the sudden nullity of the official documents that once bored him. He has been ferrying messages between the military and transport officers packing evacuees onto trains bound for nowhere. Returning to the command office, he finds "his chief, the man of precedent, order and many carbon copies, was staring, haggard and bewildered, at a typewritten document signed by the military commandant. . . . And obtaining, incidentally, his first glimpse into a world till now unthinkable—where precedent was not, where reference was useless and order had ceased to exist (83; ellipses in original).[18]

---

[18] Jenkinson, for whom war both produces and consumes archives at a hectic pace, entertains all possibilities but the one explored by Hamilton: that war could render administrative documents—indeed all documents—altogether worthless.

Theodore Savage's middle act presents itself as a narrative of strict retrogression through the stages of the civilizing process: "A people retracing its progress from chaos retraced it step by step" (102). Each loss of plenitude triggers a loss of social organization, safety, and trust. Returned to a predatory bare life, the war's survivors form marauding groups only as long as they have something to plunder in common, then turn on one another or revert to brutish solitude. But regression does not erase memory, and the recovered civilizational earliness is haunted by memories of the developed civilization that preceded the collapse. This haunting flatters neither the present, whose barbarism is underscored by the memory of lost accomplishment, nor the past, the naiveté of whose accomplishments the barbarous present exposes. Taking refuge in a ruined house, Savage discovers an elderly, dying man who asks him if he remembers who wrote the poem, "My mind to me a kingdom is." Neither man can summon the name of Sir Edward Dyer. "Well, even if we've forgotten who wrote it," says the old man, "there's one thing about him that's certain; he didn't know what we know—hadn't lived in our kind of hell. The place where you haven't a mind—only fear and a stomach. . . . The flesh and the devil—hunger and fear; they haven't left us a world! . . . But if there's ever a world again, I believe I shall have learned how to write. Now I know what we are—the fundamentals and the nakedness . . ." (119–20). A dying man's use of the future anterior ("I shall have learned how to write") contingent on the barred return of a world; a troping of literature's loss through the imminent death of one who avows the experiential poverty of lost literature: these are the marooned and canceled temporalities *Theodore Savage* produces by crossing retrogression with memory's persistence in the wake of disaster.

Hamilton's novel spends its final act tracing the tentative reassertion of social ties at the level of family and tribe. After an interval of foraging and starving alone, Savage pairs up, out of pity, with Ada, a young Cockney woman and former factory worker. At first they merely forage and starve together; later, after he gives her some underwear he has scrounged from a corpse-filled house, they become lovers, and he learns to forget his lost Phillida and look no longer on Ada "through the fastidious eyes of the civilized" (169). He abandons, too, "the code of civilization in dealings between woman and man," beating her for her refusal to help him find and prepare food (188). Their hierarchical compact is soon replicated when they are permitted to join a settlement of other survivors, conditional on their renouncing "the devil's knowledge" (230)—science, mechanics, and literacy—in order to ensure that high-technological warfare is never again possible. After rebelling inwardly against it, Savage comes to accept this condition and to stop hoping in secret that still-civilized humans will deliver him from his tribal existence. He lives out the rest of his days, raising children according to the codes imposed by the tribe. In his final years, he becomes the last local survivor of the Ruin of Man, revered and reviled as part Adam, part Merlin, part Frankenstein. To his illiterate descendants, his tomb—haunted of course—and the sound of his name stand for a dead civilization, its lost achievements, and its catastrophic legacy.

Before burying its protagonist, *Theodore Savage* spends some of its last pages characterizing his inner life during his maturity and dotage. In part it is a "vivid memory-life in which he delved, turning over its vanished treasures—the intangible treasures of dead beauty, dead literature, learning and art" (301). Having taken the vow of ignorance, Savage cannot pass these wonders on to his children, who anyway are being raised in a "primitive manhood without letters, knowing of the world that was past and gone only legends derived from [their] elders" (270). He becomes an encyclopedia without a reader. Revolving in his mind the great artists and scientists whose names and works he must suppress, he is less a living archive of pre-Ruin achievement than its living grave:

> Not only the memory of actual men whose fame had once been blown about the world; but the memory of sound, of music, and of marvels in stone, uplifted by the skill of generations; the memory of systems, customs, laws, wrought wisely by the hand of experience; and of fanciful people, more real than living men and women. With him and his like would pass not only Leonardo, Caesar and the sun of Messidor, but Rosalind, d'Artagnan and Faust; the heroes, the merrymen, the women loved and loving who, created of dreams, had shared the dead world with their fellows created of dust . . . Once deemed immortal, they had been slain by science as surely as their fellows of dust. (303–4; ellipses in original)

The interwar encyclopedic modernist works that I discuss in the second half of this book exhibit a more full-blown tendency toward inventory in relation to catastrophe. But where those works presuppose their own transmissibility and marshal encyclopedic form as a riposte to exterminative warfare's totalizing logic, *Theodore Savage* is committed to a foreclosed and cyclical view of history. When he is not lamenting the "pity of oblivion" (303), Hamilton's protagonist is observing the inevitable beginnings of the next cycle: the emergence of clans, castes, priesthoods, and polytheism as well as the preconditions of aristocracy, slavery, and hereditary monarchy. As inevitable as the ignorance that fosters these early social orders is the eventual resurgence of knowledge, its flowering in another Enlightenment, and its terminus in another Ruin. "They stood, the zealots [who judged Galileo], for that ignorance which, being interpreted, is life; and Galileo for that knowledge which, being interpreted, is death . . ." Even as he deplores the ignorance enforced by his contemporaries, Savage also accepts it as the one force that can delay the mobilization of science for destruction. In a cycle where knowledge must lead to death, ignorance can at least sustain bare life, ensuring for a time that humanity need "not fall on its own weapons, but live, just live, like the beasts!" (315).

Concomitant with the aging Savage's deterministic portrait of the future is his retrojection of that future into past cycles of civilizational boom and bust. Savage's discovery of the past in the future is Hamilton's from Abbeville, although his is precipitated not by the immediate experience of bombardment but by his silent ethnographies of his tribe, whose unschooled attempts to describe the pre-Ruin technologies to their children cause fact to slip into analogy, hyperbole, and fairy tale. "The aeroplane was a bird extinct and monstrous—larger, many times larger, than the flapping heron or the owl; the bomb was more dreadful than a lightning stroke; the tram, train or motor a gigantic wheelbarrow that ran without man or beast to drag it" (280). As the memory of science declines, and as each generation recombines and elaborates on its predecessors' distortions, what were quotidian terms and figures in the old world complete their transformation into myth.

> He came to understand that all wonders were facts misinterpreted and that (given time and ignorance) a post-office underling, tapping out his Morse code, might be seen as a geni[e] or an Oberon—the absolute master of obedient sprites who could lay their girdles round the earth; and he pictured a college-bred, sober-suited Hercules planning his Labours in the office of a limited company—jotting down figures, estimating costs and scanning the reports of geologists. Figures and reports, like his tunnels and dams, would pass into the limbo of science forgotten and forbidden, but the memory of his labours, his defiance of brute nature, would live on as the story of a demi-god; and the childhood that was barbarism would explain his achievements by a giant strength that could tear down trees and move mountains. (282)

Modernity likes to endow the mythic past with a gigantism beside which the contemporary looks reduced, even Lilliputian. In a vertiginous play of scale, this passage both repeats and reverses that optic, with the readerly present made mammoth by a post-apocalyptic future: the accountants, clerks, and engineers of 1922 become the titans who made the world before it went to smash, and whose broken edifices still litter the countryside. By cross-pollinating past and future, this scalar play produces a temporal vertigo as well: "What had once appeared prophecies [Savage] saw to be memories; the Day of Judgment, when the heavens should flame and men call upon the rocks to cover them, belonged to the past before it belonged to the future. The forecast of its terrors was possible only to a people that had known them as realities; a people troubled by a dim race-memory of the conquest of the air and catastrophe hurled from the skies" (284). Prophecy read as the garbled recollection of disaster: this is *Theodore Savage* at its most self-diagnostic.

And at its most totalizing. Although Hamilton's novel offers an exhaustive, determinist account of human history and futurity—an account from which it allows no deviation—these foreclosures are not its most unyielding gestures. That distinction goes to the novel's status as a closed evidentiary system, immunized against disproof by the narrative's core premise. According to *Theodore Savage*, the recursive nature of history is only legible just before and just after catastrophic knowledge-loss: before, by an intuition that cannot be proven; and after, by a witnessing that cannot be recorded because it is in the nature of knowledge-loss to efface the conditions for such a recording. Absent written records, the history of civilizational ruin can be transmitted only through the encryptions of oral culture and mythology over many generations; those encryptions will only become decryptable at the next catastrophic cusp, and too briefly to play a role in averting the catastrophe-in-progress. A novel that looks from a distance like an admonitory fable addressed to its author's contemporaries in fact thematizes its non-contemporaneity with them; the only readers who could read it empirically would be those positioned at similar historical cusps to its protagonist's, and therefore similarly marooned between an era of bloody-minded technological advance and one of forced ignorance. *Theodore Savage* thus constructs a radically discontinuous, transtemporal community of readers whose evidence cannot be exported to others—a community the 1922 reader can join only by a leap of evidentiary faith that eerily replicates the renunciation of empiricism demanded of Hamilton's protagonist after the Ruin. That the novel also constructs its intermittent legibility as the symptom of a macro-historical repetition compulsion does not relax the absolutism of its premise. There is no exit from a syndrome that can be apprehended so briefly, so belatedly—a syndrome whose central property is to prevent the future from reading the diagnoses of the past.

Declining Fertility

Along with other apocalyptic "next war" fictions of the twenties and thirties, *Theodore Savage* contributes to a literary genealogy whose Cold War iterations are better known. These are what I have called nuclear fables of the first type (e.g., *A Canticle for Leibowitz*, "The Masters," and *Riddley Walker*). Like Hamilton's novel, these later fables stage the extinction or near extinction of the symbolic order while leaving biological reproduction largely intact; in fact, their sense of literacy's fragility seems to require a contrastingly robust portrait of human procreation as a baseline from which to measure the loss and, in some cases, the rediscovery of writing. This structure would seem to make reproduction the primary vector of human futurity and the archive merely secondary, positing a continuous biological "we" in order to ask what our species might endure or become without writing, culture, science, and other important developments that are finally extrinsic to human being. However, such a reading ignores the first rule of speculative fiction: that the deleted element is conceptually and often ideologically elevated over what remains. *Theodore Savage* and other fables in its line identify the canceled or resurgent written archive as the difference between an ungrievable, rudimentary, merely biological being and a transgenerational symbolic one whose loss is worth mourning in advance, even if mourning can do nothing to forestall that loss. Prizing transmissible written knowledge as the futurity that matters, these fables implicitly cast nonliterate societies as subhuman indices of the futurelessness that awaits "civilization" on the other side of catastrophe. At the same time, they provide crucial alternatives to the reproductive futurism that characterizes their rival apocalyptic genre, the fable of species extinction.[19] As such, they help us think about how attempts to unforeclose the future can produce occlusions of their own, and about what we miss by discounting all forms of hopelessness as apolitical.

To illustrate this point, let's briefly consider one of the cardinal articulations of species extinction with reproductive futurism. When Jonathan Schell's *The Fate of the Earth* first appeared in 1982, its most talked-about passage was a graphic description of what would happen if a twenty-megaton bomb were detonated over the center of Manhattan. The ensuing account of how a full-scale nuclear change would likely extinguish humankind along with the majority of earth's species, leaving a "republic of insects and grass," completed the book's infernal vision. Largely owing to this vivid thought experiment, Schell's book helped resuscitate the antiwar movement in the United States, and its cautionary portrait of a dead, irradiated planet was absorbed into mass culture such that, read now, it chastens but does not surprise. But there *is* a still-astonishing moment in *The Fate of the Earth*. This occurs in a section called "The Second Death," where Schell adopts "the view of our children and grandchildren, and of all the future generations of mankind, stretching ahead of us in time." A nuclear extinction event, he argues, would wipe out not only the living but all of the unborn as well; the "second death" would be the death of a longitudinal, progenerative human future, the death of the supersession of generations and thus, as he puts it, "the death of death."[20] That we live in the shadow of this second-order death, says Schell, is nowhere more apparent than in our growing ambivalence toward—and here is the surprise—*marriage*, an institution that consecrates a personal relationship by connecting it to the biological continuity

<hr>

[19] My essay "Queer Temporalities of the Nuclear Condition" reads Miller's *A Canticle for Leibowitz* along these lines; in *Silence of Fallout: Nuclear Criticism in a Post-Cold War World*, ed. Michael Blouin, Morgan Shipley, and Jack Taylor (Newcastle-upon-Tyne, UK: Cambridge Scholars, 2013).

[20] Jonathan Schell, *The Fate of the Earth: and The Abolition* (Stanford: Stanford University Press, 2000), 154, 119. Further references are cited in the text.

of the species. "[By] swearing their love in public," he writes, "the lovers also let it be known that their union will be a fit one for bringing children into the world." In a world overshadowed by extinction, the biological future that endows love with social meaning begins to dematerialize, and love becomes, in response, "an ever more solitary affair: impersonal, detached, pornographic. It means something that we call both pornography and nuclear destruction 'obscene.'" Although Schell is not explicit about what forms of sexual detachment he laments here, "The Second Death" clearly implies that any sex decoupled from biological continuity and seeking refuge in licentious, solitary, emotionless, or momentary enjoyment—any sex that deviates from a reproductive notion of the future—is a symptom of our extinction syndrome. Thus when Schell, oddly quoting Auden, says that the peril of extinction thwarts "Eros, builder of cities," he doesn't need to invoke "sodomy, destroyer of cities" for the link between queerness and extinction to be forged (157–58). By installing a reproductive model of the future at the heart of his admonitory project, Schell stigmatizes as futureless anyone who stands beyond the pale of reproductivism: not just the homosexual, but also the unmarried, the divorced, the impotent, the childless, the masturbator, the hedonist, the celibate.

We can imagine, then, just what kind of account Schell might give of Hamilton, a self-described "spinster" who by 1918 had concluded humanity was doomed to bomb itself repeatedly back to primitive, illiterate states.[21] But however much we might resist Schell's reading of extinction as the transcendental signified of dissident sexuality, we should neither misattribute a politically hopeful view of futurity to Hamilton nor reduce her spinsterism to a symptom of wartime traumatization. Her view of the future was indeed dire—recall the devastating passage in *Life Errant* where she confesses, "I find it impossible to take any real interest in long-distance political 'planning' of any sort or kind." In the same work, she expressed her relief at being the last in her biological line and thus having "no younger generation to fear for."[22] But well before the war

---

[21] Hamilton's spinsterism was, at the very least, a principled abstinence from marriage and reproduction. She professed admiration for conventual celibates on grounds that they abstained, in addition, from indulging the "animal passions" (247). To what degree Hamilton was herself celibate in this more restrictive sense is not known. Her biographer, Lis Whitelaw, identifies her as a lesbian on the basis of "the community within which she chose to live her life"—mostly suffragists, many of whom lived together in pairs or trios. Like most of these friends, Hamilton left no archive of private papers that might have referred to passionate relationships or sexual practices; for reasons she would have appreciated, the absence of such an archive is itself difficult to read. My discussion of Hamilton is not premised on a particular understanding of her sexual preference. I do follow Benjamin Kahan in wishing not to conflate spinsterism or celibacy with either same-sex eroticism or its denial. See Cicely Hamilton, *Marriage as a Trade* (London: Women's Press, 1981), 247, subsequently cited in the text; Lis Whitelaw, *The Life & Rebellious Times of Cicely Hamilton, Actress, Writer, Suffragist* (London: Women's Press, 1990), 114; and Benjamin Kahan, *Celibacies: American Modernism and Sexual Life* (Durham, NC: Duke University Press, 2013), 10.

[22] The full passage: "Because, as I have said elsewhere, I never see a city that looks to me enduring, never see a wall that looks to me solid, I do not regret that there are none of my own blood to come

had sharpened her sense of civilizational foreboding and political fruitlessness, Hamilton was already defending spinsterism in relation to a partially barred future. That defense was less a predisposition toward her postwar convictions than a resource when apocalypse came calling. It provided her with a reason to keep writing even once she could no longer envision a posterity that could read her, let alone imagine safeguarding such a posterity through polemic. Here is the final section of Hamilton's *Marriage as a Trade* (1909):

> If humanity had only been created in order to reproduce its kind, we might still be dodging cave-bears in the intervals of grubbing up roots with our nails. It is not only the children who matter: there is the world into which they are born. Every human being who influences for the better, however slightly, the conditions under which he lives is doing something for those who come after; and thus, it seems to me, that those women who are proving by their lives that marriage is not a necessity for them, that maternity is not a necessity for them, are preparing a heritage of fuller humanity for the daughters of others—who will be daughters of their own spirit, if not in the flesh. The home of the future will be more of an abiding-place and less of a prison because they have made it obvious that, so far as many women are concerned, the home can be done without; and if the marriage of the future is what it ought to be—a voluntary contract on both sides—it will be because they have proved the right of every woman to refuse it if she will, by demonstrating that there are other means of earning a livelihood than bearing children and keeping house. (144)

Hamilton's prewar treatise offers the brutal state compatible with strict reproductivism as the counterfactual to a civilized state, one in which the making and maintenance of the world flow also through nonbiological channels. *Theodore Savage*, in turn, will depict the loss of civilization as a reversion to a strictly reproductive vision of futurity in which the notion of a "daughter of the spirit" is as unthinkable as the "kinship" Hamilton claims with Homer, Shakespeare, Goethe, and Rousseau elsewhere in her advocacy of single life. Yet treatise and novel share not only a wish for those nonbiological kinships but also a refusal of the compulsory meliorism that typified Edwardian feminist and technologist thought. *Marriage as a Trade* does not just appeal, *Middlemarch*-like, to the future valuation of incremental betterments made by those who rest in unvisited tombs. If renouncing the familial home and

---

after me. For myself, I have had the good and ill and experience of life, and I have the assurance that life, as we know it, is not all; but all the same I do not care to think too often of the future, and if I had a younger generation to love, I should care to think still less. When my brother Raymond was killed [in World War I, a few weeks from the Armistice] I realized that his death would mean the passing of my father's family, and my first instinct was of sorrow, but a sorrow that did not last. Being as little courageous for others as I am for myself I am well content to have no younger generation to fear for" (285–86).

refusing marriage and maternity are rhetorically subordinated to the "voluntary contract[s]" of future generations, *Marriage as a Trade* elsewhere models a certain voluntarism in the spinster's relationship to that futurity: the single woman, it implies, no more requires the elective, equitable marriages of future wives as her justification than a life requires an archive left to the benefit of posterity to make it meaningful. Given the degree to which futurity is generally seen as entailed by the voluntary—given, that is, our reflexive sense that to choose is perforce to choose in and toward the future, and that not to live toward the future is necessarily a benighted and pitiable condition—Hamilton's refusal to obtain the future's certification of her life and her life-writing may be the most distinctive aspect of her work.

Which may explain why Hamilton would destroy her private papers after producing, in *Life Errant*, what her biographer has called "one of the most uninformative autobiographies ever written."[23] It's as if the chief function of *Life Errant* were to stage the irrecuperability of all that it failed or refused to document and to insist on the poverty of what was communicable to posterity. In trying to read the partial archive of Hamilton's life and work—an archive that contains divergent narratives about its own status as partial—we should take care, of course, not to conflate the optative futurity of the feminist spinster with the foreclosed one of the traumatized air war survivor. The former refuses to assimilate celibacy, in the primary early-twentieth-century sense of "living unmarried," to reproductivist or reformist narratives, whereas the latter replaces the narrative of progress with the equally determinist one of cyclical collapse. But if we decline to link these futurities at all, we miss *Theodore Savage*'s critique of reproduction's adequacy, its refusal to be consoled by biological survival for the archive's utter loss. We miss, too, seeing how Hamilton's will to live in the absence of biological descendants is tributary to her later will to write in the absence of posterity. Benjamin Kahan has characterized the celibate as doubly *untimely*, possessed of both a superseded monasticism and an "unwritten future" with respect to conventional scripts of sexual development.[24] Still, despite the uncanny historical narrative that obsessed Hamilton, it is her contemporaneity with her moment, her wakefulness in the interval between an unreadable past and an unreachable future, her *timeliness* that outburns the rest. For after the First World War Hamilton did remain, movingly, awake and at work. Even as she faced the barred future unveiled by her "mental shock," she helped found the feminist newspaper *Time and Tide*, participated in the Open Door Council, kept involved in international women's suffrage efforts, and wrote a great deal—by

---

[23] Whitelaw, 4. For Whitelaw, *Life Errant* is especially obtuse regarding Hamilton's interpersonal losses and attachments and the political enjoyment and commitment others documented in her prewar suffrage work.

[24] Kahan, 6.

my count, three novels, six plays, ten travel books, a parodic history of the twentieth century, articles in favor of contraception and abortion rights, and her memoir. The conviction that civilization was nearing the next in a series of unavoidable collapses, however much that conviction mooted her work's value-toward-posterity, its transmissibility, and its futurity, could not yet wholly cancel—in fact crucially underscored—the importance of staying with the work. For Hamilton, a vigil was nonetheless worth keeping for being, as she saw it, issueless.

Jenkinson's *Manual*

Jenkinson's *Manual for Archive Administration* was commissioned by the Carnegie Endowment for International Peace, whose motivating interest in the preservation of war records is legible in the book's subtitle: *Including the Problems of War Archives and Archive Making*. The *Manual* was among the first titles in a series on the Economic and Social History of the War whose general editor, James T. Shotwell, had been managing editor of the eleventh *Encyclopaedia Britannica* (1910–11). Shotwell's preface, in its queasy oscillation between part and whole, exhibits the widespread sense that the war's scale both demanded and impeded a total portrait. On the one hand, a "reconsideration of the whole field of war economics" had become necessary thanks to the war's having "releas[ed] complex forces of national life not only for the vast process of destruction but also for the stimulation of new capacities for production." Having been "a single event," the war must be studied "as a whole."[25] On the other hand, the vastness of the war, coupled with the still-classified status of much of its archive, hindered an integrated approach. So Shotwell's series would proceed piecemeal, drawing on the wartime experience of its contributors to produce a patchwork impression of war economics. This necessity it claimed as a historiographic virtue: although unavoidably "partial," its contributors' views could also be considered "an intrinsic part of the history itself, contemporary measurements of facts as significant as the facts with which they deal." Yet somehow the series' project of holistic portraiture would be accomplished by way of, rather than despite, the partial and contradictory nature of its constituent works. As Shotwell put it, "The responsibility of the Endowment is to History itself—an obligation not to avoid but to secure and preserve variant narratives and points of view, in so far as they are essential for the understanding of the War as a whole" (ix–x).

---

[25] Hilary Jenkinson, *A Manual of Archive Administration, Including the Problems of War Archives and Archive Making* (Oxford: Clarendon Press, 1922), v–vi. Further references are cited in the text.

Jenkinson's *Manual* is rooted in the same problems of war, scale, point of view, and historical responsibility. Unlike Shotwell, however, Jenkinson was agnostic on the subject of the First World War's singularity. He recognized, certainly, that the centralized and local arms of the war bureaucracy had produced a paper trail at unprecedented rates. New communications technologies such as the telephone had created fresh problems in record-making and preservation; clerks armed with typewriters and carbon paper had cranked out multiple copies of documents on paper whose quality and durability had declined as the war progressed and more and more pulp was diverted to armament factories. Even more ephemeral than these documents had been the local branches of the war bureaucracy, organizations that were coterminous with the war and left, after the Armistice, miles of records with no clear custodian. Yet "Even the problems which seem at first to be peculiar to War Archives," Jenkinson declared, "turn out upon examination to be no more than intensifications of the old ones." As a result, a book commissioned to address the singular problem of war archives became "a general treatise applicable to Archives of all periods and illustrated from Archives of the Past," with a brief concluding chapter on war's archival ramifications. Had Jenkinson accepted the premises of his commission and written a monograph about war archives as a discrete, exceptional phenomenon, his book would likely have joined similar studies in obscurity.[26] However, by refusing that premise and relegating the war to a marginal, largely unexceptional role in a general treatise, Jenkinson made a bid for a broader audience and a longer shelf life. The *Manual* would reward that decision, laying the foundations for the professionalization of archivists, going into a second edition in 1937, and becoming first a cornerstone and then a classic of English-language archive theory.

The iconic status of Jenkinson's 1922 *Manual* has recently come under attack by scholars of records and information management who argue that Jenkinson under-acknowledged his precursors and fell short of his European contemporaries' precision.[27] According to this critique, his treatment of central categories of archive theory—quality, context, custody, appraisal, disposal, arrangement, classification, and access—did little more than collate the ideas of earlier thinkers. While concurring to some extent, I make a different argument here, one that locates Jenkinson's innovation in a place both

---

[26] See, for example, the monograph by Jenkinson's former Public Record Office colleague Hubert Hall, *British Archives and the Sources of the History of the World War* (London: Oxford University Press, 1925).

[27] See Margaret Procter, "Life Before Jenkinson: The Development of British Archival Theory and Thought at the Turn of the Twentieth Century," *Archives* 33.119 (October 2008): 136–57, and Luciana Duranti, "Cunningham's commentary," posting to <aus–archivists> listserv, January 6, 1997, qtd. in Procter, 141n7.

he and his critics have tended to underplay: the temporal ethics of archival custodianship. In essence, Jenkinson charged the archivist to suspend any historiographical agenda of *his* own (the figure is always gendered male) in order not to instrumentalize the archive; to adopt the interests and point of view of the archive; and to be the representative of future researchers whose interests he must not try to anticipate lest he deform the archive in their image. I describe this ethics as *temporal* because it constructs the archivist's responsibilities and loyalties as an eccentric orientation in time. Jenkinson's archivist must act as the contemporary not of his own contemporaries but of the archives—and, to a lesser extent, of a future he forbears to unveil. He must be a figure out of time, preserving the alterity of the dead and the autonomy of the unborn without either merging with them (what living archivist could?) or joining his contemporaries in using the past and the future as means to present ends. This begins to sound like a general rather than just a professional code of ethics, and Jenkinson would claim as much in 1940, when he described his archive theory as a "standard for the better conduct of life," adding, "had [the archivist's] doctrine of the sanctity of evidence . . . been generally accepted in the world, the world would not now be at war."[28]

When Jenkinson's portrait of the archivist is mentioned today, it tends to be as part of a narrative about the archivist's professional speciation from the historian. Margaret Procter, for example, refers to the Institute of Historical Research's launch, in 1921, of a School of Advanced Historical Study that formalized the distinction between historians and archivists, creating a demand for distinct portraits of those figures that Jenkinson's *Manual* happened to meet. But Jenkinson distinguishes the archivist from the historian and the archive administrator less on descriptive or logistical grounds than on *normative* ones, and with a passion that transcends professional advocacy. What's more, what I take to be his great innovation—the reconstruction of archive theory around a nonsynchronous ethics—is the plain view in which the war is hidden. As archivists, both Jenkinson and his critics prize narratives and procedures of continuity above all else. Confronted with the war, Jenkinson blends its discontinuities back into a general condition encompassed by a general treatise; affronted by Jenkinson's iconic status, his critics bring the overhyped *Manual* back into a relation of continuity with its predecessor texts. But Jenkinson's ethics, for all that its commitment to the dead and the unborn looks like a transtemporal continuity, is in fact premised on discontinuity and alterity. We must not criticize the dead for culling their archives, says the *Manual*, for in doing so we would presume to know their

---

[28] Hilary Jenkinson, "Reflections of an Archivist," *Contemporary Review* 165 (June 1944): 361. Further references are in the text. Although published during the war's penultimate year, Jenkinson's essay was written four years earlier, during the early months of the Blitz.

business better than they did. Nor must we create or curate our archives today with posterity in mind, for in doing so we would skew the historical record and curb the freedoms of future researchers to make what they can of us. Jenkinson's is an interwar ethics: suspended between a past and an impending discontinuity, the present enjoys a visibility horizon close to zero. If the *Manual* can demote the war to an afterthought, it is because the war's most scandalous ramification—its sense of the radical alterity of the past and the future—has already been smuggled into the very heart of the book and resignified as a transtemporal ethics. That relabeling is a powerful and appealing one in that it insists on the freedom of the dead to have acted as they did and on the freedom of the unborn to act as they will. But in making the present, through the figure of the archivist, the guardian of those freedoms, it voids the present of the very capacity it must guarantee to other times. It says there was and will be freedom; but there *is* none for us.

In order to appreciate both the grounding and the innovative leaps of Jenkinson's archival ethics, we need to look briefly at the *Manual*'s general archive theory, which followed earlier writers in stressing the importance of a record's processual origins, its place in an unbroken and legitimate chain of custody, and its meaning's dependence on the contextual totality of the archive.[29] The last of these the *Manual* inherits directly from its chief precursor, Muller, Feith, and Fruin's *Handleiding voor het ordenen en beschrijven van archieven* (1898). The so-called "Dutch Manual" treated as axiomatic what European archivists knew as *le respect des fonds*, a "maintenance of the integrity of archival collections" rooted in a faith in the distributed but inviolate truth of a given archival totality.[30] Jenkinson translates *fonds* roughly as "archive group," which he defines as "the Archives resulting from the work of an Administration which was an organic whole, complete in itself, capable of dealing independently, without any added or external authority,

---

[29] Charles Crump's essay on "records" in the eleventh *Encyclopedia Britannica* defined a record as "a document regularly drawn up for a legal or administrative purpose and preserved in proper custody to perpetuate the memory of the transaction described in it." Charles Johnson, like Hall and Crump a colleague of Jenkinson's at the Public Record Office, defined archives in 1919 as "one or more groups of documents no longer in current use, each group of which has accrued in the custody of an individual or a department in the ordinary course of business, and forms an organic whole, reflecting the organization and history of the office which produced it . . . we may regard as archives any series of documents arising in the ordinary course of business and put away for future reference." Note that neither Crump nor Johnson forbids an archive's being oriented toward posterity; Crump's diction ("preserved . . . to perpetuate the memory") even implicitly invokes posterity as a legitimate indirect object for the archive. See Charles Crump, "Records" in *Encyclopedia Britannica*, 11th ed., vol. 22 (New York: Encyclopaedia Britannica, 1911), 955–66; and Charles Johnson, *The Care of Documents and Management of Archives*, Helps for Students of History, no. 5 (London: Society for Promoting Christian Knowledge, 1919), 7, qtd. in Procter, 145–46.

[30] S. Muller, J. A. Feith, and R. Fruin, *Handleiding voor het ordenen en beschrijven van archieven* (Groningen: Erven B. van der Kamp, 1898); citation is to the English version, *Manual for the Arrangement and Description of Archives*, trans. Arthur H. Leavitt (New York: Wilson, 1940), 34n26.

with every side of any business which could normally be presented to it" (84). Several rules follow from this presumption of an archive group's integrity and self-sufficiency. Because its historicity inheres partly in the way its compiling administrators arranged it, an archive group must remain in that *ordre primitif* rather than being reorganized according to the archivist's preference or the historian's convenience. Having their meaning as a totality, the records constituting an archive group must not be separated from one another; documents lose their archive value when they are torn from the *fonds* to be displayed in museums or bundled thematically with documents cherry-picked from other *fonds*. The last moment at which archives may legitimately be culled is the moment *before* they pass out of the hands of their administrators and into the hands of the archivist: whereas the destruction of records is a routine right of an archive's compiler, the archivist cannot anticipate which documents will fall outside the interests of all future researchers and may safely be destroyed. To ensure that culling and other tampering have not occurred in the wake of an archive's transfer, its possession by "an unblemished line of responsible custodians" must be demonstrable (11). Without such a guarantee, both the legal admissibility and the evidential value of the records could be badly compromised.

So far, none of this differs from the Dutch Manual in more than emphasis. But tucked away in an early "corollary" on posterity is a foreglimpse of the nonsynchronous ethics the *Manual* will elaborate in later sections. An archive, writes Jenkinson, consists of documents

> . . . drawn up or used in the course of an administrative or executive transaction . . . of which [those documents themselves] formed a part; and subsequently preserved in their own custody for their own information by the person or persons responsible for that transaction and their legitimate successors. To this Definition we may add a corollary. *Archives were not drawn up in the interest or for the information of Posterity."* (11; emphasis added).

Jenkinson's definition captures what he took to be the two most important indices of an archive's quality: *impartiality* and *authenticity* (12). An archive's impartiality (Jenkinson also calls it a "gift") depends on its having been generated and maintained by the members of an active business or institution for their own reference and *not* with an eye toward the future's historical or juridical assessment of their activities. Archives are *impartial* in proportion as they are the instruments of those who produce and maintain them in the ordinary course of business, and partial in proportion as they are altered in the proleptic image of the future's use of them. An archive's *authenticity* depends on its having remained in the custody of the business or institution that generated it and therefore been shaped only by its creators and custodians, not disfigured through forgery or culling by those outside its functional ambit. The impartial archive is free from prejudice, the authentic archive free from tampering. Because the presumed audience of archival prejudice and tampering is posterity, Jenkinson's corollary ("Archives were not drawn up in the interest or for the information of Posterity") is really more of a first principle. Impartiality and authenticity measure an archive's quality because they testify to its *indifference* to posterity—and thus, paradoxically, its *use* to posterity. In order to instrumentalize an archive to their interpretive agendas, researchers must be confident that the archive was, during the period of its creation, fully instrumentalized by its creators to their own present-tense needs. If we living researchers are to attempt to see the faces of the dead for our own purposes, we must feel certain that the dead did not alter their expressions in a prospective attempt to meet our gaze.

Because he holds the past to have preserved archives for its own information and not for posterity's, Jenkinson is quick to defend past archive administrators for destroying even documents we wish, today, they had saved. The Elizabethan Court of Requests, he says, could not have known, nor was it bound to anticipate, how much interest the future would take in a deponent named William Shakespeare; as long as it hewed to its own standards of values in destroying records signed by deponents, we have no right to deplore the loss of the Bard's signature (118–19). Even past archivists are not to be too harshly judged for destroying records they thought valueless; "the truth is simply that they were unable to predict the directions which would be taken by the historical interests of the next hundred years." But when Jenkinson turns to the question of whether living archivists might destroy useless-seeming documents in the present, he grants them no such lenience. Because they can see the unfortunate consequences of past archivists' blindness to future historical interests, archivists in the present must be held to higher standards—even if "it is difficult to see how any one can in conscience propose in our own time to do any better for the interests of the future" (124). The unforeseeability of the future must underwrite both a less reckless archival practice than inhered in the past and a radical modesty on the part of the archivist:

> It does not seem much to demand that any one who is to take upon himself the responsibility of destroying irrevocably Archives which have come down to us from the past should do so on something more than a consideration of his own interests and those of the time in which he lives: he should surely regard himself as a trustee for the future as well as for the present. But in that case who is to fill the rôle? Who can project himself into the future and foresee its requirements? . . . For example, we have been speaking and thinking throughout this section of the interests of the Historian; but can we even answer for it that in the future the Historian will be the person most interested in the Archives we are leaving behind us? We are left by such considerations as these with a growing conviction that destruction

of any of the Archives we have received from the past is a course that a conscientious Archivist must find it difficult to commend. (123–24)

Jenkinson's modesty is so radical, in fact, that he can define the archivist's
powers only by reducing them: the archivist will have to be a "trustee for the
future" by *declining* to "project himself into the future and foresee its require-
ments." But something is coming into view, too, through the process of its
near cancellation: the archivist as a professional species with discrete duties,
capacities, ethical codes, even a distinct orientation in time. The Dutch
Manual may have been addressed to archivists, but it consists mainly of
conventions and guidelines; it almost never features the archivist as a figure
of description, analysis, or entreaty. Jenkinson's bold move is to hasten the
archivist's professional speciation by binding the conventions and guidelines
of Muller and others around an idiosyncratic ethics. From this particularizing process, the archivist emerges as a figure in whose vigilance modesty
and longevity are fused. In the veiled future, the historian may wander away
from archival work or even become extinct as a professional life form. But the
archivist, Jenkinson implies, will persist.

Having been thus distinguished from the historian, the archivist should
not, by Jenkinson's lights, undertake historical research himself. The reasons
for this abstinence surpass whatever time and attention such research might
siphon away from his primary duties. The historian's instrumental conception of the archive—his use of it in pursuit of particular arguments and meth-
odologies—is a perilous orientation for the archivist to adopt even part-time,
and not one Jenkinson believes can be contained. "[M]ost of the bad and dangerous work done [upon archives] in the past," he laments, "may be traced
to external enthusiasms resulting in *a failure on the part of the Archivist to
treat Archives as a separate subject*"—that is, as ends in themselves rather than
as means to historiographic ends (106–7; emphasis in original). Although he
will insist that the archive was an instrument in the hands of its compiling
administrators, and although he maintains the archive for the sake of others'
instrumentalizing of it in the present and future, the archivist himself must
withdraw from that economy of use.

> He is concerned to keep [archives'] qualities intact for the use, perhaps,
> in the future, of students working upon subjects which neither he nor any
> one else has contemplated. His work consequently is that of physical and
> moral conservation and his interest an interest in his Archives as Archives,
> not as documents valuable for providing this or that thesis. How then is
> he to undertake work involving judgement and choice on precisely those
> matters which are not his concern? as well expect a Palaeontologist (to bor-
> row once again the old simile) to be interested in the manufacture of bone
> tooth-brushes as ask the Archivist (in his official capacity) to pronounce
> judgement upon the merits as historical evidences of a set of archives. (125)

Here, the fanciful "old simile" is borrowed from the Dutch Manual, which describes the archivist as rebuilding the main lines of an archive's organization from key documents in the manner that a paleontologist reconstructs a prehistoric skeleton.[31] Jenkinson's reworking of the simile constructs a grotesque diorama of instrumentalizing uses of the archive, implicitly casting the historian as an industrialist who wastes old and precious things in the manufacture of base, ephemeral ones. But the simile resonates with and deepens many other elements of the 1922 Manual besides. Above all, it activates a range of surprising similarities between the fossil record and the archive. Both are formed according to organic processes that disregard posterity: the fossil bed's complex happenstance parallels the institution's internal making and keeping of records. Not only are the fossil record and the archive, in effect, forms of writing without an addressee but their capacity to bring unadulterated news of the past positively requires this lack of address. And both, soberingly, are records of *extinction*: the fossil record of species, clades, and regional biota; the archive of businesses, institutions, and regimes. In this landscape of extinction, the historians are trawling for raw materials they will use variously to inform, comfort, unsettle, discredit, and justify the living. But the archivist is on the side of the useless dinosaurs, forbearing to commodify their beautiful remains.

And he is doing so in order that the researchers of the future will be able to go on making their fossil toothbrushes. Jenkinson's archivist incarnates a logic of surrogacy and even sacrifice that is distinctly religious in cast: like the anchorite, he keeps a vigil from which the rest of us are exempt; like the paschal lamb, he goes to the slaughter-bench so that others may remain in the world and continue to mix their desire with it. He must be the contemporary neither of his contemporaries, who are free to pursue their agendas, nor of the future researchers he represents, who must remain a blank to him and who, anyway, belong to multiple generations. In a sense he has no contemporaries, unless they are his fellow archivists; as Jenkinson puts it, "the Archivist should be a modern only so far as strictly modern questions of buildings, custody, and the like are concerned: for the rest, he should be all things to all Archives, his interests identified with theirs, his period and point of view theirs" (107). A steward of the extinguished; a blind trustee for the future; a member of an "unblemished line of responsible custodians." Where we might have looked for a portrait of the archivist as a mild and owlish functionary, we find in Jenkinson a

---

[31] See Muller et al., 66–72. In 1954, the American archive theorist T. R. Schellenberg would wickedly extend the "old simile" by complaining that he was "tired of having an old fossil cited . . . as an authority in archive matters. I refer to Sir Hilary Jenkinson, former Deputy Keeper of Records at the British Public Records Office, who wrote a book that is not only unreadable but that has given the Australians a wrong start in their archival work." Schellenberg intended his *Modern Archives: Principles and Techniques* (1956) to supplant Jenkinson's *Manual*. T. R. Schellenberg to Albert C. Shwarting, July 7, 1954, Personal Letters File, Schellenberg Papers; qtd. in Jane F. Smith, "Theodore R. Schellenberg: Americanizer and Popularizer," *American Archivist 44* (Fall 1981): 319.

much stranger figure, a member of a secular holy order who withdraws from the libidinal economy of argument in the service of the archive's intrinsic value and of all research still to come. For if to appropriate the raw materials of the past in the service of present argumentative drives is to enact a standard historiographic sexuality, then the holy order of archivists enacts a celibate one. Channeling its historical desires neither toward the reproduction of its own arguments in the present nor toward an end-time jouissance it will live to experience, that order is canted toward ongoing futures it will never see—futures in which its superintendence may bear the fruit of unforeseeable research by unimaginable researchers.

What I have characterized as the historiographic celibacy of the archivist emphasizes all that is exceptional about Jenkinson's reinvention of that figure. But in at least one respect—his impartiality—the archivist is an exemplary historical actor rather than an exempt one. Recall Jenkinson's corollary: "Archives were not drawn up in the interest or for the information of Posterity." At least as regards archive making, the good-faith historical actor does not mug for posterity's camera. Only the archives produced spontaneously by these unselfconscious historical actors can tell us the truth, and they can tell us *only* the truth. By extension, historiographically self-conscious actors blemish the historical truth-content of the archives they produce. Their living-toward-posterity— their historically self-conscious sense—is not itself historical; in causing them to mar the impartiality of their generation's archive, it prevents them from being the contemporaries of their contemporaries. I have used the same formulation in describing the archivist, and it remains a question whether the archivist's secession from contemporaneity (to say nothing of Jenkinson's own production of an ostensibly transhistorical theory of archives) is in homologously bad faith. But the archivist, at least, does not pass partial archives off as impartial ones unless he deforms the records he generates in the course of his own work. More, his declared intention toward the archives he oversees is to defend them against deformation toward some particular, necessarily tendentious, image of posterity. So despite being every kind of outlier in respect to historiographic desire, Jenkinson's archivist models the basis of all good-faith historical action: a recognition that we injure the historicity of our archives if we fill them with "propaganda for posterity," and the historicity of our deeds if we perform them to curry favor with a future we cannot anticipate.

War Archives: Theory and Performance

It is now possible to see how an archive theory begun in 1920 as a highly specific portrait of the archivist eventually became, in its author's eyes, "a standard for the better conduct of life" that could have prevented the Second World War had it been more widely embraced. But before joining Jenkinson in 1940, when he made this claim, we need to stay a moment longer with the *Manual* to consider its treatment of the events and conditions that precipitated Jenkinson's book. "War Archives," the *Manual*'s brief concluding section, restores to the First World War the exceptional status it is denied elsewhere in the text. The war, says Jenkinson, "could produce nothing that was not a very special case," thanks in part to the fact that "during the war the majority of the people entered, we may say, into State employment" (163–64). But by itself the scale of the war did not pose a problem for archive *theory*; the principles and qualities we have already encountered still applied. Scale created practical problems, but the theoretical ones arose chiefly from the war's interference with the bureaucratic conditions and time frames of document production. Local and public organizations (Jenkinson worried less about State archives, which were maintained by long-standing, experienced governmental organizations) came into being suddenly, generated archives that were managed by inexperienced people, went through constant changes in staffing and function, and vanished after the Armistice (165). No sooner had the war ended than historians began to clamor for access to its archives, and their demands were often met before the archive in question had been properly set up. Jenkinson's central plea in this regard was that a concerted and centralized effort establish the links among different archive groups, catalogue and prepare the documents, and place them in the custody of permanent institutions. This, he stipulated, should be done before historians were permitted to work with the materials. The special interests of future researchers could be served only by putting off the special interests of present ones.

Here the practical problem of scale came to the fore. A Royal Commission had reported that the British war archive—produced in only four years—was as bulky as the total previous contents of the Public Record Office (21n1). Until culled, the "enormous stock of fresh experience which has been accumulated during the War" would remain hidden from researchers "in a mass of documents so colossal that the question of their housing alone (apart from those of their handling, sifting and use) presents quite novel features" (20–21). But where Jenkinson's general theory required archives to be weeded by their compiling administrators, most wartime institutions had been defunct for several years, their administrators returned to their peacetime pursuits. Jenkinson proposed a stunning solution that fused imaginative compromise with adherence to principle:

> It follows that we must compromise—do our best to restore these War Archives to the position of Archives of the Future, Archives yet in the making and therefore weedable; and from that again follows the necessity of getting to work with the greatest possible rapidity and in every other way assimilating as closely as possible the position of these documents to that of documents still belonging to current business—the only stage, it will

be remembered, in a documentary career at which we proposed to permit destruction. . . . [T]he co-operation should be secured of persons who were officially concerned with the making of the documents now in question: they alone can bring them back, as it were, into a temporary state of currency for the purposes of a reasoned selection based on their position in the administrative work of the office; and from every point of view they obviously are the persons most qualified to deal with them rapidly and efficiently. (167, 173)

Because the agencies in question had expired prematurely, without setting their documentary effects in order, Jenkinson would revive them, re-conscripting their former administrators to an undead war bureaucracy empowered to weed documents *as if the war were still on*. This scenario— never realized, unsurprisingly—both venerates and abandons the *Manual's* immanent theory of historicity. Spontaneity, impartiality, authenticity, unselfconsciousness about posterity: the very archive values in whose name Jenkinson would resurrect the war bureaucracy would be present in it only as surrogates—as mock spontaneity, ersatz authenticity, impartiality with an agenda. One might expect the opposite of Jenkinson—a defense, say, of the war archive's gigantism, redundancy, and premature abandonment as the authentic conditions of its historicity. But his proposal to revive the war bureaucracy illustrates how fundamentally his general theory presupposed a certain gradualism and proportion in the lives of archive-making institutions. As long as institutions came into being gradually, culled as they went along for internal purposes, and expired with some warning, the archival present remained self-identical. But the war had so severely violated these parameters that its archive could cease neither with the hostilities nor with the shuttering of local agencies; the war had, in a unique manner, divided the archival present from itself. In order to be realigned with a gradualist archive theory, the war bureaucracy had to be given a gift of fictive time, a grace period during which document-weeding could continue, thanks to a simulated legitimacy, long after the cessation of the document-making events. The archival repository of a true historicity would be stabilized through a carefully orchestrated performance of historicity.

Even as "War Archives" stages the reassimilation of the war's exceptional scale and tempo to Jenkinson's general theory, it performs the inverse gesture: a recognition of the war as the extreme case demanding that the general theory itself be rethought. "In fine," Jenkinson writes in an earlier section, "it is largely the addition of this abnormal mass of new Archive matter to our existing collections which compels us to face the fact that we must make at any rate a beginning of settling our archive problems, old and new, if we are to deal satisfactorily with the present and safeguard the future of research work" (21). If the war is the occasion for setting down a general theory that will settle "archive problems, old and new," it also exerts a compulsory weight in excess of a general or motivating case. Part of that weight, moreover, resides in the future, and in the future of war; for as much as the recent war may have challenged archivists through its new ways of both engendering and endangering written documents, there is the implication in Jenkinson that future wars will further amplify these problems, and to unforeseeable degrees.[32] In the future, that is, the archival present may be even more self-divided during war, may come to bear even less resemblance to the gradualism putatively modeled by the general theory. The war archives of the future might require, in response, even more extravagant, long-lasting measures than the temporary revival of the war bureaucracy proposed in "War Archives." They might require a general archive theory that accommodates—as a rule rather than an exception—collective performance, nonsynchronous conceptions of the present, and a discontinuous view of the past and the future.

As I have discussed it above, Jenkinson's *Manual of Archive Administration* already is such a general theory. Of course, when it is read as the successor to the Dutch Manual, with its gradualist grain held to the light, the 1922 *Manual* seems to swear allegiance to a historiography of continuity buttressed by a holist *respect des fonds* and a positivist faith in the truth of archives. But read with particular attention to its archival ethics, Jenkinson's great work can be seen to turn the cardinal archive value of impartiality into a secondary effect of historical discontinuity. Impartiality emerges, that is, as a double refusal either to claim to know better than the past or to angle for legibility to the future. And we violate impartiality not by straying from some imagined neutrality but by presuming that the dead were simply less-informed editions of the living, that the unborn will share our needs and drives, our criteria and priorities. Seen again through the lens of its concluding section on "War Archives," the gradualism and positivism of the *Manual*'s preceding sections look more performative, strategic, aspirational; less like a consolidation of prewar archive science and more like an interwar cri de coeur that the storms of history not be permitted to consume, as they do in *Theodore Savage*, the very archive through which the future might avoid their full-scale repetition. Read this way, the *Manual* comes into focus as the first catastrophist archive theory. It sees the discontinuities between past and present, present and future, not as fatal hazards to the archivist's work but as vulnerable

---

[32] Jenkinson's *Manual* is particularly despondent about the threat posed to archives by aerial bombardment, and about how little can be done to diminish that threat: "After our experience in the late war of the penetrating power of heavy bombs dropped from aircraft, it is doubtful whether any provision can be made against such a danger, these bombs being generally fitted with a 'delay action fuse'; but some form of 'arresting' and 'bursting courses' in the shape of stone or concrete roofs and floors would at least do no harm" (46). As a severe impediment to the archivist's provisioning and pre-visioning abilities, bombardment begins to look like a historical referent, or even a proximate cause, for what elsewhere functions as an archival ethics of veiled futurity.

charges, the principal objects of the archivist's humility and vigilance. Given events that rend the archival present and cultural perforations that divide epochs—that is, given catastrophe—it entreats us not to force our tendentious view of the archive on the future, which must be free to do its own forcing to its own unguessable ends. This is all Jenkinson's theory knows, finally, of continuity: the persistence through time of raw archival materials for others to instrumentalize as they must, and archivists' collective performance of exemption from the instrumentalizing work of the living.

Thoughts on Archives in an Air Raid

In the fall of 1940, while Virginia Woolf was composing her "Thoughts on Peace in an Air Raid," Jenkinson wrote what he later called "a kind of Philosophy of Archives hammered out first while I was waiting for bombs to fall on Chancery Lane," the location of the Public Record Office where he had worked on and off since 1906.[33] The essay, "Reflections of an Archivist," named some of the dangers posed to archives by the war, among them destruction by enemy bombardment and pulping for the waste paper needed in munitions production and other areas of the war economy. In its role as "a profession of faith" (356), it described the archivist's duty to a noninstrumental notion of the truth: "not merely to be as truthful as he can himself, but to be the guardian for the benefit of others of countless truths of all kinds—truths which interest him personally and truths which do not; yes, and truths of which he himself does not perceive the existence" (360). The piece contains the grand claim we have already encountered: that "had [the archivist's] doctrine of the sanctity of evidence . . . been generally accepted in the world, the world would not now be at war" (361). Jenkinson goes on in the essay to root fascism in a contempt for historical truth, a contempt strong enough to countenance filling the archives with propaganda to flatter and exculpate the powerful and to seek the esteem of an autocratic posterity. Although the historically self-conscious actor was not, ipso facto, a fascist, such an actor at the very least made fascism harder to combat. In the front lines of that struggle was the archivist, who kept watch over the means by which fascism would be warded off in the future: an unblemished archive containing the true facts of the case for future historians. Thus while the archivist sought to *avoid* changing the world by making claims based on the archives, he would preserve those archives in the condition that would optimize their usefulness to others in defeating or preempting fascism. And

---

[33] Hilary Jenkinson, "The Future of Archives in England," rpt. in *Selected Writings of Sir Hilary Jenkinson* (London: Alan Sutton, 1980), 329.

in doing so he would exhibit both the impartiality and the "doctrine of the sanctity of evidence" that were central to a good-faith, implicitly antifascist mode of historical action.[34]

Perhaps the most extraordinary moment in Jenkinson's "Reflections" is its materialist reverie on the future significance that might be latent in fragile archival materials—signs that would become legible thanks to a transgenerational collaboration between future students armed with new techniques and the archivists who had represented their needs without presuming to know them.

> [T]he qualities or elements in question may be not merely infinitesimal, as it might seem, in importance (the precise location, for instance, of the holes through which one sheet is sewn to another); they may be actually imperceptible to all ordinary forms of examination. There may be, for example, some moral relation between two documents which nothing save their preservation, apparently by accident, in the same box remains to testify; there may be some chemical constituent in the ink or paper, invisible to the eye, unknown, if you like, even to the analyst, the modification of which by a process innocently used in the course of examination or of necessary repair would deprive the future student of evidence which would have enabled him to date, identify or authenticate. (360)

The passage is a speculative fantasia on how such a future might vindicate the dutiful archivist, reading in the organic plenitude of the archive what the present cannot apprehend there. It is a kind of prayer, too, for a future without imminent air raids, a peacetime that will let scholars pore again over every page and binding, developing new ways of perceiving, constellating, and decoding the documents that were under threat as Jenkinson wrote. As it happened, the Public Record Office in Chancery Lane survived the Blitz

---

[34] Nowhere is Jenkinson's ambition greater, or his nonsynchronous ethics more compromised, than in these formulations. The *Manual* had charged the archivist to preserve records for use by others whose agendas and professions might be utterly alien. It follows that they might also be politically repellent to the archivist; otherwise, future researchers are denied the very alterity in whose name the archivist declines to envisage them. Given the Blitz conditions under which he wrote "Reflections of an Archivist," Jenkinson's reportrayal of the archivist as intrinsically antifascist in his orientation toward evidence, truth, and history is understandable. But in a sense it renounces the vow of historiographic celibacy in which his theory is grounded, subordinating the archivist's maintenance of the archive to the production of one political future over another. At the same time, Jenkinson's claim asks an archive theory predicated on political stability how it would cope with the prospective loss of that stability, particularly in cases where a new regime might be inimical to an ethos of impartiality. It asks whether the archivist might strategically compromise his ethics in order to combat the kinds of political regimes that could forbid or dismantle it altogether. And it is the first time in Jenkinson's writings that he admits the possibility that the archivist as described in his work—the radically modest, yet quietly self-important defender of the archive and of veiled futurity—might become extinct through geopolitical catastrophe.

with only minor structural damage, and with trivial loss of records.[35] But on the morning of September 8, 1940, German bombs did fall on the War Office repository in Arnside Street, Walworth, London, destroying 60 percent of the 6.5 million First World War service records housed there and subjecting much of what remained to charring and water damage.[36] In a compulsive repetition that seemed to come from the imagination of Cicely Hamilton, one war's administrative paper trail—records of enlistment, conduct, casualty, discharge, pension, and death—had been set alight by the bombs of the next war.

Archival Fire

This chapter has paired two markedly dissimilar texts: an archive theory that would preserve documents despite wartime spasms in their production and administration, and a speculative fiction convinced it will shortly become illegible thanks to the social collapse it sees coming with the next war. To read each work by the other's generic light only deepens their seeming opposition. As a work of latent speculative fiction, Jenkinson's *Manual* envisions a future where advances in warfare and communications technology might complicate archivists' labor but never to the point of annihilating the symbolic order that is its precondition. As a work of implicit archive theory, Hamilton's *Theodore Savage* insists on the fragility not just of bureaucratic continuity but of literacy itself; for Hamilton, the archive is not a firm civilizational substrate, as in Jenkinson, but a symptom that an advanced social order is approaching the next in a numberless series of catastrophic breaks that will leave only sparse and muddled traces in the next archive. Far from preventing conflict by safeguarding the sanctity of evidence, the archivist in Hamilton's world only hastens the inevitable disaster by superintending the knowledge that produces it. Although both works imagine the future as veiled, the

---

[35] See C. T. Flower, "Manuscripts and the War," *Transactions of the Royal Historical Society 25* (1943): 21. Flower offers a fascinating description of the evacuation of documents from London before the commencement of the Second World War, precautions and protocols for safeguarding archives during the Blitz, and the Public Records Office's attempts to deal with "the risk of valuable material being swept over the rapids in a laudable but indiscriminate drive for salvage" (16).

[36] The First World War service records that survived the September 8 bombing were divided into two groups after the war: the Burnt Documents (WO 363), which are too fragile to handle and were microfilmed in the late twentieth century; and the Unburnt Documents (WO 364). "Of the 1,400 tons of records stored here only about 300 tons were salvaged. The records concerned were soldiers' documents of the First World War, records of units and formations disbanded after that war and non-current War Office branches, including maps of historical value from the Lands Branch and proceedings of courts martial from the Judge Advocate General's office. Some records of military intelligence origin were also destroyed." Michael Roper, *The Records of the War Office and Related Departments, 1660–1964* (Kew: Public Record Office, 1998), 287.

nature and consequence of that veiling are antithetical. For Jenkinson, the future's alterity is a function of its openness: its needs and agendas cannot be anticipated, and the archivist must be a stay against any attempts to do so. For Hamilton, the future's alterity is an effect of its foreclosure: thanks to an inevitable disaster that we *can* anticipate, the future's continuity with the predisaster order will be severed. Its alterity will lie, above all, in its incomprehension of the present.

The oppositions between the two works spring from a fundamental difference in their orientation toward empiricism. The "doctrine of the sanctity of evidence" that grounds the *Manual*'s ethics is rooted in the belief that empiricism is self-preserving and self-replicating. Although future techniques, professions, and research agendas may be unimaginable today, they will still, according to Jenkinson, be evidence-based, and will benefit from our efforts to preserve varieties of evidence we cannot use or even perceive ourselves. Hamilton, in contrast, is convinced at Abbeville that empiricism must lead, and has already led, to the liquidation through high-tech warfare of its own generative conditions: the scientific method begets engines of mass death, which in turn beget social collapse. That Jenkinson and Hamilton part ways at the question of empiricism's valence is itself worth noting. If we allow the *Manual* and *Theodore Savage* to stand in metonymic relation to their respective discourse worlds, as I have suggested we do, the empiricism question begins to emerge as a central rift in interwar thinking about the constellation *archive–warfare–futurity*. A great deal follows, in other words, from how interwar subjects answered the question, is the experience of the Great War evidence to be used in the prevention of a worse sequel, or is it proof of empiricism's bent to extinguish itself? Note that these are not symmetrical choices. The Jenkinsonian position sees the experiment as still in progress, the outcome unknown, the future unforeclosed and hopeful; the Hamiltonian sees the experiment as concluded, the future sealed. The dissymmetry between the two makes this a difference not just about empiricism's historical trajectory but about ethical orientation toward the future, and about the efficacy of individual and collective action in the world.

In another sense, however, Hamilton's and Jenkinson's disparate stances toward the future amount to a difference that makes no difference. Whether the future is veiled by imminent disaster or by history's gradualist drift toward the unforeseeable, the result is the same: one abstains from rooting one's acts in a depiction of the future that conveniently resembles the present. Jenkinson's archivist may act for the sake of future researchers but must not attempt to know their minds; he clears a space for them without claiming their endorsement or authorization, acts as their trustee without acting in their names. Hamilton continues, after the war, to write and act despite being convinced that both her books and her acts will soon be made unreadable by a social collapse; there are reasons to stay at work, says her oeuvre, even without the hope of being recognized by readers or descendants like oneself. There is a similar refusal in Jenkinson and Hamilton to invoke the authority of the dead. Little as the *Manual* would have us condemn the archivists of the past, it is just as little interested in "tradition" as an ethical rationale; the archives of the past must be preserved not to honor or mollify the dead but for the sake of the unfathomable future. And as much as *Theodore Savage* indulges in elegiac catalogs of lost masters and forgotten generations, its very premise rules out their persistence as cultural or ethical authorities. What remains, for both of these singular yet paradigmatically interwar writers, is the present. Stripped of presentist constructions of the dead and the unborn to lend majesty to their actions, both Jenkinson and Hamilton incline toward a radical histori-cal modesty—a sense that one's actions can be taken to signify, in their scope and stakes, only within the narrowed aperture of the now. Yet as we saw with Jenkinson's archivist, this circumscription of the temporal range of ethics is anything but an alibi for shortsightedness. Instead, it loads the slim remain-ing interval with a terrible, even a limitless, responsibility, given the loss of a long historical continuum against which one's actions might be seen in per-spective. As the darkness beyond its shrunken circumference intensifies, so does the spotlit brightness of the present.

It is in the light of this intensified present between veils—those of the past and the future—that the dissident desire of Hamilton and Jenkinson can be seen most clearly. I have used the word "celibacy" in connection with both writers: literally, to describe Hamilton's prewar defense of spinsterism and her postwar relief at being the last in her biological line, and figuratively, to characterize Jenkinson's portrait of the archivist as withdrawing from the libidinal economies of research and posterity-courting historical agency. Both celibacies reject the constructions of the future that predominate in their respective registers—the sexual reproductivism that understands futu-rity as a matter of biological descent, and the archival instrumentalism that sees the future as both produced and solicited by tendentious uses of the archive. Having withdrawn desire from these particular futurities, however, they also decline to channel it toward the past in something like the queer "touch across time" described by Carolyn Dinshaw.[37] Nor are the celibacies of Hamilton and Jenkinson signs of desire's repression or absence. Theirs is a desire in and for the present: a desire for the intrinsic value of one's work, never mind its sequelae; a desire that the present be sufficient to justify the work of keeping watch or sounding warning.

This present-directed desire is precisely *not* the reactive sexual dissidence bewailed by Schell's "Second Death," in which nonreproductive desire is just a

---

[37] Carolyn Dinshaw, *Getting Medieval: Sexualities and Communities, Pre- and Postmodern* (Durham, NC: Duke University Press, 1999), 21.

symptom of the future's apparent foreclosure. But it would be naive to detach Hamilton's postwar defenses of spinsterism, in particular, from the imminent Ruin in whose shadow she felt such relief at having no descendants. Rather, her real-time conviction that the 1920s were an interwar period happened to provide both a referent and an intensifier for principles she already held and desires she already felt. And if I am right in calling Jenkinson's the first catastrophist archive theory—the first theory to affirm the archive values of impartiality and authenticity in the shadow of past and prospective discontinuities—then we might, after all, say the same of his portrait of the archivist's dissident desire: that it was neither reducible to nor wholly separable from its author's sense that he was writing during a pause between upheavals so exceptional that they must alter the rule. It would be oversimplifying to characterize the time of "interwar," apprehended as such by those who lived through it, as a queer temporality across the board. But its evidently narrowed horizons were deeply compatible with desire that sought neither the past nor the future as the time of its vindication.

Which brings us back to that perpetual interwar period, the Cold War, with its two nuclear fantasias: one in which the species survives the extinction of the symbolic order, another in which the symbolic order survives the extinction of the species. Cleaving resolutely to a human species-horizon in its fable of repeated literacy loss, Hamilton's novel is an obvious predecessor of the first nuclear fantasia. Jenkinson's *Manual* nowhere names the human extinction-event on which the second fantasia will center. But in its paleontological account of the archive as fossil bed—as an archive of extinctions—and in its provisions for an utterly strange researcher, the *Manual* calls in essence for a posthuman archivist, one who represents the absolute other: not necessarily a historian, not even necessarily human. (The reciprocal figure of the alien archivists in Clarke's "The Star," Jenkinson's archivist could well be superintending the human archive for future alien readers.) The *Manual* is thus the unlikeliest antecedent of the nuclear extinction narrative, in which the supersession of the present by an unforeseeable, even posthuman future is no argument against the archive's remaining intact, usable, legible. Custodianship, in the radical imagination of the *Manual*, would have to transcend not just the agendas, professions, and disciplinary formations of the present but the species horizon as well.

Read for their scenarios, Hamilton's *Savage* and Jenkinson's *Manual* appear to be the antecedents of two mutually exclusive Cold War fantasias. But the two works' deeper affinities, as I have discussed them, suggest that the fantasias of species extinction and social collapse, respectively, are variations on a single problematic. Both Hamilton's and Jenkinson's texts, as they ponder the archive's vulnerability in the shadow of modern warfare, refuse to count on the future's resemblance to the present. And yet what draws the veil before the future but the archive itself? For the future-war doomsayer, the archive of human knowledge incubates the very technologies that cause radical historical breaks, such that one civilization can know its predecessor only through the residue of myth—that is, *not* through an archive. For the modernist archive theorist, it is the vastness of the archive that permits historians in the present to exhaust their interests and agendas and be superseded by future researchers whose needs, questions, methods, and profession we cannot foresee and must not attempt to divine. Both cases theorize what Derrida will belatedly call the *archiviolithic*, the repetition-compulsion or death drive that is internal to the archive. "[E]ven in that which permits and conditions archivization," writes Derrida, "we will never find anything other than that which exposes to destruction, and in truth menaces with destruction, introducing, a priori, forgetfulness and the archiviolithic into the heart of the monument. Into the 'by heart' itself. The archive works always and a priori against itself."[38] The archiviolithic is that archival penchant for self-effacement that would leave no intelligible archive *of* that effacement. It names the place where modernist archive theory and interwar speculative fiction most intimately touch: in recognizing how the fire that would consume the archive is an archival fire.

The archives we have encountered in this chapter have no addressee. For Jenkinson, archives both accumulate and survive as the fossil record does: in a manner that is heedless of posterity. For Hamilton, the archive does not survive at all, insofar as the catastrophes it makes possible guarantee its illegibility to future readers. We turn toward a more intentional form now in pivoting from the archive to the encyclopedia. Where the archive is generated by internal administrative processes and only incidentally opened to external users, the encyclopedia is a purpose-built repository, composed from the start for the sake of its readers. Where archives contain raw material to be quarried in the production of knowledge, encyclopedias condense and explicate knowledge that has already been produced. Archives build up; encyclopedias are built. But while the encyclopedia may be more intentional than the archive in its genesis, it is not more univocal, more coherent, or more total. Archives make no truth claims, so they cannot become obsolete. Because an archive's organization is a function of its production and use, that organization cannot be faulted for arbitrariness. By the same token, the only coherence an archive need have is a functional coherence for its originators. When encyclopedias boast of being ageless total monuments to order, they court all three charges: obsolescence, arbitrariness, and

---

[38] Jacques Derrida, *Archive Fever: A Freudian Impression*, trans. Eric Prenowitz (Chicago: University of Chicago Press, 1996), 12; translation emended thanks to Stephen Dodson. For a discussion of the archiviolithic that touches on the *Encyclopédie*, see Michael J. O'Driscoll, "Derrida, Foucault, and the Archiviolithics of History," in *After Poststructuralism: Writing the Intellectual History of Theory*, ed. Tilottama Rajan and Michael J. O'Driscoll (Toronto: University of Toronto Press, 2002), 284–309.

incoherence. Yet these vulnerabilities in the encyclopedia are its cardinal virtues if you oppose coherentism, immutability, and a totalizing portrait of the known, as the editors of the late eighteenth-century French *Encyclopédie* did, and as the early-twentieth-century novelists they inspired did in their turn. The archive and the encyclopedia: two adjacent dreams of total information, two Enlightenment projects in parallel, each vexed by its own internal fire. Parallel, but converging at the vanishing point—where all encyclopedias become archival through obsolescence.

PART TWO

A mile out of Dublin he stopped short: *Edward Young*
"I am unpacking my library. Yes I am—   *Walter Benjamin*
Its precious ashes, its black unmalleable coal."   *Michel Foucault*

{ 4 }

Encyclopedic Modernism

ENCYCLOPÉDIE. Laugh at it pityingly for being quaint and old-fashioned; even so: thunder against.

—Gustave Flaubert, *Le dictionnaire des idées reçues* (pub. 1911)

A war machine.

—Gustave Desnoiresterres on the *Encyclopédie*, quoted in the "Encyclopaedia" entry in the *Encyclopaedia Britannica* (1910–11)

On the last day of the 1964–65 New York World's Fair, Donald C. Burnham, the head of Westinghouse Electric, emceed at a strange interment: the final lowering of his company's time capsule down a fifty-foot-deep "immortal well." There, under Flushing Meadows, Time Capsule II would repose a few feet from its predecessor, the Time Capsule of Cupaloy, which Westinghouse had assembled and buried in 1938. A seven-ton granite monument would mark the site, indicating that the two reliquaria should remain undisturbed until the year 6939. "In these Time Capsules," Burnham said, "men 5,000 years from now can find a record of civilization—a record which could be more priceless to them than the Rosetta stone, or the Pyramids, or the Dead Sea Scrolls have been to us." The committee tasked with the "encyclopedic chore" of producing this record of twentieth-century civilization had filled seventeen cans of archival-quality microfilm with selections from hundreds of sources—"encyclopedias, magazines, newspapers, technical papers, pamphlets, catalogs, transcripts, and 29 texts written especially for the capsule by international experts," said a press release—and had supplemented this archive with scientific experiments, sound recordings of modern music and world leaders' greetings, and the signatures of nearly a million World's Fair visitors, including President Johnson and Pope Paul VI. There were proud samples of postwar Scientific Developments, from birth control pills and antibiotics to a plastic heart valve, a laser rod, and a computer memory unit.

FIG. 4.1. *Loading Westinghouse Electric's Time Capsule II, October 1, 1964. Printed by permission of the Thomas and Katherine Detre Library and Archives, Sen. John Heinz History Center.*

And there were the Articles of Common Use, a kind of Cold War consumer survival kit including filtered cigarettes, tranquilizers, contact lenses, plastic wrap, freeze-dried food, detergent, credit cards, a bikini, and a Beatles record, all encased in a leak-proof, argon-filled glass envelope.[1] After eulogizing Time Capsule II, Burnham pressed a button to commit it to the earth. Gleaming and torpedo-shaped (Fig. 4.1), the 465-pound Kromarc stainless steel capsule looked like nothing so much as a nuclear missile being winched into its silo.

Even Westinghouse's 1938 capsule had testified to the symbiotic growth of weapons and informational payloads. The *Book of Record of the Time Capsule of Cupaloy*, which the company sent to libraries and museums around the world in the hopes of aiding the capsule's future recovery, is an exercise in geopolitically strained optimism: "[H]istory teaches us that every culture

---

[1] Westinghouse Electric Corporation, "Time Capsule II Deposited for 5,000 Years at World's Fair," press release, October 16, 1965; and Westinghouse Electric Corporation, "1965 Commemorative Brochure," n.p. The Beatles record was a seven-inch single, "A Hard Day's Night" b/w "I Should Have Known Better."

passes through definite cycles of development, climax and decay. And so, we must recognize, ultimately may ours," the introduction reads. "We choose . . . to believe that men will solve the problems of the world, that the human race will triumph over its limitations and its adversities, that the future will be glorious."[2] But the *Book of Record*'s list of late-1930s newsreels archived inside the capsule records a mobilizing world—the U.S. Pacific Fleet on maneuvers, the Soviet army marching in Red Square, a demonstration of American war machines, and footage of the bombing of Canton showing "Terror-stricken civilians in street." Time Capsule II would gesture toward the nuclear balance of terror as its enabling condition. The 1938 capsule had contained a message to the future from an Albert Einstein disquieted by the prospect of war; its successor featured the physicist's 1939 letter to President Roosevelt announcing the feasibility of atomic weapons.[3] Among the Cold War mandarins who made up Time Capsule II's selection committee were Vannevar Bush and James B. Conant, former members of the National Defense Research Committee that had overseen the Manhattan Project. Before stepping down as president at Harvard in 1953, Conant had asked the university librarian to draw up, in Robert J. Lifton and Greg Mitchell's account, "a report on books and other printed material that would constitute a record of our civilization—to be microfilmed in ten copies and buried in different places around the country. Conant explained that the atomic bomb might cause our present civilization to 'come to an end,' and we should try to avoid what happened when Rome fell and almost all written records were lost."[4] Although lacking Conant's provision of multiple, dispersed copies, Time Capsule II was similarly envisioned as a comprehensive archive made necessary by the prospect of apocalypse.

Provisioning, burial, outlasting catastrophe inside a hardened bunker: Time Capsule II expanded the logic of the backyard fallout shelter to the scale of a civilization's informational legacy. But if nuclear weapons gave the disaster-proof archive both a singular referent and a greater urgency, the creation of the first capsule in 1938 proves that such a project antedated the nuclear condition. As we have seen, the 1920s and '30s were replete with apocalyptic "next war" scenarios in speculative fiction as well as in military theory and civil defense

---

[2] Westinghouse Electric Corporation, *Book of Record of the Time Capsule of Cupaloy: Deemed Capable of Resisting the Effects of Time for Five Thousand Years, Preserving an Account of Universal Achievements, Embedded in the Grounds of the New York World's Fair, 1939* (Utica, NY: G. Leonard Gold, 1938), 5, 18.

[3] A sentence from the 1938 message reads, "Furthermore, people living in different countries kill each other at irregular time intervals, so that also for this reason any one who thinks about the future must live in fear and terror." Ibid., 49. Time Capsule II's August 2, 1939, letter, signed by Einstein, seems to have been written largely by physicist Leó Szilárd.

[4] Robert J. Lifton and Greg Mitchell, *Hiroshima in America: Fifty Years of Denial* (New York: G. P. Putnam's Sons, 1995), 226–27.

planning. In the face of their rampant depictions of humanity bombed back to a preliterate condition, building a repository for civilization's crowning discoveries and achievements would have seemed a crucial undertaking well before 1945. Far more surprising than the existence of the 1938 Time Capsule is the fact that it shared one of its core motivations with a knowledge-compassing form prominently featured in its microfilm library: the encyclopedia. Not the familiar *Britannicas* and *Americanas* of the twentieth century but the eighteenth-century *Encyclopédie* (1751–1772), that acme of Enlightenment optimism. As the *Encyclopédie*'s editor Denis Diderot wrote in 1755 in his famous metadiscursive entry, "Encyclopedia,"

> The most glorious moment for a work of this sort would be that which might come immediately in the wake of some catastrophe so great as to suspend the progress of science and interrupt the labors of craftsmen, and plunge a portion of our hemisphere in darkness once again. What gratitude would not be lavished by the generation that came after this time of troubles upon those men who had discerned the approach of disaster from afar, who had taken measures to ward off its worst ravages by collecting in a safe place the knowledge of all past ages![5]

Working in the anticipation of some disaster-to-come, Diderot and his collaborators saw that their glory would come from having enabled the survivors of some sudden darkening to rekindle the Enlightenment. For their part, Conant and Bush had helped give the disaster-to-come a new face and imminence through their oversight of the Manhattan Project. In 1965, with their colleagues on the Time Capsule II Selection Committee, they looked for an atonement Diderot and his coeditor Jean le Rond d'Alembert would have understood: they became nuclear encyclopedists.

Against Epic

Part two of this book turns to a literary site where the encyclopedia and twentieth-century warfare converge: a cluster of interwar modernist narratives that aimed to convey a comprehensive portrait of societies that the rise of total war discourse had made seem at once more visible and more vulnerable. Inasmuch as these literary works sought to archive a city, national culture, historical moment, or worldview against the eventuality of its erasure, they were the unlikely predecessors of the Westinghouse Time Capsules,

---

[5] Denis Diderot, "Encyclopédie," *Encyclopédie*, vol. 5 (1755), rpt. as "The Encyclopedia" in *Rameau's Nephew and Other Works*, trans. Jacques Barzun and Ralph H. Bowen (Indianapolis: Bobbs-Merrill, 1964), 290. Further references are cited in the text as "E." Barzun and Bowen translate only part of Diderot's full entry—hence my referring below to other translations and to the French edition.

although they staked their survival on dissemination rather than on hardened, hermetic burial. My main examples, to be taken up at length in the two chapters following this one, are James Joyce's *Ulysses* (1922) and Ford Madox Ford's *Parade's End* tetralogy (1924–28), with Robert Musil's *Der Mann ohne Eigenschaften* (1930–43) being touched on more briefly. Others include Marcel Proust's *À la recherche du temps perdu* (1913–27), Italo Svevo's *La coscienza di Zeno* (1923), Thomas Mann's *Der Zauberberg* (1924), Alfred Döblin's *Berlin Alexanderplatz* (1929), and Hermann Broch's *Die Schlafwandler* (1931–32). Previously, when these books have been read together at all they have been understood as part of a much longer tradition of "modern epics" or "world texts" stretching back as far as the early seventeenth century. Such a longitudinal approach has helped us to see affinities and similarities among works that are, in some cases, centuries apart. But it has also tended to emphasize these shared traits without considering their more immediate historical provocations and correlates. What's more, to create a centuries-long genre and genealogy of *opere mondo* is to accede to a claim made, at least implicitly, by the works themselves: that their singularity is so extreme that we must scour remote places and times in search of their scarce counterparts. Critics who overinvest in this *rara avis* pose of modern epics can be driven, in turn, to extreme formulations on the works' behalf—claims of elephantine gestation, prevision, and even literary messianism, all of which we will encounter below. I take a different approach in what follows, limiting my focus to a constellation of interwar works and reading their insistence on singularity as an index of what they most crucially share: the attempt to furnish an alternative world-picture to modern warfare's portrait of the social totality. Such a counter-portrait needs to present itself as unique in order not to seem one among many soft options. Yet the interwar period produced modern epics in numbers sufficient to belie such singularity-claims and to demand an account of these texts that relates them to the aftermath and the possible resurgence of what the same period was learning to call total war.

"Modern epic," the term by which these works are most commonly known, is not only a consequential misnomer but also a misrecognition entangled in the same coherentist political logic these works sought to challenge.[6] As Herbert Tucker writes of epic scholarship generally, "Our unanimity as theorists of epic savors of codependency with the unanimity that, we all agree, is

---

[6] Among literary scholars, the term "modern epic" is mostly closely associated with Franco Moretti's *Modern Epic: The World System from Goethe to García Márquez*, trans. Quintin Hoare (London: Verso, 1996), further references to which will be cited in the text. But the term has a broader currency that antedates Moretti's study. In a 1986 review in the *Atlantic Monthly*, for example, the novelist Martin Amis called Joyce's *Ulysses* "degraded epic, modern epic"; see Martin Amis, "The War Against Cliché: James Joyce's *Ulysses*," rpt. in *The War Against Cliché: Essays and Reviews: 1971–2000* (New York: Vintage, 2001), 442.

constitutive of epic itself."[7] A device for producing and authorizing consensus among its listeners and readers, epic has produced an impressive degree of critical consensus about itself into the bargain. That critical consensus takes, as both its object and its tacit sponsor, the notion of organic national totality of which epic is the default genre. And as Hegel pointed out in his lectures on fine art, both national holism and its signature literary genre are galvanized by war: "conflict in a state of war [is] the situation most suited to epic. For in war it is precisely the whole nation which is set in motion and which experiences a fresh stimulus and activity in its entire circumstances, because here the whole has an inducement to answer for itself."[8] A hundred years before the expression's first use, something like total war is presupposed in Hegel's characterization of epic: a nation wholly animated by war produces epic accounts of itself as an integrated, self-identical, self-fulfilling totality. Given how the genre's traditional dedication to "inviolable societal unison" (Tucker, 15) makes it a willing conscript in times of fully mobilized warfare, we will not be surprised to find critics in the century of total war recruiting even highly resistant texts into the ranks of national epic.

In challenging what Tucker calls the "strong-modernist heterodoxy" (6) that reads *Ulysses* and its genre-mates as evidence of a spontaneous post-1918 resurgence of epic, I also contest the orthodox view that epic belonged to some long-superseded age and could only be revived inorganically.[9] That orthodox view can be traced from Hegel's lectures into the twentieth century, when it was taken up, albeit with widely differing inflections and argumentative motives, by Georg Lukács, Walter Benjamin, and Mikhail Bakhtin.[10] Epic, according to this still-dominant view, belonged to an irretrievably distant

---

[7] Herbert F. Tucker, *Epic: Britain's Heroic Muse, 1790–1910* (New York: Oxford University Press, 2008), 13. Further references are cited in the text.

[8] Georg Wilhelm Friedrich Hegel, *Aesthetics: Lectures on Fine Art*, vol. 2, trans. T. M. Knox (Oxford: Oxford University Press, 1975), 1059. Further references are cited in the text. Hegel adds that to be compatible with epic, a war must occur "between nations [rather than between dynasties or civil factions] hostilely disposed toward one another" and seeking "the justification claimed by a people at the bar of history, a claim which one people pursues against another"—a war "grounded in a higher necessity" than "a mere capricious attempt at subjection" (1061). These are exterminative wars in which civilizations duel for the right to survive—in essence, "total wars" in the sense in which Ludendorff would use the phrase in the 1930s. Fascinatingly, Hegel's stipulations about epic and unlimited war produce the one moment of speculative fiction in his lecture: "If now in contrast to [past] epics we contemplate others that may perhaps be composed in the future, then these might have nothing to describe except the victory, some day or other, of living American rationality over imprisonment in particulars and measurements prolonged for infinity. For in Europe nowadays each nation is bounded by another and may not of itself begin a war against another European nation; if we now want to look beyond Europe, we can only turn our eyes to America" (1062).

[9] As proponents of the strong-modernist heterodoxy Tucker names Hugh Kenner, *The Pound Era* (Berkeley: University of California Press, 1971); Paul Fussell, *The Great War and Modern Memory* (New York: Oxford University Press, 1975); Mary Ellis Gibson, *Epic Reinvented: Ezra Pound and the Victorians* (Ithaca: Cornell University Press, 1995); and Vincent Sherry, *The Great War and the Language of Modernism* (New York: Oxford University Press, 2003). See Tucker, 6n10.

[10] See Georg Lukács, *The Theory of the Novel: A Historico-Philosophical Essay on the Forms of Great Epic Literature*, trans. Anna Bostock (Cambridge, MA: MIT Press, 1971); Walter Benjamin, "The

moment of orality, plenitude, and cultural consensus from which the rise of the novel, whether as an embodied longing for epic's lost totality or as a welcome relief from its monologism, measures our distance. Here I make a divergent claim: that far from being an anachronism during the 1920s and '30s, epic was so congruent with the emergent discourse of total war as to seem utterly contemporary. As the name of unlimited warfare became speakable again after its brief metropolitan interdiction and consignment to the colonial periphery, what Hegel called the "total conspectus of the whole of the national spirit" ceased to be an asynchronous genre (1045). The rise of total war discourse effectively placed the present *inside* the political logic of epic, a logic that made war both the crucible and the connective matrix of any given national totality. To write in full-throated epic mode in the age of total war would be to accept the premise of Achilles' shield: that full militarization is the best, and maybe only, occasion for world portraiture. Set beside such an epic premise, the fragmentariness and internal fissuring of long modernist fictions begin to look less like the flaws through which a longed-for totality seeped away and more like a critical refusal of epic's all-too-vital political logic. These distended interwar works, that is, did not decline *from* epic but simply declined it, refusing to embrace its renewed contemporaneity. To read them as latter-day epics pure and simple, then, would be to mistake as the object of their mourning what is, in fact, the object of their resistance.

But if the world texts of interwar modernism refused the bellicose holism of epic, they did not shy away from that genre's massive scale, its radical inclusivity, or its ambitions to paint a comprehensive picture of national life. Rather than concede the project of collective portraiture to unlimited war, they looked to provide a counter-portrait of their respective totalities. Needless to say, these alternative world pictures differ in many ways from one another. Some pointedly confine their action to a single day or a single year, whereas others chronicle a span of years. Some make stylistic instability a principle of construction, even a subject of metacommentary; others leave their subtle fluctuations of technique unmarked. They take a variety of positions, often within a single text, with regard to the viability of the nation as a political form and its relationship to imperial circuits of production, consumption, exploitation, and violence. But they also share something crucial, an unwillingness to counter the totalizing political logic of epic with some equally totalizing alternative. These are works, in other words, that understand the project of synoptic representation as at once necessary and impossible: necessary insofar as the project must not be surrendered to total war;

Storyteller: Observations on the Works of Nikolai Leskov," in *Selected Writings, Vol. 3: 1935–1938*, trans. Edmund Jephcott, Howard Eiland, et al., ed. Howard Eiland and Michael W. Jennings (Cambridge, MA: Harvard University Press, 2002), 143–66; and M. M. Bakhtin, *The Dialogic Imagination*, trans. Caryl Emerson and Michael Holquist, ed. Michael Holquist (Austin: University of Texas Press, 1981).

impossible in that the putatively total view is always at its root a partial one—tendentious, belated, occlusive, a view from somewhere that presents itself as a view from nowhere.[11]

Where the conventions of epic signal a self-enclosed world that already knows what it needs to know about itself, the techniques of modernist counter-epics index competing bodies, idioms, and systems of knowledge and their imperfect possession by communities that are themselves contested objects of knowledge and identification. The episodes of epic tend to build on one another through confident, if modally varied, aggregation; those of counter-epic radically reinterpret, and frequently undermine, one another. And where epic authorizes itself by routinely fulfilling its own prophecies, the interwar *opera mondo* either eschews prophecy altogether or indulges in it for the sake of putting it on display as one form of historical utterance among many. Such properties are irreducible to a single critical function. But in respect to the present context, they are the means by which modernist counter-epic interrupts its own tendency to replicate the totalizing energy of epic in the course of resisting its political logic. Internal compartmentalization, conflicted discursive zones and organizational schemata, self-contradictory systems of internal cross-reference—these are the means by which the genre delimits and impedes the project it nonetheless cannot refuse to undertake, a project that must be comprehensive while emphatically avoiding coherentism. And the name I wish to give this repertoire of necessary–impossible negotiations is *encyclopedism*.

This may seem like precisely the wrong term to oppose to the national self-assurance of epic. We hardly think of the encyclopedia as a conflicted, self-disrupting project that welcomes formal instability, contradictoriness, or play. Quite the opposite: it has the reputation of subjecting all topics to the descriptive rationalism that is both its premise and its house style, of bullying the world into compliance with its organizational grids and drives, of typifying Enlightenment arrogance in its claim to encompass the known. The encyclopedia stays unacquainted with the precariousness of its undertaking—with the caprice of its organizational rubrics, with the ephemerality of its contents, with knowledge's inseparability from representation. Instead, encyclopedias are seen as adhering to a conventional subject/object distinction whereby

---

[11] The 1920s encyclopedic novels I refer to are partial antecedents of the Mass-Observation movement of the 1930s insofar as it was, in James Buzard's words, "unable to decide whether the British culture it went in search of was something amenable to—even longing for—totalization, or something anathema to it." See his "Mass-Observation, Modernism, and Auto-ethnography," *Modernism/modernity* 4.3 (September 1997): 93–122. Buzard likens Mass-Observation's *May the Twelfth* (1937) to modernist day-books such as *Ulysses, Mrs. Dalloway, The Waves*, and *Under the Volcano* in its use of both immersive and disruptive auto-ethnographic techniques, and of both mythologizing and normalizing gestures, to counteract the state's totalizing auto-ethnographic accounts of George VI's coronation.

knowledge is instrumentalized, even propertized, for the convenience of a subject who does not deform the epistemological field by appearing within it. Compelled by standardized editorial procedures to hierarchize its contents, the encyclopedia scales the length of its entries to their perceived importance. And its modern incarnations tend to be riveted, often in name, to nations, as if only for the sake of national totalities could so monumental a project as the *Encyclopaedia Britannica* or the *Encyclopedia Americana* be undertaken. Self-enclosed, confident, unitary, nation-based: the encyclopedia in reputation sounds like nothing so much as a "total conspectus of the whole of the national spirit," in Hegel's phrase, and thus more like epic's heir or double than like its adversary. This seeming allegiance is pulled taut by the frequent listing of "encyclopedism" among the traits and techniques of epic (simile, catalogue, ekphrasis, heroic founding narrative, *descensus Averni*), as if the encyclopedia were simply an epic mode or subgenre.[12] The two are further trussed together by literary critics who give the name "encyclopedic narrative" to a genre indistinguishable in their accounts from epic, or who solder the two into new generic assemblages—"epic-encyclopedic novels"—that threaten to eliminate not just the oppositions but even the simple differences between the contributing genres.[13]

Largely catalyzed by Michel Foucault's *Les mots et les choses* (1966), and in particular by its discussion of Borges's Chinese Encyclopedia, recent scholarship on the *Encyclopédie* has sought to undo our tendency to conflate Diderot and d'Alembert's project with its more regimented, less overtly self-reflexive descendants by spotlighting both the contingencies of the *Encyclopédie* and its unapologetic cognizance of them. The revised portrait of that work is in many ways antithetical to the common view of the encyclopedia I summed up above. A profoundly metadiscursive project, it drew attention to its several and conflicted organizational axes, to their arbitrariness, and to the corrective, satirical, and subversive functions of cross-reference. It was, and knew itself to be, a work of uneven execution and ghastly disproportion, a work whose many contributors were enjoined to contradict one another. Written in French to signal its competition with encyclopedias in other national languages, it tried to ensure its future legibility by anchoring its key terms in dead, supposedly fixed languages. Although planted emphatically in the French nation and culture, it was an intellectually and materially multinational undertaking that was several times suspended and condemned by the

---

[12] Tucker writes that epic catalogue and simile, together, "put the *encyclo-* into the modern *paideia* that fell to epic as the genre that, in theory, knew it all" (29). See also Massimo Fusillo, "Epic, Novel," trans. Michael F. Moore, in *The Novel*, Vol. 1, ed. Franco Moretti (Princeton: Princeton University Press, 2006), 41.

[13] See my discussion of Edward Mendelson's "Gravity's Encyclopedia," below. On the epic-encyclopedic novel, see Fusillo, "Epic, Novel," 54.

French parliament for fomenting "a spirit of independence and revolt" and for "the corruption of morals and religion."[14] Its editor, meanwhile, claimed to write for a posterity when "the name *Frenchman*—a name that will endure forever in history—will be sought after in vain on the surface of the earth" ("E," 306). A monument to knowledge, it insisted that its contents could be superseded, its structure validly laughed at, and the conditions of its legibility effaced by linguistic drift, scientific revolutions, and natural and political disasters. None of which is to downplay the *Encyclopédie*'s vaulting ambition "to know and describe the universal system of nature and of art." That ambition, rather, was understood by the project's editors to entail a world of checks and caveats, monstrosities and incongruities. It was just this collision of zeal and flaw that would make the encyclopedia a compelling example for interwar practitioners of long-form narrative, allowing them to address the problem of epic while rejecting its solutions.

As a way of clearing space for the readings that follow in chapters 5 and 6, the present chapter prizes the encyclopedia loose from epic. It does this in three parts. The first draws on recent studies of Diderot's *Encyclopédie* to develop a portrait of that project's historical, political, epistemological, and formal volatility. The second considers how these volatilities persisted in later encyclopedias, particularly the eleventh edition of the *Britannica*, which appeared in 1910–11 and was of crucial significance to a number of Anglophone modernists. And the third revisits three influential constructions of the genre in question—Edward Mendelson's work on encyclopedic narrative, Franco Moretti's on modern epic, and Leo Bersani's on encyclopedic fiction—in the hope of unsettling some of the habits of thought ingrained in (and by) this work. These habits include, on the one hand, overcrediting the singularity claims immanent in the novels themselves, to the point of installing them in narratives of prophecy, messianism, history-transcending generic coherence, and outlandishly long gestation; and, on the other, a tendency to condemn the novels for the putative sins of their interpretive communities, as if a work could fully dictate the terms of its reception and canonization. These habits seem opposed, one exhibiting an excess of credulity, the other an excess of critical animus. But they share a coherentism on the part of the critic, a conviction that the capacious fiction is at one with its apparent claims for itself, which are of a piece with the work's interpreters. This is not just to misread encyclopedic fictions as epic, it is to do so from within a coherentist critical habitus—to be inside the lamp of epic, reading all objects by its light.

---

[14] Nelly S. Hoyt and Thomas Cassirer, "Introduction" to *Encyclopedia: Selections by Diderot, d'Alembert, and a Society of Men of Letters*, trans. Nelly S. Hoyt and Thomas Cassirer (Indianapolis: Bobbs-Merrill, 1965), xi.

In chapter 2 I argued that Virginia Woolf undertook, over the course of many works and years, an immanent critique of total war; that her pacifism inhabited and even imitated certain logics of the war machine rather than rejecting or opposing it outright. In the wake of that reading, my dichotomous treatment of the epic and the encyclopedia here may seem strange. Why insist on such discrete formal lineages in thinking about the antecedents of interwar modernist narratives? Why not embrace the hybrid genre of "epic-encyclopedic novel"? As I said earlier, the traits shared by the epic and the encyclopedia—massive inclusivity and national authority—can distract us from their deep incompatibilities. Even if we eventually read the narrative works in question as novelistic compounds of epic and encyclopedia, we fail to appreciate the instability of those compounds if we do not first understand their constitutive elements. Two disparities between epic and encyclopedia will be especially important for us. The first is their respective treatments of disaster. Although the Enlightenment encyclopedia does not quite anticipate twentieth-century fiction in representing the effacement of its own conditions of legibility, the catastrophic imagination is nonetheless fundamental to it. It was conceived as a bulwark against knowledge-loss, whether by natural or political disaster or by the sheer superfluity of discourse. Pulled in opposite directions by these two scenarios, the genre comprehends its own impossibility, understanding itself as disproportionate, transitory, and full of the wrong amounts of the wrong things. Epic, in contrast, presupposes its own unbroken transmissibility and thus cannot truly imagine the disaster of its protagonist culture.[15] Nor, being confident of its adequacy to the task of total representation, can epic imagine a superfluity of discourse in which what matters could drown. This first set of distinctions overlaps with a second, having to do with epistemology. Epic conceives of its knowledge-world as fully mapped and integrated; it transmits knowledge as a given along vectors of unbroken continuity and community. The encyclopedia imparts knowledge as a produced thing, indeed stages its production, while being aware of its ephemerality. As against the leisurely pace of epic, the encyclopedia is in a hurry to transmit knowledge that is changing even as it is being transmitted; to store it up as a provision against its loss; to produce comprehensive knowledge maps without disguising their contingent and artifactual qualities. It is unafraid of

---

[15] Epic, for all its interest in epochal nation-founding events, can neither represent a catastrophic event befalling its chosen society nor invoke the possibility of such an event as a spur to its being. Catastrophe, for epic, is something that happens to other societies, the survival and uninterrupted transmissibility of the protagonist nation being the genre's fundamental premise. Because this rage for continuity outstrips even its rage for order, epic cannot house the encyclopedia, with its discontinuous imagination, even as one among the many modes it does routinely incorporate (georgic, pastoral, ballad, etc.).

obsolescence, contradiction, or incompatible orders of order—prospects that epic also does not fear, but only because it cannot recognize them.

We begin to have a sense, then, of the repellent forces that would have to be overcome by a work that fused the epic and the encyclopedia. But at the same time that we take care not to conflate the two genres, we should bear in mind the effects—and, it may be, the tactical advantages—of their susceptibility to conflation. For it is partly owing to their similarities that the encyclopedia could provide novelists with a properly scaled alternative to modern warfare's portrait of the world on a shield. Provide them, too, with a certain cover for energies deeply at odds with the twentieth century's promotion of epic to a geopolitical super-genre. For inside the Greek gift of epic, interwar modernists harbored the oppositional spirits of Diderot, d'Alembert, and other encyclopedists, of whom they were better readers than we are today. Where we might describe the *Encyclopédie* as organizing "essential general knowledge in taxonomic displays granting privilege to the tabular synopsis of reason" (Tucker, 21), interwar narrative commemorates, and sometimes seems to emulate, the protracted years of composition, revision, and censorship that separated the serial publications of those displays. It remembers as well the encyclopedists' sense of their rubrics' arbitrariness—that far from projecting all knowledge onto a single homogenous table, the *Encyclopédie* was crisscrossed by multiple rubrics and haunted by the sense that its organization might have been utterly different. And where more recent encyclopedias appear to materialize knowledge as stable, self-enclosed, and invulnerable, interwar encyclopedic fiction reminds us that the prospect of catastrophic knowledge loss was a motivating premise for Diderot et al., who imagined the inevitable obsolescence of their work as a welcome consequence of its survival.

Revisiting the *Encyclopédie*

Diderot's great project was an engine of metadiscourse. Its first public self-description, the 1750 "Prospectus" by Diderot, preceded the work itself by seven months; its second, d'Alembert's celebrated "Discours préliminaire des editeurs," absorbed the substance of the "Prospectus" into a longer preface to the *Encyclopédie*'s first volume, published in June 1751. After an *arrêt du Conseil* interrupted publication in 1753, D'Alembert retorted with an "Avertissement" in the third volume. But the project's fourth and final metatext was its most telling, its most daring, and its most symptomatic. This was Diderot's long "Encyclopédie" entry, which appeared, in due alphabetical course, under "e" in Volume 5 of the *Encyclopédie* in 1755. The entry classifies the encyclopedia as a philosophical concept, indulges in an atypical moment of etymologizing, then sets off in a tone of stately self-importance:

ENCYCLOPEDIA, noun, feminine gender. (*Philosophy.*) This word signifies *unity of knowledge* [*enchaînement de connaissances*]; it is made up of the Greek prefix εν, *in*, and the nouns κύκλος, *circle*, and παιδεία, *instruction, science, knowledge*.

In truth, the aim of an *encyclopedia* is to collect all the knowledge that now lies scattered over the face of the earth, to make known its general structure to the men among whom we live, and to transmit it to those who will come after us, in order that the labors of past ages may be useful to the ages to come, that our grandsons, as they become better educated, may at the same time become more virtuous and more happy, and that we may not die without having deserved well of the human race.

It would have been difficult to set for oneself a more enormous task than this of dealing with everything that relates to man's curiosity, his duties, his needs and his pleasures. Accordingly, some people, accustomed as they are to judging the feasibility of an enterprise by the poverty of their own resources, have asserted that we would never finish our task. ("E," 277)

There is an odd drift inside the grandeur of those first paragraphs: from generic distance ("*an* encyclopedia"), the reader is led along a chain of deictics ("among whom *we* live," "those who will come after *us*," "*our* grandsons") to the present unfinished work ("a more enormous task than *this*") and the hopes of its mortal authors ("that *we* may not die without having deserved well"). For a project anchored in rational distance and aiming to present each thing in its "true proportion," as the same entry later claims, such a quick, defensive cancellation of the generic in favor of the specific is, at the very least, stunningly peculiar.[16] There is the strange sense, too, of a speaker intending to stay outside the descriptive frame only to find himself—only to inscribe himself, impulsively—at its center, as if he had suddenly fused with the object of description.

Readers of the original fifth volume would have noticed something else anomalous about Diderot's "Encyclopédie" entry: although it subordinates its privileged subject to the alphabetical structure of the work, the entry was not paginated in the same manner as the rest of the volume. According to his friend Jean-Jacques Rousseau, Diderot composed the essay while he was ill, the stresses of the project and its reception having undermined his health. Submitted belatedly, the piece had to be inserted by the printer at the last minute. This was no serene, distanced moment of metadiscourse, then, but a sickroom rush job, a materialist account of knowledge whose originary

---

[16] See Denis Diderot, *Diderot: Oeuvres complètes*, vol. 7 (*Encyclopédie* III, Lettres D–L), ed. John Lough and Jacques Proust (Paris: Hermann, 1976), 215. Further references, all to vol. 7, are cited in the text as *DOC* followed by page number, in my translation except where otherwise noted.

conditions left their mark on the material text.[17] Even if we decouple the
piece from its author's illness, the "Encyclopédie" entry reads, at points, like
a high-functioning *écriture malade*: digressive, mottled, indiscreet, yet possessed of a feverish liveliness and range. One of its achievements is to read the
encyclopedic project itself as necessarily unwell, out of sorts, out of scale—as
variously overstuffed and starved. Surveying the volumes so far published,
Diderot writes,

> Here we are swollen and exorbitant, there meager, small, paltry, dry and
> emaciated. In one place we resemble skeletons; in another we have a
> dropsical air; we are alternately dwarfs and giants, colossi and pygmies;
> straight, well-made and proportioned; crooked, hump-backed, limp-
> ing, and deformed. Add to these oddities a style of discourse sometimes
> abstract, obscure or *recherché*, more often careless, long-winded and slack,
> and you have to compare the entire work to the monster in *l'Art poétique*, or
> to something even more hideous. (*DOC*, 214)[18]

The work's disproportion and inconsistency, Diderot continued, arose partly
from the need to write and publish quickly in the hopes of encompassing
the state of knowledge before it became obsolete. To an extent, these faults
might be addressed in subsequent editions, which would both update and
rebalance the original. But monstrosity was also an ineliminable feature of
a work whose far-flung contributors could not be expected to homogenize
their habits of thought, their ways of writing, or their sense of their subjects'
importance relative to the whole; a work whose manifold self-conceptions
and schemata were sometimes deeply at odds with one another and with the
work itself. What's more, the *Encyclopédie* and its editors were conversant
with its indelible strangeness. Whatever its other functions, it was to be a
compendium of self-contradiction and ill-assortedness in all their forms and
magnitudes—an encyclopedia of incongruities.

A central project of scholarship on the *Encyclopédie* since about 1980 has
been to restore a sense of the work's volatility, contingency, and formal complexity by tracing the figures and fissures in its self-descriptions and watching them play out over the surface of the work as a whole. This scholarship
tends to emphasize three related aspects of the *Encyclopédie*'s metatexts: their
multiple figurations and orderings of the work; their acknowledgement and,
indeed, defense of arbitrary organizational schemata; and their concern with

---

[17] Rousseau wrote in a November 23, 1755, letter, "L'article encyclopédie qui est de Diderot fait
l'admiration de tout Paris, et ce qui augmentera votre étonnement, c'est qu'il l'a fait étant malade."
See *DOC*, 174n1. On the materialist view of knowledge in Diderot's entry and throughout his work
generally, see Wilda Anderson, "Encyclopedia Topologies," *MLN* 101 (1986): 912–29.

[18] I have slightly emended the translation of this passage in P. N. Furbank, *Diderot: A Critical
Biography* (London: Secker & Warburg, 1992), 130–31.

futurity.[19] In developing a sense of the work's allure and importance for inter-war modernist narrative, I will reactivate each of these before turning to a fourth, the imagination of disaster.

Tree, world map, broad avenue, landscape, theater, labyrinth: these were the figures by which Diderot and d'Alembert sought to capture the *Encyclopédie*'s conception of knowledge as respectively branching, concentric, successively intersectional, encompassed, tiered, and complex. As a set of analogies for a knowledge-system, they clearly overlap without being fully compatible. A tree-like order branches in both time and space; an atlas presents an array of spatially nested, static overviews; landscape and stage show us objects ranked by depth plane in lateral Cartesian space. Taken as an ensemble, this staging of metaphor-as-series is a second-order figuration of a work whose vaunted *totality*—itself a spatial figure, perhaps modernity's master-figure for spatiality itself—can only be produced, apprehended, and perfected dia-chronically.[20] Hence Diderot's definition of *encyclopédie* as "enchaînement de connaissances" (*DOC*, 174): a rounding up of knowledge, or of the sciences, one link, one entry, one cross-reference at a time. This notion of a totality that is diachronically made, used, and grasped structures the *Encyclopédie* at its most basic level. Its metatexts follow both Francis Bacon and the British ency-clopedist Ephraim Chambers in presenting a diagrammatic "tree of knowl-edge," in which every entry is placed in an arborescent order stemming from history, philosophy, and poetry and their respective roots in the human facul-ties of memory, reason, and imagination. But as we have already seen with the "Encyclopédie" entry itself, the published work was not laid out treewise but instead subjected to the brute unbranching successiveness of the alphabet.

---

[19] And there are more than three, particularly if one is reading the *Encyclopédie* back from the vantage of interwar encyclopedic modernism. Recent scholarship has also focused on the work's installation of the human observer at the center of the field of observation, an innovation that dis-pensed with both the fiction of human nonimplication in the observed and the divine center of ear-lier encyclopedias. Several scholars have attended, too, to Diderot's construction of the *Encyclopédie* as a "body" that owes its being partly to the "dismemberment" of predecessor volumes (a claim made the more compelling by the fact that a number of the entries were appropriated nearly ver-batim—taken bodily, as it were—from Chambers's *Cyclopaedia* and other sources). On the central-ity of "man," see James Creech, "'Chasing After Advances': Diderot's Article 'Encyclopedia,'" *Yale French Studies* 63 (1982): 192, and Joanna Stalnaker, *The Unfinished Enlightenment: Description in the Age of the Encyclopedia* (Ithaca: Cornell University Press, 2010), 105–6. On the bodily, see Christie V. McDonald, *The Dialogue of Writing: Essays in Eighteenth-Century French Literature* (Waterloo, ON: Wilfred Laurier University Press, 1984), 80. On plagiarism, see John Lough, *The Encyclopédie* (New York: David McKay, 1971), 80–81.

[20] McDonald reads the "Encyclopédie" entry in similar terms, as staging the limits of the ency-clopedic method itself—as the place where a project that sought to determine the exact bound-aries of its topics nonetheless could "only speak of itself through analogy—through a network of images—which measures and at the same time plays upon those limits within which it must work." See McDonald, *Dialogue of Writing*, 75.

If, as Cynthia Koepp says, "The tree of knowledge looks more like a pile of leaves" when the alphabet is done with it, those leaves were nonetheless endowed with a memory of the dismembered tree. This was the function of the parenthetical locator terms with which each entry began—(*Philosophy*), for example, in the "Encyclopédie" article—and of the *renvois* or cross-references with which it concluded. Still, these did not prevent the alphabetical order from creating, as Diderot put it, "burlesque contrasts; an article on theology would find itself relegated to a position next to one on mechanical arts" (*DOC*, 217). Some commentators have read the alphabetical burlesque as the project's most radical move, its way of scrambling the hierarchies, and particularly the disdain for manual work, incarnate in knowledge trees such as Bacon's and even d'Alembert's. Koepp again: "in the *Encyclopédie* 'mendiant' precedes 'noblesse,' and 'chaircuitier' comes before 'clerc.' One can read more about the production of iron ore than about coats of arms."[21] But the virtues of alphabetical order—its convenience as a mode of access, its liquidation of hierarchy—precipitated out of a deeper, even more radical perception of necessity. Here I mean the encyclopedists' conviction that any tree of knowledge was perforce an arbitrary schema passed off as an authoritative one, and that instead of colluding in such a ruse it was better to embrace the more explicit arbitrariness of the alphabet.[22] Witness this moment in d'Alembert's "Discours préliminaire," where a modesty bordering on self-abnegation meets a Borgesian turn for counterfactual inventory:

> One could construct the tree of our knowledge by dividing it into natural and revealed knowledge, or useful and pleasing knowledge, or speculative and practical knowledge, or evident, certain, probable, and sensitive

---

[21] Cynthia J. Koepp, "The Alphabetical Order: Work in Diderot's *Encyclopédie*," in *Work in France: Representations, Meaning, Organization, and Practice*, ed. Steven Laurence Kaplan and Cynthia J. Koepp (Ithaca: Cornell University Press, 1986), 238. Koepp goes on to offer a complex account of the *Encyclopédie*'s focus on labor and craft. The project's aim of rendering orally transmitted artisanal practices into print, ostensibly to prevent their loss, made the same practices intelligible to those who would govern and dominate their use and execution. Thus conservation doubles as "a subtle and comprehensive expropriation," seeking "to remove the inefficient and inarticulate world of work from the hands and mouths of the workers and place it in printed form before the eyes of an enlightened 'management' whose ordered purposes it would serve" (Koepp, 257). It is worth remembering that comprehensive representation can, whatever the intention of its author, abet the domination of the thing or persons represented; recall Charlton going off to help police the Iraqi protectorate with a copy of *Ulysses* under his arm as an "official handbook" to the region.

[22] Of course the alphabet both is and isn't arbitrary. Its particular sequence may not be hierarchical in origin, but convention has made it second only to numerical order in troping sequentiality itself; thanks to the same convention, particular letters may be redolent of firstness, earliness, middleness, lateness, lastness. In works published alphabetically, the uneven correlation of production time with the ABCs often vitiates the distributive uniformity supposedly guaranteed by the order's arbitrariness. Koepp notes that Des Essarts's *Dictionnaire universel de police* (1786–90) ended prematurely with an entry on "police": in this case, "universality," says Koepp, "excludes words beginning with the letters *q* through *z*." See Koepp, "The Alphabetical Order," 234.

knowledge, or knowledge of things and knowledge of signs, and so on into infinity. . . . We are too aware of the arbitrariness which will always prevail in such a division to believe that our system is the only one or the best. It will be sufficient for us if our work is not entirely disapproved of by men of intelligence. . . . [O]ne should not attribute more advantages to our encyclopedic tree than we claim to give it. . . . It is a kind of enumeration of the knowledge that can be acquired—a frivolous enumeration for whoever would wish to let it go at that alone, but useful for whoever desires to go further.[23]

On the heels of a long rationale for the tree of knowledge, d'Alembert backs away, dubbing it arbitrary, provisional, useful only to the extent that it provokes its own supersession. Such passages reveal that the *Encyclopédie* was always the Chinese Encyclopedia out of Borges in its insistence that it could have been otherwise—that there are an infinite number of ways to organize order, each of them ludicrous from the perspective of the others. Even the alphabet as a solution to the problem of hierarchy is made implicitly arbitrary here. Taking d'Alembert's cue, you might well choose to abandon the twenty-six letters and parcel knowledge out, instead, into eighteen Homeric episodes, each with its own style, organ, color, and art. Or you might, if you were Musil, store the Viennese honey of the known in a vast hive of essayistic cells linked only perfunctorily by narrative. In either case, you would be presenting a picture of what a society knew, but one rooted in the view from somewhere, patterned less on the monolithic reputation of the encyclopedia and more on its actual connectivity, its miscellaneity, its eccentricity.

A moment ago I mentioned the *renvois*, or cross-references, which Diderot described as the *Encyclopédie*'s most important feature because they elevated it from a static work to a dynamic one. Together, the cross-references' two seemingly opposed functions embody the project's deep ambivalence about totality. On the one hand, the *renvois* were the very stuff of the work's internal coherence—what Diderot called "that unity so favorable to the establishment of truth and to its propagation" ("E", 295). They counteracted the deranging effects of alphabetical order by indicating an entry's place in the dispersed tree of knowledge. By directing readers of one article to another related one, they also obviated the need for repetition while ensuring that the *Encyclopédie* as a whole would be more wide-ranging than a specialized treatise. On the other hand, Diderot insisted, the *renvois* should set entries in opposition to one another and even undermine the authority of tendentious entries:

[23] Jean le Rond d'Alembert, *Preliminary Discourse to the Encyclopedia of Diderot*, trans. Richard N. Schwab and Walter E. Rex (Indianapolis: Bobbs-Merrill, 1963), 49–50, 58.

There should be great scope for ingenuity and infinite advantage for the authors in this latter sort of cross-reference. From them the work as a whole should acquire an inner force and a secret efficacy, the silent results of which will necessarily be felt with the passage of time. Each time, for instance, a national prejudice seems to merit respect, it will be necessary, in the article specially devoted to it, to discuss it respectfully and to surround it with all its panoply of probability and attractiveness; but by giving cross-references to articles where solid principles serve as the foundation for diametrically opposite truths, we shall be able to throw down the whole edifice of mud and scatter the idle heap of dust. This method of putting men on the right path works very promptly upon good minds, and it operates unfailingly, without the least undesirable effect, secretly and unobtrusively, upon all minds. ("E," 295–96)

For all that it might reassemble "the knowledge that lies scattered over the face of the earth," the *Encyclopédie* must also be adept at "scattering" knowledge-constructions when their foundations were weak. This it would do not by omitting or openly refuting them, but by means of subterfuge—by marshaling the "silent efficacy" of antagonistic cross-references under cover of a public deference. Diderot's embrace of secrecy, particularly in rectifying the opinions of the weak-minded, gives one pause. Yet the passage does more than advocate monologism by stealth, raising as it does the possibility that the *Encyclopédie*'s tacit positions may turn out to be errors or prejudices that some future editor will need to overthrow. In this sense, the work was truly, as Christie McDonald puts it, "homeostatic or self-regulating," equipping its heritors with the means to correct its unavoidable monologisms. Its coherence and futurity, both, lay in its capacity to be at odds with itself.[24]

The "Encyclopédie" entry alone contains rival ways of envisioning the futurity of the great project. We have already encountered Diderot's invocation of "those who will come after us" and "the ages to come" as the chief beneficiaries of the encyclopedists' labors. Posterity would, in turn, reward those labors by recognizing in them "the eternally lasting evidence of our talents enshrined in the monuments we raise to ourselves" ("E," 297). But if the future was to be the time of the *Encyclopédie*'s vindication, it would also be the time of its replacement by later, more perfect editions, each of these drawing closer to the "true encyclopedia" without ever reaching it. (Diderot: "I am forced to confess that hardly two-thirds of an Encyclopedia such as ours would be included in a true encyclopedia" [*DOC*, 236].) With its eye prospectively trained on a more proportionate and epistemologically stable ideal, the *Encyclopédie* is, in a sense, a materialized anticipation of

---

[24] McDonald, 85.

the *Encyclopédie*-to-come. Its expectant temporality leads James Creech to identify prolepsis—in its ancient Greek roots, a "taking beforehand"—as the project's master-trope. For Creech, the work's most basic proleptic channels are the *renvois*, which perennially refer readers toward some future when the work of definition will at last be completed.[25] But there are broader, stranger prolepses at work in the *Encyclopédie*, forms of anticipation that verge uncomfortably, for this avowedly rational monument, on prophecy:

> [Y]ou must know the state of mind of your nation, foresee the direction of its future development, hasten to anticipate its progress so that the march of events will not leave your book behind but will rather overtake it along the road; you must be prepared to work solely for the good of future generations because the moment of your own existence quickly passes away, and a great enterprise is not likely to be finished before the present generation ceases to exist. ("E," 288)

Under the encyclopedist's job description, read "national prophet," at least to the extent that accurate forecasting could delay the project's unavoidable obsolescence. The passage hauntingly captures the untimeliness of the *Encyclopédie*: owing to the work's magnitude, its makers could not be the contemporaries of its principal readers, "whom we esteem and whom we love, even though they have not yet been born" ("E," 297). To reach and serve unborn readers, the encyclopedists would need to write as if they were themselves from the future, and thus, like Jenkinson's archivist, not the contemporaries of their contemporaries. Such a remit overturns the common portrait of the encyclopedist as one who sifts and condenses present knowledge for present readers.

At the heart of the *Encyclopédie*'s proleptic imagination, one more self-authorizing narrative towers over even the conceit of a prospective writing for the unborn. This is the notion that the work might one day act as a repository against the loss of accumulated human knowledge. Diderot provided two scenarios for such a loss. In the first, the proliferation of printed matter would become so great that "it will be almost as convenient to search for some bit of truth concealed in nature as it will be to find it hidden away in an immense multitude of bound volumes" ("E," 299). With recorded knowledge growing as vast and unnavigable as the world, the *Encyclopédie* would save its readers, in this first scenario, by condensing the known back down to a useable scale. But the work's "most glorious moment" would arise from Diderot's second scenario. In the event of "some catastrophe so great as to

---

[25] Creech, 187. Indeed, for Creech, writing in 1982, the *renvoi* structure "refers us to Derrida, anticipates Derrida" (191)—particularly the Derrida of "Hors Livre"—in its stark materialization of *différance* and its implication that semantic plenitude can only be spoken of in the future anterior tense (the "will have been" of definition).

suspend the progress of science and interrupt the labors of craftsmen and plunge a portion of our hemisphere in darkness once again," he wrote, the survivors would lavish gratitude on those who "had discerned the approach of disaster and had taken measures to ward off its worst ravages by collecting in a safe place the knowledge of all past ages!" ("E," 290). D'Alembert, in the "Discours préliminaire," went farther, unspooling a scene by turns counter-factual and proleptic:

> Let us hope that posterity will say, upon opening our Dictionary: such was the state of the sciences and the fine arts then. May the history of the human mind and its productions continue from age to age until the most distant centuries. May the Encyclopedia become a sanctuary, where the knowledge of man is protected from time and from revolutions. Will we not be more than flattered to have laid its foundations? What an advantage would it have been for our fathers and for us, if the works of the ancient peoples, the Egyptians, the Chaldeans, the Greeks, the Romans, etc., had been trans-mitted in an encyclopedic work, which had also set forth the true principles of their languages? Therefore, let us do for centuries to come what we regret that past centuries did not do for ours. We daresay that if the ancients had carried through that encyclopedia, as they carried through so many other great things, and if that manuscript alone had escaped from the famous Library of Alexandria, it would have been capable of consoling us for the loss of the others.[26]

Gone is the modesty with which d'Alembert acknowledged the arbitrariness of the work's structure. Here the *Encyclopédie* emerges not only as sanctuary and time capsule, but also as a stay against the next Dark Age and a com-pensation for the last one. If its ancient equivalent might have consoled us for the loss of the rest of the Library of Alexandria, this new Encyclopedia would enact a retroactive consolation, ending our protracted mourning by preventing the next catastrophic knowledge-loss. A kind of safe house or protective fold in *Aufklärung*-space, it would do nothing less than save the Enlightenment project from its most drastic ramification: revolution.

The *Encyclopédie*'s most "glorious" function—to act as a knowledge cache in the event of some massive historical discontinuity—points to the work's vividest difference from epic. For epic, a people are crucially renewed and defined by conflict; for Diderot and d'Alembert's project, conflict poses the single greatest threat to a society's defining achievements. The fantasy of pre-serving the Enlightenment against such a threat might have led the encyclo-pedists to mimic epic's conceit of "inviolable societal unison" by adopting a putatively self-identical, totalizing form. But instead of making epic holism

---

[26] D'Alembert, 121–22.

safe for peacetime, the *Encyclopédie* did something like the inverse: it made history's volatility the impetus for amassing knowledge while insisting, at the same time, on the volatility of that mass. Catastrophe is not the dark inverse of the encyclopedic project but one of its central self-authorizing narratives; one of its signal traits, too, insofar as catastrophe (etymologically an "overturning") is what awaits most amassed knowledge in time, and is thus the operation both documented and abetted by the project. For the encyclopedists, knowledge could not be produced by denying the contingency of its arrangement, the brevity of its dominion, or the fragility of the historical conditions best suited to its persistence. The *Encyclopédie*'s embrace of volatility was the fire at its heart. Imagine being an ambitious, knowledge-crammed writer living in the immediate aftermath of the First World War, the Bolshevik Revolution, and the Easter Rising. Imagine seeing in the rise of air war, the Treaty of Versailles, continued anticolonial agitation, and the rise of fascism the emergent conditions for another global convulsion. Imagine how the shopworn claims of the French encyclopedists might suddenly have shone.

The Eleventh

That new luster would have been both muted and transmitted by the celebrated eleventh edition of the *Encyclopaedia Britannica*. Published in 1910–11, some 150 years after Diderot's *Encyclopédie*, "the eleventh" stood, with supplements, until the Great Depression and was the standard reference work used by Anglophone writers of the period, including a number of those later dubbed modernists.[27] In contrast to Diderot's project, the eleventh swore allegiance to national and imperial sovereignty, announcing on its first page that it was

---

[27] Joyce mined the eleventh in composing both *Ulysses* (in which an earlier edition of the *Britannica* is also mentioned as being on Leopold Bloom's bookshelf) and *Finnegans Wake*. Borges adored and pored over the eleventh *EB*, citing it as the source of much of his learning and spending part of his prize money from the 1929 Second Municipal Prize of the City of Buenos Aires on a secondhand set of the edition. In 1958, Beckett received a copy of the eleventh, minus the last volume, from the bookseller Jake Schwartz and consulted it constantly both as a resource for his work and for pleasure. On Joyce and the *EB*, see James S. Atherton, *The Books at the "Wake": A Study of Literary Allusions in James Joyce's "Finnegans Wake"* (New York: Viking, 1960), 87; Theoharis C. Theoharis, "Unveiling Joyce's Portrait: Stephen Dedalus and the *Encyclopaedia Britannica*," *Southern Review* 20.2 (April 1984): 286–99; and Len Platt, "'Unfallable encyclicing': *Finnegans Wake* and the *Encyclopedia Britannica*," *James Joyce Quarterly* 47.1 (Fall 2009): 107–18. On Borges, see James Woodall, *Borges: A Life* (New York: Basic, 1996), 76; and *All There Is to Know: From Abracadabra to Emile Zola . . . Here Is the Highest Monument to Victorian Culture—Readings from the Illustrious 11th Edition of the Encyclopaedia Britannica*, ed. Alexander Coleman and Charles Simmons (New York: Touchstone, 1994), 15. On Beckett, see James Knowlson, *Damned to Fame: The Life of Samuel Beckett* (New York: Simon & Schuster, 1996), 407.

DEDICATED BY PERMISSION

TO

HIS MAJESTY GEORGE THE FIFTH

KING OF GREAT BRITAIN AND IRELAND
AND OF THE BRITISH DOMINIONS BEYOND THE SEAS
EMPEROR OF INDIA

AND TO

WILLIAM HOWARD TAFT

PRESIDENT OF THE UNITED STATES OF AMERICA

FIG. 4.2.

It was louder as well in proclaiming its completeness, accessibility, and internal consistency—in editor Hugh Chisholm's Prefatory Note, its "high ambition of bringing all extant knowledge within the reach of every class of readers" by offering "a fresh survey of the whole field of human thought and achievement."[28] Where the previous edition had contained around 17,000 entries, many of them long treatises, the eleventh offered over 40,000 of a more digestible length; it also, controversially, included biographies of still-living people.[29] Overhauling rather than merely updating the *Britannica*, its editors had "arrange[d] their material so as to give an organic unity to the whole work and to place all the various subjects under their natural headings" while their assistants remedied the "inconcinnities" among entries (*EB*, I.xiv). Diderot's serialized *Encyclopédie* had required that each volume anticipate

---

[28] *Encyclopaedia Britannica: A Dictionary of Arts, Sciences, Literature, and General Information*, 11th edition, 29 vols., ed. Hugh Chisholm (Cambridge: Cambridge University Press, 1910–11), I.ix. Hereafter cited in the text as *EB*, followed by volume and page numbers. A fusion of British cultural capital and American venture capital—it was edited by the scholarly Tory journalist Chisholm and financed and promoted by the U.S.-born entrepreneur Horace Everett Hooper—the eleventh was a thoroughly transatlantic project, with editorial offices in both London and New York. Offering shorter essays, a clearer style than earlier *Britannica*s, and expanded treatment of U.S. and Canadian subjects, the edition was canted toward the massive U.S. reading public, which Hooper sought to reach for both populist and profiteering reasons.
[29] Coleman and Simmons, eds., 30.

events in order to mitigate its obsolescence and its disharmony with later volumes. Contrastingly, the twenty-eight content-volumes of the eleventh were published in two batches a few months apart, with the result that "the salient facts up to the autumn of the year 1910 might be included throughout, not merely as isolated events, but as part of a consistent whole, conceived in the spirit of the historian. Thus only can the fleeting present be true to its relation with later developments, which it is no part of the task of an encyclopaedia to prophesy" (*EB*, I.xix). Although like any encyclopedia it would become an anachronism, the eleventh would be superseded wholesale rather than piecemeal because it had not straggled into being. Even in its obsolescence, it would remain a unified "sum of human knowledge" as of its completion date, and therefore "true to its relation with later developments."

Yet despite Chisholm's declaration of its completeness and internal congruity, the 1910–11 *Britannica* came to be more celebrated for its eccentricity. As an adolescent living in Bath in 1917, Kenneth Clark eschewed most novels, which "young people read . . . as a short cut to growing up," in favor of the eleventh *Britannica*, the work he most valued:

> It is indeed a masterly piece of editing, for it retains the best of the old articles—Macaulay's splendid eulogy of Pitt and Swinburne's "rave notice" of Victor Hugo; Mark Pattison on Grotius and Erasmus, and contributions from the best critics of the nineties—Gosse, Leslie Stephen, Morley and John Addington Symonds, all doing their best, which subsequent contributors to encyclopedias have not done. . . . one leaps from one subject to another, fascinated as much by the play of mind and the idiosyncrasies of the authors as by the facts and dates. It must be the last encyclopedia in the tradition of Diderot which assumes that information can be made memorable only when it is slightly coloured by prejudice. When T. S. Eliot wrote "Soul curled up on the window seat reading the Encyclopedia Britannica" he was certainly thinking of the eleventh edition, and he accurately describes my condition.[30]

Clark's tribute recognizes several important aspects of the edition. First, far from junking all material from previous editions in the name of freshness, it preserved many classic entries from the ninth edition (1875–89). A truly multigenerational work, it placed essays by eminent Victorians such as Matthew Arnold, T. H. Huxley, and Andrew Lang among those by still-emergent twentieth-century figures—Bertrand Russell, for example, who wrote the "Geometry" entry, and Ernest Rutherford, who contributed an essay on "Radioactivity." Thus Chisholm's portrait of the "fleeting present" was no snapshot but a temporally heterogeneous image taken with an exposure time

---

[30] Kenneth Clark, *Another Part of the Wood: A Self-Portrait* (New York: Harper & Row, 1974), 68.

of at least thirty-five years. Nor, in fact, were the entries by its fifteen hundred contributors homogenized in voice or viewpoint. Pace Chisholm, the eleventh was a self-contradictory and polyphonic text that conspicuously set aside the convention of a strict house style. Although lacking the *Encyclopédie*'s subversive *renvoi* structure, it had nonetheless managed, in Clark's view, to retain the Diderotian insight that knowledge is irremediably and memorably prejudicial, and that this prejudice must be the basis rather than the dirty secret of any encyclopedic project.

There is one more reason to tarry with Kenneth Clark. By enlisting Eliot's 1929 Ariel poem "Animula" in his tribute to the *Britannica*, Clark read the eleventh by the light of a modernism seemingly excluded from its pages. Because the edition was important for a range of modernist writers, scholars have tended to come to it in a similar spirit, as something modernism allows us to see by virtue of the disparity between the two. The eleventh, says this reading, neither canonized nor embodied nor adumbrated modernist writing; it had no truck with Anglophone modernism, which anyway was nascent when the edition was being completed. Modernism, for its part, carefully measured its distance from the eleventh *Britannica*. Even if that distance was partly a nostalgic one (as in Clark's gloss on Eliot), the edition epitomized the Victorian and Edwardian worldviews—their totalizing proclivities, their epistemological arrogance—that modernist writers would either oppose or strive to outdo by other means. The eleventh thus gets conscripted to a periodizing story about modernism's crisp, detectable inception, a story in which the 1910–11 *Britannica* embodies all that modernism outmodes and overthrows, even providing some of the inert raw material for that repudiation. Gillian Thomas, for instance, sees the edition as having "represented a very precise historical moment, not only teetering on the brink of the 1914–1918 war, but poised on the cusp of Modernism, appearing in December 1910, the precise moment at which Virginia Woolf asserted that 'human character changed.'" Thomas adds that with so many of its articles carried over from nineteenth-century editions, the eleventh's "aesthetic world is essentially late Victorian rather than Edwardian"—that "in style and taste, it was a prelude to the world of Arnold Bennett and H. G. Wells rather than that of D. H. Lawrence and James Joyce," neither of whom would, in any case, have met its imminent criteria for "men of letters."[31]

However, by entraining both himself and Eliot in the eleventh's Diderotian lineage, Clark also offers a counter-narrative to this one, stressing continuity instead of discontinuity across the divide of 1910 and the war.[32] That

---

[31] Gillian Thomas, *A Position to Command Respect: Women and the Eleventh "Britannica"* (Metuchen, NJ: Scarecrow Press, 1992), vii, 3–4, 89.

[32] This counter-story is even starker in Eliot's poem, which Clark misquotes (the lines in question actually read, "The pain of living and the drug of dreams/Curl up the small soul in the window seat/Behind the *Encyclopaedia Britannica*"). Here the book is both refuge and pleasure, and it is

continuity was based in peculiarity and multiplicity of voice, in the mind's playful leap from subject to subject, and in the bond between memory and contingency. Modernism knew better than the eleventh *Britannica*, says one story. The eleventh was what modernism knew, says another. As against both of these, Clark's tribute sees the eleventh as having schooled a number of modernist writers in the Diderotian imagination—as having taught them not *what* to think but *how* to think.[33] This is to shift our attention away from the encyclopedia as a knowledge treasury and toward its role in modeling the assembly and animation of knowledge, its way of inducing the formation of new knowledge even through its inescapable prejudices.[34] Such a view of the encyclopedia—as more provocation than repository—may seem to nullify its ability to preserve knowledge in the face of catastrophe. But as we have already seen of Diderot's *Encyclopédie*, that project's reparative function did not require the fiction that its contents were stable, final, or consonant. On the contrary, the *Encyclopédie* would fight the volatility of history with an internal volatility of its own, prizing a restless cast of mind even above positive knowledge and aspiring to transmit that restlessness to the future.

Encyclopedic Narrative

Before turning, in this book's final chapters, to the fictive descendants of the *Encyclopédie* and the eleventh *Britannica*, I devote the rest of the present chapter to three important accounts of their novelistic subgenre. The first attempt to name and characterize "encyclopedic narrative" took place

---

unclear whether it offers sanctuary through reading, through the provision of a physical barrier, or some combination of the two—an immersion in the text behind the rampart of the work. What's more, through a series of preposterous reversals, the poem disrupts the linear temporality of lost innocence and other discontinuities that seem to underpin its movement from childhood through adolescence to a bridled maturity. "Living first in the silence after the viaticum" (or last sacrament of communion, given to the dying), the unnamed soul that once curled up behind the *Britannica* seems reserved for one among several fates that require prayer: "Pray for Guiterriez, avid of speed and power/For Boudin, blown to pieces, / . . . Pray for Floret, by the boarhound slain between the yew trees." Yet the poem concludes with a second reversal as dramatic as its claim that life begins after last rites: "Pray for us now and at the hour of our birth." T. S. Eliot, *The Complete Poems and Plays: 1909–1950* (Orlando, FL: Harcourt, 1952), 71.

[33] Here I echo Wilda Anderson's reading of the *Encyclopédie*: "It will not tell [future generations] *what* to think, however, it will introduce them into the conversation recorded in the cross-references and teach them *how* to think and how to feel. Reading will be a training experience that quite literally shapes the judgment of the future philosophers, which will allow them to speculate efficiently and therefore pass from being readers to being authors themselves as they 'correct' or extend the work of their predecessors" (925).

[34] The more egregious prejudices of the eleventh include its wholesale avoidance of psychology and psychoanalysis, its paucity of women contributors and subjects, its intermittent racism, and its thoroughgoing imperialism.

in the third decade of the Cold War and was triggered by the arrival of a novel that looked like the subgenre's newest exemplar. In 1974, the jurors for the Pulitzer Prize in fiction unanimously recommended Thomas Pynchon's *Gravity's Rainbow* (1973) but were overridden by the Pulitzer board, which found the novel "turgid," "overwritten," "unreadable," and "obscene" and elected to give no fiction award that year rather than accede to the jury's choice. Provoked in part by the board's decision, Auden scholar Edward Mendelson rose to the defense of Pynchon's novel by installing it in a rarefied lineage that consisted of Dante's *Commedia* (1308–21; 1472) Rabelais's Gargantua and Pantagruel books (1532–64), Cervantes's *Don Quixote* (1605–15), Goethe's *Faust* (1808), Melville's *Moby-Dick* (1851), and Joyce's *Ulysses*—a genealogy of works he called encyclopedic narratives. The two essays in which Mendelson elaborated a theory of the genre proved highly influential, not just for subsequent readers of *Gravity's Rainbow* but also for scholars of the earlier works through which Mendelson sought to glamorize it.[35] In no small degree, we have been reading the supposed precursors of Pynchon's novel ever since through the optics of that book's early reception, as if to illustrate T. S. Eliot's claim that new works retroactively alter the "ideal order" of literary monuments from which they spring.[36] When it comes to *Ulysses* and its genre-mates, this reading back through Pynchon has been salutary in a number of ways. As I will argue in this book's conclusion, *Gravity's Rainbow* may well have been the first post-1945 text of any kind to grasp the relationship between its interwar precursors' encyclopedism and total war; we might even go so far as to say that Pynchon's novel *is*, among other things, a reading of encyclopedic modernism from across the nuclear divide. But because Mendelson was less interested in the form and history of the encyclopedia than in the project of aggrandizing *Gravity's Rainbow*, encyclopedic narrative was conflated, even at the moment of its christening, with epic. That this conflation often happened at the very moments when Mendelson sought

---

[35] Edward Mendelson, "Gravity's Encyclopedia," in *Mindful Pleasures: Essays on Thomas Pynchon*, ed. George Levine and David Leverenz (Boston: Little, Brown, 1976), 161–95, hereafter cited in the text as "GE," and Edward Mendelson, "Encyclopedic Narrative: From Dante to Pynchon," *Modern Language Notes* 91 (1976): 1267–75, hereafter cited in the texts as "EN." For studies that deploy encyclopedic narrative or one of its cognates as a central generic term, see Trey Strecker, "Ecologies of Knowledge: The Encyclopedic Narratives of Richard Powers and His Contemporaries," *Review of Contemporary Fiction* 18 (1998): 67–71; Alan Clinton, "Conspiracy of Commodities: Postmodern Encyclopedic Narrative and Crowdedness," *Rhizomes: Cultural Studies Emerging* 5 (2002): n.p.; and John Christopher Cunningham, "The American Encyclopedia: The Book of the World in the New World" (PhD diss., Duke University, 1996). For a reading of Pynchon and Diderot against the more totalizing elements of Mendelson's theory, see Luc Herman and Petrus van Ewijk, "Gravity's Encyclopedia Revisited: The Illusion of a Totalizing System in *Gravity's Rainbow*," *English Studies* 90 (2009): 167–79.

[36] See T. S. Eliot, "Tradition and the Individual Talent," in *Selected Prose of T. S. Eliot*, ed. Frank Kermode (Orlando, FL: Harcourt, 1975), 38.

to distinguish encyclopedic narrative from epic suggests more than his dis-tance from, say, the *Encyclopédie* or the eleventh *Britannica*. It also attests to the susceptibility of misrecognition that encyclopedic modernism used to such tactical advantage, passing off as epic what was, in fact, antithetical to epic at the deepest level. In what follows, I engage closely with Mendelson's work in order to disaggregate what I see as the right term ("encyclopedic") from the interpretive wrong turns to which it has led. Yet this disentangle-ment will lead, in turn, to a reentanglement—in Pynchon's words, a "pro-gressive *knotting into*"—of epic and the encyclopedia, insofar as the interwar texts at issue harnessed the memory of epic form in producing and powering their encyclopedic effects.[37]

At first, Mendelson's account of encyclopedic narrative seems full of Diderotian echoes, particularly as regards the genre's scale, intricacy, and internal heterogeneity. Encyclopedic narratives, he says, exhibit a gigantism of scale and ambition, take an interest in statecraft and social organiza-tion, and include both a history of language and a compendium of literary styles. Exemplars of the genre tend to be at once urban and imperial in ori-entation: they imagine their chosen communities, even if they are infernal or shipboard ones, as city-like in their density and intricacy, and they generalize their social and political matrices as models for the nation or world. These are not only monstrous works but also *monstra* in the arcane sense of being "omens of dire change," and they announce a new dispensation, covenant, epoch, or regime:

> Each major national culture in the west, as it becomes aware of itself as a separate entity, produces an *encyclopedic author*, one whose work attends to the whole social and linguistic range of his nation, who makes use of all the literary styles and conventions known to his countrymen, whose dialect often becomes established as the national language, who takes his place as a national poet or national classic, and who becomes the focus of a large and persistent exegetic and textual industry comparable to the industry founded upon the Bible. ("EN," 1272, 1268; emphasis in original)

Notice how the internally variegated form of the encyclopedia, with its bid to include a range of social, linguistic, and stylistic codes, is already harnessed here to a developmental model of national holism—the nation as distinct, integrated, and self-aware—that belongs more typically to the political logic of epic. Notice, too, the quasi-messianic status that Mendelson attributes to the (lone, male) encyclopedic author whom such a nation "produces" at a cer-tain point in its individuation, as if such a figure and his work were a kind of national entitlement or birthright.

---

[37] Thomas Pynchon, *Gravity's Rainbow* (New York: Viking, 1973), 3.

When epic begins to draw near, Mendelson attempts to ward it off by making two distinctions between epic and encyclopedic narrative. The first involves exogenous fields of knowledge. Epic, he says, exhibits an "unconcern with fields of knowledge outside [the writer's] experience"—in the case of ancient epic because "no such fields exist, or none of any importance," and in the case of modern epic because "the only knowledge that matters is the knowledge through which the mind creates itself" (Wordsworth's *Prelude* serves as the example here). Encyclopedic narrative, by contrast, includes "an account of an art outside the realm of written fiction" plus "a full account of at least one technology or science" ("GE," 162, 164). One might quibble that *Ulysses*, say, treats embryology far less extensively than *Gravity's Rainbow* does ballistics and organic chemistry, or that neither text could be said to offer a "full account" of its chosen arts and sciences. But the encyclopedic narratives in Mendelson's canon do exhibit an epistemophilia to which the epic catalogue (e.g., the *Iliad*'s ship list) is only faintly analogous. If epic already yearns to animate and portray a world in its totality, encyclopedic narrative intensifies that yearning by a semaphorics of erudition and incorporation: it signals its writer's massive ingestion of specialized knowledge in an era when such knowledge needs to be acquired, when it can no longer be absorbed simply by moving within epic's putatively knowable and self-contained world.

Far more surprising is the second contrast Mendelson offers between epic and encyclopedic narrative, what he calls the "prophetic quality" of the latter. Whereas epics tend to be set in a remote and mythic past, commenting only obliquely or analogically on their historical present, encyclopedic narratives lag just behind the present in order to install themselves as its harbinger. But Mendelson goes farther, arguing that the encyclopedist's trompe l'oeil auguries confer a real prophetic authority:

> The main action . . . occurs about twenty years before the time of writing, allowing the book to maintain a mimetic (or, more precisely, satiric) relation to the world of its readers, while permitting it to include prophecies that are accurate, having been fulfilled between the time of the action and the time of the writing. These "accurate" prophecies then claim implicitly to confer authority on other prophecies in the book which have not yet been fulfilled. ("GE," 163)

We have encountered Diderot's injunction to the encyclopedist: know "the state of mind of your nation" well enough to foresee its development, "hasten to anticipate its progress so that the march of events will not leave your book behind but will rather overtake it along the road." Yet it is one thing to indulge in forecast as a hedge against obsolescence, and another to embrace the full-blown prophetic mode that we meet with so routinely in epic. Nor is it clear why repackaging hindsight as prevision should authorize a work to make *real* prophecies about a future that is still to come. It is clear, however, that for Mendelson the genre's oracular quality is neither accidental nor merely rhetorical: "An encyclopedic narrative," he writes, "prophesies the modes of human action and perception that its culture will later discover to be its own central concerns" ("GE," 178). The strangeness of these texts, then, is partly the strangeness of the future, which reveals itself first to the encyclopedic author and only later—and sometimes, we are to assume, through the very agency of the encyclopedic narrative—to the culture at large.

Oddly, Mendelson goes on to describe the prophetic quality of encyclopedic narrative as an "openness in time . . . echoed by its peculiar indeterminacy of form." A work given to prophecy might be considered open in time insofar as its forecasts are speculative, hopeful, or admonitory; after all, making predictions can be central to our experience of the present and of our freedom and responsibility within it. But actual prevision requires a future that is legible because determined in advance, and criticism that ascribes real premonitory powers to a work reveals a deterministic tendency in either the text or the critic. Mendelson locates it in the text, though more explicitly in the register of characterological and generic codes than in relation to futurity. Encyclopedic narrative, he finds, exhibits a coercive energy with respect to its characters: "Most encyclopedic works include characters who try unsuccessfully to live according to the conventions of another genre . . . Their failure to deflect the immensity of [the] encyclopedia into the channels of familiar convention points to the intolerance of the encyclopedic form for the small claims of personal expectation and perspective" ("EN," 1270). Given that encyclopedic narratives are also "encyclopedias *of* narrative"—that is, radically inclusive compendia of literary codes—their intolerance for other generic precepts and for the small claims of characters who attempt to live by them suggests an intimate relation between inclusivity and control in these narratives: they teem with characters and literary codes partly in order to subordinate both to a totalizing system. It may not be so surprising, then, to find in such texts a prophetic conceit that is neither speculative nor probabilistic but deterministic, proclaiming its dominion over the future as insistently as the genre stages the fruitlessness of living by any but its own conventions.

Encyclopedic narrative's relation to futurity becomes still more vexed when we return to the messianic logic of Mendelson's account. Of *Gravity's Rainbow* he writes, "because Melville has already fulfilled the encyclopedic role in North America, Pynchon's international scope implies the existence of a new international culture, created by the technologies of instant communication and the economy of world markets" ("GE," 164–65). *Already fulfilled the encyclopedic role*: these works, each a singularity in its context, are awaited, and by arriving they both fill a vacuum and fulfill a prophetic expectation: they "take their place," a place that was in a sense theirs, and only theirs, in advance. Even their subsequent canonization and interpretation get likened, in Mendelson's account, to scriptural exegesis. Yet these works that seem to fulfill prophecies of their arrival and to take the place reserved for them are also the ostensible makers of prophecy, giving us news of future or emergent national cultures; they are ambidextrously prophet- *and* messiah-texts. Some even joke about this doubleness: in *Ulysses* a character observes that "[Ireland's] national epic has yet to be written" even as the text implicitly—and probably facetiously—offers itself as filling the opening expressed in its own pages.[38] The joke here contains an insight that might have detained Mendelson: texts that both make and satisfy predictions may stand revealed as *self-fulfilling* prophecies, canceling through a kind of textual narcissism the oracular authority they attempt to win. If the prophet's authority is to persist, the object of the prophecy must be other than the prophet. But encyclopedic narrative à la Mendelson is, for all its internal heterogeneity, intolerant of elements that stray from the genre's conventions or attempt to pull focus from its portrait of the social totality. As a genre it seems arrayed against the sort of alterity a true prophecy foretells; its answer to every question is likely to be its own form, its prophecies an elaborate form of self-regard that has little to say in the face of the future's radical illegibility. Thus encyclopedic narrative's will to prophecy doubly exposes the genre's totalizing drives: these are texts, evidently, that both see the future as predetermined and see only themselves, and not the ineliminably other, as the future. It remains difficult to imagine how such texts could produce, as Mendelson says of *Gravity's Rainbow*, "the increase of freedom through the revelation of necessity" ("GE," 169). Difficult, too, to see how encyclopedic narrative meaningfully departs from the ground of epic.

The figure of a long-awaited encyclopedic author endowed with prophetic powers would be strange enough without a certain nuclear echo: the equally messianic narrative according to which an emergent nation produces, *at* and even *as* a particular stage in modernization, a nuclear weapon as the calling card of its maturity on the world stage. Encyclopedic narratives, at least before the advent of *Ulysses*, have tended to be slow of reception, often becoming "the focus of a large and persistent exegetic and textual industry" only decades after they are published. It is the nuclear weapon, not the strenuous epochal book, whose coming is awaited by the nation at large and whose unambiguous arrival brings into being—in fact, necessitates as a precondition of its being—an industry of technician-interpreters, the storied "nuclear priesthood." It is as if Mendelson had lifted the developmentalist trajectory of encyclopedic narrative from the nuclear plot of national *Bildung* that quietly undergirds *Gravity's Rainbow*, projecting that post-1945 narrative of "going nuclear" or "joining the nuclear club" onto literary reception since Dante.[39] This atomic retrofit of 600 years of literary

---

[38] James Joyce, *Ulysses: The Corrected Text*, ed. Hans Walter Gabler with Wolfhard Steppe and Claus Melchior (New York: Vintage Books, 1986), 158 (episode 9, line 309).

[39] According to the *OED*, the expression "nuclear club" was first used to denote nuclear-weapon states in 1957. Mendelson's fusion of the Book and the Bomb in the crucible of national *Bildung* may even have shaped subsequent encyclopedic narratives. Although Rushdie's *Midnight's Children*

history is a distortion, to be sure. But in respect to interwar encyclopedic narratives, at least, it is a revealing distortion, inviting us to read those works as unimaginable without a nation's having become integrated, and thus newly visible to itself, through a global economy of injury-production. What it reveals is the eerie congruence of total war with the advancement of totalizing, coherentist theories of literature—so much so that when Mendelson reaches for the encyclopedia, he ends up taking the epic down from the shelf. For it is the epic, not the encyclopedia, that fulfills its own prophecies; epic that *must* unfold as it does, as against the sideshadowing tendencies of the encyclopedia; epic that is fused with messianic narratives of national emergence, and that subscribes to so self-contained a vision of the nation that a lone work could be sufficient to encompass it.

Modern Epic

The major elaboration and revision of Mendelson's work on encyclopedic narrative is Franco Moretti's *Modern Epic*, whose title calls a halt to talking about epic under the Mendelsonian cover of the encyclopedia.[40] *Modern Epic* begins by insisting on both the genre's structural ties to ancient epic and the "supranational dimension of [its] represented space," in contrast to ancient epic's national space (2). For Moretti, every modern epic registers what Mendelson says only *Gravity's Rainbow* does: "the existence of a new international culture, created by the technologies of instant communication and the economy of world markets" ("GE," 164–65). Thus Moretti uses the term "world text" interchangeably with "modern epic" to designate works fired in the kiln of the modern world-system's emergence. This emergence he locates in a single, though protracted, historical period—from 1800 to 2000. Where Mendelson explains the scarcity and epochal singularity of encyclopedic narrative

---

(1980) swears allegiance to all manner of epic and oral forms, it also exhibits many of the traits of encyclopedic narrative à la Mendelson, not the least of which is its simultaneous staging of becoming-book and becoming-nuclear. As many commentators have noted, Saleem Sinai makes his narratorial valediction through a conflation of nuclear and population bombs, an image dissolving at once into demographic minima and atoms: ". . . fission of Saleem, I am the bomb in Bombay, watch me explode, bones splitting breaking beneath the awful pressure of the crowd . . . Yes, they will trample me underfoot, the numbers marching one two three, four hundred million five hundred six, reducing me to specks of voiceless dust . . ." Salman Rushdie, *Midnight's Children* (Harmondsworth, UK: Penguin, 1980), 552.

[40] Moretti openly acknowledges Mendelson's work as what put him "on the right track." But with respect to all but one of Mendelson's key claims—that scarcity and cultural singularity are hallmarks of the genre in question—he is hilariously and unaccountably dismissive: "Well, I shall not call them encyclopaedias, and I shall propose a different geographical distribution" (4). Moretti goes on in a note to attribute the term "Encyclopedia" to Northrop Frye in *Anatomy of Criticism*, adding, "I have preferred 'epic' because of its narrative connotations" (4 n2).

according to a quasi-messianic logic, Moretti prefers an organic one: "The same is true indeed of literary genres as of animal species: not all reproduce at the same rate. Some, like the novel, rely on numbers and breed like wildfire. Others concentrate their hopes on a few specimens, of fairly long and arduous gestation" (4). That literary species "concentrate their hopes" for survival on particular specimens imagines a literary version of natural selection in which several members of a particular species vie for the constrained resources of their cultural milieu. But Moretti's census of the genre is both more histori- cally compressed and more populous than Mendelson's, including the afore- mentioned *Faust, Moby-Dick, Ulysses, Der Mann ohne Eigenschaften*, and *Berlin Alexanderplatz*, as well as Richard Wagner's *Der Ring des Nibelungen* (1853), Flaubert's *Bouvard et Pécuchet* (1881), Karl Kraus's *Die letzten Tage der Menschheit* (1922), Eliot's *The Waste Land* (1922), Ezra Pound's *Cantos* (1925– 69), John Dos Passos's *U.S.A.* trilogy (1930–36), Broch's *Der Tod des Vergil* (1945), and Gabriel García Márquez's *Cien años de soledad* (1967). Although still elite—Moretti allows that the scarcity and "sacred" status of world texts are constitutive of the form—such a list describes a genre less jealous and less mutually exclusive than in Mendelson's account: these texts may compete for attention but not to fulfill a single epochal role.

Given Moretti's fascination with Darwinian models of literary evolution, we might expect *Modern Epic* to argue that its focal texts are more highly developed, more perfectly fit to survive than other texts with less felicitous mutations. But Moretti's Darwinism emphasizes mutation over perfection or fitness, seeing "precisely in morphological imperfection proof of the evolu- tionary path" (5). A Hegelo-Larmarckian literary historian would read muta- tions in literary form as responding to some adaptive need on the part of a genre: just as the Lamarckian giraffe gets a longer neck out of a need to reach higher leaves, modern epic might evolve a new formal device out of a need to address some aspect of modernity. For Moretti, however, envisioning literature as "a field in which variations only arise if predestined to success" both ignores the existence of vast numbers of failed variations and smacks of a determinism whereby the predestined adaptive success of variations "in a sense foreshadow[s] the course of evolution."[41] Instead, chance mutations in literary form get selected for or against by the canon-forming efforts of the ruling class; as a pas de deux between chance formal innovation and social necessity, literary evolution cannot be predicted. Modern epic, by these lights,

---

[41] Franco Moretti, "On Literary Evolution," in *Signs Taken for Wonders: Essays in the Sociology of Literary Forms*, trans. Susan Fischer, David Forgacs, and David Miller (London: Verso, 1988), 267, 262. For a critique of Moretti's literary Darwinism grounded in modern epic's dedication to nonnormative sexualities, kinship forms, and models of biological time, see Václav Paris, "Everyday Epic: Evolution, Sexuality, and Modernist Narrative" (PhD dissertation, University of Pennsylvania, 2014).

is neither perfectly adapted to modernity out of some internal necessity nor endowed with privileged access to a future in which it plays a founding role. Quite the contrary:

> This is another odd feature of the modern epic: it is an almost supercanonical form, yet one that is virtually unread. . . . The fact that world texts depend so closely upon the scholastic institutions, moreover, is a sure sign that something is amiss: that they are not self-sufficient. And they are not self-sufficient because they do not really work all that well. They are masterpieces, of course; but often, as people used to say of *Faust*, flawed masterpieces. And sometimes, to be candid, they are semi-failures. . . . [Their flaws] reveal a kind of antagonism between the noun and the adjective: a discrepancy between the totalizing will of the epic and the subdivided reality of the modern world. The imperfection of world texts is the sure sign that they live in history. (5)

If these world texts sit at the center of an interpretive industry, they do so not because we are still learning to decode their prophecies but because they are not self-sustaining, requiring an external prop. (Note how the university here is cast not as an indispensable corrective to market failure but as an island of misfit toys—as a place with so little relation to the mainstream that to be read there is to be "virtually unread.") Mendelson mourns the damage done to encyclopedic narrative's "charismatic illegality" by parasitic scholarly bureaucracies (e.g., "the Joyce industry"). But for Moretti the modern epic is ontologically damaged, non-self-identical, and kept alive in the face of popular indifference by an exegetical life-support system.

If these flaws prevent the modern epic from reaching more readers, however, they also safeguard it against what Moretti calls its "totalitarian temptation," a temptation he finds in every modernist world text with the exception of *Ulysses* (again both the genre's median and its outlier). These texts exhibit a certain rage to order in the face of the world's growing complexity, but the materials out of which they seek to produce and enforce this order are so heterogeneous as to defuse that rage. "Culturally impure, transnational, with no longer any sense of the 'enemy,' hypereducated, indulgent towards consumption, enamoured of eccentricities and experiments: hard to make reactionary works with such ingredients," Moretti writes. "Hard, above all, to do so with *fragments*. . . . the modernist epic cannot sacrifice the fragment: for it would lose the most immediate, the most telling, of its effects" (228). Mendelson's account, too, recognizes that encyclopedic narrative's totalizing drive must confront its limits: "because they are products of an epoch in which the world's knowledge is larger than any one person can encompass, they necessarily make extensive use of synecdoche." But the difference between Mendelson's synecdoche and Moretti's fragment matters: the former is an economizing tactic, a way for an emerging national consciousness to present itself in shorthand; the latter is created by the detonation of models of cultural purity and national self-identity. More ragbag than monolith, Moretti's modern epic is the obstacle to its own most dangerous tendencies, the necessity of its materials countering the necessity of its response to the world's overwhelming complexity. It is failed but elite; recondite yet not, finally, totalitarian.

Unsurprisingly, the prophetic conceit in Mendelson has no place in Moretti's centrifugal account of the subgenre. In fact, *Modern Epic* equips us to understand that conceit as a symptom—as an effect of the genre's heterogeneity and of its relation to historical flux—rather than as a true power of prevision. Whether we regard these texts as announcing the emergence of a national culture (Mendelson) or of an international world-system (Moretti), they belong to periods of paroxysmal change. To the extent that they sit on the threshold between the prehistory and the history of new political entities and cultural matrices, world texts direct their systematizing gazes in two directions, toward the past and toward the future. One might construe the genre's manic drive to display knowledge as a compensatory response to the upheaval of the nation's or world-system's emergence. Prediction would act as a stay against the volatile, unpredictable energies of historical crisis; prophecy-making would then be understood as a recognition, albeit an encrypted one, that the emergent political form is still to come, still miscellaneous, still radically open. Furthermore, if these texts are indeed multivoiced, the prophecies they utter are deprivileged by their competition or interdependence with other voices, registers, and discourses. Set beside linguistic zones that are variously mock-epic, scientific, bureaucratic, and journalistic, prophecy gets exposed as one mode among the many jostling for attention and primacy during a historically dynamic period. Rather than being intoned or even ventriloquized by encyclopedic narrative, as Mendelson imagines it, prophecy gets entered, catalogued, and exhibited there.

But there is another way to understand the genre's prophetic tendency as a symptom, one that points up the limitations of Moretti's approach as well. What Mendelson's account calls "prophecy" might be less hyperbolically described as a canny reading of the emergent. In such an account, encyclopedic narratives would identify nascent phenomena rather than foretell the advent of unborn ones. But the question then arises—and soon it will be time to ask it of *Ulysses*—why particular writers and works possess this ability to recognize the emergent. In addressing this question we will get no help from Mendelson, whose messianic model of encyclopedic narrative imagines the text less as an outpost from which to view the emergent than as an early incarnation of a future the text then helps to emerge. That future, we should also note, is expressly—and problematically—a *national* one: Mendelson's model pins encyclopedic narrative to the emergence of integrated national cultures, assigning a unique status to the national epic as catalyzing the growth of an interpretive industry and thereby stabilizing the new nation's language and culture. But Joyce's book, for one, was written in three European cities and set in the capital city of a colony that had just, at the time of the book's publication, emerged from years of anticolonial struggle only to be partitioned into the Unionist Northern Ireland and an Irish Free State vexed by civil war. Far from becoming immediately the focus of an Irish exegetical industry, *Ulysses* was first studied where it was written: outside Ireland. The book's joke that "Ireland's national epic remains to be written" might not be a bid to fill that gap so much as a recognition of the specific challenges "Ireland" posed to the categories of nation, nationality, national language, and national culture— the very categories Mendelson imagines the book will stabilize. But where Mendelson's model relies on an overly general catchall narrative of *national* becoming, we find no greater specificity in Moretti's two-hundred-year shift to a *supranational* world-system. The notion of a macro-transition to an international culture and world market might help to explain the heterogeneity of modern epic, but when asked why or how specific exemplars of that genre might "read the emergent," it loses its explanatory particularity. In Moretti's model, the West remains monolithically in transition during this period, whereas the example of Ireland reminds us at what different rates various localities might attain the status of nation-states or enter supranational orders. It reminds us, too, how many different itineraries modernization and decolonization can follow, and with what different results.

In response to these reminders, we need to disentangle the genre of encyclopedic narrative from the social-theoretical trellises on which it has so far hung: undifferentiated narratives about modernization as national becoming (Mendelson) or as globalization (Moretti). As Arjun Appadurai, Dipesh Chakrabarty, and other proponents of "alternative modernities" theory have observed, Eurocentric paradigms that imagine a singular modernity are incommensurate with the diverse and unpredictable forms of sociocultural organization that have arisen in Latin America, Africa, South and East Asia, and other postcolonial spaces. These universalizing paradigms view the postcolony, along with underdeveloped populations within the first world (e.g., impoverished, rural, and nomadic communities), as simply belated with respect to fully developed nation-states and as needing, with the help of development projects underwritten by the international community, to catch up along a single, predetermined path to modernization. Because such paradigms can only understand the postcolony's unique accommodation or resistance to modernization as further evidence of its belatedness, they are incapable of imagining how the colony or postcolony might witness and even theorize the emergence of global phenomena *before* the imperial nation-state does. The earliness of a text written in or about such a space, then, would need to be reassimilated to teleological models of a univocal modernity. That assimilation could take several shapes. It could cleanse the text of its associations with the periphery and claim it as a metropolitan or even cosmopolitan artifact. Or it might dismiss precisely what was threateningly clear-eyed or prognostic in the text as fanciful, childish, ill-bred, monstrous, or obscene. Having been resignified as proof of the periphery's backwardness, these potentially critical elements of the text would then confirm the totalizing self-portrait of Euro-American modernity. A text that not only contained such critical elements but also seemed to theorize an emergent counter-totality—one based, say, on limitless violence rather than on a world market or a cosmopolitan political order—would challenge that self-portrait all the more energetically and therefore require a more aggressive resignification.

I will have more to say in the ensuing chapters about how specific interwar modernist works move among total war, colonialism, and asynchronous temporalities. Here, I wish to stay with the question of what we miss when we read such works in exclusive relation to historical narratives of unbroken, centuries-long development. For Hegel, remember, "the situation most suited to epic" is the state of war, inasmuch as it stimulates an entire nation to the epic projects of integrated activity, holistic self-portraiture, and self-justification. *Modern Epic* theorizes the world system while avoiding both the "small wars" through which that system is advanced or consolidated and the world wars that contract it in spasm—a fact that marks the extent to which Moretti has had to deform epic out of all (Hegelian) recognition in making it account for modernist texts.[42] Strangely, this avoidance may be the thing *Modern Epic* most directly inherits from early-twentieth-century theorists who, following Hegel, portrayed epic as the genre of intact holism from which the novel takes leave. Whether this valediction inspired relief or regret in the particular theorist, it marked, and continues to mark, as impossible the very resurgence of comprehensive portraiture that was the signal feature of total war discourse. Because it defines epic through its obsolescence in modernity, such a view cannot imagine epic's recrudescence as political logic, and therefore cannot entertain the need for a counter-epic that would contest war's monopoly-claim on total representation. As earlier chapters in this book have argued, the problem during the interwar years was not totality's loss but its all too forceful reassertion through the logic of total war. The long modernist narratives that took shape during those years were built not on an *epic*

---

[42] Moretti does allow that one aspect of modern epic declines from *Faust* through the turn of the twentieth century, only to undergo a resurgence "around the First World War," adding that this surge is an example of "punctuated equilibrium" in literary evolution—an evolution not constant but instead "like the life of a soldier, made up of long periods of boredom, and brief moments of terror" (75). But the aspect in question is *polyphony*, one we should be ready by now to associate much more strongly with encyclopedism than with epic. Moretti comes no closer than this to saying that war or discourses about it might jar the world system sufficiently to reenergize latter-day epic. Nor does he come near the dialectical corollary to the boredom/terror model of literary development: that war as *event* might eclipse or conceal the systemic, perpetual aspects of war, and that modern epic might reveal these as well.

armature to foreground the lost totality of the present, but on an *encyclopedic* armature to contest the resurgent totality of the present.

Pace Bersani

Both Mendelson's and Moretti's work on long-form narrative might be described as biological: it approaches the subgenre morphologically, addresses the conditions of its emergence and mutation, and describes the ecological niches in which it might hope to survive. In contrast, Leo Bersani's work on encyclopedic fiction is heavily normative, inveighing against the "culture of redemption" he claims these novels incarnate. We might approach Bersani's polemic through a series of questions that the *Encyclopédie*, by coupling disaster with comprehensive representation, has taught us to ask. Can literary works really mitigate the experience of disaster, or even of disaster's seeming imminence? Does literature with historically redemptive ambitions forfeit other possibilities or responsibilities? Having held out a redemptive promise to its readers, can it justify the expense of time, attention, and even freedom it asks of them? Might such literature debase or diminish trauma by presupposing the adequacy of the aesthetic—to say nothing of a particular work's deployment of the aesthetic—to repair or annul history's ruination? In response, Bersani categorically denies that "a certain type of repetition of experience in art repairs inherently damaged or valueless experience":

> Experience may be overwhelming, practically impossible to absorb, but it is assumed—and this is especially evident in much encyclopedic fiction— that the work of art has the authority to master the presumed raw material of experience in a manner that uniquely gives value to, perhaps even redeems, that material. This may sound like an unattackable truism, and yet I want to show that such apparently acceptable views of art's beneficently reconstructive function in culture depend on a devaluation of historical experience and of art. The catastrophes of history matter much less if they are somehow compensated for in art, and art itself gets reduced to a kind of superior patching function, is enslaved to those very materials to which it presumably imparts value.[43]

Encyclopedic fiction, Bersani proceeds to argue, aims less to repair a broken culture than to replace it with a literary surrogate whose formal

---

[43] Leo Bersani, *The Culture of Redemption* (Cambridge: Harvard University Press, 1990), 1; further references are cited in the text. The block quotation is from the book's Prologue; the subsequent paraphrase of Bersani's critique of encyclopedic fiction is taken primarily from the chapter "Against *Ulysses*," the central example of encyclopedic fiction in an account that also addresses *Bouvard et Pécuchet*, *Moby-Dick*, and *Gravity's Rainbow*.

coherence "depreciates" the real world as formless in comparison. The very traits through which encyclopedic fiction would seem to check its coherence-claims and reassure us as to its openness—radical intertextuality, parody and pastiche, interpolation, stylistic pluralism—Bersani reads as the text's encrypted bids to consolidate its authority: readers are prevented by source-hunting, differentiating among distinct narratorial zones, and other annotative busywork from really interpreting the text, the historicity of whose intertexts is subsumed under its "timeless design." Thus the reader is asked to withdraw from the world in order to help sustain, through ceaseless explication, a text that offers itself as an improvement on the world's incoherence; to cultivate a bottomless memory for the text at the expense of any historical or cultural memory that does not serve the work of annotation; and to pay "an uninterrupted attention not exactly to [the work] itself but to its instructions for its own further elaboration" (170, 175). In return, the reader is implicitly promised that "the possession of [the text's portrait of] culture will transcend anxiety and perhaps even redeem history" (178). This promise, along with the culture of redemption it encapsulates, Bersani claims, negates *life* by deeming it reparable through art's surrogacy, and it negates *art* by reducing its role to reparation.

The terms in which Bersani describes the culture of redemption—valuation and devaluation, depreciation, compensation, and above all redemption (from the Latin *redimere*, "to buy back")—make clear that, for him, such a culture's scandal lies in its imputing a logic of general equivalence where one should not exist. Redemptive aesthetics treats two incommensurate things, the work of art and the catastrophes of history, as if they were fungible, thereby diminishing and even negating both. But what *about* them stands to be degraded? In the case of the work of art, the imperiled thing is clearly the work's immunity to exogenous criteria and premises, particularly those of philosophy, whose stable, unified truth-claims and "perfectly intelligible ideas" encyclopedic fiction only deforms itself by attempting to ape. (Here the chief example is Proust's *Recherche*, which suffers from "a strong (but happily unsuccessful) movement away from novelizing and by a depreciation of [its] own fictions" [2].) Bersani says little about how, exactly, the catastrophes of history are demeaned by redemptive aesthetics, beyond asserting that they "matter much less" when we imagine art may compensate for them. But to forbid transactions between the catastrophes of history and the work of art on these grounds is, in effect, to anoint or consecrate historical traumas, cordoning them off from profane, everyday categories such as the aesthetic and the logic of equivalence. Trauma having been thus sacralized, the art that would represent it in the hope of facilitating a collective working-through becomes a kind of sacrilege. At the same time, the very phrase "the catastrophes of history" condenses a move made repeatedly, if more diffusely, throughout

The Culture of Redemption: the conflation of history, of "the raw materials of experience," and, in places, of sexuality itself with trauma.[44] By at once quarantining and ontologizing trauma in this manner, Bersani bars the way not just to equivalence-based transactions between art and catastrophe but also to interactions of any sort between them. This amounts to a strange apotheosis of the offending logic of equivalence: although it is only one of many ways in which two systems might interact, it gets promoted in his account to the exhaustive case through which all interaction is normatively foreclosed.

One result of this sweeping interdiction is that Bersani's account cannot entertain any distinction between redemption and reparation. Here I use the term *reparation* not as a synonym for "restitution" or "compensation" (as in the phrase "war reparations") but, in a less economistic and juridical sense, as signifying mending and repair; not a making whole so much as a "making ready again" (as in *reparare*) that does not depend on notions of commensurability, completeness, or even adequacy. Such a notion of reparation—as an imperfect recovery from one disaster in preparation for another that may be on the horizon—comports with the interwar period's signal temporality, in which the memory and anticipation of devastating conflict produced vertiginous interference patterns. Reparation in anticipation: according to recent Kleinian scholarship by Eve Sedgwick and others, such a linkage will at first sound like a category error. "The first imperative of the paranoid," writes Sedgwick, "is *There must be no bad surprises*, and indeed, the aversion to surprise seems to be what cements the intimacy between paranoia and knowledge per se, including both epistemophilia and skepticism."[45] By these lights, anticipation would be the core temporality of a paranoid position, not a reparative one, and knowledge would be the paranoid's best tool and first defense. But if the encyclopedia since Diderot might once have looked like the paranoid genre par excellence—as the ultimate stockpiling of knowledge to deter bad surprises—it should be clear by now how far this was from the case. The French encyclopedists never thought knowledge could prevent the bad surprise of natural or political catastrophe, both because they regarded the disaster as unforeseeable and because they understood knowledge itself, in its instability and transience, as an ongoing disaster.

By the same token, encyclopedic modernism between the wars, although epistemophilic in the extreme, did not aim to preempt bad news by knowing it in advance. Its imperative was not *There must be no bad surprises* but *Given*

---

[44] Bersani writes, "In this book I have been arguing that, in a culture of redemption, sexuality and history are catastrophes that art has the task of repairing and redeeming. Reparative cultural symbolizations repeat those catastrophes in order to transcend them, which means that they scrupulously reenact the failures they are meant to make not happen" (108).

[45] Eve Kosofsky Sedgwick, *Touching Feeling: Affect, Pedagogy, Performativity* (Durham, NC: Duke University Press, 2003), 130; emphasis in original. Further references are cited in the text.

the uncancelable prospect of bad surprises, let us not allow the shadows that they cast to be our sole portrait. Although there is no paranoia without anticipation, there are nonparanoid responses to anticipation, and sometimes there is reparation precisely where one looks for paranoia. Yet it is not the reparation that Sedgwick celebrates or Bersani deplores in their respective readings of Klein, a reparation that reassembles the part-objects attacked by the ego in its paranoid position into "something like a whole—though . . . *not necessarily like any preexistent whole*" (Sedgwick, 128) or an idealized, "sublimated object" that, while "nothing more than a function of the attacked object . . . is disguised as transcendence" (Bersani, 21). Reparative encyclopedism embraces neither the fiction of perfected knowledge that would preempt bad surprises nor the fiction of perfected experience that would permit one to transcend anxiety or the catastrophe of history. It mends what is known on the road to its likely obsolescence; for its readers' sake, it thematizes the misrecognition of the partial for the total, even as it allows that no pedagogy can exempt one from the violence of history or desire.

Bersani's critique of encyclopedic fiction is directed as much at the works' scholarly reputations and communities as it is at the works themselves. Certainly it eschews any engagement with the complex formal and epistemological interface between the encyclopedia and the novel. Having spent time considering this interface, however—and having connected it to particular memories and anticipations of disaster rather than generalizing about the catastrophes of history—I wish to counter Bersani's argument with something like its inverse, both here and in the ensuing chapters. Encyclopedic fiction, says Bersani, has to negate the world in order to supplant it with a coherent aesthetic likeness. But as I have contended, interwar encyclopedic modernism arose in response to a heightened sense of the emergent world-war system's *self*-negating potential, one that vastly outstripped any literary form's capacity for world-negation. As they register that system's conjugation of totality and fragility, the works in question forbear to exhibit anything like the bumptious coherentism Bersani attributes to them. In contrast to the kindred holisms of epic and total war, encyclopedic modernism is, like the *Encyclopédie* itself, a presumptively shattered totality. Where for Bersani the genre claims to transcend anxiety through the authoritative sublimating work of culture, I would say that anxiety approaches its cultural apotheosis in encyclopedic modernism. In other words, far from claiming to transcend anxiety, the genre's interwar manifestations are both catalyzed by geopolitical anxiety and consequently drawn to a formal-epistemological lineage highly anxious about the Enlightenment's self-negating energies. Yet instead of merging those anxieties, as Bersani would do, with the catastrophes of history in order to isolate them from art, exchange, and the quotidian, encyclopedic modernism radically mixes the traumatic with the everyday. As with Diderot's project, its portraiture of the commonplace is inseparable from anxieties about both the disaster-to-come and the arbitrariness of our orders of order. Encyclopedic fiction between the wars is where the aesthetic abides with past and possible catastrophes precisely by *not* claiming to redeem them—but also by refusing to disavow all interaction between catastrophe and the aesthetic.

At the *Encyclopaedia Britannica*'s bicentennial banquet in 1968, Robert Hutchins, chairman of its Board of Editors, praised the work for manifesting "a vision in which science and technology, instead of threatening to exterminate us, will repeal the curse of Adam and enable all men everywhere to achieve their full human possibilities."[46] As so often in its modern history— think of the Westinghouse time capsules in 1938 and 1965—the form's promise could be articulated only through the catastrophe it was meant either to stave off or to mitigate. Diderot and d'Alembert knew nothing of world war or of nuclear weapons, yet they had characterized their *Encyclopédie*, too, as a knowledge-ark for the next deluge. Thus we find another continuity where we are used to seeing rupture. This chapter has argued for the existence of other unwonted through-lines: the eleventh *Britannica*'s transmission of Diderotian epistemology across the epochal seams of December 1910 and the First World War, for example, and the persistence of epic's political logic in the very period when the form was being eulogized as irrecoverable. Against the backdrop of these continuities, the next chapters will further press the case for *differentiating* interwar encyclopedic modernism from a five-century tradition of encyclopedic narrative or a two-century run of modern epics corresponding to the emergence of the world system. The reasons for doing so include the fact that the First World War both altered and exposed elements of the world system's self-description: altered it by elevating war to a primary means of constructing totalities, and exposed, at least for some observers, the partiality, in every sense, of this construction. Encyclopedic modernism between the wars may not have been the first literature to insist that the total is a special case of the partial; but it had specific, still-emergent reasons for renewing this insistence. And in the tradition of Diderot et al., it found richly generative formal and epistemological resources to apply to the task.

Not that the works of fiction addressed in the following chapters "look" like encyclopedias. Although they contain proleptic and analeptic jumps, they possess a recoverable diegetic chronology that is alien to the modern encyclopedia, whose alphabetic structure facilitates the reader's ergodic course through the text. Unlike lipogrammatic writings by the likes of Georges Perec, Walter Abish, and Christian Bök, encyclopedic modernist

---

[46] Carol Zaleski, "The Great EB," *The Christian Century* (March 24, 2011). See also *Banquet at Guildhall in the City of London, Tuesday 15 October 1968: Celebrating the 200th Anniversary of the Encyclopaedia Britannica and the 25th Anniversary of the Honorable William Benton as Its Chairman and Publisher* (United Kingdom: Encyclopaedia Britannica International, 1968).

narratives do not use the alphabet as a generative device or as a strong organizing conceit. Their internal modular structures (chapters, episodes, books) exhibit neither definitional aims nor a desire to provide an exhaustive account of a particular subject. And they replicate neither the *renvoi* structure of the *Encyclopédie* nor an equivalent to the eleventh *Britannica*'s exhaustive one-volume index. Yet in comparison with both nineteenth-century realism and other modernist fiction of the interwar period, these works are warped *toward* encyclopedic traits in ways that interfere with the codes of narrative sequence, novelistic optics, and fictional world making. Although their chapters are not quite "entries," neither are they topically blank units of episodic progression: Musil inclines toward the essayistic, Ford and Döblin toward the set piece, and Joyce toward discrete style-worlds whose techniques are motivated by the clash of diegesis with competing organizational matrices. Even if the alphabet serves no explicit portal-function in these works, the alphabetical lumpiness of many serially published encyclopedias (the 1768 *Britannica* devoted the first of its three volumes to A–B and the last to M–Z) finds an analogue in their internal dissymmetries, most spectacularly in *Ulysses*' late-chapter bloating.[47] Diderot's beloved *renvois* are commemorated by the wormholes of cross-reference and self-contradiction that traverse these works, and in their way of pitting one internal unit's style-world or epistemology against another's. Although not formally self-indexing, these works have driven their readers to create concordances, annotations, character censuses, maps, charts, handbooks, and, indeed—as if the works were autonomous worlds—whole new *encyclopedias* in striving to understand them. And in all of the works in question, the novel's traditional focus on particular individuals through time is intermittently decentered by sidelong glances at would-be protagonists and house styles, by attempts to narrate the masses that populate city and battlefield, and ultimately by an ambition to comprehend a whole society. In thus engaging with the encyclopedia, these works did not take a poker-faced Enlightenment project and travesty it; rather, they magnified what was already bulbous, distended, ridiculous, off-kilter, and self-divided in the encyclopedia and used it as a curb on the projects of massively inclusive representation they nonetheless undertook.

Some famous works are more often invoked or consulted than read. Envision one begun modestly but grown, over the years of its writing and serialization, into a behemoth. Internally reticulated, it outfitted each of its compartments with a kind of discourse-world unto itself, a world with its own voice, preoccupations, governing terms, agendas, and resonant bodies of expertise. Yet these sections shared a number of links—informational,

---

[47] See Richard Yeo, *Encyclopaedic Visions: Scientific Dictionaries and Enlightenment Culture* (Cambridge: Cambridge University Press, 2001), 5.

satirical, subversive, even censorship-evading—and a profound cumulative effect, of building a "body" one organ at a time. It was a book rooted at once in the creaturely, sensory, material experiences of humanity and in the dream of an immutable, transcendent, and eternally transmissible language. That division was amplified by the work's organization along multiple, often incompatible, axes or logics, some concrete, others extravagantly abstract. Bowdlerized by one of its creator's close associates, it was dogged by spurious imprints and, on more than one occasion, censored as corrupting its readers and thus stripped of its copyright privilege. The beneficiary of patronage structures, the work was sold by subscription and made its maker famous. And although strongly affiliated with one nation, it was composed, printed, read, and given asylum in many. A Rabelaisian book of the world, it goes by at least two names.

5

The Shield of *Ulysses*

The sphere of the city is the habitual and the commonplace. Perhaps this assumption will do more than anything else to date Joyce's work. . . . times change, and the established routines of city life are interrupted by air-raid sirens.

—Harry Levin, *James Joyce: A Critical Introduction* (1941)

I want . . . to give a picture of Dublin so complete that if the city one day suddenly disappeared from the earth it could be reconstructed out of my book.

—James Joyce, speaking about *Ulysses* to Frank Budgen

One of the names of the book of the world is *Ulysses*. Its name for the world is Dublin, the city Joyce wanted to archive in its pages. His claim that *Ulysses* could serve as a blueprint for a second Dublin if the first one vanished gets repeated all the time by Joyceans, almost none of whom believe it.[1] In dismissing Joyce's claim as hyperbole, the same scholars pass over its premise—Dublin's sudden disappearance from the earth—as merely the platform for an authorial boast. A few commentators, however, have taken Joyce's premise seriously, connecting it to the violent period during which he was writing *Ulysses*.[2] They remind us

---

[1] Frank Budgen himself noted the absence of pictorial description in *Ulysses* in comparison with *Dubliners*. Richard Ellmann responded to the claim with similar skepticism: "Other novelists are, however, much more likely to present a city in reconstructable form. Joyce offers no architectural information, only places to bump elbows, or to lean them, to see out of the corner of an eye, to recognize by a familiar smell. The city rises in bits, not in masses." See Frank Budgen, *James Joyce and the Making of "Ulysses," and Other Writings* (London: Oxford University Press, 1972), 69, and Richard Ellmann, *Four Dubliners: Wilde, Yeats, Joyce, and Beckett* (New York: George Braziller, 1988), 68. Yet the frequency with which Budgen's anecdote is cited suggests a fascination with something more than its dubious reconstructability claim. For a short genealogy of critical responses to the anecdote, see Joseph Brooker, *Joyce's Critics: Transitions in Reading and Culture* (Madison: University of Wisconsin Press, 2004), 75–76.

[2] See James Fairhall, *James Joyce and the Question of History* (Cambridge: Cambridge University Press, 1993), 194–95; Enda Duffy, *The Subaltern Ulysses* (Minneapolis: University of Minnesota

that the years 1914 to 1921 brought stark evidence of the growing erasibility of cities, and of the vulnerability of urban populations to mass death or displacement. Joyce made the comment while walking with Frank Budgen along the Universitätstrasse in Zurich, the city for which he and his family had left Trieste, seeking refuge from the sort of urban warfare that would escalate over the course of the First World War. As both an active port and the "City of Desire" in *Italia irredenta*, Trieste was marked by Italy for "redemption" from five centuries of Austro-Hungarian rule. When Italy entered the war in May 1915, military authorities ordered a partial evacuation of the city; as British citizens, the Joyces had to decamp. By the time they left for neutral Switzerland in late June of that year, they and the rest of Trieste's inhabitants had endured daily artillery fire and four air raids by Italian planes.[3]

Within a year Joyce would also have read reports from Dublin about the 1916 Easter Rising, during which 500 people died and 2,500 were wounded, most of them civilians cut down by crossfire.[4] Cities had of course been sites of mass death before this. But the Easter Rising differed from the urban barricade fighting of the past in the use, principally by British soldiers, of newly precise and destructive weapons. Fired from the ground, from rooftops, and from gunships in the River Liffey, the new cannons, incendiaries, and machine guns rapidly reduced whole blocks of the city center to ruins. The resemblance between these ruins and the shelled-out remains of Great War towns was not lost on Dubliners, one of whom wrote in a letter, "I have just returned from walking round the [General Post Office] and Sackville Street. If you look at pictures of Ypres or Louvain after the bombardment it will give you some idea of the scene." Contemporary postcards and booklets depicting the wreckage bore the caption "Ypres-on-the-Liffey."[5] As Hugh Kenner once observed, most of *Ulysses* was composed in the knowledge that the cityscapes featured in its central episodes "would never be seen again as they had been."[6] In the knowledge, too, that the emerging doctrine and practices

---

Press, 1994), 123–25; Mark A. Wollaeger, "Reading *Ulysses*: Agency, Ideology, and the Novel," in *Joyce and the Subject of History*, ed. Mark A. Wollaeger, Victor Luftig, and Robert Spoo (Ann Arbor: University of Michigan Press, 1996), 100; and Enda Duffy, "Disappearing Dublin: *Ulysses*, Postcoloniality, and the Politics of Space," in *Semicolonial Joyce*, ed. Derek Attridge and Marjorie Howes (Cambridge: Cambridge University Press, 2000), 37–41.

[3] Richard Ellmann, *James Joyce*, rev. ed. (New York: Oxford University Press, 1983), 383. Henceforth cited as *JJ*. In an April 28, 1919, document about the English Players affair, Joyce referred to himself hyperbolically as "a prisoner of war liberated on parole to Switzerland in July 1915 by the Austrian Government in consideration of my health." James Joyce, *Letters of James Joyce*, 3 vols., ed. Stuart Gilbert and Richard Ellmann (New York: Viking, 1966), vol. 2: 439. Further references are in the text as *L* followed by volume number.

[4] Keith Jeffery, *Ireland and the Great War* (Cambridge: Cambridge University Press, 2000), 51.

[5] The letter writer is Mary L. Norway in *The Sinn Fein Rebellion as I Saw It* (London: Smith, Elder, 1916), 68; qtd. in Jeffery, 45. The phrase "Ypres-on-the-Liffey," which appears to have circulated rather broadly, appears as a caption to a postcard published by Bairds of Belfast (Jeffery, 52) and in an unsigned booklet, *Dublin and the "Sinn Fein Rising"* (Dublin: Brunswick, 1916).

[6] Hugh Kenner, *Ulysses*, rev. ed. (Baltimore: Johns Hopkins University Press, 1987), 93.

of total war were projecting this condition of eradicability to all cities, whose names, like the names of Arras and Reims, Ypres and Louvain, might become shorthand for their destruction. What more pressing reason to put all of Dublin in a book than to archive the city against its potential erasure?

As we approach the generic standoff between epic and encyclopedia through war's relation to total representation, it would be useful to have some touchstone for that relation—an emblem of city- or world-portraiture under pressure of war. Readers of *Ulysses* will find the book's artifactual counterpart not in Homer's *Odyssey*, with its nested scenes of oral transmission, but in the *Iliad*, which describes the object Hephaestus, old artificer and soul of the smithy, most memorably forged: Achilles' shield, which the warrior's mother procured for him after Hector claimed his armor from the slain Patroclus. Not content to forge a common shield, the smith god creates what Robert Fagles translates as "a world of gorgeous immortal work" on the shield's glittering expanse. It is world-creation in miniature, the closest thing to Genesis I in Greek epic: "There he made the earth and there the sky and the sea and the inexhaustible blazing sun and the moon rounding full and there the constellations . . ." Against this ground, Hephaestus places the figures of "two noble cities filled with mortal men," a stereoptic portrait of work versus war, the civil polis versus the city under siege:

> . . . With weddings and wedding feasts in one
> and under glowing torches they brought forth the brides
> from the women's chambers, marching through the streets
> while choir on choir the wedding song rose high
> and the young men came dancing, whirling round in rings . . ..
>
> But circling the other city camped a divided army
> gleaming in battle-gear, and two plans split their ranks:
> to plunder the city or share the riches with its people,
> hoards the handsome citadel stored within its depths.
> But the people were not surrendering, not at all.
> They armed for a raid, hoping to break the siege—
> loving wives and innocent children standing guard
> on the ramparts, flanked by elders bent with age
> as men marched out to war.[7]

This last image of civilians standing guard on the ramparts twins the shield with the besieged Ilium and presages that city's sacking. We might mistake elements of the passage—the young men no longer dancing but marching

---

[7] Homer, *The Iliad*, trans. Robert Fagles (New York: Penguin, 1990), 483–84.

out; the women, children, and elders left behind—as little different from the modern notion of "conventional warfare," with its gendered and generational divisions of labor. But examined more closely, the shield shows us that when armies attack cities rather than clashing on a remote battlefield, the civilians who dwell in the besieged city are effectively militarized—both conscripted to the work of soldiers and made possible targets of wartime violence, including the pillaging of the city once it has fallen. The raid named in the passage turns out to involve just such a targeting of noncombatants: the herdsmen guarding the belligerent army's flocks, slaughtered with their livestock as a way to break the siege. And once the link between the army and its supply train is made, even the ensuing peacetime scenes of farming and animal husbandry, feasting and courtship, retain their ghostly implications in the war economy. Depicting civilian life in the shadow of civilian mass-death on the surface of a defensive weapon, Achilles' shield suggests that every element of political, private, economic, and civil life is both knit up with and imperiled by warfare; it is a premodern panorama of what we have come to call total war. It encapsulates, too, what I earlier called the political logic of epic—the logic whereby war offers the primary occasion for an organic, coherentist portrait of a social totality.

This chapter describes Joyce's *Ulysses* as a latter-day counterpart and rival to Achilles' shield. It thus anticipates W. H. Auden's 1952 poem, "The Shield of Achilles," to which I turn at the chapter's end. In the intervening pages I argue that the synoptic portraiture *Ulysses* both attempts and renounces is that of Hephaestus's masterpiece, not just a portrait of the social totality at war but a portrait of total war as *the* occasion for perceiving and theorizing the social totality. Against this political logic of epic, *Ulysses* calls on encyclopedic form to model comprehensiveness without coherentism, a view of the whole that insists on the partiality of synoptic viewing. Downriver from Diderot and just upstream of the Westinghouse Time Capsules, Joyce's is an always partial conspectus made *necessary*—not, like epic, made *possible*— by the prospect of total war and the threat such war poses to the living, the archive, the built environment, and the future. The chapter interferes with several standard chronologies and taxonomies. Because it construes a text set in 1904 as conversant with a mode of warfare not named until 1916 and not yet common parlance by the time of the book's publication, my discussion will have to account for what looks like a premonitory or prophetic quality in Joyce's book, a capacity to read what is emergent or to come. It also reads a text set in Dublin as registering a world war in which Ireland was not territorially involved. And in addressing a total mode of warfare understood by Joyce's contemporaries as subsisting between or among metropolitan nation-states, such an argument would seem to ignore *Ulysses'* location in an occupied colonial capital, a location on whose specific features much valuable scholarship in postcolonial Irish studies has been grounded. Far from severing total war and colonial occupation, however, I renew my earlier insistence on the historical linkages between the two, drawing attention to how *Ulysses* uncovers those links in the face of their occultation by a range of discourses and genres, including but not limited to military theory, international law, and a number of other interwar modernist city texts.

In the previous chapter I envisioned a colonial text bearing advance news of reorganized violence in the world system, then sketched the contortionist readings by which such earliness would need to be reassimilated to metropolitan narratives of colonial belatedness. *Ulysses'* interwar reception is a case study in just this sort of resignification, which took two principal shapes among Western metropolitan critics. One group—the likes of Valéry Larbaud, Ezra Pound, and T. S. Eliot—de-Celtized the book's earliness, aligning it (sometimes agonistically) with European cultural, intellectual, and scientific traditions.[8] The second group rewrote *Ulysses* as a monument to colonial belatedness, describing the book and its author in terms of a backwardness of class (Virginia Woolf called *Ulysses*, in her diary, "An illiterate, underbred book, it seems to me; the book of a self-taught working man, & we all know how distressing they are"), of race ("It is enough to make a Hottentot sick" wrote a reviewer for the *Sporting Times*), or of both class and race.[9] The verdict as to *Ulysses'* retrogression was particularly strong when it came to the book's violence. Woolf, again, wrote, "it seems to me the conscious and calculated

---

[8] Moretti repeats this move: "Of course, it is a well-known fact that Joyce is Irish and that *Ulysses* takes place in Dublin. But if Joyce were an Irish *writer*, comprehensible and containable without any loose threads within Irish culture, he would no longer be Joyce; if the city of *Ulysses* were the real Dublin of the turn of the century, it would not be the literary image *par excellence* of the modern metropolis. Cultural phenomena cannot be explained in the light of their *genesis* (what ever has emerged from the studies that interpreted Joyce on the basis of Ireland?); what counts is their objective *function*. And there is no doubt that *Ulysses* fully belongs to a critical turning point of international bourgeois culture—a status it would not have achieved in the investigation of Ireland's peripheral and backward form of capitalism (which was, moreover, dependent on the destiny of British capitalism: yet another reason to move from the effect to the cause)." Franco Moretti, *Signs Taken for Wonders: Essays in the Sociology of Literary Forms*, trans. Susan Fischer, David Forgacs, and David Miller (London: Verso, 1988), 189–90, emphasis in original.

One need not view Joyce or *Ulysses* as "comprehensible and containable without any loose threads in Irish culture" to take exception to Moretti's equally reductive dismissal of the book's site-specifically Irish bases. The singular modernity argument is the invisible driveshaft of Moretti's move here: hosting merely a "peripheral and backward form of capitalism," the colony plays "effect" to the metropole's "cause." Rather than loiter in the colony's belated space, we should read the texts that only incidentally originate there from the sites of their true functionality, the capitals of international bourgeois capitalism. My reading of *Ulysses*, in a sense, reverses Moretti's itinerary, arguing that if we read the text back into the particulars of its colonial setting we can see, from that vantage, the incubation of total war's techniques in the colonial periphery before their full-blown use in the metropole.

[9] Virginia Woolf, *The Diary of Virginia Woolf, Volume II: 1920–24*, ed. Anne Olivier Bell with Andrew McNeillie (New York: Harcourt Brace Jovanovich, 1978), 189; "Aramis," "The Scandal of *Ulysses*," *Sporting Times* 34 (1922): 4; rpt. in *James Joyce: The Critical Heritage*, vol. 1, ed. Robert H. Deming (London: Routledge and Kegan Paul, 1970), 192.

indecency of a desperate man who feels that in order to breathe he must break the windows."[10] The scenario imagines the book as an incommensurately violent response to the author's backward condition. What such a view cannot entertain—or cannot bear to entertain—is the obverse possibility: that *Ulysses* is a forward look at an emergent condition of incommensurable violence, a condition emerging first in colonial spaces. To be seen properly, the text's colonial forwardness must not be viewed through the singular modernity optics that produced the twin distortions of its interwar reception (*Ulysses* as the first masterpiece of the European avant-garde; *Ulysses* as a handbook of colonial backwardness). The forward-looking elements of *Ulysses* need to be recovered, too, from the internal resistances—its diegetic time-lag, its conspicuously backdated prophecies, its Homeric endoskeleton—that the text sets up against them. When we correct for these resistances and distortions, we see that the book's origins and setting in an occupied colonial metropolis gave *Ulysses* a privileged view of the imperial world system, and at a threshold moment in the production of violence and the abrogation of its containment by law.

Such a view is possible, in part, because Dublin's status as a colonial metropolis gives the lie to the stark binarism of metropole versus colony on which much colonialist discourse as well as early postcolonial criticism relied. My claim here partly echoes Fredric Jameson's observation that Ireland possessed a "national situation which reproduce[d] the appearance of First World social reality and social relationships—perhaps through the coincidence of its language with the imperial language—but whose underlying structure [was] in fact much closer to that of the Third World or of colonized daily life." In Jameson's discussion, the special case of Ireland makes it the ideal laboratory for a thought-experiment—one that ultimately confirms the center–periphery dyad, maintaining the colony as a space of "brute force, naked power, open exploitation" as against the legalized and occulted exploitation, and the anomie, of the metropole.[11] His experiment, in other words, finds in Dublin and in Joyce's novel the exception that proves the rule. I contend that *Ulysses* and its city together constitute an exception that dismantles the rule. It reminds us, first, that other cities shared Dublin's hybrid status as colonial metropolis, even if they did not produce world texts on the scale of Joyce's. Second, and more crucially, the Joycean example shows us how the center–periphery dyad masks growing resemblances between metropolitan and colonial spaces. These resemblances include the spread of commodity culture, consumerist

---

[10] Virginia Woolf, "Character in Fiction" (1924), in *The Essays of Virginia Woolf, Volume III: 1919–1924*, ed. Andrew McNeillie (San Diego: Harcourt Brace Jovanovich, 1988), 434.

[11] Fredric Jameson, "Modernism and Imperialism," in Terry Eagleton, Fredric Jameson, and Edward W. Said, *Nationalism, Colonialism, and Literature* (Minneapolis: University of Minnesota Press, 1990), 60, 59.

economics, metropole-identified educational institutions, and nascent civil law regimes to colonial cities. Most importantly for our purposes, they also include the recognition that extreme forms of colonial policing were cognate with the total war whose belated arrival in the metropole was beginning to seem imminent. Revising Edward Mendelson's claims about the prophetic dimensions of encyclopedic narrative, this observation about total war's colonial provenance allows us to understand at least one of *Ulysses'* prophetic registers in a geopolitical rather than a magical fashion: if total war between metropolitan nation-states is being assembled and road-tested in the colonies, then a colonial account of these practices will be received in the metropole as prophetic—or, if you prefer, as literally avant-garde, arriving in the vanguard of the full-blown phenomenon.[12]

Ulysses' Encyclopedism

Earliness, prophecy, anachronism: these varieties of untimeliness are not traits typically associated with the modern encyclopedia. But as we learned by tarrying with Diderot, the *Encyclopédie* brought proleptic methods to bear for the sake of future readers, its editor insisting that the encyclopedist "hasten to anticipate [the nation's] progress so that the march of events will not leave your book behind but will rather overtake it along the road." However, before considering how *Ulysses* heeds this temporal directive, we first need to develop a general account of the book's encyclopedic form. The notion that it has one begins with Joyce himself, who described it in a 1920 letter to Carlo Linati as "a kind of encyclopedia."[13] The claim is expanded on by the schema

---

[12] As it happens, this way of understanding *Ulysses'* earliness comports with turn-of-the-century narratives in the emergent field of geopolitics that were also theorizing the movement of violence through the imperial world system. In 1904, the year in which Joyce's novel is set, the head of the Royal Geographic Society, Halford Mackinder, published an essay called "The Geographical Pivot of History." There he discussed the ramifications of "the virtually complete political appropriation" of the world, the fact that imperial expansion had finally lapped against the globe's far shores. Henceforth, Mackinder said, "Every explosion of social forces, instead of being dissipated in a surrounding circuit of unknown space and barbaric chaos, will be sharply re-echoed from the far side of the globe, and weak elements in the political and economic organism of the world will be shattered in consequence. There is a vast difference of effect in the fall of a shell into an earthwork and its fall amid the closed spaces and rigid structures of a great building or ship." H. J. Mackinder, "The Geographical Pivot in History," *The Geographic Journal* 23.4 (April 1904): 422.
Backdated to this historical cusp, *Ulysses* appears to prophesy such a crisis in the imperial world system out of which the mass violence concurrent with its composition would unfold. The Easter Rising, in particular, embodied the link between total war and so-called "low-intensity conflict": the ruins of central Dublin in 1916 exhibited the effects of artillery fire not into the earthwork of the preindustrial society but into "the closed spaces and rigid structures" of a colonial metropolis.
[13] James Joyce, *Selected Letters*, ed. Richard Ellmann (London: Faber and Faber, 1975), 271. Joyce described his "damned monster-novel" in the same letter as "the epic of two races (Israel-Ireland) and at the same time the cycle of the human body as well as a little story of a day (life)." *Novel, epic,*

Joyce sent Linati in the same letter and another he prepared a year later for Larbaud. These grids assigned to most or all of the book's eighteen episodes a color, a technic, a science or art, an organ, a symbol or range of symbols, and an array of Homeric correspondences. The schemata are now read less for their decryptive power than for their divergences and omissions, and for their function as high-literary signaling devices at the time of the book's publication. As to the latter, they seem to insist both that *Ulysses* is meticulously organized and that its internal reticulations are based more on categories of knowledge and experience than on the raw narrative seriality of the conventional "chapter." With the multiplicity of the book's organizing categories suggesting one might divide the world along a number of axes, the full extent of each axis seems engridded in the book's grand scale. The 1921 schema's syllabus of "Arts" (Theology, History, Philology, Economics, Botany and Chemistry, Religion, Rhetoric, Architecture, Literature, Mechanics, Music, Politics, Painting, Medicine, Magic, Navigation, Science) starts to look whimsical and incomplete if we stare at it long enough, but the first and strongest impression it conveys is of an inclusivity that is curricular in its scope and ambition. Here is a work of imaginative literature that wants to compete, if not with the universe, at least with the university.

Like both the university and the encyclopedia, *Ulysses* is built of multiple discourse worlds connected by pathways that call attention to those worlds' differences as well as to their adjacency. Although its episodes unfold for the most part sequentially, the first three run concurrently with the next three. ("Telemachus" and "Calypso" begin at 8 a.m., "Nestor" and "Lotus Eaters" at 9 a.m., etc.) Thus the episodes associated with the arts of Theology, History, and Philology happen alongside, respectively, those affiliated with Economics, Botany and Chemistry, and Religion. This structure draws the book closer to the encyclopedia's massive simultaneity, its nonsequential warehousing of its entries. As if to underscore this formal proximity, episodes one and four contain a diegetic *renvoi*: "A cloud began to cover the sun slowly, wholly."[14] The verbatim repetition of this narratorial sentence and its roughly synchronic appearance in the two episodes indicate that it refers in both instances to the same cloud. Yet as with the *Encyclopédie*'s cross-references, the cloud's appearance calls as much attention to disparities as to similarities between the contexts in which it appears: this is the same cloud seen from two distinct

---

cycle, story, encyclopedia—each of these generic taxa has its rewards and its proponents. My aim in this book is not to portray *Ulysses* as encyclopedic to the exclusion of the others but to trace the historical reasons for its misrecognition as a primarily epic work, including the misrecognitions of its encyclopedic gestures *as* epic ones.

[14] James Joyce, *Ulysses: The Corrected Text*, ed. Hans Walter Gabler with Wolfhard Steppe and Claus Melchior (New York: Vintage Books, 1986), 1.248, 4.218. Further citations are in the text by episode number and line number.

locations, beginning to cover the sun at nonsynchronous moments from each vantage. This holds true, as a rule, for the book's many other intratextual wormholes and hyperlinks. Episode ten, "Wandering Rocks," goes so far as to elevate the *renvoi* to a fundamental structural element, fastidiously cross-referencing a series of eighteen sections—each foregrounding a particular profession, institution, demographic, or area of economic activity—plus a final round-up focalized through the gaze of the viceroy as he is drawn through the streets of the city in a parade of imperial power. A microcosm or micropedia of *Ulysses* in its numerology and modular-synchronic structure, "Wandering Rocks" flaunts its encyclopedism, setting that form in an uneasy relation with the surveillant British colonial administration it appears now to serve, now to evade. For as much as modern encyclopedias are transnational in their production, they tend to sail under national flags. "Wandering Rocks" suspends Joyce's encyclopedia between Britannica and Hibernica.

A second aspect of *Ulysses'* encyclopedism is illuminated by its source texts. In researching and writing the book, Joyce made extensive use of almanacs, anthologies, dictionaries, directories, maps, encyclopedias, and even tidal charts. The 1904 *Thom's Official Directory of the United Kingdom of Great Britain and Ireland*, on which he relied heavily, included alphabetical listings of Dublin's streets and residents, lists of trades by category, information about U.K. and city government, clergy, and public institutions, and a chronology of Irish history starting in 140 CE. Thanks to *Thom's*, *Ulysses* teems with references to actual residents, addresses, businesses, and institutions.[15] But it also echoes the reference book's organizational logic. The "Aeolus" episode, in which wind and journalism meet, blows through hundreds of varieties of rhetorical trope, from asyndeton to zeugma; "Oxen of the Sun," written with the aid of literary anthologies, is told in a roughly chronological series of parodies of celebrated prose styles by (male, British) writers; and "Sirens" performs an inventory of musical forms. In a 1919 letter to his patron Harriet Shaw Weaver, Joyce alluded to an exhaustive, totalizing energy in *Ulysses'* compartmentalized structure: "the progress of the book is in fact like the progress of some sandblast . . . each successive episode, dealing with some province of artistic culture (rhetoric or music or dialectic) leaves behind it a burnt up field. Since I wrote the Sirens I find it impossible to listen to music of any kind" (*L1*, 128–29). This scorched-earth encyclopedism inverts the claim that Dublin could be rebuilt out of *Ulysses*: here, the text consumes—both incorporates and burns up—the matter it takes on board, even if it does so in the name of some future reconstitution of that matter from the text.

---

[15] On Joyce's use of *Thom's*, and on the errors he variously inherited, propagated, and introduced, see Sam Slote, "The Thomistic Representation of Dublin in *Ulysses*," in *Making Space in the Works of James Joyce*, ed. Valérie Bénéjam and John Bishop (London: Routledge, 2012).

Such reconstructions, though not yet so dramatic as the rebuilding of a whole city, have been numerous. Any canonical "primary" text forms a hub whose spokes—articles, monographs, editions, adaptations—refer to it. But *Ulysses*, in addition to being a primary text in this manner, has served as a reference book for a myriad projects whose aim is less to comment on or interpret or stage *Ulysses* than to build out of it. At least two novels extrapolate whole narrative lives of *Ulysses'* protagonists from the details embedded in Joyce's book.[16] The subject of dozens of concordances, word lists, and annotations, *Ulysses* has also spawned a mini-industry in literary cartography whose most recent offering boasts eighty-one maps, illustrations showing characters' movements, lists of their postal addresses, and an account of Joyce's use of *Thom's Guide*.[17] And now computer modeling is enabling scholars to come a step closer to rebuilding vanished bits of Joyce's Dublin out of the book. Although 7 Eccles Street, the Georgian townhouse inhabited by the Blooms in *Ulysses*, was demolished during the mid-twentieth century to make way for a new hospital wing, a team of scholars and designers has combined literary, photographic, and archival evidence via AutoCAD and FormZ applications to recreate the space as a digitally animated three-dimensional model.[18] These last examples illustrate two points: first, *Ulysses'* encyclopedism is a matter not only of internal traits and authorial lore but also of textual genealogy, the book being both built from and generative of encyclopedias. And second, scholarship on *Ulysses* is a site where we can see drives fundamental to the text itself—in this case, the drive to meet demolition with a longing to reconstitute the world out of its textual surrogate—continuing to perform tangible work.

Joyce once boasted that he had "a grocer's assistant's mind"—one given, presumably, to the patient enumeration, display, and exchange of objects under the awning of commerce (*L*3, 304).[19] So far, critical discussion of *Ulysses'* fetish for lists and catalogs has tended to follow suit by linking it to shopkeeping, ascribing even the text's mock-epic rosters to its author's proclivity for totting up and taking inventory. The encyclopedism of *Ulysses* is commercial,

---

[16] See John Henry Raleigh, *The Chronicle of Leopold and Molly Bloom: "Ulysses" as Narrative* (Berkeley: University of California Press, 1977), and Peter Costello, *The Life of Leopold Bloom: A Novel* (Lanham, MD: Roberts Rinehart, 1992).

[17] See Ian Gunn, Clive Hart, and Harald Beck, *James Joyce's Dublin: A Topographical Guide to the Dublin of "Ulysses"* (London: Thames & Hudson, 2004).

[18] See Ian Gunn and Mark Wright, "Visualizing Joyce," in *Hypermedia Joyce Studies* 6.1 (2006): n.p. The model of 7 Eccles Street is at www.no7.org.uk.

[19] A remark Joyce made to his friend Claud W. Sykes while he was working on *Ulysses* in 1918 captures a similar absorption with commonplace utilities, here explicitly opposed to epic and placed in a gradient of national culture: "To me an Irish safety pin is more important than an English epic" (*JJ*, 423). The Irish safety pin does not need the machinery of epic to imbue it with importance; indeed, the passage seems to insist that *Ulysses* is not an epic of the Irish safety pin.

says this argument, whose proponents cite Joyce's habit of quizzing visiting Dubliners on the sequence of shopfronts along a particular street in their shared hometown.[20] Franco Moretti has argued that "in *Ulysses*, social relationships appear only through the prism of consumption," and that Joyce's book provides a "monumental autopsy" for the classical capitalism that ends with the postwar birth of monopoly capitalism, stranding the obsolete British free market economy in a crisis of overproduction.[21] Michael North, responding to Moretti's work on modern epic, takes issue with its tying that elite genre's encyclopedism to the emergence of a world economic system that was already accessible to the masses: "this supranational dimension can hardly count as an aesthetic innovation if an ordinary consumer in a place like De Kalb, Illinois, could buy dry goods decorated with motifs from King Tut's tomb. The world text, with its crazy mixture of Greece, Germany, India, and Rome, exists within a world economy where the mixtures are, if anything, even more indiscriminate."[22] North importantly reminds us here that a "world text," no matter how complex or inclusive, is always less so than the world, and that part of such a text's aesthetic and ideological function can be to misrecognize a part of the world for the whole. Yet for North "the world" remains loosely synonymous with "the world economy," and economic systems are, implicitly, the sole pinhole through which the social totality can be viewed *in camera*.[23]

To suggest that *Ulysses* imagines or grapples with total war as a portrait of the social totality is not to disarticulate total war from economic systems. As we have already seen, military theorists and international jurists after the First World War regarded civilians as contributing to an integrated national war economy and therefore as legitimate and effective targets. But the fact that total war theory requires economic assumptions in no way guarantees the obverse—that is, that economistic theories make a central place for war in their portrait of the social totality. What's more, economics is necessary

---

[20] See, for example, Duffy, "Disappearing Dublin," 46. Here Duffy is citing, rather than reproducing, the critical tradition that celebrates the putative encyclopedism of Joyce's "mimetic specificity."

[21] Moretti, "The Long Goodbye," 189, 185.

[22] Michael North, *Reading 1922: A Return to the Scene of the Modern* (New York: Oxford University Press, 1999), 24.

[23] At points, *Ulysses* seems explicitly to identify economics as its master discourse. The book's apparent self-description as "this chaffering allincluding most farraginous chronicle" (14.1412) in "Oxen of the Sun" squarely places its inclusivity in a scene of commercial transaction (*chaffer* means to "haggle," "dicker," or "bargain," and the word *farrago*, whence *farraginous*, is a word for "hodge-podge" or "mixed fodder," derived from a word meaning "grain"). As if to confirm Joyce's temperamental affiliation with the grocer's assistant, the penultimate episode contains Bloom's itemized budget for June 16, 1904, although the detailed accounting it offers is less extraordinary than the fact that the rest of the text so carefully tracks the exchange of money, goods, and services that the reader can see what transactions the budget distorts and suppresses. *Ulysses* can look poised to catch all fish in the net of the balance sheet.

but not sufficient for theorizing total war, which targets the civilian not only to diminish the state's productive capacities but also in the hopes of terrorizing the masses into rising against their own government and precipitating a surrender. The civilian, in the eyes of total war, is not only a laboring and consuming body but also a fulcrum for leveraging an enemy state's capitulation. Such a deployment of the enemy's civilians against the state may have certain economic lineaments (one expends resources on, say, terror-bombing campaigns with which to incite civilian insurrection), but this sort of violence is no longer a temporary means to the end of restoring economic life under a different regime. Much as one might be tempted to think of total war as a special case of economic life—as, adapting Clausewitz, economics by other means—a fully ramified total war theory asks us to entertain the inverse possibility: that economic systems are means of maintaining conditions for perpetual war, including the ongoing underdevelopment and domination of civilians by their own military elites. *Ulysses* does not subordinate economic systems to total war or vice versa. But it stages the struggle between these portraits of the social totality, animated by the very lust for totalizing representations it finally rejects. The formal body of the text is caught in these competing flows, whipsawed by their rival lines of force.

"Nestor," the book's second episode, seems to affirm the primacy of the economic in the way its central figure, Stephen's employer Garrett Deasy, assembles anti-Semitism, imperialism, and British cultural capital under the banner of thrift. But the episode begins with Stephen conducting a history lesson on Pyrrhus and the first Battle of Asculum, in the midst of which he imagines the destruction of a city or world in Blake-tinged language that will recur at a more explicitly apocalyptic moment later in the text: "I hear the ruin of all space, shattered glass and toppling masonry, and time one livid final flame. What's left us then?" (2.9–10).[24] His student's recalling Pyrrhus's words about Asculum ("Another battle like that and we are done for") prompts another devastating vision: "From a hill above a corpsestrewn plain a general speaking to his officers, leaned upon his spear. Any general to any officers. They lend ear" (2.16–17). As several commentators have pointed out, the remainder of the chapter is shot through with wartime rhetoric and allusions that belong less to the book's 1904 setting than to the moment of its

---

[24] The passage combines fragments from Blake's *A Vision of the Last Judgement*, with its eschatological visions of "a Great City on fire," and from *The Marriage of Heaven and Hell*, with its profession that "the world will be consumed by fire at the end of six thousand years." See William Blake, *The Complete Writings of William Blake*, ed. Geoffrey Keynes (London: Nonesuch Press, 1957), 608, and *The Complete Poems*, ed. Alicia Ostriker (Harmondsworth, UK: Penguin Books, 1977), 187. Stephen's shards of Blake and his trauma survivor's question "What's left us then?" commemorate not only burned Troy but bombed Trieste and another bombed and burning city Blake seemed elsewhere (*Poems* 195) to have foreseen: "The fire, the fire, is falling!/Look up! look up! O citizen of London, enlarge thy countenance[!]"

composition in 1917.[25] By that critical year—the year of the Bolshevik revolution and of the Great War's deepest settling into attrition and failed offen-
sives—the pupils Stephen instructs in "Nestor" would be of combatant age.
By figuring the boy's hockey game as battle, his thoughts seem to foreshadow
that grim diegetic future even while recalling wars past:

> Shouts rang shrill from the boys' playfield and a whirring whistle.
> Again: a goal. I am among them, among their battling bodies in a med-
> ley, the joust of life. You mean that knockkneed mother's darling who
> seems to be slightly crawsick? Jousts. Time shocked rebounds, shock by
> shock. Jousts, slush and uproar of battles, the frozen deathspew of the slain,
> a shout of spearspikes baited with men's bloodied guts. (2.316–18).

"Nestor" goes on to import the intergenerational agon of soldier versus general, a dominant cultural narrative about the Great War, into Stephen's meeting with Deasy; and it alludes repeatedly to cataclysmic violence (the "toppling
masonry" and Pyrrhic victory mentioned above; the "European conflagration" imagined in Deasy's letter about foot-and-mouth disease [2.327]). The
episode's saturation in Great War spectacle and rhetoric makes its reference
to the prophetess Cassandra (2.329) a nontrivial one: "Nestor" is an epicenter
of *Ulysses'* backdated prophecies, and is so pervaded with the wartime context
of its writing that Robert Spoo has claimed it bears comparison with the war
poetry of Wilfred Owen and Siegfried Sassoon.[26]

We'll return to the question of war and prophecy shortly. For now it's sufficient to note that these uncanny traces in "Nestor" of a diegetically future
war, in concert with the episode's fixation on ancient wars, may compete with
the economic for the status of master discourse, but that the economic has the
last word. In the final sentence, the very sunlight falling on Deasy gets figuratively monetized: "On his wise shoulders through the checkerwork of leaves
the sun flung spangles, dancing coins" (2.448–49). This same sun, as Stephen
sardonically notes earlier in the episode, supposedly never sets on the British
Empire, and the associative chain links Deasy to the financial and cultural
business of imperialism. Stephen's, by contrast, is the consciousness through
which the images and lexicon of war enter the chapter, interrupting Deasy's
master discourse. If the discourses of war and economics are rivals in the
episode, their rivalry depends on their remaining discrete enough to be thus
personified in the episode's two central figures. Moreover, economics seems
linked to nearly all the episode's major themes—race, religion, imperialism,

---

[25] See E. L. Epstein, "Nestor," in *James Joyce's "Ulysses": Critical Essays*, ed. Clive Hart and David
Hayman (Berkeley: University of California Press, 1974), 17–28; Robert Spoo, "'Nestor' and the
Nightmare: The Presence of the Great War in *Ulysses*," *Twentieth Century Literature* 32 (1986): 137–54;
Fairhall, 165–70; and Alistair Stead, "Great War *Ulysses*," *James Joyce Broadsheet* 71 (2005): 4.

[26] Spoo, 138.

gambling, literary culture—*but* war. This dramatic isolation of war signals that "Nestor," despite its martial references and rhetorics, conceives of war not as a general condition but as an event that occasionally interrupts the peacetime pursuits (commerce, literature, empire, etc.) that aggregate around the figure of Deasy; the episode, that is, imagines war as "conventional" rather than either total or perpetual. A second marker of war's conventionality here is its explicit gendering. Deasy tells Stephen, "A woman brought sin into the world. For a woman who was no better than she should be, Helen, the run-away wife of Menelaus, ten years the Greeks made war on Troy" (2.390–92). Women are those who start wars, not those who perish in them or labor in war industries, and in this single respect Stephen aligns with Deasy: his mental images of war are of muddy battlefields, schoolboys-turned-soldiers, old men presiding over the slaughter of young ones. Elsewhere in the first half of *Ulysses*, Bloom thinks of female casualties in connection with the burning and sinking of the *General Slocum*: "All those women and children excursion beanfeast burned and drowned in New York. Holocaust" (8.1146–47). By confining the mass death of women and children to a nonmilitary disaster, this instance highlights the exclusive masculine gendering of war and therefore its conventionality. War as "Nestor" and other early episodes in *Ulysses* imagine it cannot proffer itself as a master discourse because it is not yet total war; it is war as the exceptional rather than the general case, the bounded rather than the total.

Still, the raw materials of connections later episodes will develop between colonialism and total war are present as early on as "Nestor." Despite its seemingly distinct threads (wartime violence versus peacetime commerce, culture, and imperial adventurism), the episode is haunted by memories of "peacetime" violence in colonial spaces. While gazing at a manteltop portrait of Albert Edward, Prince of Wales (since 1902, King Edward VII), the Ulsterman Deasy asserts the length and complexity of his own historical memory, claiming to remember the famine of 1846, reminding Stephen that the Protestant Orange lodges lobbied for the repeal of the 1800 Act of Union before O'Connell did, adding "You fenians forget some things." In response, Stephen's interior monologue runs thus: "Glorious, pious and immortal memory. The lodge of Diamond in Armagh the splendid behung with corpses of papishes. Hoarse, masked and armed, the planters' covenant. The black north and the true blue bible. Croppies lie down" (2.272–76). Deasy's more-radical-than-thou speech stirs in Stephen's mind first the Ulster toast to the Protestant William of Orange, then a cluster of images evoking late-eighteenth-century Ireland: the clash of Protestant and Catholic paramilitary associations at the Diamond near Loughgall in 1795; the Protestant victory and consequent founding of the secret Orange Order (whose initial members swore to "exterminate all the Catholics in the Kingdom of Ireland"); the forced migration of thousands of Ulster Catholics, whose houses the Orangemen papered with the injunction "go to hell or Connaught"; the Wexford rebels ("Croppies") of 1798. Stephen's thoughts tell stories of violent Irish resistance to violent British occupation, and of secret paramilitary groups (i.e., civilians organized in a military manner) coercing civilians. These stories vex the distinctions—between peacetime and wartime, commerce and conflict, civilian and soldier—that lie at the heart of conventional warfare's historiography. Thus "Nestor," whose art Joyce's schemata designate as History, revokes the guarantee that Athena, disguised as Mentor, offers about the episode's Homeric namesake—that Nestor "will tell you history and no lies."[27] Without yet offering a fully realized critique of them, Joyce's "Nestor" replicates the biases of metropolitan historiography: its masculinist take on war, its emphasis on conflict between imperial nation states, its view of conventional warfare as an interruption in the business of civil society and economic life, and its peripheralizing of colonial violence.

These are precisely the biases that later episodes of *Ulysses*, above all the 5,000-line "Circe," will assail. But even this longest of *Ulysses*' episodes does not, finally, construct war as a counter-totality to economic models, nor does it fuse violence and economics in some super-unified field of exchange. Instead, it takes total war theatrically to its limits, insisting on its colonial history and its availability as a master discourse only to lay these at the feet of an open future. For *Ulysses*' totalizing drives confront their absolute limit in the future, which, pace Mendelson, gets exempted from the purview of the text despite its premonitory strains. These include probabilistic forecasts à la Diderot and geopolitical forms of earliness of the kinds I discussed earlier, those first sightings from the crow's nest of the colonial metropolis. But as we will see in numerous textual instances and at least one avant-textual one—a blatant "prediction" of the Great War that Joyce deleted from a draft of the "Cyclops" episode—*Ulysses* stops short of the kind of fulfilled prophecy that endorses classical epic's claims to self-sufficiency and organic world-portraiture. Its forecasts are less premonitory than admonitory. Rather than garner authority by foreclosing the future, they aim to hope and warn.

Encyclopedia Prophetica

Prophecy might well have been absent from Joyce's book, its absence serving as one of the indices by which the novel's 1904 setting measures its distance from the oracle-haunted world of Homer, the prophets of the Hebrew Bible, the vaticinations of early Christian mystics, and certain early modern seers. But instead, as we have begun to see, *Ulysses* teems with allusions to prophets and prophetic texts, with diegetic instances of prognostication, with skeptical

---

[27] Homer, *The Odyssey*, trans. Robert Fitzgerald (New York: Farrar, Straus and Giroux, 1998), 35.

anatomies of prophecy's social function. It is as if Joyce's book were an encyclopedia of prophecy. As such, *Ulysses* undertakes to demystify prophecy through aggregation, by assimilating it to its historical moment, and by making it one of many discourses competing for attention. Yet this deprivileging of prophecy is not the end of the story, for the novel also engages in acts of prescient, if conditional, *hope* that may be the true locus of untimeliness in the text, as against prophecy's false untimeliness. "Behold, I make all things new," intones the Book of Revelation. Even as *Ulysses* historicizes apocalyptic prophecy, the original news that stays news, it renovates future-directed utterance toward opener, less authoritative, less historical registers.[28]

As if to travesty the empty glamour-grab of self-fulfilling prophecy, *Ulysses'* most conspicuous (and frequently cited) forecast concerns itself, Ireland, and epic. In the "Scylla and Charybdis" episode, one of the Anglo-Irish littérateurs speaking with Stephen in the National Library says, "Our national epic has yet to be written" (9.309), a formulation in which the work appears at once to predict Irish nationhood and to designate itself as that emerging nation's epic. Certainly the prospect of an Irish nation-state attracts a good deal of *Ulysses'* forward-thinking energy.[29] But to read the "national epic" line as the text's straight self-nomination, as many readers have done, is to ignore every one of the book's other political forecasts. Deeply ambivalent in their nature and import, these could not be farther from, for instance, Mendelson's narrative of triumphant state-formation and literary messianism. For *Ulysses* never makes or alludes to a prophecy of national becoming without in some way blunting or annulling it. Sometimes this happens through carnivalesque interruption, as when the final words of Robert Emmet's speech from the dock—"When my country takes her place among the nations of the earth, then and not till then let my epitaph be written. I have done"—are broken up by the mingled sounds of a passing tram and Bloom's passing gas (see 11.1284–94). That syntax—"x will not happen until y transpires"—should be familiar to us from literary modes that consecrate prophecy at moments of regime change: the tragic ("Macbeth shall never vanquished be until / Great Birnam Wood to high Dunsinane Hill / Shall come against him") and the epic ("Troy

---

[28] Here I follow Arthur Danto in understanding prophecy to be a historical statement about the future: "The prophet is one who speaks about the future in a manner which is appropriate only to the past, or who speaks of the present in the light of a future treated as a *fait accompli*. A prophet treats the present in a perspective ordinarily available only to future historians, to whom present events are past, and for whom the meaning of present events is discernible." Arthur C. Danto, *Analytical Philosophy of History* (Cambridge: Cambridge University Press, 1968), 9.

[29] Indeed, Enda Duffy has argued that *Ulysses* is "*the* book of Irish postcolonial independence," both because it registers those (diegetically future) events that were concurrent with its composition and that led to the foundation of the Irish Free State and because it attempts to model subaltern subjectivities and communities that might come into being after independence (Duffy, *Subaltern "Ulysses,"* 1, emphasis in original).

will not fall until Philoctetes brings his bow from Lemnos"). *"Fuit Ilium!* The sack of windy Troy.... The masters of the Mediterranean are fellaheen today," says Professor MacHugh in "Aeolus," just after claiming that John F. Taylor's speech about the youthful Moses and the Egyptian high priest has "the prophetic vision" (7.909–11). Yet whether we think Taylor's speech eloquent or just windy, its "prophetic" qualities have more to do with vatic tone than with any accurate prediction of the Irish language revival's achieving Mosaic fullness. And this is true again and again in *Ulysses*: the *making* of political prophecy is an occasion for *checking*, and often for *mocking*, political prophecy.

But you can mock prophecy without detracting from its claim to be sacred, privileged speech. If instead you seek to *deconsecrate* prophecy, the surest way is not to mock it but to insist on its historicity—on its lack of untimely vantage, its being an artifact perfectly synchronous with its moment. *Ulysses* is a veritable museum of prognostication, curating its exhibits with care, ensuring that we may track prophecy to its historical ground. Sometimes this ground is closer to the present than it seems. Bloom, toward the end of "Nausicaa," recalls "Mother Shipton's prophecy that is about ships around they fly in the twinkling" (13.1065–66). He is thinking here about famous lines in which the Tudor prophetess from Yorkshire was thought to have predicted the steam engine, the railway, the diving suit, the submarine, the dreadnought, the air balloon, the telegraph, the gold rush, and the end of the world in 1881:

ANCIENT PREDICTION
(Entitled by popular tradition "Mother Shipton's Prophecy")
Published in 1448, republished in 1641

Carriages without horses shall go,
And accidents fill the world with woe.
Around the world thoughts shall fly
In the twinkling of an eye.
The world upside down shall be
And gold be found at the root of a tree.
Through hills man shall ride,
And no horse be at his side.
Under water men shall walk,
Shall ride, shall sleep, shall talk.
In the air men shall be seen,
In white, in black, in green;
Iron in the water shall float,
As easily as a wooden boat.
Gold shall be found and shown
In a land that's now not known.
Fire and water shall wonders do,

England shall at last admit a foe.
The world to an end shall come,
In eighteen hundred and eighty one.[30]

But this wasn't, in fact, a Tudor-era prediction: by 1904, the passage Bloom recalls was widely known to have been introduced by one Charles Hindley into an 1862 edition of a book on Mother Shipton.[31] Hindley's misattribution of backdated prophecies to a long-dead prophet—his faked "revival" of a Renaissance text—is a classic example of something called *vaticinationes ex eventu*, the disfigurement of the archive to make the past appear to predict an already realized future. By including this example of *ex eventu* prophecy, then, *Ulysses* fortifies its readers against the very technique by which Mendelson says encyclopedic novels secure their prophetic authority, exhibiting the production of false apocalyptic prophecy as itself a legibly historical act.

If we turn to what genetic critics call the avant-texte of *Ulysses*—that is, the totality of its surviving prepublication drafts—we find an extraordinary refusal of *ex eventu* prophecy at the compositional level. Among the forgone textual futures of *Ulysses*, in a 1919 draft of the "Cyclops" episode, there is a backdated prophecy of the Great War. In the draft, a pubgoer named O'Madden Burke tells his fellow drinkers,

there's a war coming on for the English and the Germans will give them a hell of a gate of going. What they got from the Boers is only what you might call an hors d'oeuvre. . . . But this time, whether they win or lose, . . . They'll be up against an army that'll kill a man for every man they kill. Wait till you see.[32]

---

[30] Qtd. in William H. Harrison, *Mother Shipton Investigated: The Result of Critical Examination in the British Museum Library, of the Literature Related to the Yorkshire Sibyl* (London: W. H. Harrison, 1881), 12–13. The claim that the prophecy was first published in 1448 seems to be an instance of spectacular carelessness, as the year of publication antedates the traditionally held year of Mother Shipton's birth by forty years.

[31] The book was *The Life and Death of Mother Shipton*, originally edited by Richard Head and published in London in 1684, reprinted in 1862 with additions by Hindley. The April 26, 1873 issue of *Notes and Queries* reported "Mr. Charles Hindley, of Brighton, in a letter to us, has made a clean breast of having fabricated the Prophecy quoted at page 450 of our last volume, with some ten others included in his reprint of a chap-book version, published in 1862." Qtd. in Harrison, 43. Hindley's admission of the hoax did not prevent hysteria from breaking out in rural parts of England as the year 1881 drew near. The 11th edition of the *Encyclopaedia Britannica* (Cambridge: Cambridge University Press, 1911) records, "The suggestion that Mother Shipton had foretold the end of the world in 1881 was the cause of the most poignant alarm throughout rural England in that year, the people deserting their houses, and spending the night in prayer in the fields, churches and chapels."

[32] Buffalo MS V.A.8, p. 19v; James Joyce, *The James Joyce Archive*, ed. Michael Groden, Hans Walter Gabler, David Hayman, A. Walton Litz, and Danis Rose (New York: Garland, 1977–79), 13:120; James Joyce, *Joyce's Notes and Early Drafts for "Ulysses": Selections from the Buffalo Collection*, ed. Phillip F. Herring (Charlottesville: University Press of Virginia, 1977), 169. In his recent discussion of the passage, Groden notes that in the next draft Joyce replaced "the English" with "the Sassenachs" (a Celtic term for Saxons or English people generally), "they" with "the imperial yeomanry," and "army" with "conundrum." See Michael Groden, *"Ulysses" in Progress* (Princeton: Princeton University Press, 1977), 145, and *"Ulysses" in Focus: Genetic, Textual, and Personal Views* (Gainesville: University of

The utterance not only foretells the war's scale, bloodiness, and key adversaries but also links a conflict between imperial nation-states to colonial warfare through the figure of the "hors d'oeuvre," a course that is at once outside the main meal and its certain harbinger. Had this prophecy remained in the published text, it would have exemplified just the sort of rigged authority-bid that Mendelson ascribes to premonitory encyclopedic narratives. But Joyce deleted the passage from the episode prior to the fair-copy Rosenbach Manuscript, with the result that the longitudinal flow of revision now stages the same rejection of prophecy that the published text performs at the level of theme and rhetoric. The remaining adumbrations of the Great War and of the prospect of the peace of nations in the published *Ulysses* are, as we have seen in the case of "Nestor," much more oblique ones, and they are often cheek by jowl with language about the future's resistance to divination.[33]

What is true of forged prophecy is also true of good-faith prediction: both acts are historically intelligible ways of being in a particular present—of being, after all, the contemporaries of our contemporaries. In the penultimate "Ithaca" episode we learn that a drawer in the Blooms' walnut sideboard contains "a sealed prophecy (never unsealed) written by Leopold Bloom in 1886 concerning the consequences of passing into law of William Ewart Gladstone's Home Rule bill of 1886 (never passed into law)" (17.1787–90). Here prophecy—again, pointedly failed—appears where *Ulysses* has taught us to expect it: filed away in the archive, among dirty postcards and pen nibs and a toddler's drawings. A form of expression in which the knowledge, fears, and desires of a particular moment can be read with special clarity, prophecy, for

---

Florida Press, 2010), 131; the subsequent draft to which Groden refers is Buffalo MS V.A.6, p. 3; Joyce, *Archive* 13:134c; Joyce, *Notes and Early Drafts*, 180–81. For an engaging discussion of how the classical unities of "Cyclops" are haunted by allusions to post-1904 events, see Susan de Sola Rodstein, "Back to 1904: Joyce, Ireland, and Nationalism," in *European Joyce Studies 8: Joyce: Feminism/Post/Colonialism*, ed. Ellen Carol Jones (Amsterdam: Rodopi, 1998), 145–85.

[33] As Groden notes (*"Ulysses" in Progress*, 145), a prediction about the First World War enters the "Aeolus" episode in a late revision, where Myles Crawford makes a reference to the Archduke Franz Ferdinand's June 9, 1904, visit, as an emissary of his father Emperor Franz Joseph I of Austria, to Edward VII of England: "Sent his heir over to make the king an Austrian fieldmarshal now. Going to be trouble there one day" (7.542–43). In contrast to the prophecy deleted from "Cyclops," this one is brief and swept along by a stream of other references to Austria. Because Crawford is scanning Deasy's letter on foot-and-mouth disease while he speaks, it is not clear whether "Going to be trouble there one day" is his own prediction or one he is reading from the typescript. This is prophecy with an ambiguous prophet.

The "Eumaeus" episode also contains what looks like a prophecy of the First World War: "But a day of reckoning ... was in store for mighty England ... There would be a fall and the greatest fall in history. The Germans and the Japs were going to have their little lookin, he affirmed. The Boers were the beginning of the end. Brummagem England was toppling already and her downfall would be Ireland, her Achilles heel" (16.996–1003). Any clairvoyant authority the utterance might have had is weakened by its only partial accuracy—to say nothing of the fact that it is spoken by the cabman's shelter's clearly mendacious proprietor, who may or may not be "Skin-the-Goat" Fitzharris.

all its yearning to part the curtains of the future, may be the historical artifact par excellence.

I want to pause, though, over Bloom's prophecy to observe that the "Ithaca" narrators, who can cross even the boundary between factual and counter-factual—telling us, for example, to what purpose Bloom *could have* applied the boiled water (11.275–76), what careers he *could have* pursued (11.787–94), or why he *would have* smiled if he had smiled (11.2126–31)—these narrators decline to unseal the envelope and expose the verbatim contents of Bloom's prophecy. Why? At the very least, this act of narratorial reticence bespeaks a deep sympathy with Bloom, a choice to leave unread what he has either forgotten about or decided not to open. If Bloom has made a decision—the likelier reading, given that he has taken pains to conserve the envelope among other important documents that he revisits—it seems to be the decision to preserve his forecast unopened until the prospect that inspired its writing may be fulfilled. That is, as long as Irish Home Rule remains unachieved, the prophecy will remain unread by both Bloom and the narrators.

This would seem to resurrect the syntax of "not until . . . only then" that *Ulysses* has elsewhere mocked, there as here in respect to future-conditional political change. But there's a difference: whereas the delimiting clauses in my earlier examples—Emmet's "*When* my country takes its place" and the weird sisters' "*Until*/Great Birnam Wood to high Dunsinane Hill / Shall come against him" and the prophet Helenos's "*until* Philoctetes brings his bow"—camouflage prophecy in the language of contingency, Bloom saves his sealed forecast in the truly contingent hope that the conditions for opening it *might* arrive. For starker contrast, set Bloom's gesture beside the eschatological couplet Charles Hindley ascribed to Mother Shipton: "The world to an end *shall* come /In eighteen-hundred and eighty-one." A simple future utterance like this one radiates certainty until it fails to transpire, whereupon its prophetic authority is discredited and dispelled. But to leave unopened your eighteen-year-old forecasts about the consequences of a still-unrealized political condition—such an act may be susceptible to disappointment, but not to discrediting. Unlike the brittle prophetic utterance, Bloom's reserve (which is also the text's) has the resilient, ongoing quality of an act of vigilance, the result not of one but of a series of decisions to keep waiting, keep hoping. Ernst Bloch, the great theorist of political hope, had this to say of prophecy that manipulates the present through false guarantees about the future:

> There was a man who exchanged paper money of his own making for cash, imprinted with the words "Payable in the Currency of God's Kingdom on Judgment Day." Which sounds like a model for the enormous swindle perpetrated by the Thousand-year Reich. . . . It was the vilest caricature of Adventism, of the false Messiah, of the expectation of Christ's Second Coming on the day after tomorrow—and nothing came of it, except blood.

"God arrives next Tuesday at 11:25 a.m. at the Illinois Central, hurry there to welcome him!" In this way a religious or (so to speak) utopian psychosis was started once in Chicago.[34]

As the ever-imminent Dr. John Alexander Dowie, a.k.a. Elijah III, who "Is coming! Is coming!! Is coming!!!" in *Ulysses* (8.15) reminds us, "The Deity ain't no nickel dime bumshow" but "a corking fine business proposition" (14.1585–87). The "swindle" of the confident short-term divination always charges a heavy up-front fee in worldly currencies while promising hundredfold profits in the world to come. In contrast to this swindle of certitude, Bloch describes a *"well-founded"* hope that

> must be unconditionally disappointable . . . because it is open in a forward direction, in a future-oriented direction; it does not address itself to that which already exists. For this reason, hope—while actually in a state of suspension—is committed to change rather than repetition, and what is more, incorporates the element of chance, without which there can be nothing new. Through this portion of chance, however sufficiently determined it may be, openness is at the same time also *kept open*. At least to the extent that hope, whose field of action this is, pays in the coin of hazard so as not to be indebted to the past.

The kind of disappointment entailed in well-founded hope, Bloch adds, is its "creative 'minus' . . . as distinguished form the false 'plus'" of overconfident prophecy.[35] I have been suggesting, in effect, that *Ulysses* is an encyclopedia of the "false 'plus,'" seeking through its catalog of accidental, falsified, and commodified prophecies to fortify its readers against such confident swindles. Where it would leave us is in a space of the "creative 'minus,'" a space of potential, even ongoing, disappointment that we have nevertheless come to understand as indissociable from a rigorous hope.

That's a rather fine description of the book's final three *nostos* or homecoming episodes, and particularly of "Ithaca." Written in the form of a catechism whose questions do not so much elicit answers as knowingly anticipate them, the episode could have been a deterministic paradise. In promising, as Joyce put it, to let "the reader know everything and know it in the baldest coldest way" (*L1*, 159–60), "Ithaca" poses as the terminus to speculation, interpretation, and curiosity—as the answer-key at the back of the textbook. Its epic intertext, moreover, aligns this forestructuring with paroxysmal violence: in Homer the *nostos* entails a cold-blooded slaughter of the suitors and

---

[34] Ernst Bloch, *Literary Essays*, trans. Andrew Joron et al., (Stanford: Stanford University Press, 1998), 339–40. The piece, entitled "Can Hope Be Disappointed?" was Bloch's inaugural lecture at the University of Tübingen, delivered on November 17, 1961.

[35] Ibid., 341, 340; emphasis in original.

unfaithful servants by Odysseus and Telemakhos, as if the raider of cities had made a Troy of his home. Yet in gestures that are by turns hilarious, whimsical, and devastating, "Ithaca" repeatedly defaults on—disappoints—the promise of its form to foreclose interpretation or futurity. Yes-or-no questions are met with indirect answers, or drowned in surplus information, as in the famous water odyssey (17.163–228). Flat-toned queries inspire echolalia ("a shock, a shoot, with thought of aught he sought though fraught with nought" [17.284–85] in a response to a question about the advantages of shaving at night), outbreaks of cutesiness (the enumerations of Milly Bloom's feline traits—"cf mousewatching cat" [17.900]), and sudden lyricism ("The heaventree of stars hung with humid nightblue fruit" [17.1039]). Enigmas ("Who was M'Intosh?") remain unsolved and answers are deformed in the image of characters' anxieties, fantasies, deceptions, and self-deceptions—or in sympathy with their hopes, as with Bloom's unopened prophecy. The reader who consults "Ithaca" with the aim of knowing everything in the baldest coldest way finds pages of ludic inclusivity, stunning omissions, rival temporalities, ill-assorted codes and dictions hunkering under the pretense of a house style. Finds, that is to say, encyclopedism. Crucially, though, this paradise of the creative minus refuses to dissociate itself entirely from the false pluses of epic and of fulfilled prophecy. Its bloody Homeric overtones, its conversance with the imagination of disaster, Stephen's incredible violation of hospitality in singing an anti-Semitic ballad to his Jewish host—these facets of "Ithaca" keep it from being an oasis of playfulness or celestial calm.[36] Unconditional

---

[36] Although "Ithaca" displaces violence into its less kinetic registers, it remains nonetheless preoccupied with disaster: "the deluge" (17.749), "a submerged, petrified city" (17.1975), "decimating epidemics: catastrophic cataclysms which make terror the basis of human mentality: seismic upheavals the epicentres of which are located in densely populated regions" (17.1003–5), "sublunary disasters" (17.1152), "holocaust" (17.2051), "Armageddon" (17.2056), "a cataclysmic annihilation of the planet in consequence of a collision with a dark sun" (17.2181–82). The episode's encyclopedia of last things makes Revelation, rather than the *Odyssey*, its chief intertext. The whole of "Ithaca," with its drive to list and tabulate, occurs in the shadow of the following apocalyptic answer to the question of what could nullify the calculations of Stephen's and Bloom's relative ages: "The cessation of existence of both or either, the inauguration of a new era or calendar, the annihilation of the world and consequent extermination of the human species, inevitable but impredictable" (17.462–65). Even when offered as speculation, this irruption of apocalyptic scale and finality into the domestic setting of "Ithaca" flings into a momentary abyss two characters whose communion the chapter is supposed to enact, however briefly and imperfectly. As vividly as Homer's description of the slaughter of the suitors, such moments in "Ithaca" forge a connection between domicile and radical violence, even obliteration; they insist that every Ithaca may host, beget, even become, an Ilium.

On Stephen's singing of "Little Harry Hughes," see Marilyn Reizbaum, *James Joyce's Judaic Other* (Stanford: Stanford University Press, 1999); Vicki Mahaffey, "Sidereal Writing: Male Refractions and Malefactions in 'Ithaca,'" in *"Ulysses"—En-Gendered Perspectives: Eighteen New Essays on the Episodes*, ed. Kimberly J. Devlin and Marilyn Reizbaum (Columbia, NC: University of South Carolina Press, 1999), 254–66; and Margot Norris, *Virgin and Veteran Readings of "Ulysses"* (New York: Palgrave Macmillan, 2011), chap. 10.

disappointability can no more be decoupled from the prospect of violence than it can be reduced to it.

No passage in "Ithaca" better captures the fusion of hazard, caprice, and openness, of disappointment and hope, than the excursus on clown and coin in Bloom's musings. Stephen has declined Bloom's proposal of asylum and the two men discuss counterproposals—scenarios in which Italian lessons, vocal coaching, and intellectual dialogue could be exchanged for the benefit of Stephen and both Blooms. But then the question comes: "What rendered problematic for Bloom the realization of these mutually selfexcluding propositions?" And the answer is one of those moments where polite conversation crumbles, exposing a fund of loss. Bloom doubts things will work out with Stephen for two reasons: first, "the irreparability of the past"—because dead sons do not come back to life and the intuitive particolored clown is not his child; and second,

> ... The imprevidibility of the future: once in the summer of 1889 he (Bloom) had marked a florin (2/–) with three notches on the milled edge and tendered it in payment of an account due to and received by J. and T. Davy, family grocers, 1 Charlemont Mall, Grand Canal, for circulation on the waters of civic finance, for possible, circuitous or direct, return.

> Was the clown Bloom's son?

> No.

> Had Bloom's coin returned?

> Never. (17.973–88)

That "Never" has an undeniable affective truth for a man whose dead son and dead father are never coming back, who has made many unrewarded donations to various goodwill economies, and who has even been punished for those donations. And it is grammatically true that the coin has *never*—that is, *not ever*—returned. But in a temporal sense, that "never" is hyperbolic, is not strictly true; it would be more accurate to say "not yet." (Which raises the question: under what conditions and for what reasons is *not yet* misrecognized here for *never*?)[37] What's more, even were the marked coin to return,

---

[37] The same question and observations apply to those two instances of *never* in the description of Bloom's "sealed prophecy (*never* unsealed)" concerning "Gladstone's Home Rule bill of 1886 (*never* passed into law)" discussed above (11. 1788–90; emphasis added). Although it is true that the particular Home Rule bill in question was *not ever* passed into law, the general political condition of Home Rule is one that has simply *not yet* come to pass by June 1904. In relation to that future-conditional Home Rule, Bloom's prophecy has *not yet* been unsealed. Michael Rubenstein discusses the clown and coin passage in compatible terms, reading "the waters of civic finance"—both economic infrastructure and public utilities—as sites where *Ulysses* thinks both social totality and political hope; see his *Public Works: Infrastructure, Irish Modernism, and the Postcolonial* (Notre Dame, IN: Notre Dame University Press, 2010), 87–92.

it would not demonstrate the *previdibility*, or foreseeability, of the future; its return, no less than its failure to return, would demonstrate the *imprevidibility* of the future.[38] The future's resistance to divination, and its attendant capacity (or even tendency) to disappoint our hopes—these are the positive conditions rather than the costly outcome of paying in the coin of hazard for the chance that something unforeseen will happen. That more is at stake here than coin or clown or even a new friendship becomes apparent in the next exchange:

Why would a recurrent frustration the more depress him?

Because at the critical turningpoint of human existence he desired to amend many social conditions, the product of inequality and avarice and international animosity. (17.989–92)

Tied up in the question of Bloom's future-conditional disappointments is nothing less than utopian political hope, a hope whose referent seems to supersede the political form of the nation-state while memorializing some of its sorrows in the phrase "international animosity." This isn't to suggest that Joyce's book is exclusively awaiting the perpetual peace of some cosmopolitan postnational order—only that the political futures it takes the trouble to conjure are not limited to an Irish nation whose epic it could become. *Ulysses* keeps vigil over more than one unopened envelope.

In "Aeolus," Lenehan says of the prophet Moses that he died "with a great future behind him" (7.875–76). As we've seen, preposterous truth often thrives in the patter of clowns, and Lenehan is one of *Ulysses*' best. Here his jest reminds us that the future is always *seen from somewhere*, whether from Egypt or Pisgah, and that past hopes and preparations for the future, although they recede, may be recovered and rehabilitated as resources in the present. History, that is, may be a repository of forgone possibilities, unrealized desiderata, utopias that keep feeding our plans. Paul Ricoeur could almost be glossing Lenehan when he laments, "We have so many unfulfilled plans behind us, so many promises that have still not been held, that we have the means of rebuilding the future through reviving our heritage in its multiple forms."[39] Or Ernst Bloch again:

[Hu]mankind is not yet finished; therefore, neither is its past. It continues to affect us under a different sign, in the drive of its questions, in the

---

[38] The *OED* records a use of *imprevisibility* in 1887. But Joyce's use of *imprevidibility* in "Ithaca" is the first known appearance of the word in English and thus, in a term appropriate to the passage, a coinage. Like the florin coin (a British two-shilling piece named after a thirteenth-century Florentine coin) with which it is thereby linked, the word *imprevidibility* is marked by an Italian origin, in *imprevedibilità*, "unforeseeability," "unpredictability," or "capriciousness."

[39] Paul Ricoeur, *Amour et justice* (Tübingen: J. C. B. Nohr, 1990), 58; qtd. in and trans. Jérôme Bindé, "Toward an Ethics of the Future," in *Globalization*, ed. Arjun Appadurai (Durham, NC: Duke University Press, 2003), 112–13.

experiment of its answers; we are all in the same boat. The dead return transformed: those whose actions were too bold to have come to an end (like Thomas Münzer); those whose work is too all-encompassing to have coincided with the locality of their times (like Aeschylus, Dante, Shakespeare, Bach, Goethe). The discovery of the future in the past, that is the philosophy of history, hence of philosophical history as well.[40]

And, we might add, of a philosophy of literature as an encyclopedia of not yet completed futures, one that seeks ways of changing literature into a literature of changing the world. Reviving mothballed forms and dormant emplotments, checking for a pulse among left-for-dead texts—that would be a rereading very different from striving to catch up to a work deemed, as Joyce's book has so often been, ahead of its time. We have a great future behind us, and one of its names is *Ulysses*.

Urban Violence and Amity Lines

But it was neither as a repository of futures past nor as a simulacrum of a vanished city that *Ulysses* appeared to Air Commodore L. E. O. Charlton in late 1922. He viewed it, remember, as an "official handbook to the country of his sojourn"—as a present-tense guide to the new British mandate of Iraq, whose aerial policing he would first help administer and soon come to protest.[41] Charlton made the remark in his 1931 memoir, with the benefit of nearly a decade's hindsight. Nonetheless it's a stunning claim, one that no academic reader of Joyce's book would think to make for many decades. If scholars were—or are—"still learning to be James Joyce's contemporaries, to understand our interpreter," as Richard Ellmann famously wrote in 1959, it may be that certain nonscholarly readers have been better positioned to read *Ulysses* as contemporaries, better equipped to see its congruity with other spaces where law, violence, and spectacle took nonmetropolitan forms.[42] We can only guess what more Charlton had to say about *Ulysses* in general and about the "Circe" episode in particular. But as that fifteenth episode is the book's

---

[40] Ernst Bloch, "Dialectics and Hope," trans. Mark Ritter, *New German Critique* 9 (Autumn 1976): 8. The essay was originally a chapter in Bloch's *Subjekt–Objekt, Erläuterungen zu Hegel* (1951). Thomas Münzer was a radical theologian in early-sixteenth-century Germany about whom Bloch elsewhere wrote, "Above all, Münzer is history in a fruitful sense; he and his cause and all things past that are worth recording are made to obligate us, to enthuse us, to support more and more that which is always meant to be for us" (Ernst Bloch, *Thomas Münzer als Theologe der Revolution*, 1921); qtd. and trans. in Bloch, *Literary Essays*, 129.

[41] L. E. O. Charlton, *Charlton* (London: Faber & Faber, 1931), 269.

[42] The claim of Joyce's earliness and his readers' belatedness opens the first edition of Ellmann's celebrated biography of Joyce; see Richard Ellmann, *James Joyce* (New York: Oxford University Press, 1959), 1.

most extended engagement with war, international law, colonial violence, and the figure of the civilian, one imagines it would have been the center of his "official handbook" reading, the unlooked-for literary guide to his experiences in Baghdad and Diwaniya. And if he had witnessed either kind of RAF "bombing demonstration"—the triumphalist metropolitan spectacle or the colonial use of sovereign violence to deter resistance—he might have found elements of both in "Circe"'s damaged pageantry.

Charlton's invocation of the handbook genre, applied to "Circe," seems almost as facetious as his use of the descriptor "official." Episode fifteen is written in the form not of a manual or vade mecum but of an unperformable script that ricochets crazily among theatrical, naturalistic, surrealist, and other modes. This extreme technical play is irreducible to a single historical referent, but some of the most provocative scholarship on the episode has linked it to the revolutionary upheavals of the Irish War of Independence (1919–1921), during whose violent central year "Circe" was written and rewritten. For Enda Duffy, the episode's clashing modes pose a central question about the use of terrorist methods by anticolonial movements: "How can the project of liberation, which aims to enable the construction of new subjectivities, exist in the same breath as terrorist violence that is willing to wreck any subjectivity in its path?"[43] This perceptive way of putting the question also blinkers it in one respect: it treats terrorism as a question only for militant anticolonialists, not for imperial nation-states. Other discussions of violence in "Circe" hew similarly to the international legal distinction between the licit war of nations and the illicit terror of nonstate actors. Yet Joyce rejected this very distinction during the Great War's final months, characterizing that conflict as an act of state-sponsored terror: "Naturally I can't approve of the act of the revolutionary who tosses a bomb in a theatre . . . On the other hand, have those states behaved any better which have drowned the world in a blood bath?" (*JJ*, 446). Far from granting the insurgent a monopoly on terror, "Circe" is remarkable for its refusal to do just that. It asks *both* state and nonstate actors its crucial question: How are emancipatory, subjectivity-making projects to coexist with a will to unlimited violence?

The episode's most vivid rejection of the war–terror divide brings *Ulysses'* encyclopedism to bear on a scene of urban disaster, once again fusing the city's name with its destruction:

---

[43] For Duffy, the episode stages both the question and a response to it at the level of mode, juxtaposing realism and modernism in order to point up the limitations of each in compassing the problem of terror. In critiquing these two modes, he argues, "Circe" challenges the reader to envision a third, postmodern one in which the uses and abuses of realism and modernism are instructively copresent and the subaltern's future status as a speaking agent, neither hypertrophied nor abject, can be imagined. See Duffy, *Subaltern "Ulysses,"* 132 and chap. 4, passim.

DISTANT VOICES

Dublin's burning! Dublin's burning! On fire, on fire!

(*Brimstone fires spring up. Dense clouds roll past. Heavy Gatling guns boom. Pandemonium. Troops deploy. Gallop of hoofs. Artillery. Hoarse commands. Bells clang. Backers shout. Drunkards bawl. Whores screech. Foghorns hoot. Cries of valour. Shrieks of dying. Pikes clash on cuirasses. Thieves rob the slain. Birds of prey, winging from the sea, rising from marshlands, swooping from eyries, hover screaming, gannets, cormorants, vultures, goshawks, climbing woodcocks, peregrines, merlins, blackgrouse, sea eagles, gulls, albatrosses, barnacle geese. The midnight sun is darkened. The earth trembles. The dead of Dublin from Prospect and Mount Jerome in white sheepskin overcoats and black goatfell cloaks arise and appear to many. A chasm opens with a noiseless yawn. . . . Factory lasses with fancy clothes toss redhot Yorkshire baraabombs. Society ladies lift their skirts above their heads to protect themselves. Laughing witches in red cutty sarks ride through the air on broomsticks. Quakerlyster plasters blisters. It rains dragons' teeth. Armed heroes spring up from furrows. . . . On an eminence, the centre of the earth, rises the field altar of Saint Barbara.*) (15.4659–89)[44]

We might take this as *Ulysses'* prophecy that the end of the world will emanate from the periphery, or at least from practices incubated there. At the same time, Joyce's vision of urban apocalypse is so antic and so miscellaneous as to disrupt prophecy's self-importance and epistemological privilege. The passage's compendious energy remakes Dublin into Every City, the composite backdrop to Crucifixion, Armageddon, World War, London fire, Theban civil war, witches' Sabbath, Easter Rising, 1798 Rebellion, suffragist revolt, proletarian revolution, and horror film. It is a short encyclopedia of eschatology, and it insists that the world also ends, in a sense, when political epochs are overturned in mass movements. One thing, at least, we can recover from this strange jumble of recycled tropes and unprecedented events: the catastrophe here seems to flow equally from bomb-tossing factory lasses and armies mobilized within a civilian space, from terror waged by both insurrectionists and states. But we look in vain, finally, for a cause of this disaster, which unfolds automatically rather than in response to some intention. Terror here is a spontaneous combustion; the inversion of the world, culminating in a chiasmic tourney among infighting Irish patriots (*"John O'Leary against Lear O'Johnny"*) and a black mass celebrated on the altar of the pregnant Mina Purefoy's belly. It is an event in which everyone and no one is an agent, and

---

[44] As Roy Gottfried has pointed out to me, St. Barbara is the patron saint, in modernity, of artillerymen, miners, and other who use explosives. Her patronage stems from her early association with lightning, which was the punitive instrument of her pagan father's death after he beheaded her for being a Christian.

the cartoonishness of the passage—its anarchic census of grotesques still pursuing their agendas as the world ends—is eerily constitutive of the total violence it embodies.

We see more clearly how the "Dublin's burning!" passage juxtaposes insurgent violence, counterinsurgent reprisal, and total war when we restore it to the context of the surrounding pages. The potpourri apocalypse in "Circe," we find, does not spring from standard evocations of the portentous Last Days; instead, it arises out of worldly references to imperial pomp, international law and arbitration, and colonial warfare. These references are threaded through 400 lines of escalating tension between two characters on a crowded street in Dublin's red-light district, finally culminating in a public act of soldier-on-civilian violence in a colonial space—a one-blow dust-up framed as a synecdoche for mass conflict. The dissymmetry of this conflict exposes the hollowness of the scenes that precede it—scenes that stage monarchial self-congratulation and the "fair fight" rhetoric of international rules of warfare. But it does more: the British soldier's attack on the colonial civilian is in some sense *produced by* the discourses of benevolent empire and cosmopolitanism, the civilian's ironic, drunken ventriloquism of those discourses being part of what spurs the drunk soldier to strike him. Far from being a check on such an act, international law is presented here, in the episode's quasi-allegorical register, as an alibi and even a delivery system for colonial violence.

Toward the end of "Circe," Bloom follows Stephen out of Bella Cohen's brothel into the street, where the redcoat Private Carr accuses Stephen of having insulted Cissy Caffrey, Carr's hired company for the evening. The voices of the crowd set up the nature of the confrontation, naming the participants by category: "No, he didn't. I seen him. The girl there. He was in Mrs. Cohen's. What's up? Soldier and civilian" (15.4378–79). Soon after this, Stephen drunkenly muses on the asymmetries of a face-off between soldier and civilian, at the same time implying that a one-on-one confrontation of this kind stands in for something larger: "Doctor Swift says one man in armour will beat ten men in their shirts. Shirt is synechdoche. Part for the whole" (15.4402–3).[45] Having introduced the prospect of military violence against unarmed colonial civilians, the discourse then slips laterally to the question of war and peace between states. Stephen says, "Struggle for life is the law of existence but human philirenists [i.e., peace-lovers], notably the tsar and the king of England, have invented arbitration. (*he taps his brow*) But in here it is I must

---

[45] Swift's "A Letter to the Whole People of Ireland" (1724) presents an even more savage dissymmetry, along the way illustrating how reason and force are at once invincible and incompatible forms of argument: "For, in reason, all government without the consent of the governed, is the very definition of slavery: but, in fact, eleven men well armed will certainly subdue one single man in his shirt." Jonathan Swift, *The Drapier's Letters, and Other Works, 1724–1725*, ed. Herbert Davis (Oxford: Basil Blackwell, 1959), 62–63.

kill the priest and the king" (15.4434–37). The focus here is on Stephen's mental fight against internalized authorities, but the historical references are nonetheless serious ones: to Tsar Nicholas II, who in 1898 convened the first Hague Conference, which established the Permanent Court of Arbitration, the first global mechanism for settling interstate disputes; and to Edward the Seventh, known as "Edward the Peacemaker" for promoting international goodwill and for the treaties of arbitration he forged in 1903 and 1904 with France, Spain, Italy, Germany, and Portugal.[46] Yet the tone of Stephen's utterance is ironical, and his mention of the imperial monarchs reminds us that the Court of Arbitration sought to curb violence between imperial nation-states, not between those states and their colonies. Only three months after the 1899 Hague Conference, British troops departed for the Boer War, a conflict invoked repeatedly during the final pages of "Circe" alongside references to two other wars of expansion or imperial competition: the Zulu War and, through a snatch of Tennyson's "The Charge of the Light Brigade," the Crimean War.[47]

Thus Stephen's internal memo—"But in here it is I must kill the priest and the king"—is not just about the need for regicide and clericide in the mind; it is also about how the cosmopolitan ideal crystallized in international arbitration exempted colonies from its peaceful vision. Carr, however, mistakes Stephen's note-to-self as a more specifically seditious remark: "What's that you're saying about my king?" (15.4447). At this, who should appear but Edward the Peacemaker himself, mumbling about "Peace, perfect peace"—the title of a popular late-nineteenth-century hymn and a seeming nod to the sort of cosmopolitan order Kant imagined in *Toward Perpetual Peace*. But again the utopian pieties of this vision get immediately undercut by the episode's shifting portraiture, as Edward the Peacemaker morphs from Kantian cosmopolite into a knuckles-and-know-how referee of the fair duel. Says Edward to his public, "We have come here to witness a clean straight fight and we heartily wish both men the best of good luck" (15.4460–61). This description of conflict as "clean," "straight," "hearty," and manly seems ridiculous in the century of total war, but it squares with the vision of regulated pugilism incarnated in the Hague Conventions of 1899 and 1907, and with the understanding that the

---

[46] Fairhall (194) notes that in *A Portrait of the Artist as a Young Man*, the character McCann, modeled on Joyce's friend Francis Skeffington, is an advocate of "the Csar's rescript, of Stead, of general disarmament, arbitration in cases of international disputes" and other cosmopolitan pacifisms. Stephen meets these views, much as he does in "Circe," with derision: "Three cheers for universal brotherhood!" James Joyce, *A Portrait of the Artist as a Young Man* (New York: Viking, 1964), 196.

[47] These include a reference to the Boer commander De Wet (15.4522); a cameo by the popular song figure Dolly Gray, whose soldier sweetheart is called to the South African front (15.4417); Private Compton's accusing Stephen of being pro-Boer, and Bloom's performance of loyalism in response: "We fought for you in South Africa, Irish missile troops. . . . Honoured by our monarch" (15.4602–7).

use of force need not be constrained outside the amity lines circumscribing the club of signatory nations.[48] "Circe" underscores the compatibility of these international regimes with continued colonial repression outside the amity lines by accompanying each sanctimonious regal utterance with a scene of mass violence or brutal reprisal. Having shaken hands with the combatants and their seconds to "General applause," the Peacemaker "levitates over heaps of the slain"—perhaps a Boer War battlefield—and sings, in the ballad manner of Buck Mulligan's Joking Jesus, "My methods are new and are causing surprise. / To make the blind see I throw dust in their eyes" (15.4464, 15.4476–79). Later, the Croppy Boy, a figure from a song about the 1798 Rebellion, is publicly hanged (he has confessed to a British captain disguised as a priest that "I bear no hate to a living thing, / But I love my country beyond the king"). After the hangman has plunged his head into the corpse's belly and crowned himself with the dead rebel's smoking entrails, Edward VII contentedly sings "On coronation day, on coronation day, / O, won't we have a merry time, / Drinking whisky, beer and wine!" (15.4562–64). Again, the repeated association of Edward with particular rules of arbitration and warfare makes these scenes more than general satires about sovereignty's bloody foundations; they are also the colony's bitter riposte to the elite family of nations and its cosmopolitan pieties.

"Circe" further invokes this colonial counter-discourse by following the mention of Edward VII's coronation with the figure of John Edward Redmond, one of the armed heroes named in the "Dublin's burning!" passage as having sprung from dragons' teeth.[49] During Edward's coronation on August 9, 1902, Redmond, the head of the Nationalist party he had reunited

---

[48] Here is how a standard British textbook on jurisprudence from the period puts it: "The 'family [of] nations' is an aggregate of States which as a result of their historical antecedents have inherited a common civilisation, and are at a similar level of moral and political opinion. The term may be said to include the Christian nations of Europe and their offshoots in America, with the addition of the Ottoman Empire, which was declared by the Treaty of Paris of 1856 to be admitted to the 'concert Européen.' Within this charmed circle, according to the theory of International Law, all States are equal. Without it, no State, be it as powerful and as civilized as China or Japan, can be regarded as a normal international person." Thomas Erskine Holland, *The Elements of Jurisprudence* (Oxford: Clarendon Press, 1880), 267. The passage stood with only minor emendations (e.g., the addition of Japan to the family of nations) through the book's thirteenth and final edition, published in 1924.

[49] This conceit of warriors sprung from dragons teeth—an allusion to the founding of Thebes by Cadmus and five warriors sprung from the sown teeth of a dragon Cadmus had slain—invokes a moment in Irish oratory when English law is rewritten as an encrypted form of warfare: Walter Hussey Burgh said in a 1779 speech to the Irish Parliament, "Talk to me not of peace. Ireland is not at peace. It is smothered war. England has sown her laws as dragons' teeth, and they have sprung up as armed men." Burgh was speaking on the occasion of the Parliament's embodiment of the Irish Volunteers, an armed force loyal to the Crown but dedicated to the Irish Parliament's legislative authority. See *Ireland and Her People: A Library of Irish Biography*, vol. 4, ed. Thomas W. H. Fitzgerald (Chicago: Fitzgerald, 1910), 395.

after the Parnell split, gave a dissenting coronation speech on the steps of the Dublin City Hall. To England Redmond said, "You may proceed with your coronation jubilations and celebrations, you may assemble all the nations of the world in London to witness an exhibition of the loyalty, and what you call the unity of the empire, but you cannot hide from your guests the skeleton at your feast." That skeleton was the fact that Ireland "lies at your very heart oppressed, impoverished, manacled, and disloyal, a reproach to your civilization, and a disgrace to your name." Redmond's speech insists, furthermore, that this skeleton be recognized not as an uninvited guest but as the creation of British imperial rule. England's new constitutional monarch, he pointed out, was acceding to a throne that had presided over the annulment of the Irish Constitution with the Act of Union in 1800 without enforcing the British Constitution in Ireland. The result was a colonial regime under which the state of exception—the revocation of legally ensured rights and privileges—had become the general rule; in which the bare life of the citizen remained untransformed into the good life; in which citizenship itself was a legal fiction and the law more often facilitated than interdicted violence.

> Never for one hour since then has the English government of Ireland rested upon anything except naked force and unabashed corruption. Never for one hour has the British Constitution been in force in this country, whose own Constitution was destroyed. Why, the mere fact that in one hundred years, eighty-seven coercion acts have been passed by the English Parliament for Ireland, in spite of Irish protest, is sufficient to establish the facts that I have adduced. Martial law, suspension of the Habeas Corpus Act, suspension of trial by jury, suppression of free speech—these have been the permanent blessings conferred on Ireland by the destruction of the Irish Constitution. No single reform, large or small, has ever been obtained by purely constitutional methods.
>
> . . . People talk of the devastation in the Transvaal and Orange River Free State. Horrible, inhuman, and disgraceful as that was, it was as nothing compared to what happened in Ireland under the so-called constitutional rule of the English Parliament. The Transvaal, after all, was in a state of war. But in Ireland, in a state of peace, the homes of the people have been leveled, the population of our country has been largely exterminated or expatriated, and our fair and smiling fields have been laid waste and desolate.[50]

Redmond says plainly what the more violent scenes in "Circe" persistently imply: that the state of exception had been the rule in Ireland since the dissolution of the Irish Parliament with the 1800 Act of Union, and possibly earlier;

---

[50] John Edward Redmond, "Ireland and the Coronation," rpt. in *The World's Famous Orations, Vol. VI: Ireland, 1775–1902*, ed. William Jennings Bryan (New York: Funk & Wagnalls, 1906), 264; 259–61.

that thanks to this state of exception, the colony was treated during a putative time of peace as if it were a wartime adversary; that the distinction between war and peace signified among imperial nation-states but not between those states and their own colonies, which fell outside the amity lines. If "Circe" goes farther than Redmond it is in extending the permanent state of exception beyond the borders of the colony, a gesture it performs by giving us Dublin not as a remote outpost for the containment of violence but rather as the epicenter from which the end of the world ripples out. It implies, too, that international rules of warfare will finally be overwritten just as readily as the British Constitution has been ignored and suspended in the colony; that metropolitan citizens will, in their turn, become skeletons at the feast of sovereignty.

Theater of Total War

So far I have considered the episode's engagement with total war, colonialism, and law at the level of content—its enormous range of reference and allusion, its descriptive passages, the utterances and events it conveys. But the status of an utterance or event in such an episode is radically unstable. Consider the "Dublin's burning" passage: it is triggered not by Private Carr's hitting Stephen, which takes place several pages later, but by Cissy's (and then the crowd's) calling for the police to prevent Carr's long-threatened attack on Stephen. The ensuing scenes of pandemonium, Irish patriotic infighting, and black mass—including the voice of Adonai shouting first "Dooooooooooog!" and then "Goooooooooood!" (15.4711, 15.4716)—take up two pages but make no discernable impression on the characters (Stephen, Cissy, Carr, Bloom, et al.) in the "realist" narrative. On the heels of these spectacular but ineffectual scenes of apocalypse, the single knockout blow Carr finally gives Stephen seems at once anticlimactic and reassuringly concrete: it appears to seal the difference between the text's fanciful elaborations and their gritty substrate in real events. Yet as many commentators have pointed out, the supposedly real events in "Circe" are neither universally borne out by later episodes as having "really" happened nor perfectly separable from the episode's dreamlike interpolations.[51] "Circe," then, appears to stage a duel or duet between at least two incompatible modes, the documentary and the hallucinatory, only to expose

---

[51] See, for example, Hugh Kenner, "Circe," in *James Joyce's* Ulysses, ed. Clive Hart and David Hayman (Berkeley: University of California Press, 1974), 341–62; Hugh Kenner, *Joyce's Voices* (Berkeley: University of California Press, 1978), 91; C. H. Peake, *James Joyce: The Citizen and the Artist* (London: Edward Arnold, 1977), 263; Daniel Ferrer, "'Circe,' Regret and Regression," in *Post-Structuralist Joyce: Essays from the French*, ed. Derek Attridge and Daniel Ferrer (Cambridge: Cambridge University Press, 1988), 132.

both as fabricated codes whose mutual exclusivity is at best conjectural.[52] All this in a long episode that recirculates and elaborates on vast amounts of material from earlier parts of the text, whose contents burst the bounds of the dramatic convention in which it is written, and whose fantastic registers draw on an array of dramatic genres, from farce to melodrama to pantomime.

I said above that the formal elements of "Circe" are too complex to be ascribed to a single historical referent or correlate. But in its convulsive stagecraft and its paratactic descriptions of mayhem and mass violence (*"Cries of valour. Shrieks of dying. Pikes clash on cuirasses. Thieves rob the slain"*), the episode can be said to evoke or restage, among other spectacles, the theater of war.[53] This metaphor, as Paul Fussell has influentially shown, spoke to large areas of experience, memory, and cultural production in the Great War that was being waged during the early years of *Ulysses'* writing. It captured, for instance, the theatrical dimensions of military costume, the central-casting typology of rank, the conscript's military "role" as against his civilian identity, and the combatant's saving division into actor and spectator during battle. It connected British soldiers' widespread use of theater lingo at the front (e.g., their referring to raids as "shows" and "stunts," or the practice in trench magazines of reporting battles in the idiom of London theatrical advertisements) with the hunger some of those same soldiers exhibited for theatergoing when they were on leave. Above all it pertained to the sudden metamorphoses that the twentieth-century battlefield had made routine: transformations of a scene of waiting into one of panic, of towns into ruins, of upright men into shattered corpses. The theater, its lexicon, and its generic conventions were ways of domesticating the phantasmagoric and powerfully dissociative aspects of life at the front. But the entangled idioms of war and the stage also testified to the untameably alien experience of industrialized mass violence—the way all life, as Fussell puts it, "had turned theatrical."[54]

---

[52] In his editor's introduction to *Reading Joyce's "Circe": European Joyce Studies* 3 (Amsterdam: Rodopi, 1994), Andrew Gibson helpfully surveys the scholarship on "Circe," describing its gradual movement from a mimetic, psychologizing approach (sorting the episode into realist vs. hallucinatory zones in order to determine which events actually occur) to a discursive one (tracing the interplay among and construction of multiple registers—theatrical, self-referential, naturalistic, phantasmagorical, etc.—without privileging one as representing what "really" happens). In league with the discursive approach, my reading here entangles elements of "Circe" that were previously treated as separable. In the episode's theater of total war, the theatrical metaphor attempts to manage war's violent transformations of the visual, and self-referentiality is both a function of and a riposte to the totality claims of the conflict in question.

[53] James Fairhall suggests, along similar lines, that "Circe" "vie[s] with the Great War as *Gesamtkunstwerk*" (Wagner's term for the total work of art) by formally replicating some of modern warfare's most marked characteristics: "it is filled with ironies, disjunctions, jerky energy, and hallucinatory violence and transformations" (212).

[54] Paul Fussell, *The Great War and Modern Memory* (Oxford: Oxford University Press, 1975), 191–95.

Even if we allow that the transformative and apparitional dynamics of "Circe" recall those of a theater of war, we still have to reckon with its being a theater where no *conventional* war is represented, where the colonial metropolis supplants the battlefield, where civilians vastly outnumber soldiers, and where the central act of martial violence is a fracas comprised mostly of verbal threats.[55] Yet these may not be objections to reading "Circe" as a theater of war so much as indicators of the kind of war the episode theatricalizes, and of the distance between its dramaturgy and that of the Great War trenches we saw referenced in "Nestor." By transposing warfare's sudden metamorphoses to the civilian space of the city, and by deploying anticipation and verbal threat not just as preludes to but also as modalities of violence, "Circe" mounts a theater of *total* war. The total war put on by the episode, we should note, differs from the understanding of the phrase that was dominant when *Ulysses* was published. The episode's setting in a colonial city, its synecdochic use of a redcoat's attack on a colonial civilian, its insistence on the symbiosis between international rules of warfare and violent colonial occupation, its modeling the structural homologies between anticolonial terrorism, state reprisal, and total war—all these factors embody the text's dissent from the dominant construal of total war as inhering between nation-states. Fittingly, this dissent is not so much formulated as it is staged: whereas the military figures to whom the text refers in its early pages (e.g., Nelson and Wellington) seem remote from its civilian setting, by the end of "Circe" we have been shown the city as battlefield and the citizenry as both targets (Stephen) and combatants (*"Factory lasses with fancy clothes toss redhot Yorkshire baraabombs"*).[56] A scrim lifts, revealing the colonial city not as unbridled war's backwater but as its proving ground. War, then, supplies both a logic and an object of metamorphosis in the episode; "Circe" stages a double transformation scene in respect to the limits and politics of sovereign violence.

It was while Joyce was writing this total-war theater that he described *Ulysses* to Linati as "a kind of encyclopedia," and genetic scholars have identified "Circe" as the epicenter of the book's becoming encyclopedic. After

---

[55] In the case of Carr's assaulting Stephen, the actual blow signifies less than do the dozen pages of threats ("I'll wring the neck of any fucking bastard who says a word against my bleeding fucking king" [15.4720–21]) and the phantasmagoria they seem to trigger. Far from being a salve or compensation for violence, the episode's apparitions and disappearances prolong the anticipation of assault, partly constituting the state of impending violence that is itself shown to be a powerful form of coercion in the episode's colonial metropolitan setting.

[56] Kevin Dettmar has reminded me, though, that Nelson and Wellington are, through their respective monuments, quotidian, even cardinal figures in the civilian setting of Dublin: *Ulysses* places Nelson's pillar at the very "Heart of the Hibernian Metropolis" (7.1–2), and the Wellington Monument was, in Joyce's day, essentially the city's western perimeter stone. Battlefield Dublin, realized in the Easter Rising and surrealized in "Circe," can be said to have been symbolically and ideologically latent in an urban landscape that so prominently featured such monuments.

drafting it, Joyce began to revise and expand other episodes in the curricular direction indicated by the schema he had sent Linati.[57] It's as if, having set up an act of public soldier-on-civilian violence in a colonial metropolis, and having tied that local act into a world system of unevenly distributed law and war, *Ulysses* had to expand to something like the scale and complexity of that system—not in order to ratify its view of conflict as the occasion for apprehending social totalities, but so as to contest that view. This resistant scaling up is most obvious in *Ulysses*' many lists, which Joyce inflated massively in his late revisions. The catalogues in classical epic present exhaustive, coherentist views of domains that tend to the warlike. The Trojan battle order and Greek ships rehearsed in the *Iliad*, the *Aeneid*'s rosters of Italian heroes and Tuscan fleet commanders— all of these take war as the occasion for world-portraiture. Contrastingly, in the "Cyclops" episode alone Joyce inventories an old plumber's debts (12.33–51), foreign delegates witnessing a public execution (12.555–69), clergy attending a committee meeting on the revival of Gaelic sports (12.927–38), socialite wedding guests with fanciful horticultural names (12.1269–78), Irish tourism sites (including Fingal's Cave, which is in Scotland) depicted on a pub napkin as if it were a medieval tapestry (12.1451–61), and a procession of saints and martyrs, including a detailed roster of their clothing and accessories (12.1676–1719). *Ulysses* not only demilitarizes the contents and occasion of epic catalogue but also undermines that mode's coherentism through verbal pratfalls and naked violations of both category and ontology. When Muhammad, Adam and Eve, Herodotus, The Man that Broke the Bank at Monte Carlo, The Woman Who Didn't, Gautama Buddha, and Lady Godiva can appear in a census of "Irish heroes and heroines of antiquity" (12.176–99), every noun and adjective in that selection rubric has fractured under the pressure of incongruity.

The encyclopedism of "Cyclops" attempts to smuggle the world in through the gap between inventory and miscellany. "Circe," too, is massively encompassing as well as allusive, quarried from an enormous range of found texts, from Queen Victoria's diaries (via Lytton Strachey) and Havelock Ellis's sexological writings to threepenny soft-porn magazines. Yet the primary object of the latter episode's radical inclusivity is *Ulysses* itself, and its writing prompted Joyce to thicken and multiply the *renvoi*-like cross-references within and among episodes throughout the book.[58] Such a degree of cross-referentiality

---

[57] Groden, for example, writes, "As 'Circe' grew more complex, so did Joyce's plans for *Ulysses*. In September [1920] the book was not really 'a sort of encyclopedia,' but his imagination obviously seized on this while he worked on 'Circe.' Growth and expansion became extremely important." *"Ulysses" in Progress*, 177. See pp. 178–200 for Groden's account, foundational for genetic scholarship on *Ulysses*, of how Joyce's 1920 and 1921 revisions extended and intensified the book's encyclopedism.

[58] Ronan Crowley's work on "Circe" makes use of the National Library of Ireland's recently acquired prepublication materials pertaining to the episode. Preserving Groden's core narrative about how "Circe" catalyzed the book's encyclopedic turn particularly as to intratextual reference, he notes that Joyce began heavily mining typescripts for earlier episodes shortly after moving to

might, in another kind of work, have fed the impression of coherentist world-portraiture. But consider, as an extreme version of the general case represented by "Circe," the following passage in which Stephen, the other brothel patrons, and several of the prostitutes waltz to a player piano's rendition of "My Girl's a Yorkshire Girl":

STEPHEN

Dance of Death.

> (*Bang fresh barang bang of lacquey's bell, horse, nag, steer, piglings, Conmee on Christass, lame crutch and leg sailor in cockboat armfolded ropepulling hitching stamp hornpipe through and through. Baraabum! On nags hogs bell-horses Gadarene swine Corny in coffin steel shark stone onehandled Nelson two trickies Frauenzimmer plumstained from pram falling bawling. Gum he's a champion. Fuseblue peer from barrel rev. evensong Love on hackney jaunt Blazes blind coddoubled bicyclers Dilly with snowcake no fancy clothes. Then in last switchback lumbering up and down bump mashtub sort of viceroy and reine relish for tublumber bumpshire rose. Baraabum!* . . .* (15.4138–50)

Despite being *Ulysses'* most densely self-referential passage, this is no stable lattice of nested directories, no neat intratextual spreadsheet.[59] Instead, we have something like the visual smear effect produced by a spinning camera. Details from numerous earlier episodes return, often in ironic shorthand ("*Conmee on Christass*" recasting Father Conmee's sanctimonious tram ride as Christ's entrance into Jerusalem), and fuse with lyrics from the pianola's song. Although the "Dance of Death" invoked by Stephen is mimetic, a medieval literary and visual genre depicting death's indiscriminate power over the social totality, the ensuing stage directions are governed not by representation but by kinesis; not by a totalizing portraiture but by a phenomenology of the blur and dip, effects that emanate from the past and present diegetic events of whirligig ride, waltz, bicycle race, and the thumping procession of Liffey-borne porter barrels. "*Sort of viceroy*" reminds us that we last heard "My Girl's a Yorkshire Girl" in "Wandering Rocks," played by a regimental band at the same time that the British viceroy was passing in cavalcade through central Dublin. But whereas imperial sovereignty is constantly on display elsewhere in "Circe," here it is tellingly leveled with other echoes and spun with the language of a music hall song.

Paris in July 1920. Crowley also discusses Joyce's use of Queen Victoria, Ellis, and the "racy three-penny." See Ronan Crowley, "Fusing the Elements of 'Circe': From Compositional to Textual Repetition," *James Joyce Quarterly* 47.3 (Spring 2010): 341–61, esp. 354, 346, 352.

[59] On the prepublication versions of this passage, including the presence of many of its elements in the episode's first draft, see R. G. Hampton, "'Toft's Cumbersome Whirligig': Hallucinations, Theatricality, and Mnemotechnic in V.A.19 and the First Edition Text of 'Circe,'" in Gibson, ed., *Reading Joyce's "Circe": European Joyce Studies* 3, 143–78, esp. 159–62.

Apropos of sovereignty, this linguistic dervish-dance occurs, significantly, in a stage direction—that is, within the discursive zone that more often calls the dance than dances.[60] We might recall here that the long stage direction that follows the utterance "Dublin's burning!" is not a guideline or even a requisition for onstage representation but a mimetic fiat: within the textual frame, factory lasses with fancy clothes "really do" toss redhot Yorkshire baraabombs. But the "Dance of Death" stage directions are a welter of participles, nouns, and prepositions, lacking the main verb on which the mimetic authority of stage directions generally relies. To the extent the episode's stage directions are its organizing, supervisory presence, the "Dance of Death" directions stage the meltdown of that totalizing presence, the grocer's assistant gone bacchic. This liquidation takes place, paradoxically, *through* the passage's intratextual retentiveness. The return of its constituent signifiers from earlier in the text is at once so obtrusive and so distorted as to exceed the demands of simple cross-reference, with the result that the signifier as such eclipses the project of total representation that it was supposed to serve. By interrupting its bid to encompass the world in order to be the encyclopedia of itself, *Ulysses* engages in an immanent critique of any totalizing project, enacting the tendency of a supposedly total model or portrait to refer more insistently, more accurately, and more meaningfully to itself than to the world.

"Circe" travesties not only spatial totality-forms but temporal models of plenitude as well. Apocalyptic (and some messianic) temporalities imagine the eschaton—the end of the world—as the singular event to which all history leads and all signs point; its arrival closes the circuit of prophecy and thus comes to stand for a semantic as well as a cosmological fullness. But "Circe," for all its admonitions, catastrophes, and spectacular unveilings, disports with apocalyptic time in order to dismantle it. Far from culminating in some singular eschaton, it gives us a world that ends so frequently (e.g., the cameo of "THE END OF THE WORLD," the "Dublin's burning" sequence, Carr's blow to Stephen, the velvet-Elvis messianism of Rudy Bloom's apparition on the episode's final page) that the *kairos* or critical end-time of apocalypse is reassimilated to *chronos*—to undifferentiated sequence or "one damn thing after another," one damn apocalypse after another.[61] This treatment of *kairos* as a special effect or hallucination of *chronos* happens at the level of the signifier as well as at that of the diegetic "event." The sentence "*Factory lasses with*

---

[60] As Martin Puchner observes, the unperformability of "Circe" amplifies rather than mutes the authority of its stage directions: "as long as they are mere directives, they can be disobeyed, and in fact they are all the time. As soon as they are directed at a reader, however, their prescriptive force can range unchallenged." See his *Stage Fright: Modernism, Anti-Theatricality, and Drama* (Baltimore: Johns Hopkins University Press, 2002), 87.

[61] The terms *kairos* and *chronos* as they are used here, as well as the characterization of the latter as "one damn thing after another," are Frank Kermode's, from *The Sense of an Ending: Studies in the Theory of Fiction* (Oxford: Oxford University Press, 1967), 44–50.

fancy clothes toss redhot Yorkshire baraabombs," from the "Dublin's burning" stage directions, dresses figures of violent civilian insurgency in the lyrics and percussive punctuation—*baraabum!*—of that popular song. More echo than eschaton, it describes the radical alterity and novelty of the end of the world in spectacularly secondhand language. Again, the text's encyclopedism acts as the unlikely delivery system for its critique of coherentism: so many jostling temporalities have been incorporated here that they prevent one another's dominance, ruling out the privileged and singular temporalities of prophecy, epic catalogue, or world-ekphrasis.

My opening example of ekphrasis in classical epic was the shield of Achilles, not just a defensive weapon but also "a world of gorgeous immortal work," and thus a world described as well as a description of the world. To this confident, self-enclosed masterwork *Ulysses* acts as a latter-day counterpart and riposte. In this it anticipates the artifact described by Auden's "The Shield of Achilles" (1952), seen by the warrior's mother over the shoulder of Hephaestus as he makes it.[62] Auden's Thetis searches the shield's surface for the antique plenitudes of epic but this time finds a dire series of twentieth-century scenes. Where Homer's shield places peacetime and wartime cities at its center, Auden's favors disconnected peripheral spaces—the concentration camp or prison fenced in barbed wire, "arbitrary" and vacant places, or teeming but featureless, unsparing ones. In one of these an army far away from its sovereign or generals is dispatched to engage a far-off adversary:

> Out of the air a voice without a face
>> Proved by statistics that some cause was just
> In tones as dry and level as the place:
>> No one was cheered and nothing was discussed;
>> Column by column in a cloud of dust
> They marched away enduring a belief
> Whose logic brought them, somewhere else, to grief.[63]

Epic would have represented the whole chain of command from gods to hoplites, ascribed motives, meted out punishments, brought the adversaries face to face, shown us their families and the worlds to which the survivors would return. Auden's poem pronounces that totality unrepresentable, moving the sites of both executive decision and decision-at-arms offstage and implying that such

---

[62] Philip Bobbitt's *The Shield of Achilles: War, Peace, and the Course of History* (New York: Anchor, 2003) also unfolds in the space between the *Iliad*'s account of the shield and Auden's, which respectively function as its foreword and afterword. According to Bobbitt, these bookends should remind readers "that our moral and practical decisions have real consequences in the use of force" and that "war is a product as well as a shaper of culture" (xxxi).

[63] W. H. Auden, "The Shield of Achilles," in *Selected Poems: Expanded Edition*, ed. Edward Mendelson (New York: Vintage, 2007), 207, 206.

displacements enable the powerful to disavow responsibility toward the power-less. *Ulysses* also shatters the holism of Achilles' shield, holding up in its place Stephen Dedalus's image of Irish art, "the cracked lookingglass of a servant" (1.146)—the avowedly partial reflection of a traumatized, subordinated social totality. Yet Joyce's response to epic world-description differs from Auden's in staying with rather than renouncing the question of totality. By now we should recognize in the figure of the cracked looking glass an emblem not of damaged or failed encyclopedism but of *any and all* encyclopedism. Although it lacks the epistemological and cosmological certainties on which epic depends, it may signify the more urgently for being produced by the interplay of so many voices, codes, and situated glimpses. Its fissured, provisional surface notwithstanding, it attempts to restore connections at once disavowed and required by the impe-rial world system, connections among sovereignty, law, and force. Beholding it, both imperial soldier and colonial civilian speak the city's name: *Dublin*, the first of many names for the somewhere else where they would come to grief.

Scattering

Walking along Sandymount Strand on the morning of June 16, 1904, Stephen Dedalus recalls some of his youthful conceits as an intellectual and would-be writer. His thoughts mock his younger self but exhibit tenderness toward that self too—a tenderness that extends to the written record, which may permit one to be read after death, but which is itself precarious, in its own way mortal.

> Books you were going to write with letters for titles. Have you read his F? O yes, but I prefer Q. Yes, but W is wonderful. O yes, W. Remember your epiphanies written on green oval leaves, deeply deep, copies to be sent if you died to all the great libraries of the world, including Alexandria? Someone was to read them there after a few thousand years, a mahamanvantara. Pico della Mirandola like. Ay, very like a whale. When one reads these strange pages of one long gone one feels that one is at one with one who once . . .
> (3.139–46, ellipses in original)

Earlier I described *Ulysses* as being somewhere between Diderot and the Westinghouse Time Capsules in its encyclopedism. This passage affirms that location and lineage. Alphabetical but dispersed like the Cupaloy book to the world's archival safe houses, Stephen's writings would repose in at least one nonexistent library, Alexandria, whose destruction by fire in antiquity had been a motivation for the French *Encyclopédie*.[64] There, whether for "a

---

[64] The ancient Library of Alexandria seems to have been burned several times, the last in 642 CE. The Bibliotheca Alexandrina, the first library to be built near the site of the destroyed library, was not inaugurated until 2002.

few thousand years" or for 311.04 trillion (the length of an age of Brahma, or *mahamanvantara*), they would await those who might commune with the long-dead writer through the scene of reading. In imagining these future scenes, the young Stephen mantles himself in prophecy by alluding ("epiphanies written on oval green leaves, deeply deep") to the Cumaean Sibyl. Consulted by Aeneas in Virgil's epic, this famous oracle wrote the names and destinies of Romans on leaves that she arranged in order on the floor of her cave. If the winds arose to scramble the leaves, the prophecies would be irretrievably lost and a veil again drawn before the face of the future.[65] With their Sibylline traces, Stephen's thoughts give us the essence of *Ulysses*' encyclopedism: a yearning, in the face of violently deranging forces, for continuity and for a social portraiture so total as to comprehend the future. And alongside that yearning, the recognition that large-scale social portraiture lies not in coherentism but in arranging particulars in competing orders of order. Continuity is premised on dispersal: like the pages of the encyclopedia, the leaves of prophecy are *written* scattered.

One of the derangements most on *Ulysses*' mind is total war doctrine, along with the violent practices it both described and excluded from its portrait of the world. Yet for all that Joyce's book resists, exposes, and warns against the logic of total war, it is also on the lookout for the reparative and critical potentials of what it opposes. That a society's economic flourishing depends on labor, or that the psychological life of a citizenry might bear crucially on its productive capacities and political will—these observations can underwrite horrors, but they can also think against the atomization and fragmentation at the heart of both metropolitan bourgeois society and the imperialist project. Thus while the aims of total war doctrine may be to instruct one nation in prevailing over another, its implications can abet a nontotalizing holism. Such implications are best preserved alongside the rejection of total war's intent by differentiating gestures—inventories of the incongruous, clashes of temporalities and linguistic zones and literary techniques, an emphasis on discrete

---

[65] See Thomas Bulfinch, *Bulfinch's Mythology*, rev. ed. (New York: Grosset & Dunlap, 1913), 275. Bulfinch mentions another story about the Cumaean Sibyl that entails the burning rather than the dispersal of prophecy. She appeared before the Roman king, Tarquinius Superbus, offering to sell nine books at a high price. When he declined she burned three of them and offered the remaining six at the same price. Again he refused, and again she burned three books. Finally the king bought the remaining three for the price she had originally quoted for the nine. Inside them were written what became known as the Sibylline Prophecies, the destinies of the state of Rome. These were stored in a stone chest in the Temple of Jupiter Optimus Maximus and consulted only occasionally, and with great ceremony, by the members of a special priesthood. The Temple's eventual destruction by fire created a market for fake prophecies, or "pseudo-Sibylline oracles," some of which survive today. On the Sibyl of Cumae, see Michael Wood, *The Road to Delphi: The Life and Afterlife of Oracles* (New York: Picador, 2003), 115–17. The epigraph to T. S. Eliot's *The Waste Land* (1922), quoting the *Satyricon* of Petronius, refers to the Cumaean Sibyl's wish, at a point where age has shriveled her body to a fraction of its original size, to die.

but interlocking social and literary systems—gestures that refuse total war doctrine's tendency to classify all things, indiscriminately, as potential targets. And this is just what *Ulysses* does, and what, in varying means and proportions, its genre-mates do: enact an encyclopedism that is cross-referenced but self-contradictory, lacking an integrated house style, and keen to archive the improbable, the impossible, the occulted, the discordant, the benighted. This is a literary encyclopedism that recognizes that totality is a trope, and *for that reason* vies to portray it. It admits of no exempt, unsituated, or asymptomatic observer; yet it refuses to yield the right of synoptic portraiture to the crosshair optics of total war. As against that epic Olympian view, it wants to see less steadily, but more whole.

6

War Shadowing

FORD MADOX FORD'S *PARADE'S END*

On the other hand, on the occasion of their conversation at Lobscheid, Tietjens had prophesied what at the time seemed to her a lot of tosh. It had been two or three years before, but Tietjens had said that about the time grouse-shooting began, in 1914, a European conflagration would take place which would shut up half the houses in Mayfair and beggar their inhabitants.

—Ford Madox Ford, *Some Do Not . . .* (1924)

But decent augurs grin behind their masks.

—Ford Madox Ford, *Some Do Not . . .* (1924)

To speak of "the shadow of war" is to walk in the valley of cliché. The phrase gestures vaguely at war's moral darkness; at the fog or perennial dusk of battle; at the chiaroscuro in which war is often pictured; at its way of towering over people and places and of blotting out nonwarlike ideas and events. Most of all, the shadows of war are temporal, cast by a looming war on its prologue, by a past war on its aftermath, or by an ongoing war on the present, which it darkens to wartime. These figures treat time like a landscape where war's shadows slant down indifferently on a spatialized past, present, and future. It may seem strange to imagine war as a prominence casting shadows on its present or in its historical wake, but as long as these images involve an *actual* war they at least conform to our experience of shadows in space cast by real objects. How much stranger to imagine shadows cast by a *possible* war upon the time before it occurs. Such an image requires us to materialize what is at most only *probable*, endowing it with a light-blocking solidity. Yet we do this whenever we adumbrate future events in works of literature or history. As Gary Saul Morson puts it, "Foreshadowing makes the future not just an inevitability but a substantial actuality. It is invisible but there, both virtually (in its effect) and actually. In a sense, it has already happened, and we are in its shadow."[1] As the object of foreshadowing, war need not offer a special case, but it does—given war's scale and gravity and its attraction to nontemporal shadows—offer an extreme one. To speak of the shadow of a future war, even as a cliché, is to oversubstantiate the merely possible.

Morson and his intended collaborator, Michael André Bernstein, have tried to insist on both the strangeness of foreshadowing and the negative consequences it may have for freedom.[2] In projecting a realized future onto an earlier diegetic or historical moment, foreshadowing may do no more than assert a narrator's privileged knowledge of a time that remains illegible to the literary characters or historical actors for whom that time has not yet arrived. But Bernstein identifies a more pernicious variant, "a kind of retroactive foreshadowing in which the shared knowledge of the outcome of a series of events by narrator and listener is used to judge the participants in those events *as though they too should have known what was to come*" (16; original emphasis). The observer, that is, not only projects signs of an accomplished future onto its foretime but also berates the denizens of that past for having failed to read the signs correctly *then*. This post-facto foreshadowing Bernstein dubs *backshadowing*, citing as his primary example histories of the Shoah that fault Austro-Hungarian Jewry for not fleeing the genocide they should have been able to see coming. Such narratives can be seen to constrain the freedom of historical actors in at least two ways: first, by conceiving of then-future events as predetermined and thus immune to intervention; and second, by holding those persons responsible for failing to single out one among many possible futures as *the* future and acting accordingly. The antithesis to backshadowing historiographies, says Bernstein, would be a way of narrating history that "lets us hear the reasonableness of those who made the fatally wrong guesses, recording their position with the same degree of sympathetic clarity as it does the arguments of characters who turned out to be accurate in their predictions" (36). Rather than trap its agents in the foreshadows and backshadows of a unilinear, determinist model of history, such a writing would illuminate the untaken but possible paths that branched off to the side, as it were, of how events actually unfolded. Morson's coinage for this practice: *sideshadowing*.

Bernstein's cardinal example of literary sideshadowing is Robert Musil's immense novel, *Der Mann ohne Eigenschaften* [*The Man without Qualities*], which was begun in 1921 and remained unfinished at the author's death in

---

[1] Gary Saul Morson, *Narrative and Freedom: The Shadows of Time* (New Haven: Yale University Press, 1994), 49.

[2] Michael André Bernstein's *Foregone Conclusions: Against Apocalyptic History* (Berkeley: University of California Press, 1994), was written concurrently with *Narrative and Freedom*; the two books were initially to have been a single coauthored volume. Further references to Bernstein's book are cited in the text.

1942. The novel's action begins, ominously, in August 1913, and several characters are involved in plans to commemorate, come December 1918, the seventieth anniversary of the crowning of Emperor Franz Joseph. But instead of advancing with gathering speed toward the watershed date of August 1914—much less the winter of 1918—Musil tarries in 1913, as if to insist that those who lived through it did not universally or unequivocally experience it as a prelude to war's outbreak. "Time was on the move," says Musil's narrator. "People not yet born in those days will find it hard to believe, but even then time was racing along like a cavalry camel, just like today. But nobody knew where time was headed. And it was not always clear what was up or down, what was going forward or backward."[3] The backshadower conflates dwellers in the past and in the present by assigning them an equal ability to read the intervening time. But Musil claims that the prewar period was "just like today" for a different reason: it, too, faced an unfixed, still illegible future. The novel dilates the year 1913 partly in order to pack it with possible futures that could not yet be ruled out, thereby restoring the veiled quality of the future seen from that year. "It is as though *The Man without Qualities* were all sideshadows," Bernstein writes, "glimpses of diverse but equally credible futures, without any one of them being granted the aura of inevitability that is indispensable to foreshadowing" (98–99). For Bernstein, Musil's critique of backshadowing extends even to the novel's unfinished status: having decided not to end the work with the momentous outbreak of war, the novelist was in a sense obligated to leave it unfinished in order to preserve its "adequacy to the world's inherent complexity" (107).

Perhaps because he sees Musil's unfinished novel as refusing on principle to close in the authoritative manner of a "great novel," Bernstein refrains from placing *The Man without Qualities* among great genre-mates. In comparison with it, he finds even Marcel Proust's *roman-fleuve* artificially damming its deep counterfactual channels in order to achieve "a movement of closure essential to a canonic masterpiece." However, in a parenthetical moment that sideshadows his own discussion, Bernstein asks a subsequently unpursued question about genre, narrative ethics, and protagonism:

> (In this context, it is worth asking whether a novel fully committed to sideshadowing ought to center on the life story of a single, clearly identifiable protagonist at all. Even Musil, for whom sideshadowing was a central intellectual/ethical principle, had Ulrich's experiences dominate *The Man without Qualities* still more than Marcel's dominate *À la recherche du temps perdu* [1913–27]. Perhaps only in works like Joyce's *Dubliners* (1914) or Dos Passos's *Manhattan Transfer* (1925) and *U.S.A.* trilogy [1930–36], in which a

---

[3] Robert Musil, *The Man without Qualities*, 2 vols., trans. Sophie Wilkins (New York: Vintage, 1995), I:7. Further references are cited in the text by volume and page number.

whole city or historical era are the real "main characters," can sideshadowing be best enacted.) (109–10)

For all their dedication to reactivating the many futures that were possible
in a past moment, Musil and Proust are missing something Bernstein finds
in the other large-scale world texts that he names. This is a centrifugal protagonism, such that a given work's foreground is more densely populated,
more briefly and serially held, or liquidated altogether. Whereas Proust and
Musil sideshadow through essayism, grammatical mood, and diegetic event,
Bernstein gestures here toward a structural counterfactualism, one that mul-
tiplies sideshadows by representing more subjects and collectivities living in
relation to a greater variety of possible futures. This suggestion raises the possibility that other nondiegetic elements of a work—generic, modal, technical—might play an integral role in its rejection of unilinear historical models.
Sideshadowing, that is, need not be the sole province of narrative content and
subtle fluctuations of register. It might also be produced by more strenuous
formal gestures. The ethical, political, and historiographic import of those
gestures becomes clearer, in turn, when they are seen to model an indetermi-
nate futurity, for the past as well as for the present.

Of course this is not the only way to constellate freedom, futurity, and
technical innovation. In the first half of this book—in the perpetual suspense of Woolf's "The Mark on the Wall" and "Thoughts on Peace in an
Air Raid," and in Hamilton's *Theodore Savage*, with its implicit cyclicality—
we saw tortuous narratives tracing the future's foreclosure. One burden of
form in those works is to model political resolve precisely at moments when
the future appears foreordained. A meaningful politics does not, in other
words, require as its precondition a belief that the future is open, any more
than it needs a notion of posterity to validate acts in the present. This only
sounds diametrically opposed to Bernstein's intuition that form models the
future's openness. For the emphasis in his and Morson's critique of backshadowing falls not on how historical actors viewed the future but on how
the observer in the present judges persons in the past. The burden of formal
sideshadowing in world texts such as those Bernstein mentions would be
this: that although at a given moment the future may have *appeared* foreclosed, it *was* not, and the retroactive narration of a past moment as foreclosed has profoundly negative consequences for our view of the freedom
of historical actors. But there is a rider to Bernstein's policy that Hilary
Jenkinson might have supplied: the fact that futures past were not predetermined does not negate or make naive the convictions and resulting deeds
of historical actors who experienced the future as foreclosed. If we must not
now judge the dead for failing to know what we do of their future, neither
must we dismiss them for feeling as they did about what they understood
to be imminent.

The global catastrophe whose arrival *The Man without Qualities* defers and forbears to make inevitable need not, in Bernstein's reading, have been a war, much less *that* war. It is, after all, treated as homologous with the Shoah in his contrasting analysis of backshadowing in Aharon Appelfeld's *Badenhaym 'ir nofesh* [*Badenheim 1939*] (1978). But as we have seen, the First World War was the context in which the phrase and concept of total war emerged, and the 1920s the decade during which that concept was elaborated into a doctrine. To write during the twenties of the months or years just before 1914, then, was to represent not just the war's foretime but the moment before war putatively "became total," and from the vantage of a later moment when that becoming-total was hardening into a standard discursive feature about the Great War. To write an emphatically prewar novel as mammoth as Musil's during the twenties was unavoidably to place the scale of the work in some relation to a war whose defining characteristic was scalar. More than by its unfinished status, the novel deprivileges the war by making an epoch of a diegetic year on the war's very doorstep. Yet while Musil's 2,500-page work sprawls in certain dimensions, in others—its cast of characters, its array of social strata, its range of idiolects—it is surprisingly modest. *The Man without Qualities* is dilatory, to be sure, but it dilates inward, making time take more time, hollowing out subjunctive and speculative spaces within declarative and constative ones. Its encyclopedism, to the extent it exhibits this trait, is directed elsewhere than at a social totality whose portraitist total war was threatening to become. In its nearly infinite protraction of the war's foretime—indeed, in its cancelation of that time's "foreness" through sideshadowing—Musil's novel is in a sense compelled to meet the gaze of total war with a blank, unrecognizing expression. ("Total what?") In thus admirably declining to concede the war's inevitability, it also sidesteps the chance to protest total war discourse through a countermodel that "knows" of the war and can meet head-on the doctrines that emerged from it.

As a foil to *The Man without Qualities*, one wants an interwar work that represents the war and its aftermath as well as its foretime—a work whose sideshadowing occurs through innovative technical and perspectival devices and whose encyclopedism is sufficiently extrovert to attempt a comprehensive account of its society, and yet anti-coherentist in its formal self-understanding.[4] Several long interwar modernist works come near this description—Proust's *À*

---

[4] On the novelistic imperative to remember or think totality in a detotalized world, see A. J. Cascardi, "Totality and the Novel," *New Literary History* 23.3 (Summer 1992): 607–27. Cascardi largely follows Lukács in associating the world's detotalization with the loss of nature, social holism, and theological consolation as sources of form and grounds for value. Given the loss of those guarantors, says Cascardi, the novel from Cervantes forward must remember totality "by the synthesis of separate and sometimes incompatible parts" (615). Interwar encyclopedic novels, as I see them, double down on the belatedness, the heterogeneity, and above all the *constructedness* of novelistic totalities in the face of modern war's bid to retotalize the world.

la recherche du temps perdu, Döblin's *Berlin Alexanderplatz* (1929), and Broch's
Die Schlafwandler (1931–32), for example. But one meets it exactly: Ford Madox
Ford's *Parade's End* series, whose four volumes first appeared between 1924 and
1928. Ford's tetralogy takes the foreground in this chapter partly because my
characterization of it departs from critical consensus. The absence of *Parade's
End* from Bernstein's quick list of works that protagonize a whole city or historical era is symptomatic of a broader dismissal: Edward Mendelson omits
it from his catalog of encyclopedic fictions, and it is likewise missing from
both Franco Moretti's and Massimo Fusillo's rosters of modern epics.[5] For
the few commentators who read it by counterfactual lights, Ford's tetralogy
sideshadows one thing only: a more thoroughly experimental version of itself
that follows through on the foreshortened formal initiatives of the actual version or on its early volumes' emancipatory, utopian, "absolute" nostalgia.[6] In
declining these iconoclasms, goes the argument, the tetralogy either lapses
into an attitude of reactionary nostalgia or recommits to that attitude's literary manifestation, a mode of realist social history it uses to satirize Liberal
wartime deceitfulness. Meanwhile, critics who see the work as thoroughly
modernist in its embrace of formal and social fragmentariness abstain from
trying to square those disintegrative elements with the work's undeniable cen-
tripetalisms—its fealties to realist historical fiction; its weird resuscitation of
Victorian marriage, adultery, and inheritance plots; and its success in painting
so comprehensive a portrait of its era that, as we'll see, at least one contemporary reviewer likened the work to a time capsule.[7]

To view *Parade's End* as incompletely modernist or as failing to maintain
its emancipatory nostalgia is to extrapolate a counterfactual version of the
work from the actual one's most renegade traits, and then to read the actual
by the light of that imagined extrapolation. This is both a common and a
productive use of the counterfactual in literary analysis. But it is not the only
one. In addition to subjecting the work to overt or implicit sideshadowing
operations on the part of the critic, we might also (or alternatively) accord
gestures of the work itself—particularly those that seem partial, conjectural,
or semaphoric—a counterfactual function and agency. In the case of *Parade's
End*, this would mean encountering a passage like the following, from *A Man
Could Stand Up—*

---

[5] On Mendelson and Moretti, see chapter 4, above. Massimo Fusillo, "Epic, Novel," trans.
Michael F. Moore, in *The Novel, Vol. II: Forms and Themes*, ed. Franco Moretti (Princeton: Princeton
University Press, 2007), 32–63.

[6] I allude here to Vincent Sherry's and Nicholas Brown's readings, which I address below.

[7] Samuel Hynes, for instance, writes, "Ford's sense of the disintegration of England and English
culture appears in the novel in disintegrated forms and vivid impressionistic fragments." What
remains unclear in Hynes's account, however, is how so fragmentary and disintegrated a work also
manages to "embod[y] the whole historical myth . . . in one intelligible story." See Hynes's *A War
Imagined: The First World War and English Culture* (New York: Collier Books, 1990), 432–33.

> With an air of carefully pulling parcels out of a carrier's cart he produced from the cavern behind the sacking two blinking assemblages of tubular khaki-clad limbs. They wavered to erectness, pink cheeses of faces yawning beside tall rifles and bayonets.[8]

and suspending the wish that Ford had patterned the whole tetralogy after the mechanomorphism of Marcel Duchamp's *Nu descendant un escalier n°* *2* (1912). Instead, we might ask to what effect the novel, at this moment in its depiction of life at the Western Front, permits itself to conjure this auxiliary set of formal codes for a few lines, then reverts to a more conventional narration only to toggle to some other set of codes a few pages later.[9] As moments like this accumulate, Ford's work begins to look generatively restless, perpetually spinning off alternative formal trajectories for itself, some open, some foreclosed, many deeply incompatible with one another. Once primed to it, we begin to see this formal sideshadowing at the level of genre as well, and to encounter the tetralogy's activations of epic, historical realist, and pastoral energies as a series of projections, speculations, or prospects—as openings made in a subjunctive mood rather than as impasses or failures in an indicative one. To adapt Bernstein on Musil, it is as though *Parade's End* were all sideshadows, glimpses of diverse but equally credible technical and generic horizons, without any one of them being granted the aura of inevitability. And it is precisely, I contend, by means of its subjunctive relationship to form—through its perpetual undermining of form's will to forestructure narrative—that Ford's novel hopes to ward off a particular, war-torn future.

Obviating All Future Wars

In a *New York Times Book Review* of September 1950, Caroline Gordon discussed a new edition of *Parade's End*. Gordon guessed that its early readers

---

[8] Ford Madox Ford, *Parade's End* (New York: Alfred A. Knopf, 1950), 546. Further references are cited in the text. I have keyed my quotations from the tetralogy to this widely available edition. I refer occasionally to the excellent four-volume Carcanet scholarly edition, with citations keyed to its individual volumes.

[9] Jed Esty has helped me see how this particular stylistic flare-up bears directly on questions of war, form, and determinism. By the time Ford was writing *Parade's End*, prewar mechanomorphism seemed to have forecast the war's techno-determinism, providing a ready-made visual language for its production of machine-men like those Ford refers to here as "assemblages of tubular khaki-clad limbs." Yet by so impishly adopting and abandoning mechanomorphism, Ford engages in an anti-determinist manipulation of that supposedly determinist idiom—an instrumentalization of style as *techne* against techno-determinism. This sort of trickster modernism not only allies Ford with Duchamp, the arch-puppeteer of forms and styles, but also disentangles the latter's practice from more bellicose visual languages that superficially resemble it. Such passages in *Parade's End* insist that Duchampian mechanomorphs and assemblages, far from being battle-ready in the manner of much futurism and vorticism, subject war's totalizing energies to surrealist fragmentation.

had found the sequence a "not too realistic account of one soldier's disillusioning experience" in the Great War, then ruefully added that Ford's tetralogy was now "being published on what is perhaps the eve of a third world war."[10] Writing one year after the first Soviet atomic bomb test and several months into the Korean War, Gordon may well have thought the world was heading toward another calamity. But her remark was not only an incidental nod toward contemporary geopolitics; it also revived the question of the tetralogy's central aim. Ford had explicitly described that aim a few years after completing *Parade's End*: "I have always had the greatest contempt for novels written with a purpose. Fiction should render and not draw morals. But, when I sat down to write that series of volumes, I sinned against my gods to the extent of saying that I was going—to the level of the light vouchsafed me—to write a work that should have for its purpose the obviating of all future wars."[11] In her gesture toward what had happened since *Parade's End* first appeared—a second global war and now the emerging conditions for a third—Gordon marked both the tetralogy's failure and its persistent timeliness: the future war had come despite Ford's literary efforts, but those efforts could still help avert the *next* future war.

Ford's ambitions are worth recalling here not so that we may blame *Parade's End* for all subsequent wars but because its critics have tended to downplay or ignore its admonitory qualities, its orientation toward the future.[12] In doing so, they have understandably taken their cue from the work itself, which can seem fixed in the backward glance of the *ubi sunt*. The titles of the tetralogy as a whole as well as of its second, third, and fourth volumes—*No More Parades* (1925), *A Man Could Stand Up—* (1926), and *Last Post* (1928)—prepare us for an elegiac stance toward a defunct public militarism and its vanishing social protocols. Christopher Tietjens, the work's protagonist, seems in every respect a terminal figure: by his own description he is "a Tory of such an extinct type that [you] might take me for anything. The last megatherium" (490); a man of "clear Eighteenth-century mind" living in the early twentieth

---

[10] Caroline Gordon, "The Story of Ford Madox Ford," *New York Times Book Review*, September 17, 1950, sec. 7, pp. 1, 22; rpt. in *Critical Essays on Ford Madox Ford*, ed. Richard A. Cassell (Boston: G. K. Hall, 1987), 89.

[11] Ford Madox Ford, *It Was the Nightingale* (Philadelphia: J. B. Lippincott, 1933), 225. Further references are in the text. Ford expressed his hope that the tetralogy would aid in obviating future wars as early as his 1925 dedication to its second volume, *No More Parades*: "Few writers can have engaged themselves as combatants in what, please God, will yet prove to be the war that ended war, without the intention of aiding with their writings, if they survived, in bringing about such a state of mind as should end wars as possibilities." Ford Madox Ford, *No More Parades*, ed. Joseph Wiesenfarth (Manchester, UK: Carcanet, 2011), 4.

[12] See, for instance, Max Saunders's claim that "As a novelist [Ford] is concerned to represent society, not to change it. Anyway, his novels are mostly about how it has already changed. *Parade's End* is an elegy rather than a manifesto." Max Saunders, *Ford Madox Ford: A Dual Life* (Oxford: Oxford University Press, 1996), II: 225.

century; the last Protestant heir to the Groby estate, whose great tree is felled at the behest of an American tenant near the end of the cycle. On Armistice Day, the day on which volume three opens and concludes, Tietjens realizes that the Great War has made his type obsolete: ". . . to-day the world changed. Feudalism was finished; its last vestiges were gone. It held no place for him" (668). His wife Sylvia, for all that she flouts the behavioral codes of her husband's "expired" viewpoint, is no less convinced that "her world was waning" (808). And his brother Mark, shortly before dying, goes so far as to impute a degenerative tendency to the Tietjens clan, all of whom, he thinks, were "born with some kind of kink" (736). *Parade's End* is, by these many markers, an extinction narrative chronicling the last days of a doomed social order.

Yet while the tetralogy charts the expiration of "the last surviving Tory"— indeed, as we'll see, brings that figure back from death in order to watch him wane—it conspicuously avoids making him an emblem of all that it would be worth ending war to save. Although Tietjens is presented at certain moments as admirable, Ford's portrait of him is finally an ambivalent one, dwelling as much on the contradictions, follies, and numbness entailed in his brand of Tory chivalry as on its supposed virtues. *Parade's End* contains only trace amounts of elegy's bad counterfactualism, the kind that says, "If only we could go back to the lost past, we might bear the future." It imaginatively revives a member of the eighteenth-century squirearchy neither to lament his type's extinction nor to repopulate the future with his ideological progeny, but for the sake of his political celibacy. Tietjens's feudal worldview is unreproducible prima facie—and for just that reason he functions as something approaching a neutral observer, one exempt from the marketplace of viable ideologies. Who better to annotate the strange death of Liberal England than the extinct old-school Tory, an ethnographer from that other country, the past? And who better to raise credible alarms about the future than a figure without a tendentious stake in it? It is through this untimely protagonist, one not the contemporary of his contemporaries, that Ford will attempt to warn his own contemporaries away from war; through a futureless character that *Parade's End* tries to undoom the future of the world.

An admonitory project, then—but not, for that reason alone, exempt from backshadowing. A book bent on obviating future wars might well want to show, in hindsight, the shadows of the last war darkening *its* foretime; to indict the powerful for not having heeded the signs; and to urge better reading of the shadows cast by the next looming war on the present. *Parade's End* opens with signs of heavy forestructuring but soon rounds on that gambit with two surprising moves. First, to an even greater extent than *Ulysses*, it makes prophecy an object in its diegetic world. And second, it subjects prophecy, along with its enabling premise—a conception of the future as foreknowable and of the polity as self-enclosed and fully comprehensible— to traumatization in the war. Lest coherentism become an object of nostalgia through its apparent wartime loss, Ford's series builds to the following point: that far from robbing us of some epic plenitude that existed in peacetime, war is what authorizes the political logic of epic, even as it makes that nation-based coherentism look like the remedy to war. Having mounted this critique, *Parade's End* must proceed without recourse to prophecy or destiny, without the lineaments of epic. What remains are probabilistic fields and best-guess forecasts; obstructed or partial views of landscapes and totalities; and a literary form flexible enough to accommodate multiple temporalities, shattered chronologies, clashing regions of localized expertise in place of a grand synthesis, and a medley of techniques none of which is wholly adequate to the scale of the work. What remains is the fallible encyclopedia, which like Tietjens we might have scorned before the war transvalued it into just the form for our broken day.

Uncyclopedia Britannica

The famous opening of *Some Do Not . . .* (1924), the first volume of *Parade's End*, is a paradise of foregone conclusions. Two young men, elite public officials who work for the Imperial Department of Statistics, are sitting among the glossy surfaces of a "perfectly appointed railway carriage":

> The leather straps to the windows were of virgin newness; the mirrors beneath the new luggage racks immaculate as if they had reflected very little; the bulging upholstery in its luxuriant, regulated curves was scarlet and yellow in an intricate, minute dragon pattern, the design of a geometrician in Cologne. The compartment smelt faintly, hygienically of admirable varnish; the train ran as smoothly—Tietjens remembered thinking—as British gilt-edged securities. It travelled fast; yet had it swayed or jolted over the rail joints, except . . . where these eccentricities were expected and allowed for, Macmaster, Tietjens felt certain, would have written to the company. Perhaps he would even have written to the *Times*. (3)

Wealth and safety, mandarin self-satisfaction unmarked by wear and tear, reliable mechanisms for correcting unwelcome eccentricities—such a passage, set in July 1912, practically dares the postwar reader not to see it as a tableau of what will go to wrack when the world derails in August 1914. In so strongly portending the war, these sentences notify us that Tietjens, Macmaster, and the rest of their generation will be ejected from prewar lives of easy insularity. As regards the course of *reading*, however, the passage says something like the opposite: yes, this train is going just where you think it is. For although the majority of Ford's characters might be surprised by the disaster of the war, foreshadowing offers an assurance that the novel, at least, will stay on its rails to the end of a narrative line it has surveyed in advance.

Even the baleful final sentence of this volume's first part—"The knacker's cart lumbered around the corner" (144)—promises the reader a direct route to war's expected slaughter bench.

Tietjens himself will *not* be surprised by the onset of war, because he has predicted it with uncanny accuracy. Not long after the rail trip to Rye that opens the novel, he goes to Germany to escort Sylvia home, her runaway affair with another man having ended. While there, she later recalls, he "had prophesied what at the time seemed to her a lot of tosh. . . . Tietjens had said that about the time grouse-shooting began, in 1914, a European conflagration would take place which would shut up half the houses in Mayfair and beggar their inhabitants" (155).[13] Although Tietjens likens himself at one point to the prophet Jeremiah (18), Ford's novel ascribes his premonitory powers not to divine favor but to his talent for probabilistic forecasts based on precise numerical data and a broad understanding of global economic and political systems. Sylvia recalls, "He had patiently supported his prophecy [of the war] with financial statistics as to the approaching bankruptcy of various European powers and the growingly acquisitive skill and rapacity of the inhabitants of Great Britain" (155). But *Some Do Not . . .* indulges, through its protagonist, in more than just backdated prophecies. In 1917, having returned from the Front on medical furlough, Tietjens forecasts "our next war with France," the natural enemy Britain cannot help opposing. "It's the condition of our existence. We're a practically bankrupt, overpopulated, northern country; they're rich southerners, with a falling population. Towards 1930 we shall have to do what Prussia did in 1914" (162).[14] Again the method is empirical rather than magical, but here the future prophesied is still to come for the book's author and initial readers as well as for its characters. *Some Do Not . . .* seems, in this, to adhere precisely to Mendelson's model of encyclopedic fiction, making accurate post-facto prophecies in order to authorize its forecasts about the actual future, and thereby extending its rails even beyond the tetralogy's diegetic terminus on an unspecified June day in the 1920s.

Some Do Not . . . takes pains to portray Tietjens's predictive bent as more than a function of his work as a government number cruncher. It is, rather, one expression of his singular mind, whose freakish retentiveness Ford describes repeatedly as encyclopedic—indeed, as *hyper*-encyclopedic. Tietjens, we learn early on, has spent the middle months of 1912 "tabulating from memory the errors in the *Encyclopaedia Britannica,* of which a new edition [the famous eleventh, surely] had just appeared. He had even written an article for a dull

---

[13] Grouse-shooting begins on the "Glorious Twelfth" of August.

[14] The notion of a war between Britain and France ca. 1930 seems wrongheaded in hindsight. But like Tietjens, the British air war theorists of the 1920s were forecasting precisely this "next war" scenario, estimating the strength of the French air force (rather than the German one, which had been grounded by the Treaty of Versailles).

monthly on the subject" (10). But although he "despised people who used works of reference," Tietjens also benefits from the fact that others believe his mind to be just such a work: his admiring boss at the Imperial Department of Statistics calls him "a perfect encyclopaedia of exact material knowledge" (5). A subsequent chapter shows his mind tracking along such diverse subjects as ballistics, golf course architecture, racehorse pedigrees, and soft-billed birds (65). His nightlong communion with the young suffragist Valentine Wannop is a duet for quibbling epistemophiles, a lovers' discourse on the Linnaean nomenclature for the large bat, correct recitations from Ovid, and the eighteenth-century exports of the town of Rye (130–35). "You're an incorrigible fellow," his godfather, General Campion, tells him after Tietjens has set him straight on the durability of sixteenth-century English castle construction; unlike both the *Britannica* and Campion himself, Tietjens seems insusceptible to correction. "If ever there's any known, certain fact . . . How the devil do you get to know these things?" (77). These early chapters establish that the true protagonist of *Parade's End* is not Tietjens but Tietjens's mind, and that a central project of the tetralogy will be to illustrate that mind's origin, nature, function, and destination. "It was in that way his mind worked when he was fit: it picked up little pieces of definite, workmanlike information. When it had enough it classified them: not for any purpose, but because to know things was agreeable and gave a feeling of strength, of having in reserve something that the other fellow would not suspect . . ." (70). However much knowledge might be of the past, the vector of its deployment is the future—some moment when to possess it will endow one with a tactical advantage or a bulkhead against bad surprises. In the extreme case of Tietjens, Ford's *Homo encyclopaedicus*, this provisioning confers a limited prevision into the bargain, the ability to extrapolate a future from vast stores of facts.

Tietjens may disdain the *Britannica*, but the encyclopedia was Ford's touchstone for comprehensive learning. His father, whom he remembered as "a man of encyclopedic knowledge," had written the entries on Boccaccio, Bach, Handel, Beethoven, and Chopin for the ninth *Britannica*, and in 1905 Ford had assisted his uncle, the art critic William Michael Rossetti, in revising articles on Italian painters for the eleventh.[15] His own command of far-flung miscellaneous fields of knowledge often struck those around him as "omniscient." But the encyclopedic mind that inspired Ford to begin *Parade's End* was that of his great friend, Arthur Pierson Marwood, with whom he had founded the *English Review*. The youngest son of a North Yorkshire squire, Marwood was a gifted mathematician, the inventor of a "really infallible System for defeating the tables at Monaco," and the author of an article for the

---

[15] Saunders, *Ford Madox Ford*, I: 20, 195; Ford Madox Ford, *Some Do Not . . .*, ed. Max Saunders (Manchester: Carcanet, 2010), 13n.

Review called "A Complete Actuarial Scheme for Insuring John Doe against All the Vicissitudes of Life."[16] According to Ford he possessed "the clear, eighteenth-century English mind which has disappeared from the earth," part and parcel of which was "the largest general, the largest encyclopaedic, knowledge that, I imagine, it would be possible for any one man's skull to hold." He could discourse—and accurately, Ford marveled—"about the rigging of fruit schooners, about the rotation of crops on sandy soils, about the home life of Ammianus Marcellinus, the vocabulary of Walter Pater, the hidden aims of Mr. Chamberlain, systems of irrigation, the theories of Mendel, the rapture of Higher Mathematics, Napoleonic strategy, consubstantiation, or the Theory of Waves."[17] Marwood's real-life pastime of compiling errors in the *Britannica*—as many errors, he successfully wagered, as the edition had pages—would become the hallmark of Tietjens's hyper-encyclopedism. When Marwood died in 1916 of tuberculosis, the prospect of truly comprehensive knowledge of the world seemed, to his friend, to die with him.

Ford's crucial postwar vision of Marwood—half visitation, half thought experiment—occurred in the garden of Harold Munro's villa at St.-Jean-Cap-Ferrat, just after Ford had taken up residence there in November 1922. "I imagined [Marwood's] mind going all over the misty and torrential happenings of the Western Front. . . . I seemed . . . to see him stand in some high place in France during the period of hostilities taking in not only what was visible but all the causes and all the motive powers of infinitely distant places" (*Nightingale*, 221–22). The vision restores the dead friend with all his powers— powers of "going all over" and "taking in"—intact. More than intact: in Ford's idealized resurrection, Marwood shatters the limits of mere optics. He sees the invisible, takes in what is beyond the horizon, apprehends complex webs of initiative and causality. According to this origin-narrative, *Parade's End* is an alternate history in which the war *can*, after all, be totally comprehended thanks to Marwood's all-seeing, all-knowing mind. Given that the war had seemed to target memory itself in ways that seemed new, a hypermnesic's view of it would be of particular use and power. But the "as if" of alternate history is useful and powerful precisely to the extent that it is impossible in fact. Ford's thought experiment implies that Marwood's omniscience and the Great War were mutually exclusive and could only be copresent in his fiction. Like Tietjens, Marwood possessed the Tory's "extinct frame of mind."[18] One thing extinguished with him was the prospect of an entitled, confident, limitless overview; invoking that viewpoint after his death is, by Ford's own logic, as fanciful, as preposterous, as imagining a megatherium in the streets of

---

[16] Ford Madox Ford, *Thus to Revisit: Some Reminiscences* (New York: E. P. Dutton, 1921), 218.

[17] Ford Madox Ford, *Return to Yesterday: Reminiscences of James, Conrad, and Crane* (New York: Horace and Liveright, 1932), 359; Ford, *Thus To Revisit*, 59.

[18] Ford, *No More Parades*, 5.

early-twentieth-century London. To resurrect Marwood and all he incarnates in fiction, then, is finally to confirm his extinction and the extinction of his omniscient powers; it would seem to be only elegy.

But *Parade's End*, as I suggested earlier, has a more complicated relationship to the past and the future than can be compassed by elegy. While it looks back, it also provides a motivating context for the backward look, cataloguing its elegiac moments among other symptomatic responses to the recent war. Ford's account of the tetralogy's genesis does this too: the vision of Marwood looking over the Western Front does not arise in a vacuum but answers Ford's experience of panic at the recurrence of his own wartime amnesia. Shortly before having the vision, Ford had been in Paris, where he had run into a man who had been in his regiment during the war. After visiting the Notre Dame tablet commemorating the French war dead, the two reminisced about traveling together in a G.S. limbered wagon back to their battalion in 1916. Ford had been returning from sick leave in Corbie, where he had undergone dental surgery on injuries caused by an explosion at Bécourt-Bécordel, on the front—the same explosion that had wiped away three weeks of his memory and hindered him from remembering his name. Thinking about that trip, Ford realized with dismay that he could not recall whether the wagon's brake had been a lever or a wheel—a detail of the sort that fills Diderot's *Encyclopédie*. "My panic became worse. It seemed a catastrophe that I could not remember what those brakes had been like. The memory that had chosen to return after Corbie must be forsaking me again." That evening he learned of the death of Proust and, although he had not yet read a word of the *Recherche*, was inspired by the novelist's reputation as memory's encyclopedist to envision "a certain literary work to be done . . . something on an immense scale, a little cloudy in immediate attack but with the salient points and the final impression extraordinarily clear" (*Nightingale*, 195, 199). And yet earlier that same day he had felt his command of the "salient points"—the details without which he felt insecure even planning to write—slipping away.

The ensuing vision of Marwood's mind, then, answered both Ford's fear of resurgent battlefield memory loss and his desire to write on a Proustian scale: the recovering amnesiac's need to write memory's *Britannica* as a stay against forgetfulness. A Marwood who had lived to survey the war would have been proof against forgetting, being gifted with a mind perfectly capacious, perceptive, retentive. In order to make fiction in the image of such a mind, Ford would have to recondition his own imperiled memory, a project he undertook at the Munro villa by subjecting himself to "a regular Staff Examination," testing his recall "as to strengths of units, as to supply, as to ciphers, as to the menus for troops and the stabling of mules. In each case I checked myself by such textbooks as I still had and in nearly every instance I found that my memory was correct enough" (*Nightingale*, 224, 227). By this account, Marwood's mind incarnates a prewar totality that might yet be reconstituted—a model that might, through the war veteran's attempt to imitate it, help the postwar mind recover the clarity and recall it possessed before it was traumatized. But a shadow account of encyclopedism develops alongside this one in Ford's memoir and its fictional counterpart in Tietjens's prewar omniscience. This counter-narrative says that a coherentist encyclopedism, far from having been ontologically prior to the war that shattered it, is in fact a postwar phantasm generated by a damaged mind and projected back into the prewar past. Encyclopedism, in other words, may not be a once-viable project made impossible by the war; instead, it may be a project made urgent, made necessary, or in a certain sense invented by the war that seems to have demolished it as a prospect. According to this account, the total-information technology that supplements and partially restores the damaged memory becomes a fantasy-image of what that memory once was. Only a traumatized mind that must consult synoptic reference works to restore itself to a pretraumatized state could imagine that it was ever, itself, encyclopedic.

For this is just what Ford does to Tietjens in the tetralogy's most extraordinary act of sabotage: he takes the encyclopedic mind ostensibly meant to *remedy* the effects of trauma and *afflicts* it with trauma. After the first part of *Some Do Not . . .* concludes by grimly adumbrating the war, the narrative jumps forward to 1917. Tietjens is in London on leave from the front, where, we learn, the shock produced by a nearby explosion has left a three-week hole in his memory and damaged his general power of recall: of his brain, he tells Sylvia "a great portion of it, in the shape of memory, has gone" (168). The narrator elaborates: "there were whole regions of fact upon which he could no longer call in support of his argument. His knowledge of history was still practically negligible: he knew nothing whatever of the humaner letters and, what was far worse, nothing at all of the higher and more sensuous phases of mathematics" (179). It is as if the very holes blasted in his memory adhered to its encyclopedic architecture, taking out certain subjects and "regions of fact" but not others. If this loss weirdly imitates the organizational logic of a "dictionary of arts and sciences," as the *Britannica* was first described, so does Tietjens's attempt to repair it: this "eighteenth-century figure of the Dr. Johnson type" (151) is crawling alphabetically through the very reference works he used to shun in order to reconstitute his ravaged memory. He tells Sylvia:

> ". . . The Koran says—I've got as far as K in my reading of the *Encyclopaedia Britannica* every afternoon at Mrs. Wannop's—'The strong man when smitten is smitten in his pride!' . . . Of course I got King's Regs. and the M.M.L. and Infantry Field Training and all the A.C.I.s to date by heart very quickly. And that's all a British officer is really encouraged to know . . ."
>
> "Oh, Christopher!" Sylvia said. "*You* read that *Enyclopaedia*; it's pitiful. You used to despise it so."
>
> "That's what's meant by 'smitten in his pride,'" Tietjens said. (170)

Our discovery that Tietjens relies on the *Britannica* as his post-traumatic tutor resignifies the earlier references to the encyclopedia, and to his scorn for it, as adumbrations of this very moment of loss. Like the smooth-running train and the knacker's cart that bookend the prewar chapters of *Some Do Not . . .*, the language that designated Tietjens "a perfect encyclopaedia of exact material knowledge" (5) was written from what we now see to have been a postwar vantage, marking his mind in advance for damaging.

Such backshadowing would appear to confirm the forebodings of the tetralogy's opening chapters and the attendant view of history as fore-closed—as susceptible to prophecy because structured in advance. If only you had an encyclopedic mind like Tietjens's, it seems to say, you too would have seen the war coming; you too would have anticipated its damage and the compensatory fantasies and behaviors that would follow from it. But here we should remember that whereas history is not forestructured, fic-tion as a rule *is*, and can address its condition of already-writtenness to the question of historical foreclosure in at least two ways. Some works of fic-tion inflict their forestructuring on history, implying that historical events, too, are capable of being positively foreshadowed in the manner criticized by Morson and Bernstein. Other fictions do the reverse, insisting on the openness of historical futures by calling attention to bad faith conflations of literature and history *as conflations*. Ford's is a fiction of the second type. Although *Some Do Not . . .* replicates many of the traits of the first, histori-cally foreclosing type of fiction, it also subjects them to a thoroughgoing dissection, anatomizing the process by which fiction imposes its teleology on historical futures past. Ford's novel sets up as the precondition of histor-ical foreknowledge—an encyclopedic mind—what it later reveals to be the retrojection of a mind traumatized by the war it was supposed to foreknow. It understands the statement "If only you had a mind like Tietjens's . . ." not as a possible but unrealized condition but as one symptom of a trauma that no mind could have foreseen, even one capable of spotting errors in an encyclopedia. The reader who has seen that symptomatic wish return, as it were, to the novel's opening from its diegetic future, should be released from the fantasy of historical prevision based on encyclopedic knowledge. Not to traverse that fantasy would be to take up lodgings in a preposterous loop of the sort *Some Do Not . . .* exhibits as literature while seeking to pro-hibit for historiography.

Having relinquished the dream of a mind sufficiently encyclopedic to cor-rect the *Britannica*, predict the future, and make holistic sense of the war, *Parade's End* might be expected to bid farewell to encyclopedism altogether. But even as we witness Tietjens divining future wars from the depths of his traumatic amnesia and struggling to recall words (*incense, Port Scatho, Metternich, Bemerton*) that were once in his working vocabulary—even as we are shown the encyclopedic mind in the act of coming apart—the tetralogy is deepening its formal engagement with the encyclopedia. Not with some idealized work as written by Marwood or the prewar Tietjens, but with the *Britannica* to which Ford, his uncle, and his father contributed, the worldly encyclopedia as *Parade's End* has already shown it to us: sprawling, untidy, inclusive, ridden with inconsistencies, contradictions, and errors. This is the form that will suffice, Ford's novels imply, once the fantasy of the perfect encyclopedia has been abandoned. What form more sufficient to portray the world comprehensively yet without the coherentism and forestructured logic the war has made seem less credible than ever?

The encyclopedism of *Parade's End* fastens on many objects within its story world: eighteenth-century furniture; the flora and fauna of East Sussex; the hunting rituals, agricultural knowledge, and equine management practices of the Yorkshire squire; ruling-class London's social and bureaucratic networks.[19] The work's middle volumes, to which we'll turn shortly, devote much of their energy to a panoramic account of the war. But from early in its first volume the tetralogy takes a compendious interest in at least one nondiegetic object: literary technique. Ford's novel departs repeatedly from its baseline social realism through unmarked leaps in its narrative chronology, recursivities, rotations through point of view and narratorial voice, short spells of visual cubism and mechanomorphism, protracted hallucinations, typographical outbursts to mimic the sounds of guns or bugles, and metafictive curlicues such as a character's editing his own free indirect discourse on the fly. Here, for example, is Tietjens on an after-breakfast walk with Valentine the day after they have met in Rye. He imagines lunch, then in his mind plays and orchestrates a patriotic Elgar hymn:

> [. . .] Overgrown lettuce with wood-vinegar to make the mouth scream with pain; pickles, also preserved in wood-vinegar; two bottles of public house beer that, on opening, squirts to the wall. A glass of invalid port . . . for the *gentleman*! . . . and the jaws hardly able to open after the too enormous breakfast at 10.15. Midday now!
>
> "God's England!" Tietjens exclaimed to himself in high good humour. "'Land of Hope and Glory!'—F natural descending to tonic, C major: chord of 6–4, suspension over dominant seventh to common chord

---

[19] Where *Ulysses* favors an encyclopedism of curriculum (the organizational matrices of the Linati and Larbaud schemata) and inventory (the post-epic catalogs in the book's later episodes), *Parade's End* favors the epitome in its early pages, giving us brief core samples of Tietjens's squirearchical knowledge. Only when the tetralogy decamps for the Western Front does the war emerge as both the work's central catastrophe and its primary encyclopedic object. This double emergence is one of the many affinities between *Parade's End* and *Moby-Dick*, whose catastrophic and encyclopedic energies also intersect—in the whale. Or, more properly, in *whaling*: whereas for Ford war is the horizon of the catastrophe, for Melville it is capitalism as epitomized by whaling, a productive force that is disastrous for the whale and, by extension, for the environment.

of C major. . . . All absolutely correct! Double basses, 'cellos, all violins, all woodwind, all brass. Full grand organ, all stops, special *vox humana* and key-bugle effect. . . . Across the counties came the sound of bugles that his father knew. . . . Pipe exactly right. It must be: pipe of Englishman of good birth; ditto tobacco. Attractive young woman's back. English midday midsummer. Best climate in the world! No day on which man may not go abroad!" (105–6)

Some elements of the passage—its propensity for parataxis and inventory, its conceit of transcribing a character's thoughts with all their ellipses and associative leaps—would be at home in *Ulysses*, a book Ford knew well and had reviewed less than a year before beginning *Some Do Not . . .* But had this passage appeared in *Ulysses*, the narrative technique would have been sustained through both the passage itself and the episode in which it occurred, Joyce's book being rigorously modular in its encyclopedism of technique. In Ford's, contrastingly, the technical seams are extravagantly ragged, and few departures from the baseline style are sustained for long. The first paragraph in the passage above slides from free indirect discourse ("A glass of invalid port . . . for the *gentleman!*") into interior monologue ("Midday now!"). The second sets out in direct discourse ("'God's England!' Tietjens exclaimed to himself . . .") but shifts almost immediately into an interior monologue within quotes, where the previous paragraph had ended in unquoted interior monologue. The line "Across the counties came the sound of bugles that his father knew" reads like an unmarked intrusion of third-person narratorial language into Tietjens's implied first-person thoughts but is in fact (or also) a modified echo within his interior monologue of T. W. H. Crosland's "The Yeoman" (1899): "Across the counties came the sound / Of war-drums that his fathers knew."[20] Such passages—and there are many of them in *Parade's End*—suggest the novelist's attention has wandered along with that of his protagonist, plucking and discarding techniques as if they were trailside flowers.

The restlessness with which Ford takes up and drops such techniques can make the tetralogy look like a traditional social history with fantastical but stunted experimental outgrowths. In Vincent Sherry's provocative reading, *Parade's End* entertains and even embarks on a wide range of modernist formal "initiatives" that might have exposed the false syllogisms of Liberal justifications for the war, but is finally more notable for resisting or renouncing these same initiatives in order to pursue its social historical aims and its ultimate commitments to progressive time and Tory decency. In what amounts to a structuring "rhythm of opportunity and refusal," says Sherry, Ford's prose repeatedly ramps up its "counterconventional

---

[20] Ford, *Some Do Not . . .*, 133n.

energies" only to shut them down. The latter move occurs not because Ford lacked the "nerve and dare" of more thoroughgoing experimentalists but because he possessed an inverse courage: to renounce modernist initiatives he saw as willing to trade with the rational and verbal mendacity of political Liberalism even while they opposed Liberal models of progressive time. Ford's example, for Sherry, can thus serve as a foil or "pretext" for modernists such as Woolf, whose work took the formal opportunities *Parade's End* conspicuously declines.[21]

Without doubt, Ford's tetralogy is less consistently animated by counterconventional energies than is Woolf's fiction, less implacably innovative than Joyce's. Of the latter, Ford wrote, "Personally I'm quite content to leave to Joyce the leading novelist-ship of this country, think he deserves the position, and hope it will profit him."[22] This awareness of experiment as a route to position and profit rather than simply an authentic expression of historical change is crucially shared by the tetralogy, and is a key to its semaphorics of literary technique. For all that it welds modernist techniques to a world altered by the war, *Parade's End* also understands them as signaling devices with their own instrumental uses. The work's canniest move is to place both the conventions of nineteenth-century realism (third-person omniscient narration, diachronic plotting, narratorial generalizations) and departures from those conventions under a historicizing scrutiny. Within a diegetic context that thematizes historical emergence, supersession, extinction, and undeath, it calls attention to the contingency and artifactuality of various techniques by abruptly taking them up and just as abruptly casting them aside. *Parade's End*, I argue, is less an artifact of modernism declined than a social history of techniques that include but are not limited to those we have come to call modernist. The work's experimental gestures, however foreshortened in isolation, produce an aggregate effect in excess of "opportunity and refusal." By repeatedly interrupting both the tetralogy's realist *techne* and its progressive model of history, Ford's formal outbursts prevent that realism from settling into the house style of his project, even as they refuse to install "modernism" as a thoroughgoing successor regime.

Such a reading builds on Sherry's insight about the rhythm of opportunity and refusal in Ford while placing the accent of comparison differently. Rather than juxtapose Ford and Woolf, or Toryism and Liberalism, it sees *Parade's End* as a project stalked internally by its own doubles, staging a fidgety oscillation between conventional and counterconventional modes, each sideshadowing the other in a counterfactualism not just of literary technique but of

---

[21] Vincent Sherry, *The Great War and the Language of Modernism* (New York: Oxford University Press, 2003), 228–29, 233.

[22] Ibid., 233; *Letters of Ford Madox Ford*, ed. Richard M. Ludwig (Princeton, NJ: Princeton University Press, 1965), 143.

historiographic procedure as well. The work's technical sideshadowing, that is, permits us to glimpse alternative tetralogies—a cubist *Parade's End*, a stream of consciousness *Parade's End*, a historically foreclosed one, a Freudian one, a metafictive one—like the compartments of a speeding train seen strobing past from the window of a stationary coach. Serial, intermittent, and speculative, Ford's is a subjunctive modernism, posed as a thought experiment rather than accomplished as an act. "What if," it asks for a few sentences, "one were to write an analytic cubist novel?" In this, it should remind us of the work's origin in a more personal counterfactual premise, the construction of an alternate world in which the brilliant friend had lived through the war to make sense of it. Just as Ford resurrects Marwood's encyclopedic mind only to afflict it with the trauma it was to have redeemed, *Parade's End* revives the condition-of-England chronicle after the war but vexes it with modernism, refusing either the consolation of totalizing form or the mirror-image consolation of that form's absolute liquidation. Its technical sideshadowing opens windows that look out on how things might have been without escaping through those windows into a fully alternative, fully reparative world. This curbed counterfactualism does not negate the tetralogy's encyclopedism. It *is* its encyclopedism, its way of insisting on the impossibility of portraying a social totality while nevertheless undertaking the same portrayal, its way of aching for a holism it recognizes can neither be met by realist social history nor relinquished to the universal targeting logic of unlimited war.

Total Worry

The first reviewers of *Some Do Not . . .* dwelt, unsurprisingly, on its ambitious scope and exhaustive detail rather than on its subtler counterfactual elements. The U.S. novelist Louis Bromfield likened the book to a time capsule in the way it bottled the essentials of early-twentieth-century English life:

> Suddenly, without a word, Ford Madox Ford (*né* Hueffer) publishes a book which is to our day what *Vanity Fair* was to the early days of Victoria's reign, a book that presents a picture of social life surpassed in poise, penetration, and literary excellence only by Thackeray's great novel. If it were buried now, to be dug up three hundred years hence, the men who dug it up would have an extraordinarily sound picture of the England of the past quarter century. They would know about it virtually all there is to know.[23]

---

[23] Louis Bromfield, "The New Yorker," *Bookman* 60.6 (February 1925): 739; qtd. in *Ford Madox Ford: The Critical Heritage*, ed. Frank MacShane (London: Routledge and Kegan Paul, 1972), 93. A number of early reviews compared *Some Do Not . . .* with Thackeray's novel. Stuart Sherman's review for the *New York Herald Tribune* (Nov. 16, 1924, pp. 1–2) was titled "Vanity Fair in 1924," and

Bromfield appears to be so taken with the hyper-encyclopedism of Tietjens's mind before the war that he has failed to notice that mind's injury by the war, consequently mistaking for the book's achievement what is really its object of mourning and critique. But his identification of *Vanity Fair* (1848) as a precursor to *Some Do Not . . .* is insightful, and helps us draw nearer to *No More Parades* and *A Man Could Stand Up—*, the middle volumes of Ford's tetralogy. For although Bromfield does not say so, both *Vanity Fair* and *Parade's End* are historical fictions that make the massive wars occupying their central chapters the occasion for social portraiture, yet refuse the plot and frame of the war novel. Instead they cross their accounts of mass mobilization—for Thackeray, the Napoleonic Wars, culminating in the Battle of Waterloo; for Ford, the Western Front near Rouen in the Great War—with marriage and adultery plots that precede, outlast, and crucially saturate the event of war. It is within the tense matrix engridded by that crossing, with war as its x-axis and marriage as its y, that both novels unfold their vast and partial chronicles of their respective societies.

With historical fiction bearing a particular relationship to mass conscription, we have also entered Lukácsian space, specifically that of *The Historical Novel* (1937). There Lukács famously posits that the French *levée en masse* and the subsequent mobilization of European populist armies in the Napoleonic Wars "for the first time made history a *mass experience*," disseminating through the people "the feeling first that there is such a thing as history, that it is an uninterrupted process of changes and finally that it has a direct effect upon the life of every individual."[24] This feeling, says Lukács, was helped along by several phenomena related to the shift from professional or mercenary armies to mass conscription: the growth in the sheer scale of armed forces, conflicts, battlefields, and supply lines; the erosion of class barriers within the army; its greater interaction through requisition with those living where the war was being fought; the liquidation, both within Napoleon's army and in places it conquered, of the remnants of feudalism; and the use of propaganda to reveal to the masses "the social content, the historical presuppositions and circumstances of the struggle, to connect up the war with the entire life and possibilities of the nation's development" (4). The dawning recognition that, as George Steiner puts it in an allusion to Lukács's argument, "history had become everyman's milieu" in turn makes possible the historical novel, the first proper examples of which begin to appear around the time of Waterloo.[25] That battle's centrality in *Vanity Fair* does not, however, cement

---

a writer for the *English Review* (Vol. 39, July 1924, pp. 148–49) called Ford's "the biggest novel of the century . . . the twentieth century *Vanity Fair*."

[24] Georg Lukács, *The Historical Novel*, trans. Hannah and Stanley Mitchell (Lincoln: University of Nebraska Press, 1983), 23. Further references are cited in the text.

[25] George Steiner, *In Bluebeard's Castle: Some Notes Toward the Redefinition of Culture* (New Haven: Yale University Press, 1971), 13. Although Steiner does not mention Lukács here, his

the latter's status for Lukács as a historical novel. Thackeray, he says, avoids the genre's "classical" form (as practiced by Walter Scott) in favor of an artificially resuscitated eighteenth-century social fiction, which the novelist bends, in his political disillusionment, to a satire meant "to strip history of its periwig" (202). Where such a takedown of the great through their drawing room vices and follies might have worked to focus attention on humbler figures, Lukács sees Thackeray as a bitter satirist producing merely "the distortion of history, its degradation to the level of the trivial and the private," and his eighteenth-century stylistic archaisms as turning would-be positive characters into "tedious, insufferable paragons of virtue" (204, 206).

My point in calling Lukács to mind here is neither to accept his argument wholesale nor to apply it mechanically to *Parade's End* as a latter-day *Vanity Fair*. Ford's tetralogy resembles the classical historical novels of Scott even less than *Vanity Fair* does, and that dissimilarity results not from a Thackerayan satirical distance but from too great a proximity to a war that has barely begun to recede, and whose shattering effects *Parade's End* registers in the straitened counterfactualism of its technique. Still, Ford's tetralogy anticipates elements of Lukács's reading of the nineteenth-century historical novel in the way it constellates historicity, social totality, and mass warfare as both precondition and warrant for its own version of historical fiction. More than any other English-language fiction about the war, it connects not just battlefront to home front and trench to ministry, but the front and reserve lines to the bivouac metropolis of barracks, base depots, and headquarters, all joined by an octopoid war bureaucracy and by complex networks of communication, transport, command, and control. *No More Parades* details the entrenched army's dependence on the local population in relating how a French railway strike threatens to impact the war. It documents, too, both the resentments between military and civilian leaders and the tensions between career military and civilian conscripts. And in *A Man Could Stand Up—* Tietjens, the "last Tory," thinks to himself that feudalism is finished, then goes on to celebrate the Armistice with comrades of much humbler estate into whose fellowship the war has cast him. Where Lukács puts the nation at the heart of his claims about the Napoleonic Wars, however, the wartime volumes of *Parade's End* underscore the global extent of the First World War's theaters, supply lines, and colonial troop conscription as well as the war's role in imperial geostrategy. Although it lacks *Ulysses'* sense of total war's colonial provenance, the tetralogy offers a powerful corrective to Western Front–only portraits of the First World War—and, proleptically, to Lukács's nation-based

---

discussion of the *levée en masse* and the spread of the historical sense clearly has *The Historical Novel* in mind. See also his "Georg Lukács and His Devil's Pact" (1960), rpt. in *Language and Silence: Essays on Language, Literature, and the Inhuman* (New York: Macmillan, 1967).

analysis of an earlier epochal war that was also massively imperial and trans-national in scope.[26]

In *Vanity Fair*, Thackeray has the Napoleonic Becky Sharp hurl Johnson's *Dictionary* out the window of a moving carriage in a rejection of eighteenth-century rationalism. *Parade's End* begins with a figurative defenestration of that other Enlightenment tome, the encyclopedia, only to take it back on board as a damaged project strangely adequate to the war-damaged state of Tietjens's mind. In volumes two and three, Ford's encyclopedism fixates on the war. You can open an omnibus edition of *Parade's End* at random and know immediately when you've landed on *No More Parades* or *A Man Could Stand Up—* thanks to the density of (mostly unexpanded) military acronyms in those volumes, from A.V.C., D.C.M., and G.O.C.I.C. to O.T.C., R.S.M., and V.A.D.[27] This oblique illumination—an encyclopedism that enumerates but seldom explicates—holds true generally in these volumes, especially *No More Parades*. Set at the Rouen base camp, it gestures at the war's vast demographic scale and behind-the-lines infrastructure through paratactic inventories like this one:

> Tietjens considered the sleeping army. . . . That country village under the white moon, all of sack-cloth sides, celluloid windows, forty men to a hut . . . That slumbering Arcadia was one of . . . how many? Thirty-seven thousand five hundred, say for a million and a half of men. . . . But there were probably more than a million and a half in that base. . . . Well, round the slumbering Arcadias were the fringes of virginly glimmering tents. [. . .] Base depots for infantry, cavalry, sappers, gunners, airmen, anti-airmen, telephone-men, vets, chiropodists, Royal Army Service Corps men, Pigeon Service men, Sanitary Service men, Women's Auxiliary Army Corps women, V.A.D. women—what in the world did V.A.D. stand for?—canteens, rest-tent attendants, barrack damage superintendents, parsons, priests, rabbis, Mormon bishops, Brahmins, Lamas, Imams, Fanti men, no doubt, for African troops. And all really dependent on the acting orderly-room lance-corporals for their temporal and spiritual salvation. (330)

Tietjens's musings convey the specialized texture of military discourse, the complexity of the war, the variety of its participants' assignments, religions,

---

[26] A partial exception to my claim that the tetralogy ignores total war's colonial provenance: Father Consett, the Catholic priest who is friend and counselor to Sylvia Tietjens and her mother, and who is executed as part of the Casement affair. "In one or other corner of their world-wide playground they had come upon Father Consett and hanged him. No doubt they tortured him first" (414).

[27] Respectively: Army Veterinary Corps, Distinguished Combat Medal, General Officer Commanding (in Chief), Officers' Training Corps, Regimental Sergeant-Major, and Voluntary Aid Detachment.

and places of origin. Like the storm of military acronyms *No More Parades* unleashes, the passage also constructs the uninitiated reader as a civilian who is overhearing, rather than being addressed by, a war veteran recollecting the war. It's as if we had walked in on Ford in the Munro villa, quizzing himself with an edge of desperation "as to strengths of units, as to supply, as to ciphers, as to the menus for troops and the stabling of mules." The encyclopedism focalized through Tietjens in the tetralogy's wartime volumes reads as an act less communicative than inward—at once a defense against and a symptom of traumatic forgetting.

Tietjens's hermetic, unsubordinated catalogs have their foil in the perspective of General Campion, his godfather and commanding officer. Campion embodies what Patrick Deer calls "the epic confidence of the strategic view."[28] Its possessor enjoys the vertical distance of the hilltop, the mediation of the aerial photo, the schematizing privilege of the map, the temporal prerogative of the long-range war plan. Above all he enjoys the power to instrumentalize resources, places, persons, and whole realms of experience to martial ends— to subordinate in precisely the ways Tietjens fails to do. So when Campion tells his godson, "An officer's private life and his life on parade are as strategy to tactics" (465), he presumably means that private life should be a means of realizing the grand aims of one's military life, should serve those aims rather than impede them as Tietjens's marital complications have done by ostensibly sullying his reputation and shaking his men's faith in him. As Deer observes, Campion's "lofty perspective gives him access to several strategic plotlines, of which Tietjens must ironically remain ignorant." The general's instrumentalizing gaze, that is, makes him the novel's master plotter—not only along the martial axis (he is pushing for a single command of the Allied forces along the Western Front and for imperial expansionism in the East), but also along the marital or private axis. In fact, of all the characters in *Parade's End* he enjoys the greatest freedom to maneuver diagonally within the space plotted by those two axes, sending his godson up to the front line in order to insulate himself from the effects of Sylvia Tietjens's scandalous behavior. "What won combats, campaigns, and, in the end wars," he thinks to himself, "was the brain which timed the arrival of forces at given points" (469). Such a brain understands "forces" to include not only armed regiments but also the personal, medical, spiritual, sexual, social, and familial vectors of soldiers' lives, even as it seeks to align those vectors with the ends of war. "Only connect! [. . .] Live in fragments no longer," is Margaret Schlegel's refrain in Forster's *Howards End* (1910). Campion represents the weaponization of that

---

[28] Patrick Deer, *Culture in Camouflage: War, Empire, and Modern British Literature* (Cambridge: Cambridge University Press, 2009), 51.

imperative. All-connecting, all-comprehending, and comprehending all as tributary to military force: his is the brain of total war.

In its great goal of obviating all future wars, *Parade's End* might have found a powerful instrument in Campion, whose ability to connect military and private life, war and empire, strategy and tactics might have been turned from warmongering to pacifism. This is, after all, the approach Woolf's *Mrs. Dalloway* takes in appropriating the comprehensive logic of total war to countervailing ends. But it is not through Campion's mind, or through his panoramic view of war, domestic culture, history, and empire, that Ford routes his antiwar polemic. Although the work is among other things a large-canvas social history, its admonitory energies do not run in those macrohistorical or mass-political channels. Instead, they follow Ford's concern for the minute-to-minute psychological experience of the soldier (and, as we will see, the civilian)—his interest in showing "how modern fighting of the organized, scientific type affects the mind."[29] Here he is, writing again on his aims in beginning the tetralogy:

> [. . .] it seemed to me that, if I could present, not merely fear, not merely horror, not merely death, not merely even self-sacrifice . . . but just worry; that might strike a note of which the world would not so readily tire. For you may become callous at the thought of all horrors of more than a million dead: fear itself in the end comes to rest. . . . But worry feeds on itself and in the end so destroys the morale that less than a grasshopper becomes a burden. It is without predictable term; it is as menacing as the eye of a serpent; it causes unspeakable fatigue even as, remorselessly, it banishes rest. And it seemed to me that if the world could be got to see War from that angle there would be no more wars. . . . (*Nightingale*, 226)

Parade's End will admonish its readers through its portrait of *worry*. Technologies of the aggregate—the very sorts of practices employed by Tietjens and his fellow Imperial Statisticians—can induce empathic burnout in readers by overloading them with descriptions of war and enumerations of its costs. But worry, as Ford conceives it, is not only eternally self-renewing for the soldier but also inexhaustibly transmissible to a reader. Because it is finally incommensurate with its objects, to the point where "less than a grasshopper" can become a burden, worry cannot exhaust itself as do phenomena of a stable, if unassimilably massive, scale (e.g., "the thought of all horrors of more than a million dead").[30] We should note two things here. First, a

---

[29] Ford Madox Ford, *A Man Could Stand Up—*, ed. Sara Haslam (Manchester, UK: Carcanet, 2011), 3.

[30] Ford's use of the tiny animal to figure the minima of worry-inducement ("less than a grasshopper becomes a burden") recalls one of the best known passages in another of the tetralogy's precursors, George Eliot's *Middlemarch*: "If we had a keen vision and feeling of all ordinary human life, it would be like hearing the grass grow and the squirrel's heart beat, and we should die of

scalar incommensurability is figured as a key element of what the work will show ("how modern fighting . . . affects the mind"). Second, because worry is incommensurate with present danger, a description of worry at the front may instill a politically productive worry about future wars in the peacetime reader. Because fear is terminable, so is the readerly fear of fear. But worry being self-renewing, the reader who is led to worry about worry cannot, in theory, be released into numbness, forgetfulness, or complacency. War comes and goes. Worry, however much war may channel and amplify it, is always with us.

As the stuff of which *Parade's End* will build its counter-portrait of the social totality at war, worry will need to be shown as both *excessive* in its wartime intensity and as *exceeding* the war in its duration. Fittingly, in turning to wartime, the tetralogy first thematizes worry in domestic terms. The opening section of *Some Do Not . . .*, set in 1912, has just ended with the knacker's cart lumbering round the corner. It is 1917 now, and Sylvia Tietjens is remembering standing on a sea cliff in Yorkshire in the company of an unnamed man who had pointed first to gulls screaming and dropping the herring they had caught and then to a bird of prey circling high above against the sun.

> The man told her that that was some sort of fish-eagle or hawk. Its normal habit was to chase the gulls which, in their terror, would drop their booty of herrings, whereupon the eagle would catch the fish before it struck the water. At the moment the eagle was not on duty, but the gulls were just as terrified as if it had been.
>
> Sylvia stayed for a long time watching the convolutions of the eagle. It pleased her to see that, though nothing threatened the gulls, they yet screamed and dropped their herrings. . . . The whole affair reminded her of herself in her relationship to the ordinary women of the barnyard. (146)

Had the gulls and the fish-eagle appeared in Woolf or Douhet, they would have figured the experience of civilians living under threat of aerial bombardment, primed to mistake any bird for a bomber, any backfiring car for a bomb. But while *Parade's End* elsewhere acknowledges civilian anxieties about air raids (see 222, 702, 762, 829), the parable of the fish-eagle instead indexes the predatory Sylvia's effect during both peace and war on the plainer women of her acquaintance, whose husbands it is her "hobby" to captivate so as to have the pleasure of refusing their offers of assignation. Although nominally about the terror of the gulls in the face of imminent attack, the passage is at

---

that roar which lies on the other side of silence." George Eliot, *Middlemarch*, ed. Bert G. Hornback (New York: Norton, 2000), 124. *Parade's End* suggests that the twentieth century has realized Eliot's counterfactual, exposing all who live in it to that ceaseless roar by boosting the sensitivity of perception, the number of stimuli, and the feedback loop ("worry feeds on itself") the two create.

heart about the routines that develop in relation to an ongoing threat, such that those routines take on a life independent of the threat. A prospective disaster-event is twice domesticated: first into a habit of panicky vigilance, and second into an analogy for human sexual predation and possessiveness. Terror decoupled by routine from a discrete event and transmuted into a habitable structure of expectation: this is worry à la Ford, and Sylvia Tietjens is its master instigator.

She is that because she spurns Campion's dictum, "An officer's private life and his life on parade are as strategy to tactics." Just as she declines through flagrant infidelities to play the dutiful squire's wife in peacetime, she refuses the wartime role of dutiful officer's wife by talking her way into the base camp, enlisting Tietjens's men in her siege upon him, spreading rumors that he is an adulterous socialist with messianic delusions, and causing scandal by appearing in public with other men. Her outrageous behavior prompts Campion to send her husband to the front lines after her former lover in the War Office has vengefully marked Tietjens unfit for intelligence work. Yet in physically trespassing on the military space of the base camp, Sylvia simply personifies what Ford's novel insists is a general condition: the intrusion of domestic cares on minds putatively dedicated to war making. One of her counterparts in this is O Nine Morgan, a Welsh soldier who is killed during an air raid after Tietjens denies him permission to visit home on intelligence that Morgan would likely be killed by his wife's prize-fighter lover if he returned. Having died messily in Tietjens's arms, Morgan haunts him for the rest of volumes two and three. Like Sylvia, the dead Welshman exposes the futility of attempting to subordinate domesticity to war: in trying to prevent the man's private life from interfering with his military duties, Tietjens has exposed the man to a death that wrenches him from both. Graham Greene, for one, recognized how unique Ford's work was in foregrounding this futility, and its attendant worry, over the pity and terror of battle. A novel like *All Quiet on the Western Front*, he noted, "confined its horror to the physical, to the terrors of the trenches, so that it is even possible to think of such physical terrors as an escape . . . from the burden of thought and mental pain." But *Parade's End* offered no reprieve from such burdens: "The private life cannot be escaped and death does not come when it is most required."[31] Where Woolf and other novelists of the city at war recorded how home had become, disastrously, another front, Ford's message is the obverse: that, in the midst of the front, we are disastrously at home.

The inescapable "home" that deepens the worry of the soldier is not always a byword in Ford for marital trouble, or even for domestic life in general. It

---

[31] Graham Greene, "Introduction," *The Bodley Head Ford Madox Ford*, Vol. III (London: Bodley Head, 1963), 7–8.

also includes the civilian policymakers whose view of soldiery was largely instrumental, and whose motives were opaque and often suspect to those at the front. In this, too, the tetralogy diverges from most Great War combatant fiction, which tends to relate conflict as a series of suspended or realized encounters between enemy hosts rather than as the carrying out of self-serving civilian policy by disquieted armies. In the dedicatory epistle that opened the first edition of *No More Parades*, Ford wrote,

> That immense army was also extremely depressed by the idea that those who controlled it overseas would—I will not use the word betray, since that implies volition—"let us down." We were oppressed, ordered, counter-ordered, commanded, countermanded, harassed, strafed, denounced—and, above all, dreadfully worried. The never-ending sense of worry, in fact, far surpassed any of the "exigencies of troops actually in contact with enemy forces," and that applied not merely to the bases, but to the whole field of military operations. Unceasing worry![32]

Ford does not venture to say whether the army's depression or lack of confidence were justified, and this is just the point: worry is sustained by the impossibility of confirming its object; by the ongoing prospect, rather than the certainty, that one might be let down, whether by one's spouse or by one's superiors; by the recognition that one is totally beholden to the decisions of others but possesses only a partial knowledge of their motives, allegiances, and constraints. To the extent it forms a counter-totality to unbridled war, worry is a totality of the horizontal, not of the vertical in the manner of Campion. It confers no strategic viewpoint—not even on officers like Tietjens, whose job is to bear a second-order worry, a worry about soldiers' worries about "home" in all its forms:

> Heavy depression settled down more heavily upon him. The distrust of the home Cabinet, felt by then by the greater part of that army, became like physical pain. These immense sacrifices, this ocean of mental sufferings, were all undergone to further the private vanities of men who amidst these hugenesses of landscapes and forces appeared pygmies! It was the worries of all these wet millions in mud-brown that worried him. They could die, they could be massacred, by the quarter million, in shambles. But that they should be massacred without jauntiness, without confidence, with depressed brows, without parade . . . (297).

The notion that soldiers might more justifiably be massacred if only their "parade" (that is, their dignity, integrity, and bearing) were intact smacks of a Toryism nostalgic for bygone days of honorable militarism. But there's

---

[32] Ford, *No More Parades*, vi.

something else at work here too: a sense that the deaths of soldiers are even more deplorable when not only their physical but also their mental lives have been totally instrumentalized to a misdirected war machine they know, furthermore, regards them as populations. "But men," Tietjens thinks in rebuttal. "Not just populations. Men you worried over there. Each man a man with a backbone, knees, breeches, braces, a rifle, a home, passions, fornications, drunks, pals, some scheme of the universe . . ." (297).

One of Ford's fantasies in writing *Parade's End*, remember, was to see Arthur Marwood "stand in some high place in France during the period of hostilities taking in not only what was visible but all the causes and all the motive powers of infinitely distant places." That fantasy assuaged panic—Ford's fear that war trauma would claim his memory—with panorama. *No More Parades* closes with a scene of two nested panoramas, one beheld with equanimity, the other with panic. The earlier of the two, a memory from nineteen months previous, is set atop the Montagne Noire in Belgium, from where "you saw the whole war." In an elliptical jumble of free indirect discourse and interior monologue, Tietjens's recollection spreads the vista at the reader's feet: Ypres, the enemy trenches at Wytschaete, a squadron over the slag heaps at Béthune, and plumes of smoke that showed the Germans were shelling the town of Poperinghe, where two girls kept a tea shop.

> [. . .] The shells had killed them both . . . Any man might have slept with either of them with pleasure and profit. . . . Six thousand of H.M. officers must have thought about those high-coloured girls. Good girls! . . . But the Hun shells got them. . . . What sort of fate was that? . . . To be desired by six thousand men and smashed into little gobbets of flesh by Hun shells? [. . .]
>
> That was according to the rules of the service. . . . General Campion, accepting with equanimity what German airplanes did to the hospitals, camps, stables, brothels, theatres, boulevards, chocolate stalls, and hotels of his town would have been vastly outraged if Hun planes had dropped bombs on his private lodgings. . . . The rules of war! . . . You spare, mutually, each other's headquarters and blow to pieces girls that are desired by six thousand men apiece. . . . (494).[33]

As if seeing through Campion's eyes, Tietjens here enjoys a mountaintop view that links and ranks disparate parts of the war machine. Ostensibly a plaint about the double standards and confraternity of generals—their high tolerance for collateral damage so long as their command sphere

---

[33] For a parallel discussion of the two panoramas, see Deer, *Culture in Camouflage*, 55–57. Deer emphasizes the question of access to the strategic view and characterizes as "almost schizoid" Tietjens's perspective as both observer and observed. Tietjens's refusal to divorce Sylvia is, for Deer, an "instance of protest and resistance" made possible by his recognition that strategic seeing depends on a degree of access and protection to which he can never lay full claim.

remains untouched—it also recognizes the military rationale for permitting and even deliberately inflicting collateral damage. Women who keep a tea shop in Poperinghe are nodes of commerce and objects of desire for a large number of soldiers; however nonviolent in themselves, these civilians are part of a war economy that sustains combatants and are therefore, by the logic of total war, legitimate targets. This synoptic view of the Western Front may fall short of Ford's vision of Marwood in comprehending every space and motive at a glance. But it registers total war's understanding of all it sees as part of an infinitely extensive, infinitely targetable system of violence-production.

Tietjens's only Achilles'-shield view of the war is a scene of tranquility recollected in a panic at "having lost so much emotion" (494). The chronologically later scene that triggers the memory practically fuses panic with the panoramic, once again making the synoptic overview a symptom of crisis rather than a remedy for it. Campion has summoned Tietjens to inform him that he is being sent up to the front lines in consequence of Sylvia's recent visit to the base camp. Tietjens's internal reaction: "There it was then: the natural catastrophe! . . . His mind was battling with the waters. What would it pick out as the main terror? The mud, the noise, dread always at the back of the mind? Or the worry! The worry!" (477). Campion then poses the inevitable question:

> "Why *don't* you divorce?" he asked.
>
> Panic came over Tietjens. He knew it would be his last panic of that interview. No brain could stand more. Fragments of scenes of fighting, voices, names, went before his eyes and ears. Elaborate problems. . . . The whole map of the embattled world ran out in front of him—as large as a field. An embossed map in greenish *papier mâché*—a ten-acre field of embossed *papier mâché*, with the blood of O Nine Morgan blurring luminously over it. (492–93)

He takes refuge in remembering the calmer mountaintop view in Belgium, only to founder again on the present—"By heavens! Is this epilepsy? . . . No, it isn't! . . . I've complete control of my mind. My uppermost mind"—then lies to Campion that he lacks the grounds for divorce (494). Note that Tietjens's panic is triggered not by some reactivation of his battlefield trauma but by the subject of *divorce*. This is a panic of private entrapment with dire ramifications. Tietjens will not divorce Sylvia because she is Catholic, and because his public-school Tory chivalry makes exposing her infidelities—the grounds for divorce—as unthinkable as peaching on another boy to the headmaster. Having refused to divorce her, he must be sent to the front lines and to near-certain death. In turning toward the "whole map of the embattled world," Tietjens's mind attempts to escape the panic-inducing subject of private life, but the bloody wash that blurs the map signals his failure: O Nine

Morgan, that personification and cardinal object of his worry about worry, was driven to death behind the lines by the prospect of death at home. Again, panic and war death in *No More Parades* happen not at a tragic remove from private life but when private life obtrudes itself on militarized experience. Worry may blur the whole map of the embattled world, but it is also, by now, that map's enabling condition.

I referred earlier to a military hermeticism in Tietjens's mental cataloging of the war, contrasting it to General Campion's comprehensive view of how military aims are entangled in private life. Although *No More Parades* immerses its reader periodically in the martial language and experience of the male combatant, its foremost gesture is to reentangle these with the language and experience of noncombatants through the medium of worry, and to transmit that worry to a reader it constructs as a noncombatant. *Parade's End* attempts, in essence, to fuse the combatant and the noncombatant at the level of mental experience rather than to connect them, Campion-style, in an instrumental hierarchy. Ford's novel engineers this fusion at a number of levels. Through the figure of Valentine Wannop, it devotes many pages to the wartime civilian's mental anguish—as potential target, as bearing both the altered privileges and the complicities of citizenship, as deprived of information about a war to which loved ones are mobilized. This anguish it makes commensurate with the soldier's, if different in shape and tempo. By tracking Tietjens's itinerary from civilian to soldier and back again—an itinerary Ford, after all, shared—it reminds us that combatant and noncombatant are not absolutely discrete identities or species of being but diachronic phases in many, many lives. And it underscores the continuity between those phases in its portrait of a conscript army so underprepared as to be "practically civilian in texture" (467). In offering a panoramic view of its society, *Parade's End* allies itself with the panicked Tietjens, with the blood-stained map. It finds the relations among persons, things, and forces intelligible not as means to the end of total war, but as comprising a world of total worry.[34] This negative-affect model of totality will not expire with the war; worry has no noon when things are shadowless. But even its postwar shadows can host the vision of a landscape in which one could stand up free from both the enemy's crosshairs and war's particular pitch of worry, the vision of a holism unsponsored by total violence.

---

[34] Here Ford may be at his greatest remove from Lukács, who would say that the decadence of modernism lies precisely in misrecognizing as individual psychological issues what are in fact massive, structural forms of violence and exploitation. Yet Ford portrays worry less as individual, private suffering than as a structure of feeling at the level of battalion, population, social totality. We can imagine the two debating whether a totality can be conceptualized through worry, and dividing as to which term is the irritant. Lukács: "The problem is it's *worry*." Ford: "The problem is it's *total*."

Overcast Pastoral

Last Post is where Ford lays out this vision. Because *A Man Could Stand Up—* breaks off its narrative of the Armistice prematurely, some fragments of the war's last day are embedded in the tetralogy's fourth volume. Nevertheless, it is essentially a postwar book, set on a June day in the 1920s and occupied with a few afternoon hours in the West Sussex hamlet where Christopher Tietjens and Valentine Wannop, now expecting a child, have taken up residence with Tietjens's ailing brother Mark and his French wife, Marie Léonie. Pastoral in contrast to the urban, suburban, and war-torn settings of the first three volumes, *Last Post* is a departure in other ways: more given to extended stream-of-consciousness passages, and focalized through characters other than the absent Tietjens, who does not make his first appearance in the volume, outside of flashbacks, until its penultimate page. It is more conclusive at the level of event as well: now installed at her husband's ancestral estate, Sylvia has had an ancient cedar he cherishes there cut down, supposedly at the behest of the wealthy American who is about to rent the place but in fact to spite Tietjens. Yet she also decides, on learning of Valentine's pregnancy, to grant her husband the divorce he will not request himself. Uncertainties are cleared up: Tietjens's father seems not, after all, to have killed himself years before in despair over his son's scandalous private life, and the father of Sylvia's university-age son turns out to be Christopher rather than her lover. Mark Tietjens dies with a benediction to Valentine on his lips, and the reader is left to imagine a humble but happy future for her and Christopher, living in the country, raising their child, and peddling English antiques to the American collectors whose ubiquity and economic rise Christopher has accurately predicted.

One begins to see why Graham Greene denounced this paradise regained as betraying both the rest of the tetralogy and the singularity of Armistice Day, which he remembered as "an explosion without a future"—and why he omitted *Last Post* from The Bodley Head Ford as "a disaster which has delayed a full critical appreciation of *Parade's End*."[35] In doing so he cited Ford's own retraction of the volume, although without noting that Ford vacillated endlessly as to the merits of *Last Post* and whether it belonged among its predecessor volumes.[36] Subsequently, the question of whether *Parade's End* should be regarded as a trilogy or a tetralogy has become an interminable debate among its readers, critics, and adaptors. Recent editions of the text have favored the inclusion of the fourth volume, and Ford scholars have lately tended to defend

---

[35] Greene, "Introduction," 6, 7.

[36] For a detailed account of Ford's statements on this score, see Saunders, *Ford Madox Ford*, II: 254–55.

Last Post as a worthy part of the sequence. But so far the screenwriters are of the party of Greene: both the 1964 and the 2012 TV adaptations of *Parade's End* treat it as a trilogy, although the more recent version, by Tom Stoppard, imports a key incident from *Last Post*—the cutting down of Groby Great Tree—into its concluding scenes set on Armistice Day.

Here I consider several questions that *Last Post*'s outlier status helps us to pose beyond the aesthetic and intentionalist criteria native to the trilogy vs. tetralogy debate. These questions will lead us back to how the work meets the convention of foreshadowing and backshadowing war by casting shadows to the side. In fact, the anomalous or semidetachable quality of volume four might itself be understood as sideshadowing the tetralogy's literary architecture. In a way the previous volumes do not, *Last Post* asks the reader to consider what difference its own presence or absence makes to the overall arc, emphasis, and genre of Ford's series. Consider, then: as a trilogy, *Parade's End* would begin with adumbrations of war, devote the bulk of its narrative time to the war years, and conclude with the Armistice. Shifting its focus away from Sylvia to Valentine in its third, terminal volume, it would gesture toward the resolution of a domestic plot while neglecting to represent that resolution, favoring instead a triumphalist end to war, with Valentine, Tietjens, and his surviving comrades forming, in their Armistice Night bean-feast together, a victorious and jubilant nation in miniature. Envisioning not November 11, 1918, but the war overall as "an explosion without a future," such a project would close off the postwar society as implicitly unrepresentable. With its project of vast national portraiture coterminous with the total war that occasioned it, this *Parade's End* trilogy would sail much closer to the political logic of epic. It would be as if *Vanity Fair* had ended in Napoleon's abdication after Waterloo, with Amelia Osborne widowed by her husband's battlefield death alongside intimations, already, that his friend Dobbin will take his place in her affections; as if Thackeray's novel had as its sole project the depiction of the mobilized nation, of the nation *as* that which is mobilized and, once demobbed, can no longer be portrayed. Digging up either of these literary time capsules—Ford's or Thackeray's—the archaeologists of the future would know, to adapt Louis Bromfield, virtually all there is to know about England *at war*.

In the shadow of its truncation, as in its concluding modulation to pastoral, the four-volume *Parade's End* can be seen more clearly to stage a daring refusal of epic. The condition of narratability, it asserts, ends not with world war but with the dissolution of one marriage and the prospect of another; with death and impending birth; with the confirmation of legitimacy and the disposition of property; with the loss of an ancestral totem that may also have incarnated a family curse; with the contented embrace of a midsized life. If these elements of *Last Post* sound for all the world like the rudiments of nineteenth-century British fiction, we do well to remember their subjection, in turn, to a set of disfiguring pressures: spasmodic shifts in chronology and technique, wild rotations in point of view, and the persistent aftershocks of war. Yet as the final act in a sequence that without it would have clung to the lineaments of national war narrative, *Last Post* is most radical precisely in coloring outside those epic lines with the tints of Victorian domestic narrative. It also points up the fact that each of its predecessor volumes has, in subtler but equally persistent ways, vexed the project of wartime social panoramism with insubordinate matter: marriage, adultery, divorce, financial predicament, gossip and scandal, reputation and retribution, and the worry that attends and connects all of these. Greene, who lauded the first three books for refusing to portray war as an escape from private life, rejected *Last Post's* portrait of private life without war as "unashamed . . . sentimentality," deploring its defanging of Sylvia "as though Lady Macbeth dropped her dagger beside the sleeping Duncan."[37] Too feeling-prone, too domestic and small-bore in its resolution, too friendly to a disarmed femininity: *Last Post* as Greene saw it turned traitor on the other volumes' masculinism of scale and emphasis. In his and other dismissals of the final volume as mere sequel, coda, or afterthought, we are hearing its success at embarrassing epic.

Last Post, I have said, casts sideshadows on its predecessor volumes by dint of its greater conventionality, especially its resuscitation of the nineteenth-century marriage plot. It's a mark of *Parade's End's* complexity that it can sustain a roughly inverse claim: that in allotting an order-giving role to world-historical events largely focalized through a sole, central observer—Christopher Tietjens—its first three volumes most resemble the Victorian novel.[38] By the lights of such a reading, *Last Post* is the tetralogy's most counter-conventional volume in retreating from the world stage and in trading the central observer for a decentered ensemble. Thus although the final volume is most withdrawn from both world-historical chronologies and their alternatives, as regards form it is the place where Ford's lateral shadows fall most thickly. Where *Some Do Not . . .* launches the tetralogy's counterfactualism in respect to technique, *Last Post* adds to that a sideshadowing in respect to narrative point-of-view, even to protagonism. Its opening is focalized through Mark Tietjens, silent and confined to his bed on a terrace overlooking four counties. Dodging in and out of narrative registers from omniscient third-person to free indirect discourse to interior monologue, subsequent chapters shift to Marie Léonie; to the Tietjenses' gruff cabinetmaker, Cramp; to Millicent de Bray Pape, the American tenant of Groby; to Mark Tietjens, Jr., Sylvia and Christopher's son; to Sylvia; to Valentine; and

---

[37] Greene, "Introduction," 5–6.
[38] Robert Green mounts such a reading in *Ford Madox Ford: Prose and Politics* (Cambridge: Cambridge University Press, 1981).

lastly back to Mark as he is dying. This shift to the tetralogy's secondary figures tends to be read as a negative-space portrait of its protagonist—as a way of
depicting Tietjens's centrality in the thoughts of those affected by him. But the
focal consciousnesses of *Last Post* are thinking about a thousand things besides
Christopher, and their cameos do less to substantiate our view of him than to
gesture toward a work—really, to a potentially infinite series of works—centered
in preoccupations and temperaments wholly different from his. Where the flick-
ering experimentalism of the earlier volumes glimpsed a series of stylistically
and generically alternative tetralogies, *Last Post's* rapid handoffs in point of view
make protagonism itself subjunctive.

Reflecting in 1933 on *Parade's End*, Ford identified as its subject "the world
as it culminated in the war." In the same moment he acknowledged a key limitation to the structure of novelistic protagonism: "You—or at least I—cannot
make the world your central character. . . . For mankind in the bulk seems to
lose the character of humanity and to become mere statistics." His tetralogy
would require that necessary evil, an individual protagonist. Yet even in ruling
out the novel of aggregates, Ford makes a surprising confession: "I sit frequently
and dream of writing an immense novel in which all the characters should be
great masses of people—or interests. You would have Interest A, remorselessly
and under the stress of blind necessities, slowly or cataclysmically overwhelming Interest Z. Without the attraction of sympathy for a picturesque or upright
individual" (*Nightingale*, 215–16). An alphabetically comprehensive fiction without a protagonist, tracing instead the clash of masses or interests; the novel bent
to a combination of encyclopedism and macrohistory: however unwritable this
ideal seemed, it can be felt moving beneath the waters of *Parade's End*, gesturing
through alternatives to totalities that lie to the side of what it represents.

Tietjens incarnates both that ideal and its necessary frustration: he is the
statistician who prevents the work, by virtue of being its central figure, from
ascending to the statistical ideal. His seemingly paradoxical relation to the
work's synoptic ambitions, we should note, aligns him less with formal experimentalism than with the self-division of a certain strain of nineteenth-century
realism, one that culminates in the work of George Eliot. This is a realism
whose generalizing aims must contend with its particularizing technique and
ethics. Its protagonist, initially produced to exemplify a real-world type or
species, eventually undermines the classificatory premises of that initial gesture through the deepening realization and embodiment demanded of her
by plot and by its ethical imperative to illustrate her singularity. According
to Catherine Gallagher, this tension between "the impulse toward reference
and the impulse toward realization" may even be said to define realism, and
the energy generated by this tension is what propels Eliot's realist narratives.[39]

---

[39] Catherine Gallagher, "George Eliot: Immanent Victorian," *Representations* 90 (Spring 2005): 66.

Drawn explicitly in the charged field between type and singularity, Tietjens belongs less to the cohort of modernist protagonists (Leopold Bloom, Clarissa Dalloway, et al.) than with the likes of Dorothea Brooke. Although he is introduced to the reader as typifying a passé Tory worldview, he either renounces or is stripped of nearly everything—monogamy, a clearly legitimate heir, a Protestant line, unmarred familial property, prominence, "omniscience"— that he is supposed to represent. Tietjens is the exemplar turned outlier, the data point at which aggregates—Ford's Issue A and Issue Z—vanish.

That this realism problem persists in *Parade's End* does not make Ford's quartet a belated *Middlemarch* (1871–72). One of the most singular things about the tetralogy is the way it holds a core tension of realism copresent with a subjunctive experimentalism while declining to resolve one by means of the other. It declines, that is, to suggest either that formal counter-conventions can resolve the realist problem of squaring individual and aggregate representation, or that the shocks to the social totality indexed in the project by speculative modernist techniques might be wished away through an embrace of realism in the indicative mood. *Last Post* amplifies these refusals. It ratchets up the expectation of a realist solution through the foregrounding of marriage and inheritance plots precisely as its revolving stream-of-consciousness focalizations draw attention to the arbitrariness of realism's protagonist structure. Yet having pitted these energies against one another, the volume neither engineers a détente between them nor produces some synthesis of the two, instead bringing them to conclusions that remain discrete, adjacent, undialectized despite occurring in the same page space. The realist strain culminates with Mark Tietjens's entreating the pregnant Valentine from his deathbed, "Never thou let thy barnie weep for thy sharp tongue to thy goodman" (835)—that is, speak gently to Christopher before your child—and with the implication that such gentleness among individuals might be scaled up to the aggregate. The modernist strain, at the last, takes up the dying man's point of view and then transitions silently to an omniscient narrator to relate Valentine's embargo on Mark's last words: "Perhaps it would be best not to tell Lady Tietjens that he spoke. . . . She would have liked to have his last words. . . . But she did not need them as much as I" (836). A plea for civility is no sooner communicated, and by a man who has not spoken for years, than it is declared incommunicable. Groby Great Tree, freshly felled, is present in a chunk of aromatic wood, a fragment shored against the ruin of the lineage and life-world emblematized by the venerable tree.

One thing we can say about this dialectics at a standstill: it is irreducible to the element of nostalgic pastoral that is nonetheless inarguably present in *Last Post*. The same element is present in earlier volumes too, as when Tietjens, awaiting an attack on the front lines in *A Man Could Stand Up—*, daydreams of Sylvia in white crepe walking down a seventeenth-century street and thinks:

Heaven knew, we did not want a preposterous drum-beating such as the Elizabethans produced—and received. Like lions at a fair. . . . But what chance had quiet fields, Anglican sainthood, accuracy of thought, heavy-leaved, timbered hedge-rows, slowly creeping plough-lands moving up the slopes? . . . Still, the land remains. . . .

The land remains. . . . It remains! . . . At that same moment the dawn was wetly revealing; over there in George Herbert's parish . . . What was it called? . . . What the devil was its name? Oh, Hell! . . . (566)

Later, having remembered the name of Herbert's parish, he considers the young men he is commanding.

What a handful of frail grass with which to stop an aperture in the dam of—of the Empire! Damn the Empire! It was England! It was Bemerton Parsonage that mattered! What did we want with an Empire? It was only a jerry-building Jew like Disraeli that could have provided us with that jerry-built name! The Tories said they had to have someone to do their dirty work. . . . Well, they'd had it! (591)

The condemnation of the imperial present, the idealization of the rural past, the anti-Semitism alongside Anglo-Saxon "cradle of the race" (567) paeans to the Salisbury countryside—this is none other than the Little Englandism that Jed Esty has influentially traced in the London-based late modernism of the 1930s. Assuaging the loss of British universalism through an embrace of English particularism, this late-imperial turn produced what Esty calls "a new apprehension of a complete national life—an insular romance of whole-ness, or at least of layered social knowability," that was typically nostalgic in its temporality.[40] In Nicholas Brown's reading, the same two passages I have cited from *A Man Could Stand Up—* "[harmonize] with the nostalgic thrust of the entire tetralogy" and help set the stage for its concluding turn to the English countryside. For Brown, the only thing that ironizes the final vol-ume's "nostalgic, soft-focus, Merchant-and-Ivory ending" is Tietjens's demo-tion from Yorkshire squire to petty-bourgeois antiques peddler, his reduction by the vicissitudes of history and capitalism to "a purveyor of the simulacrum of his own desire."[41]

Although at Brown's distance from the 1920s *Last Post* can look like a lightly ironized, high-gloss period drama, Ford's contemporaries saw it dif-ferently. For one reviewer it conveyed "the general impression of a nightmare in a lunatic asylum"; for another it was "at times . . . terribly like a psychopathic

---

[40] See Jed Esty, *A Shrinking Island: Modernism and National Culture in England* (Princeton: Princeton University Press, 2004), 8.

[41] Nicholas Brown, *Utopian Generations: The Political Horizon of Twentieth-Century Literature* (Princeton: Princeton University Press, 2005), 102–3.

ward in some fabulous hospital for world-war wreckage."[42] Such reactions remind us how much of the damage that interests Ford outlasts the war. Sylvia remains haunted, as she was at Rouen, by Father Consett, her friend the Irish Catholic priest who was executed after the Easter Rising, and whose reproving shade presides over her decision to divorce Tietjens. When she at last tells Valentine of her decision, the latter reacts not with relief but by fainting (thankfully, for her child's sake, on a Basra rug), her guttering thoughts beset by money worries. Her first words to Tietjens on his return—the words that precipitate Mark's dying plea for gentleness—are to berate him for misplacing a set of prints owed to a client: "How are we going to feed and clothe a child if you do such things? . . . How are we to live? How are we ever to live?" (835). Meanwhile Mark's epiphanies—that his father died by accident, that Valentine must not be Christopher's half-sister and thus incestuous lover— take place only in his head and, in his aphasic state, cannot be communicated to anyone else. The war is over but worry endures, ready to be amplified by the next war should it come but awful enough without it, offering no guarantees. Violence, as well, persists in the postwar, whether in the rending memory of battlefields and air raids or in the presence of the master's domestic violence against the servant, the male servant's against his wife. Like Woolf's in "The Mark on the Wall," the pastoral of *Last Post* is shaded by the prospect—never the certainty—that the fragile equipoise the book details will be wrecked by violence, or shown to be rotten with worry.

Returning to the pair of passages from *A Man Could Stand Up—*, we find the tetralogy has prepared us for this beclouded pastoral by showing us its genesis in the trenches. There, the vision of plowlands and hedgerows is conjured as a distraction from an oncoming strafe by Tietjens, whose traumatic amnesia stops him ("Oh, Hell!") from remembering the name of Herbert's parish despite the fact that he's read past "H" in the *Britannica*. To thus posit the specific origin of a nostalgic pastoralism is to make it untenable as an ahistorical, reparative mode. It's as if *Parade's End* had anticipated the Little Englandism of the 1930s and warned against it by historicizing its emergence—not, for Ford, in imperial contraction, but in the combatant's rejection of a war he ascribes to imperial *expansionism*, and in the midst of which he longs—understandably, impossibly—for the unmilitarized landscape of home. Had the work stayed stapled to Tietjens, it might simply have adopted his utopian view of the Anglican sainthood, the quiet fields, the land, the cradle of the race. But by placing him in a variety of landscapes, moments, and syndromes, and finally by taking leave of his point of view altogether,

---

[42] Gerald Gould, [untitled review], *Observer*, February 5, 1928, qtd. in David Dow Harvey, *Ford Madox Ford 1873–1939: A Bibliography of Works and Criticism* (New York: Gordian Press, 1972), 376; William McFee, "Tietjens Once More," *New York Herald Tribune Books*, January 15, 1928, rpt. in MacShane, ed., *Ford Madox Ford: The Critical Heritage*, 113.

the tetralogy comprehends him, too, in his historicity, comprehends how his views might contribute to the "atrocities of peace" that Ford claimed provoked him to pacifism even more than did the "horrors of war."[43] In this, *Parade's End* joins "Thoughts on Peace in an Air Raid" in abhoring, all at once, the prospect of war and the wrong kind of armistice.

Looking back during the 1930s at London just after the war, Ford wrote, "[A]ll things that lived and moved and had volition and life might at any moment be resolved into a scarlet viscosity seeping into the earth of torn fields. [. . .] Nay, it had been revealed to you that beneath Ordered Life itself was stretched the merest film with, beneath it, the abysses of Chaos. One had come from the frail shelters of the Line to a world that was more frail than any canvas hut" (*Nightingale*, 64). The scene presents a grim contrast to the jubilations of November 11, 1918. Far from remedying the feeling of exposure Ford had experienced at the Front, the postwar metropolis redoubled it, outdid it. The membrane of form could be torn at any moment, dropping one into the void. As distinct as *Last Post's* rural setting is from postwar London, Ford's description of the latter gets at that volume's sense of precariousness and contingency. Sylvia, bemused by the quiet life Tietjens has made with Mark and Valentine after his turbulent years with herself, thinks, "It was as if a man should have jumped out of a frying pan into—a duckpond" (792). As we have seen, a number of Ford's critics have found *Last Post* to be just such a duckpond after the frying pan of the tetralogy's wartime volumes. It is the fire. And yet it is not a fire of foreordination. All things that live *might* at any moment be resolved into blood, says Ford, but they *need* not be. In the same passage about postwar London, he lamented, "In the old days we had seemed to have ourselves and our destinies well in hand. Now we were drifting towards a weir . . ." (63). There is foreboding in this double loss of sovereignty and destiny, but not foreclosure. Worry can take war's place as the basis of totality in *Parade's End* because all possible futures are still conditional, including the future at war.

In one of *The Man without Qualities'* most vivid images of the future's openness, Musil's narrator has this to say: "The train of events is a train that lays down its own tracks as it goes along. The river of time carries its own banks along with it. The traveler moves on a solid floor between solid walls, but the floor and the walls are strongly influenced by the movements of the travelers, though they do not notice it" (484). No view of history could be farther from the opening of *Parade's End*, with its image of ruling-class privilege and rectitude speeding on smooth rails toward the unavoidable catastrophe of war. In their perfectly appointed prewar railway carriage, Tietjens and Macmaster are elite passengers of history, prepared to complain to the *Times* if the train

---

[43] Ford Madox Ford, *Great Trade Route* (London: Allen & Unwin, 1937), 97.

jolts them. They seem to have themselves and their destinies well in hand, unaware they are the inertest of freight. But this initial figuration of history as an inescapable trunk line is relegated to the status of a spur line in Ford's work—a work that wants to be nothing but sideshadows, a network of trunk-less spurs. In the opener conception of history that *Parade's End* assembles and enacts over many pages, the travelers move about the carriage, not just influencing the conveyance through their movements but in fact helping to produce and constitute it at every moment. For Ford, as for Musil, actors and events lay down rails as they go instead of following along some extant route. This figure, more impasse than dialectical image, may be difficult to visualize. But it is the burden of works that conceive of the future as radically multiple until the moment, unrepresentable in its complexity, when the present welds one future into place. At that moment there is no way to separate history's subjects from its course—no way to tell the traveler from the track.

Conclusion

PERPETUAL INTERWAR

Life has changed into a timeless succession of shocks, interspaced with empty, paralysed intervals. But nothing, perhaps, is more ominous for the future than the fact that, quite literally, these things will soon be past thinking on, for each trauma of the returning combatants, each shock not inwardly absorbed, is a ferment of future destruction.

—Theodor W. Adorno, *Minima Moralia:*
Reflections on a Damaged Life (1949)

If you cud even jus see 1 thing clear the woal of whats in it you cud see every thing clear. But you never wil get to see the woal of any thing youre all ways in the middl of it living it or moving thru it. Never mynd.

—Russell Hoban, *Riddley Walker* (1980)

When the Postmodern Studies Association convened for the first time in 2006, the title of its inaugural symposium bespoke an uncertainty about its object of study. "Mid-century to Postmodern: The Postwar Era Reconsidered" treated postmodernism not as a field-designating term but as the terminus of a postwar era that was itself both implicitly finished and in need of rethinking. After only two days, the thirteen scholars present decided to change the organization's name to Post45. Although there is no public record of their deliberations, conferee Amy Hungerford's essay "On the Period Formerly Known as Contemporary" provides some strong clues. The Postmodern Studies Association's initial banner word had likely come to seem too closely associated with the Jamesonian neo-Marxian approach, as well as burdened by a history of valuing "experimental" writing by white men over putatively realist works by women and people of color. In contrast to what Hungerford calls "the old postmodernism," the period designation post-1945 must have seemed unevaluative, open, and methodologically neutral, implying, in her words, "a minimal set of assumptions about the way the world and culture—especially American culture—have changed since the end of World War II."[1] As a field parameter, the war's end offered the double virtues of inclusivity and punctuality.

But how punctually do wars end? In the case of the Second World War, the answer to this question may seem obvious: hostilities in the war's last theater, the Pacific, concluded on September 2, 1945, with the signing of the Instrument of Surrender by Japanese officials on the deck of the USS *Missouri* in Tokyo Bay. If you consult other indices, however, as the historian Mary Dudziak has done, you find that even so decisive a war can keep ending (and not ending) well after the fighting does. The U.S. Armed Services, she observes, continued to give Asiatic-Pacific Campaign Medals for service through March 2, 1946, and Army of Occupation Medals to those who served in Japan through April 27, 1952, the last day of the Allied occupation.[2] By the reckoning of the Disabled American Veterans, which grants membership to veterans "disabled in line of duty during time of war," Dudziak reports, "The only non-war period after World War II, other than a period of seven months in 1990, was from October 15, 1976 to November 4, 1979" (30–31). She shows, too, how even when wars end formally, a state's legal war powers can persist long after the surrender documents have been signed. In several cases during the late 1940s, for example, the U.S. Supreme Court found that "war does not cease with a cease-fire order, and power to be exercised by the President . . . is a process which begins when war is declared but is not exhausted when the shooting stops." The war power, said the Court, "includes the power 'to remedy the evils which have arisen from its rise and progress' and continues for the duration of that emergency" (38–39).[3]

For Dudziak and many other scholars, the fiction of war's punctuality is enormously consequential.[4] It props up two additional fictions: first, that wartime is the exception to the rule of peacetime; and second, that wartime states of emergency—the arrogation of powers to the sovereign or the executive, suspensions of transparency and due process—are fully and rapidly

---

[1] Amy Hungerford, "On the Period Formerly Known as Contemporary," *American Literary History* 20:1–2 (Spring/Summer 2008): 414, 418. On the 2006 symposium, see 419n3.

[2] Mary L. Dudziak, *War•Time: An Idea, Its History, Its Consequences* (New York: Oxford University Press, 2012), 151. Further references are in the text.

[3] Dudziak is quoting the decisions in *Ludecke v. Watkins*, 335 U.S. 160, 169–70 (1948), citing *United States v. Anderson*, 9 Wall. 56, 70; and *Woods v. Cloyd W. Miller Co.*, 333 U.S. 138, 141–44 (1948).

[4] The scholarship on this subject is too extensive to list exhaustively here but see, for example, Kim Lane Scheppele, "Law in a Time of Emergency: States of Exception and the Temptations of 9/11," *University of Pennsylvania Journal of Constitutional Law* 6 (2004): 1001–83; Judith Butler, *Precarious Life: The Powers of Mourning and Violence* (London: Verso, 2006); Oren Gross and Fionnuala Ní Aoláin, *Law in Times of Crisis: Emergency Powers in Theory and Practice* (Cambridge: Cambridge University Press, 2006); and Elaine Scarry, *Rule of Law, Misrule of Men* (Cambridge, MA: MIT Press, 2010).

superseded by the rule of law when peacetime resumes. Critics who would unmask these fictions insist that modern war and war powers have historically proven to be not punctual but durable, not exceptional but perpetual in their drift. These critics lately seem to include President Barack Obama, who in a May 2013 speech at the National Defense University affirmed his intention "to refine, and ultimately repeal" Congress's twelve-year-old Authorization to Use Military Force (AUMF), the legal basis for the war on terror that has kept America, as he put it, "on a perpetual wartime footing" since 9/11.[5]

If you take the postwar era to have ended on November 9, 1989, with the fall of the Berlin Wall, or on September 11, 2001, with the Al Qaeda attacks, then the notion of a post-9/11 perpetual wartime ushered in by the passage of the AUMF and the Patriot Act will inform the Cold War decades only as a reading of their aftermath. But there are also reasons not to adopt *perpetual war* as a field-defining rubric for the earlier period. For all that it insists on those years' continuous state of militarized violence-production, a perpetual war analytic fails to capture the massive asymmetries in how that violence was distributed—the difference, say, between what civilians in superpowers versus those in neocolonial proxy-war sites experienced—or the fact that despite the conventional wisdom about emergency powers, some rights grew *more* robust during the most geopolitically tense years of the Cold War.[6] Admonitions against perpetual war can rebuke the standard binarism of wartime versus peacetime. But as a field or period designator, the rubric of perpetual war does less to evade the same binarism than to reinforce it, over-consecrating the category of "wartime" by making it coterminous with the time of the state and all those whom it governs.

In place of perpetual war, then, I offer here a way of characterizing late modernity that will sound initially like a contradiction in terms: *perpetual interwar.* The expression appears to contradict itself because an interval between two discrete historical events would seem nonperpetual by definition. This is only true, however, if we apply the term *interwar* exclusively in retrospect, after the advent of a second war has notarized the foregoing period's in-betweenness. If, as I have attempted to do in this book, we treat the term *interwar* phenomenologically—as the real-time experience of remembering a past war while awaiting and theorizing a future one—we begin to see how a period could go on, even in near perpetuity, feeling like an interwar era as long

---

[5] White House, press release, "Remarks by the President at the National Defense University," May 23, 2013, http://www.whitehouse.gov/the-press-office/2013/05/23/remarks-president-national-defense-university, n.p.

[6] Dudziak (80–81) notes that in 1962, the year of the Cuban Missile Crisis, the Kennedy administration enforced James Meredith's civil right to enroll in the University of Mississippi and the U.S. Supreme Court handed down landmark civil liberties cases in *Engle v. Vitale*, 370 U.S. 421 (barring states from requiring prayer in public schools), and *Baker v. Carr*, 269 U.S. 186 (permitting the Court to intervene in state legislative redistricting).

as the prospect of military violence appeared to loom. A few approaches to "the" interwar period, 1918–1939, have already advanced along these lines.[7] By treating expectation, anxiety, prophecy, and anticipatory mourning as serious objects of historical analysis, these accounts undo the portrait of the period rendered from the privileged vantage of its certain terminus in war, even as they show us historical actors in the interwar period who saw the next war as a certainty. Foreclosed futurity, in this approach, ceases to function as a historiographic master plot by which to pity the naiveté of those who didn't see the war coming or to praise the canniness of those who did. It emerges instead as an experience that can be studied as a historical object through its evidentiary traces. Such a study gives us a contingent interwar in which the memory of one conflagration is shadowed by the suspicion or conviction that another, even worse one is in the offing. Unsealing the 1918–1939 period in this manner should restore, in turn, our access to the Cold War's interwar phenomenology, its suspension between one war and its impending sequel. Such a shift enables us as literary scholars to read, for instance, post-1945 nuclear fictions—Walter M. Miller Jr.'s *A Canticle for Leibowitz* (1960), say, or Russell Hoban's *Riddley Walker* (1980)—as the descendants and genre-mates of twenties and thirties texts such as Hamilton's *Theodore Savage* (1922) and H. G. Wells's *The Shape of Things to Come* (1933), and as no less "interwar" in their disposition.

Yet the experience of being between past and future wars is not all that's indexed by the notion of a perpetual interwar. I mean *inter + war* to denote not only "between wars" but also "in the midst of war" (as in Cicero's famous utterance, *Silent leges inter arma*: "For law falls silent in the midst of war").[8] If this alloy of interwar and midwar looks like compounding the paradox, we need only recall Britain's interwar air control experiment in Iraq to see that what one subject, community, or population experiences as an interval of peace another may experience as a time of intermittent or even continuous violence, whether in the shape of small wars, colonial occupation and policing, anticolonial uprising, civil war, or the psychic violence of war-anticipation. Rooted in a Eurocentric historiography, *interwar* has typically connoted postwar gaiety and prosperity followed by financial crisis, political spasm, and rearmament.[9] But a generation of scholarship on

---

[7] See, for example, my "Air War Prophecy and Interwar Modernism," *Comparative Literature Studies* 42.2 (Spring 2005): 130–61; Roxanne Panchasi, *Future Tense: The Culture of Anticipation in France Between the Wars* (Ithaca, NY: Cornell University Press, 2009); Leo Mellor, *Reading the Ruins: Modernism, Bombsites and British Culture* (Cambridge: Cambridge University Press, 2011), chap. 1; and Susan R. Grayzel, *At Home and Under Fire: Air Raids and Culture in Britain from the Great War to the Blitz* (Cambridge: Cambridge University Press, 2012), chaps. 5 and 6.

[8] The passage, from Cicero's *Pro Tito Annio Milone ad iudicem oratio*, is more often cited in resequenced form as *Inter arma silent leges* and translated "Among [times of] arms, the laws fall mute."

[9] Eric Hayot's chapter/manifesto "Against Periodization" offers a strong critique of how periodizing scholarship in the West tends not only to reproduce Eurocentrism in space and culture but also

colonial violence during the twenties and thirties has made the term bear other news: that even between wars someone is *inter arma*, is in the midst of a time of arms. This sounds like perpetual war redux but in fact rejects that model's way of homogenizing all conflict, no matter its scale or symmetry or intensity or legality, as *war* full stop. The analytic of perpetual interwar seeks not to "promote" all armed violence to the status of war but to trace the uneven distribution of violence across races, classes, populations, spaces of empire, and temporalities. It matters for this analytic which conflicts are declared, what names they go by, whether those involved have chosen their involvement, and whether they are protected by laws of war. Embracing neither the wartime-versus-peacetime binarism nor the too simple rejoinder that now all time is wartime, a perpetual interwar analysis demands a specific accounting of whose conflicts underwrite whose tranquility, even as it offers a general portrait of late modernity as harboring, always, three simultaneous relations to the time of armed conflict. For at every moment in the world system of late-modern injury production, conflict is recollected, ongoing, and future-conditional all at once. As scholars working in (I'd hazard) any period since at least the Napoleonic Wars can attest, this tripartite relation to the time of military violence contributes to a geopolitical suspense, one that should play a more prominent role in our theories of late modernity.

Enough scholarship crosses the 1945 divide that the general benefits of such an approach have begun to seem uncontroversial. Here I develop a more focused claim: that a range of post-1945 works, including but not limited to some of the historiographic metafictions that were cornerstones of "the old postmodernism," themselves engage in *theorizing* a transperiod approach to late modernity by means of something like a perpetual interwar. In part because it will appear so improbable a choice, I turn briefly now to Thomas Pynchon's *Gravity's Rainbow* (1973). For decades a whetstone text for honing postmodern canons, theories, and field traits, the novel has seemed particularly suited to various periodizing enterprises within that field. This was true practically from the moment it was published: Edward Mendelson described it in 1976 as heralding the arrival of "a new international culture, created by the technologies of instant communication and the economy of world markets."[10] And it remains the case, as in Brian McHale's recent claim that Pynchon's novel ushers in postmodernism's major phase, its appearance in 1973 "coincid[ing] with other indicators of

---

"to narrate the history of the aesthetic in European time, emplotting beginnings, middles, and ends in a manner that is not . . . merely neutral." See Eric Hayot, *On Literary Worlds* (New York: Oxford University Press, 2012), 156.

[10] Edward Mendelson, "Gravity's Encyclopedia" in *Mindful Pleasures: Essays on Thomas Pynchon*, ed. George Levine and David Leverenz (Boston: Little, Brown, 1976), 165.

the major phase's onset around the years 1972–74."[11] The book's punctual arrival from the perspective of literary history may be partly an effect of the chronological precision with which it unfolds, most of its diegetic events being internally traceable to particular dates, even to specific hours. The novel's third part, "In the Zone," ends on the night of August 5, 1945 in London, where two minor figures are polishing their postwar plans while, in another time zone, the plane carrying the first atomic bomb approaches Hiroshima.[12] The dawn of the nuclear weapons age, the division of Germany and Austria at the Potsdam Conference, the U.S. recruitment of German scientists through Operation Paperclip: a novel moored to these events and undertakings beats periodizing critics at their own game, constructing 1945 as a radical discontinuity, a "Year Zero," as Ian Buruma has dubbed it.[13] Like its protagonist Tyrone Slothrop, dispatched "to be present at his own assembly—perhaps, heavily paranoid voices have whispered, *his time's assembly*," *Gravity's Rainbow* imagines witnessing the birth of its Cold War time. It should be the playbook of the post-1945.[14]

Yet for all the force punctuality exerts in and through it, Pynchon's novel is also aswarm with untimely counterforces: for every chronologism an anachronism, for every teleology a bizarre analepsis, for every assembly a dispersal. Whether we understand it as his Orphic sparagmos or simply as the heat-death of his protagonism, Slothrop, we're both told and shown, is not assembled but "broken down instead, and scattered" (738). So too is the notion of a discrete, self-identical "time" of the sort that periodization implies. Despite continuing to be read as "*futurist* in its orientation," *Gravity's Rainbow* devotes much less energy to prolepsis than to analepsis, and the burden of its flashbacks, whether to seventeenth-century Mauritius or to South-West Africa in 1922, is to assert continuities between the past and the 1944–45 diegetic present. These continuities flow in a few principal channels: the exploitation and mass killing, usually outside of formal wartime, of supposedly preterite races and species by a self-appointed elect; the elect's dependence on and desire for the preterite; and, through numerous analepses to the twenties and thirties,

---

[11] Brian McHale, "Period, Break, Interregnum," *Twentieth-Century Literature* 57.3–4 (Fall/Winter 2011): 331.

[12] Steven C. Weisenburger, *A "Gravity's Rainbow" Companion: Sources and Contexts for Pynchon's Novel*, 2nd ed. (Athens: University of Georgia Press, 2006), 310, 354. Weisenburger uses (among other data) astrological allusions in the text to support his precision dating.

[13] See Ian Buruma, *Year Zero: A History of 1945* (Harmondsworth , UK: Penguin, 2013). Buruma's argument is less invested than his title suggests in the discontinuous narrative of the reboot. The later months of 1945, he shows, saw the widespread resuscitation by the Allies of their interwar colonial projects, an undertaking that included significant levels of violence outside the aegis of declared war. The second half of 1945, by these lights, was in essence post-1945—even as it resumed certain pre-1939 distributions of law and violence.

[14] Thomas Pynchon, *Gravity's Rainbow* (New York: Viking, 1973), 738; original emphasis. Further references are in the text.

the steady growth of cartelized transnational capital by way of intermittent nation-based wars. Those interwar decades are, as it turns out, the novel's favorite analeptic destination. We accompany Franz and Leni Pökler to a 1929 seance in Berlin where the spirit of Walter Rathenau, the industrialist, cartelizer, and politician who was assassinated in 1922, is contacted. In later analepses we pay visits to the interwar German film industry and witness the prehistory of Hitler's rocket program in the hobbyist Society for Space Travel. And the flashback to South-West Africa, the Herero Uprising of 1922, and its suppression by German soldiers insists that even as the potential tributaries to another world war are beginning to flow toward one another, colonial violence is ongoing. Rather than build to a "year zero" view of 1945 as sealing the preceding years in the crypt of the past, the novel engages in a seance of its own, inviting adjacent interwar periods to commune through the medium of the war.

Despite being moored to a specific historical interval, *Gravity's Rainbow* is in fact a veritable encyclopedia of means by which a time can fail or refuse to be contemporary with itself. The novel's penchant for anachronism, especially for the sixties drug lingo slung by its characters in the 1940s, sabotages the claims to historical accuracy it elsewhere seems to certify through research and careful chronology. Similarly, the gleeful speed at which the narration switches generic codes, adopts period argots, and hotwires arcane lexicons ensures that the book's content never fuses with a historically settled form with which it might be said to be concurrent. But among *Gravity's Rainbow*'s untimely traits, the most prominent is surely its obsession with hysteron proteron, the figure of reversal in which effect precedes cause, response anticipates stimulus, sequelae predate injury. There is no need here to catalog all of the novel's instances of this figure, but at least two rise to something like structural significance: the fact that the supersonic V-2 rocket arrives before its victims hear it coming; and Slothrop's pattern of having erections, and often sexual encounters, at the locations of *future* V-2 rocket strikes. The second of these phenomena is never fully explained and may, after all, be debunked in the novel's later pages. But the first reminds us that uncanny, apparently magical deformations of time may have nonmagical causes. The velocity at which modern weapons travel entails both a loss of warning and a scattering of the sensorium of violence across temporalities. By the time you've heard its final approach, the disaster is in the past.

The figure of hysteron proteron binds Pynchon's novel tightly to the prevailing nuclear conditions of its writing. These, remembering Derrida's "No Apocalypse, Not Now," had to do with *preemption*, a reversal of conventional sequence through speed: the threat of massive retaliation deters the first strike in advance; nuclear war must outstrip the laws of war that would interdict it; and griefwork, in its turn, must travel faster than war, must happen in advance of a war that might permit no survivable postwar.[15] But while these preemptive logics reach a kind of apogee during the Cold War, we have seen that they were already emergent in the military theories, international legal debates, and "next war" speculative fictions of the 1920s. All of these early interwar discourses registered the deranging effects of modern warfare's acceleration and its ratcheting up of geopolitical suspense. Together, they point to a large-scale reversal of historiographic sequence: the arrival, well before the Cold War, of many of the strategic, legal, and psychic effects we have since attributed to the nuclear condition, and the presence of a "peacetime" colonial proxy-war geometry we usually ascribe to the Cold War. In tacking back and forth between the interwar period and the transitional months of 1945, *Gravity's Rainbow* says that what looked like a radically new world order was in many ways an uncanny return, a quotation posing as a coinage.

Having aligned the interwar period and the Cold War as deep intertexts, Pynchon's novel rivets them to one another through a series of allusions to the very interwar encyclopedic fictions discussed in the preceding chapters of this book. Its opening wartime dream of evacuation by rail ("Inside the carriage, which is built on several levels, he sits in velveteen darkness" [3]) evokes the first scene of Ford's *Parade's End* tetralogy, in which Tietjens and Macmaster ride, before the war upends everything, in a railway carriage running "as smoothly . . . as British gilt-edged securities."[16] The first waking scene of *Gravity's Rainbow* echoes, as many have noted, the opening pages of Joyce's *Ulysses*. These also feature a rooftop morning ritual, spiral stairs, sunlight filtering through mullioned windows, and a group of male covivants making breakfast after a rough night, although in Joyce's "Telemakhos" episode no V-2 rocket arcs toward Dublin, threatening to demolish the Martello tower. More diffusely, Pynchon's novel recalls Musil's *The Man without Qualities* in its entropic protagonism and its distension of a brief historical interim to the scale of an epoch. My aim in mentioning these allusions is not to annex *Gravity's Rainbow*, "the old postmodernism," or post-1945 literature writ large to something like a "long modernism."[17] But I would describe *Gravity's Rainbow* as a reading of these modernist intertexts, one that identifies them as precursors in more than raw size or formal restlessness. It also defends them against any charge of naiveté or obsolescence for belonging to a world order superseded in 1939 or 1945. By reactivating *Ulysses* and *Parade's End*, in

---

[15] On speed and the inverse temporalities of the nuclear condition, see also my "Bombing and the Symptom: Traumatic Earliness and the Nuclear Uncanny," *diacritics* 30.4 (Winter 2000): 59–82; Daniel Cordle, *States of Suspense: The Nuclear Age, Postmodernism, and United States Fiction and Prose* (Manchester, UK: Manchester University Press, 2008), and Daniel Grausam, *On Endings: American Postmodern Fiction and the Cold War* (Charlottesville: University of Virginia Press, 2011).

[16] Ford Madox Ford, *Parade's End* (New York: Alfred A. Knopf, 1950), 3.

[17] Hungerford (418) suggests that it might be better to call the post-1945 period "long modernism."

particular, in its dread-filled opening pages, it identifies them as undepleted resources in contending with war's deformations of time and totality. And insofar as that suspenseful interval between launch and possible arrival is the interwar arc par excellence, it says—and this makes it a precursor of the present book—that modernism, even in the twenties and thirties, was already under the vapor trail.

Gravity's Rainbow, I have argued, offers a more unsparing critique of periodizing historiographies than most of its critics have done. The novel masquerades as an epic of scrupulous chronologism only to disclose its radical commitments to untimeliness and durativity. Pynchon's book is a transperiod work in period camouflage. And it is not unique in this. Even confining ourselves to novels that project interwar temporalities and violence-distributions beyond the 1918–1939 period, we might point to Kazuo Ishiguro's *The Remains of the Day* (1989) and *When We Were Orphans* (2000), Nicholas Mosley's *Hopeful Monsters* (1990), Michael Ondaatje's *The English Patient* (1992)—and, more recently, to the transperiod seances of Tom Carson's *C* (2011) and the thick counterfactualism of Kate Atkinson's *Life after Life: A Novel* (2013). These examples alone indicate that transperiod thinking is not an exclusive property of what Linda Hutcheon called "that most didactic of postmodern forms: historiographic metafiction." Despite her accompanying claim that "postmodernism is less a period than a poetics or an ideology" (28), its putative use of modernist technique against modernist hermeticism emboxes it historically.[18] We need to decouple any given works' historiographically oriented metafictive energies from postmodernism, not least because the skepticism such works register about historical punctuality is so often, and so effectively, leveled against the alleged start dates of the postmodern and the postwar.

And after? With the Cold War receding and "post-9/11" on the rise as a periodization of the present, does it make sense to speak of a perpetual interwar in referring to our own moment? To be sure, the prospect of a worldwide war that would both mobilize and target whole populations seems more remote than it once did. Other doomsday scenarios occupy us more urgently. Yet despite our not having plunged into global conflict since the Second World War, few populations have enjoyed an uncomplicated peacetime in recent years. In the global frame, the Uppsala Conflict Data Program reported thirty-three "armed conflicts"—those in which at least one party is a state—as having occurred in 2013, its most recent reported year, alongside a much larger number of non-state and one-sided conflicts.[19] U.S. armed forces are deployed at present in over

---

[18] Linda Hutcheon, "Historiographic Metafiction: Parody and the Intertextuality of History,"' in *Intertextuality and Contemporary American Fiction*, ed. Patrick O'Donnell and Robert Con Davis (Baltimore: Johns Hopkins University Press, 1989), 28.

[19] Uppsala Conflict Data Program, http://www.pcr.uu.se/research/ucdp/, n.p.; see also Uppsala Universitet, press release, "Two out of Five War Fatalities Occurred in Syria," June 12, 2014.

150 countries, most of them in Middle Eastern combat zones associated with the "war on terror."[20] In its domestic and foreign policies the U.S. government continues to rely on extraordinary war powers conferred by the Patriot Act and the AUMF, both of which have been in place since 2001 despite the current president's apparent willingness to end this "perpetual wartime footing." Meanwhile that footing legally underwrites the use, across enormous distances, of technological asymmetries massive enough to put target and targeter not just in vastly different time zones but also in disparate temporalities vis-à-vis war and peace. Thus a drone pilot may, from a safe stateside workplace that looks for all the world like peacetime, take the lives of those in far-off zones torn by what looks for all the world like war.[21] The one lives in a polity where aspects of the presumptive next war are debated by analogy with past wars: an interwar polity. The other is *inter arma*, amid a time of arms, in the zone where law falls silent. Yet it is predominantly the silence of law in the remote operator's state, the interwar polity where war powers outlive a war that was anyway never declared, that licenses the massive asymmetry of the drone strike. Asymmetric in intensity and totality as well as in temporality: for where the drone attack is partial for the remote operator, the executive, and the citizenry in whose name the strike occurs, it is total for the figures down below, on the receiving end of the bombs. These antinomies of law and force, partiality and totality, space and time, are among the basic elements of our perpetual interwar. Violence for now is constant; only war is intermittent.

This book began with the *bukimi* felt by the citizens of Hiroshima in the days before August 6, 1945. I'd like to close it by touching on postwar Japan, and in particular on political rhetoric that imagines Japan's resumption of full political sovereignty as a return to an interwar footing. In her compelling essay, "Trauma's Two Times," Marilyn Ivy tracks this rhetoric, which sees Japan as trapped since 1945 in a *haisengo* or "post-defeat" temporality. Ivy

---

[20] United States Department of Defense, "Total Military Personnel and Dependent End Strength by Service, Regional Area, and Country," March 31, 2014. https://www.dmdc.osd.mil/appj/dwp/get-file.do?fileNm=SIAD_309_Report_P1403.xlsx&filePathNm=milRegionCountry.

[21] Although the U.S. drone operator's stateside workplace is not a war zone, there is some evidence that these remote combatants can experience occupational burnout, combat stress, Post-Traumatic Stress Disorder (PTSD), Perpetration-Induced Traumatic Stress (PITS), or some combination of these. See Joseph A. Ouma, Wayne L. Chapelle, and Amber Salinas, "Facets of Occupational Burnout Among U.S. Air Force Active Duty and National Guard/Reserve MQ-1 Predator and MQ-9 Reaper Operators" (Wright-Patterson Air Force Base, OH: Air Force Research Laboratory, USAF School of Aerospace Medicine, 2011), and Wayne L. Chapelle, Amber Salinas, and Kent McDonald, "Psychological Health Screening of Remotely Piloted Aircraft (RPA) Operators and Supporting Units," Wright-Patterson Air Force Base, OH: Department of Neuropsychiatry, USAF School of Aerospace Medicine, 2012). For a skeptical analysis of these reports and the mainstream media discourse surrounding them, see Grégoire Chamayou, *A Theory of the Drone*, trans. Janet Lloyd (New York: New Press, 2014).

shows that for new conservatives such as Kato Norihiro, this syndrome has its origins in the trauma (*torauma* in Japanese) of a defeat sealed by the atomic bombings. Its guarantor is the Japanese constitution, drawn up and imposed by the United States and stripping Japan of the sovereign right to maintain an army, navy, or air force or to use arms as a means of settling international disputes. For Kato and other neonationalists, Japan's current political ontology is thus grounded in three humiliations: defeat in a war widely seen as unjust on Japan's part; a "foreign" constitution imposed by an occupying power; and military emasculation. The result is a pathological nation, castrated by its compulsory demilitarization, tainted at its constitutional source, and afflicted by a split personality (*jinkaku bunretsu*) arising from its inability either to justify or to apologize for its wartime past. Ending this syndrome, Kato indicates, would require something like a prioritized notion of grievability: first the Japanese war dead should be mourned in order to reunify a national subject that could then mourn the victims of Japan's aggressions in Asia, rehabilitating the last war in the process.[22] A constitution of Japanese origin would need to follow, one—and this is the key point—that restored the nation's sovereign right to maintain a military and wage war. Without that revived recourse to future war, says Kato, the last war must remain unredeemed and shameful. As Ivy neatly characterizes the position, "Japan is frozen at the moment of defeat *because* there is no more war to come. Without the futurity of war there is no real escape from the postwar. . . . The previous war needs to be repeated through a war to come, and this war to come has to always be held open in its futurity."[23] It's a hysteron proteron as uncanny as anything in Pynchon: the only way to end the postwar is by advancing to the interwar.

In describing present-day Japan as stymied, self-divided, "abnormal," and infantilized, Kato projects an aspirational portrait of "normal" nationhood

---

[22] Where Susan Sontag in "The Imagination of Destruction" (1965) reads Godzilla as registering a mass trauma over the possibility of future nuclear wars, Kato has more recently allied the monster with a different uncanny, the unwelcome return of the unmourned war dead. In the early films, he claims, Godzilla is "a revenant, the returning spirit of the Japanese who died in that war we would rather forget"—those soldiers and war victims who were seen during the war as heroic but whom postwar democratization had "left hanging in the void; no one could say for sure what they had died for." The monster's uncanniness, Kato argues, was exorcised over time by its domestication and cute-ification, a process he extends through Pikachu and other Pokémon to its terminus in the mouthless Hello Kitty. See Susan Sontag, "The Imagination of Disaster," rpt. in *Against Interpretation* (New York: Farrar, Straus, and Giroux, 1966), and Kato Norihiro, "Goodbye Godzilla, Hello Kitty," *The American Interest* (September 1, 2006), http://www.the-american-interest.com/articles/2006/09/01/goodbye-godzilla-hello-kitty/, n.p. Kato's 2006 article appears to be a domesticated and miniaturized version of his more openly nationalist book, *Haisengo ron* (Tokyo: Kodansha, 1997).

[23] Marilyn Ivy, "Trauma's Two Times: Japanese Wars and Postwars," *positions: east asia cultures critique* 16.1 (Spring 2008): 177. Further citations are in the text. I rely in this section on Ivy's paraphrase of Kato's *Haisengo ron*.

as unimpeded, unified, and endowed with a mature and phallic militarism. This portrait is an extreme one, certainly, yet it reveals something about the general structure of national sovereignty's relationship to time and trauma. For all that Kato imagines a "normal" Japan as asymptomatic, he does not wish to dissociate it altogether from trauma. To the contrary: the sovereign nation should need neither to disavow past wartime traumas nor to renounce the power of waging traumatizing wars in the future. States reserve, and are even constituted by, the right to monopolize violence in the future—and the right to have monopolized it in the past; as Ivy puts it, "Nation-states normally subsist through the assumption of war's seriality" (171). In Japan's case, she goes on to note, this model says in effect that the best therapy for war trauma, including perpetrator-trauma, is to prepare for the next war. She continues:

> Perhaps the most powerful exit strategy from the national trauma of war might be, paradoxically in light of the current debates, to renounce war and to choose abnormalcy: a chosen perverse nation-statehood, rather than one traumatically imposed. Yet as long as the nation-state—that of any nation-state whatsoever—is affirmed with all its violent, traumatic origins, the promise of future wars is always and constitutively proffered as the therapy for the traumas of past wars.

"No more and no less than when that form bears the name of Japan," Ivy concludes, will the traumatic form of the nation-state "continue to ensure the seriality of war" (185). The normative time of that traumatic nation-state is neither peacetime nor wartime nor postwar nor Cold War; it is interwar, a time limned by a past war of which the state need not be ashamed and by the unhindered right to wage war in the future.[24]

Faced with the conception of a nation-state strung taut between commemorations of a warlike past and the right to a warlike future, what could help us summon up a countermodel? Through what vision of "perverse nation-statehood," in Ivy's phrase, or of dissident political temporality can a collectivity imagine its future as something other than the time of its righteous war making or its emasculating defeat? Where Kato and other neonationalists propose to abolish Article 9 (the constitutional renunciation of the right of war) or reduce its interdictions, we could look to those Japanese citizens who support Article 9 on pacifist grounds and even question the constitutionality of Japan's Self-Defense Forces. We might reopen

---

[24] In the humanities and qualitative social sciences, we have intuited this for some time now in dwelling on political theories about law, force, and sovereignty—Benjamin's "Critique of Violence" (1921), Carl Schmitt's *Political Theology* (1922) and *The Concept of the Political* (1932)—that issue from "the" interwar period and, for all their differences, bear the watermark of that time's geopolitical suspense.

Immanuel Kant's *Toward Perpetual Peace* in the hopes of internalizing, if not a full-blown alternative to sovereignty, at least a model of it that annuls rather than presupposes the right to wage war in the future. We might revisit, too, some of the figures and acts we have encountered in these pages. There is Leopold Bloom's sealed prophecy of emancipation, neither realized nor opened nor discarded but carefully archived in the hope of its fulfillment. There is Ford Madox Ford's bid to obviate all future wars by portraying a totality of worry that takes a high enough toll without battle. There is Virginia Woolf's thinking, in an air raid, of a peace women could prolong by opting out of their procreative role in furthering the state's war-and-gender system. And there is Derrida's vision of God and the sons of Shem agreeing, in Babel, on a multilingual entente because no name was adequate to license war between them—because "they preferred to spend a little more time together, the time of a long colloquy with warriors in love with life, busy writing in all languages in order to make the conversation last, even if they didn't understand each other too well."[25]

Writing in early 1940 of a Paul Klee drawing he had owned since 1921, Walter Benjamin gave us that unassimilable image, the angel of history, facing the mounting debris pile of the past while being blown, backwards and helplessly open-winged, into the future by the storm of progress. Whether in solidarity with the ancient Jews who were "prohibited from inquiring into the future," or in protest against sovereignty's attempt to monopolize depictions of the future—or simply because the war unfolding as he wrote was the only horizon he could imagine—Benjamin says little in "On the Concept of History" about the temporal direction in which the angel is blown. Like that divine messenger, he turns his back on the turned back of the future, hoping perhaps to disenchant it and put the prophets out of business while still leaving the messianic door ajar.[26] But we know now that an angel of the interwar could not face only the past; that its gaze would travel back and forth between history's singular catastrophe and the future through which the unprecedented might at any moment arrive, whether it take the shape of the Messiah, the revolution, or the disaster. And we know that such an angel,

---

[25] Jacques Derrida, "No Apocalypse, Not Now (full speed ahead, seven missiles, seven missives)," trans. Catherine Porter and Philip Lewis, *diacritics* 14.2 (Summer 1984): 31.

[26] Walter Benjamin, "On the Concept of History," in *Selected Writings Vol. 4: 1938–1940*, trans. Edmund Jephcott and others, ed. Howard Eiland and Michael W. Jennings (Cambridge, MA: Harvard University Press, 2003), 397. The fuller passage on Jewish futurity, from §B of an early draft of the piece: "We know that the Jews were prohibited from inquiring into the future: the Torah and the prayers instructed them in remembrance. This disenchanted the future, which holds sway over all those who turn to soothsayers for enlightenment. This does not imply, however, that for the Jews the future became homogeneous, empty time. For every second was the small gateway in time through which the Messiah might enter."

pinioned between one storm it physically remembers and another it cannot *not* imagine, would keep watch over the making of archives, the burying of time capsules, the writing of strenuous and broken encyclopedias. We might like to put that trapped figure behind us or inter it in archives of its making. But the normative time of the state remains premised on war's seriality. We are interwar angels, blown sideways by a storm into a storm.

APPENDIX

Chapter Abstracts

This book aims to recover certain lost complexities of the interwar period. It argues that the 1920s, in particular, were a time of both postwar relief and wrenching anxiety about the next war. During that decade, "total war" was being adumbrated and theorized in the metropole while imperial powers quietly tested its techniques in colonies and mandates. Meanwhile, some of the interwar period's most innovative writers struggled either to find literary forms for warding off total war or to mount resistance despite the next war's seeming inevitability. *Tense Future* also finds elements of the Cold War emerging not in the year 1945 but in the twenties, which saw pre-nuclear formulations of deterrence strategy, postulations that sovereignty's master temporality was *entre deux guerres*, and a steep rise in fears that modern warfare threatened not only written archives but literacy itself.

The introduction, "Traumatic Earliness," opens with three examples of uncanny arrival, three subjects who recognize an awaited catastrophe when it comes despite its absolute unprecedentedness in their experience. These examples lead to an elaboration of what urbanist Lewis Mumford calls, in the third instance, a "collective psychosis," a psychic wounding produced by the *anticipation* of violence, particularly in cities facing imminent bombardment from the air. The ensuing account of a *pre*-traumatic stress syndrome offers a corrective to the field of trauma studies, which has focused almost exclusively on the aftermath of mass violence. After outlining how the field might address trauma bidirectionally, I connect my model of traumatic expectation to allied work in the space of "critical futurities," including nuclear criticism, queer temporalities scholarship, and histories that seek to reemplot or reactivate futures past. I then address the historiography of the interwar period, suggesting we approach its "betweenness" as both constructed retroactively and experienced by many historical actors in real time. The introduction ends with a discussion of the weak theory of modernism now structuring the field of modernist studies, and of weak theory's special suitability for opposing total war, that strongest of strong theories.

The book's body chapters fall in two parts. The first develops a critical account of total war discourse and addresses the resistant potential of acts, including acts of writing, before a future that looks barred or predetermined by war. Part two shifts the focus to long interwar narratives that pit both their scale and their formal turbulence against total war's portrait of the social totality, producing both ripostes and alternatives to that portrait in the practice of literary encyclopedism.

Chapter 1, "On the Partiality of Total War," uncovers the first uses of the expression "*la guerre totale*" in 1916, in Léon Daudet's far-right French wartime journalism, and tracks the concept forward through interwar air power theory to present-day military historiography. Analyses of internal Royal Air Force material and 1920s RAF air shows in England and Iraq bring to light connections between total war and colonial violence and the mediating role of race in these linkages. The chapter's broad analysis is wound around the armature of a complex interwar figure: L. E. O. Charlton, the RAF officer who, having set out for the Iraqi protectorate in 1922 (with a new copy of James Joyce's *Ulysses* under his arm, no less), resigned from his post a year later to protest British bombing policies in the region. Chapter 1 concludes with a discussion of Charlton's subsequent air power writings and his imperial fiction, *Near East Adventure* (1934), a story about a pair of British runaways who are given shelter by Bedouins and are the sole survivors of an RAF raid that kills their hosts. The apparent contradictions between Charlton's conscientious objection and his later air power advocacy, I argue, help make visible the imperial system of differential legal protection and violence exposure that was cemented by Britain during the interwar period.

Chapter 2, "Perpetual Suspense: Virginia Woolf's Wartime Gothic," reads a constellation of Woolf's writings—particularly "The Mark on the Wall"(1917), *Mrs. Dalloway* (1925), *The Years* (1937), and "Thoughts on Peace in an Air Raid" (1940)—as attempts to grapple with imminent, as opposed to bygone, military violence. In rejecting what she called "the thrall of plot," Woolf condemned suspense less as a Victorian narrative convention than as a permanent condition of militarized geopolitics. At the same time, through a strain of her fiction I call wartime gothic, she experimented with ways to encode, thematize, and even transmit that geopolitical suspense. Yet while her diaries, essays, and fiction dwell on the air raid and cognate scenes of future-conditional violence, they do not plead for a release from suspense under any conditions. Instead, they explore the prospect of new collectivities, intimacies, and forms of expression under threat. And, in some of Woolf's most radically feminist writing, they refuse a future unbarred on despotic, deplorable terms. By 1938, when Mumford was identifying a "collective psychosis" wrought by urban war anxiety, Woolf had spent the better part of twenty years attending equally to that condition and to its collective dimensions and ramifications, its way of both threatening and producing communal experience.

Chapter 3, "Fantasias of the Archive: Hamilton's *Savage* and Jenkinson's *Manual*," extends the previous chapter's analysis of dissidence in the face of an apparently foreclosed future. At issue here are two works published in 1922 and preoccupied with the relations among war, futurity, and the archive: suffragist Cicely Hamilton's work of apocalyptic speculative fiction, *Theodore*

Savage: A Story of the Past or the Future, and the *Manual of Archive Administration* by Hilary Jenkinson, who was then Deputy Keeper of the British Public Records Office. Although these works could not be farther apart generically, both forbear to instrumentalize the present in the name of either tradition or posterity. Instead, they advocate celibacy (marital and reproductive for Hamilton, historiographic for Jenkinson) as a desire in and for the present. The chapter's frame identifies these two works as interwar genre-mates and forerunners of two types of apocalyptic fantasia more commonly associated with the Cold War: one that imagines the persistence of humanity and the extinction of the archive, the other envisioning the extinction of humanity and the persistence of the archive.

Chapter 4, "Encyclopedic Modernism," asks why the encyclopedia should have been so important a formal template for interwar writers embarked on long, formally variegated novels. Contesting the encyclopedia's reputation as a monument to Enlightenment hubris, the chapter returns to Diderot's and d'Alembert's writings about their *Encyclopédie* (1751–72) to reactivate that project's professed multivocality, self-contradiction, and obsolescence; its compensatory bent for prophecy; and its aim to safeguard against disastrous knowledge-loss in the event of natural or political catastrophe. These features, many of which persisted in early-twentieth-century encyclopedias such as the celebrated eleventh *Britannica* (1910–11), made the genre a powerful model for interwar writers undertaking comprehensive projects that did not default to epic's militarized holism. The chapter aims to undo the conflation of epic and encyclopedic modes in influential studies of long-form narrative. Neither a synonym for encyclopedic fiction nor a form made defunct by the rise of the novel, epic emerges in my analysis as crystallizing the political logic of total war and therefore as the form most inviting refusal and immanent critique by works opposing that logic.

Chapter 5, "The Shield of *Ulysses*," reads Joyce's 1922 novel back into the wartime and immediate postwar years of its writing (1914–1921). Recent postcolonial readings of *Ulysses* have linked it to the Easter Rising and the Irish War for Independence. This chapter argues that the book also links colonial violence to modern warfare more broadly, climaxing in a blow given an Irish civilian by a British soldier against the "Circe" episode's backdrop of apocalyptic urban devastation. Referred to by its author as "a kind of encyclopedia," *Ulysses* engages repeatedly in outsized gestures of description, definition, and inventory under the twin signs of futurity and disaster. One object of this encyclopedism is war, which Joyce's ostensibly peacetime novel conjures through its Homeric intertext, its historical allusions, its portrait of Dublin under militant colonial occupation, and its subtly anachronistic references to the paroxysmal years of its writing. These violations of diegetic time are not a bid to garner the kind of prophetic authority that is sometimes granted *Ulysses*. Rather, they contribute to a reading of the colony as avant-garde—as terribly ahead of the curve—thanks to uneven distributions of law and injury. When the colony is used as a laboratory for emergent, expansive forms of violence, colonial reportage reads like prophecy in the metropole. This temporal breach is one of the many fissures Joyce's novel traces in the social totality; together, they measure the difference between the coherentist world picture offered by Achilles' shield in Homer's *Iliad* and its critical counterpart in the shield of *Ulysses*.

Chapter 6, "War Shadowing: Ford Madox Ford's *Parade's End*," opens with a brief discussion of Musil's *The Man without Qualities*, whose setting in an infinitely protracted 1913 denies the inevitability of the First World War. Building on Michael André Bernstein's and Gary Saul Morson's work, I contrast Musil's narrative and modal "sideshadowing"—his lighting up of possible but untaken roads—to Ford's twitchier experiments in formal and technical sideshadowing. Where other critics see *Parade's End* as a failed attempt at modernism in the declarative mood, I maintain that the work achieves a powerfully antitotalizing modernism in the subjunctive mood, not least in the way its final volume flips restlessly through a series of possible protagonists. The tetralogy's formal heterogeneity—its amalgam of nineteenth-century marriage plot, realist social history, and transient modernisms—finds a diegetic counterpart in the *Encyclopedia Britannica*, which *Parade's End* transvalues from failed monument to resource: Ford's protagonist keeps a running list of its many errors until he suffers traumatic amnesia on the Western Front and has to restore his lost knowledge by memorizing—what else?—the *Britannica*. The encyclopedia's mistakes and inconsistencies, I argue, make it especially fit to portray the world comprehensively yet without an epic coherentism the war had made seem less credible than ever.

The conclusion, "Perpetual Interwar," reads Thomas Pynchon's *Gravity's Rainbow* (1973) as a novelistic antecedent to *Tense Future*. Adapting the formal strategies of *Ulysses* and its genre-mates to the hyperbolized frames of colonial genocide, species extinction, area bombing, and nuclear war, Pynchon's novel surfaces what is often latent in its interwar modernist precursors: the links between metropolitan and colonial violence; the intimate if vexed relationship between total war and totalizing form; and the apprehension, well before 1945, of a traumatizing anticipation we still associate almost exclusively with the post-Hiroshima era. Where studies of peace and conflict tend to oscillate between the Kantian ideal of perpetual peace and the perpetual war supposedly ushered in by the twentieth century, *Gravity's Rainbow*'s fixation on the 1920s and '30s reads the Cold War moment of its writing as a perennialized interwar period, suspended between past and future-conditional global conflict and shot through with smaller conflicts that are denied the name and legal status of war. The book ends with a brief discussion of the interwar as the normative time of national sovereignty—as the temporality par excellence of a state defined by its unhampered claim to past and future monopolies on violence. Through what *abnormal* constellations of law, force, and time, I ask, might political collectivities hope to dwell in an alternative to perpetual interwar?

BIBLIOGRAPHY

Alnwick, Kenneth J. "Perspectives on Air Power at the Low End of the Conflict Spectrum." *Air University Review* 35.3 (March–April 1984): 17–28.

Alter, Robert. *Imagined Cities: Urban Experience and the Language of the Novel.* New Haven and London: Yale University Press, 2005.

Amis, Martin. *The War Against Cliché: Essays and Reviews: 1971–2000.* New York: Vintage, 2001.

Anderson, Wilda. "Encyclopedia Topologies." *MLN* 101 (1986): 912–29.

Arac, Jonathan. *Commissioned Spirits: The Shaping of Social Motion in Dickens, Carlyle, Melville, and Hawthorne.* New York: Columbia University Press, 1989.

Atherton, James S. *The Books at the "Wake": A Study of Literary Allusions in James Joyce's "Finnegans Wake."* New York: Viking, 1960.

Auden, W. H. *Selected Poems: Expanded Edition.* Ed. Edward Mendelson. New York: Vintage, 2007.

Bakhtin, M. M. *The Dialogic Imagination.* Trans. Caryl Emerson and Michael Holquist. Ed. Michael Holquist. Austin: University of Texas Press, 1981.

Baldwin, Stanley. *Parliamentary Debates—Commons*, November 10, 1932, vol. 270, cols. 631–32.

Beaumont, Roger A. "A New Lease on Empire: Air Policing, 1919–1939." *Aerospace Historian* 26 (Summer/June 1979): 84–90.

Beckett, Ian F. W. *"Total War."* In *War, Peace and Social Change in Twentieth-Century Europe.* Ed. Clive Emsley et al. Milton Keynes, UK: Open University Press, 1989.

Beer, Gillian. "The Island and the Aeroplane: The Case of Virginia Woolf." In *Nation and Narration.* Ed. Homi K. Bhabha. London: Routledge, 1990. 265–90.

Bell, David A. *The First Total War: Napoleon's Europe and the Birth of Warfare as We Know It.* Boston and New York: Houghton Mifflin, 2007.

Benjamin, Walter. *"On the Concept of History."* In Vol. 4: *1938–1940.* Trans. Edmund Jephcott and others. Ed. Howard Eiland and Michael W. Jennings. Cambridge, MA: Harvard University Press, 2003. 389–400.

———. "The Storyteller: Observations on the Works of Nikolai Leskov." In *Selected Writings, Vol. 3: 1935–1938.* Trans. Edmund Jephcott, Howard Eiland, et al. Ed. Howard Eiland and Michael W. Jennings. Cambridge, MA: Harvard University Press, 2002. 143–66.

Berman, Jessica. *Modernist Commitments: Ethics, Politics, and Transnational Modernism.* New York: Columbia University Press, 2011.

Bernstein, Michael André. *Foregone Conclusions: Against Apocalyptic History.* Berkeley: University of California Press, 1994.

Bersani, Leo. *The Culture of Redemption.* Cambridge, MA: Harvard University Press, 1990.

———. "Is the Rectum a Grave?" *October* 43 (Winter 1987): 197–222.

Bialer, Uri. *The Shadow of the Bomber: The Fear of Air Attack and British Politics 1932–1939*. London: Royal Historical Society, 1980.

Biddle, Tami Davis. *Rhetoric and Reality in Air Warfare: The Evolution of British and American Ideas About Strategic Bombing, 1914–1945*. Princeton, NJ: Princeton University Press, 2002.

Bindé, Jérôme. "Toward an Ethics of the Future." In *Globalization*. Ed. Arjun Appadurai. Durham, NC: Duke University Press, 2003.

Blake, William. *The Complete Poems*. Ed. Alicia Ostriker. Harmonsdworth, UK: Penguin Books, 1977.

———. *The Complete Writings of William Blake*. Ed. Geoffrey Keynes. London: Nonesuch Press, 1957.

Bloch, Ernst. "Dialectics and Hope." Trans. Mark Ritter. *New German Critique* 9 (Autumn 1976): 3–10.

———. *Literary Essays*. Trans. Andrew Joron et al. Stanford: Stanford University Press, 1998.

Bobbitt, Philip. *The Shield of Achilles: War, Peace, and the Course of History*. New York: Anchor, 2003.

Brantlinger, Patrick. *Dark Vanishings: Discourse on the Extinction of Primitive Races, 1800–1930*. Ithaca, NY: Cornell University Press, 2003.

———. *Rule of Darkness: British Literature and Imperialism, 1830–1914*. Ithaca, NY: Cornell University Press, 1988.

Bromfield, Louis. "The New Yorker." *Bookman* 60.6 (February 1925): 739.

Brooker, Joseph. *Joyce's Critics: Transitions in Reading and Culture*. Madison: University of Wisconsin Press, 2004.

Brown, Nicholas. *Utopian Generations: The Political Horizon of Twentieth-Century Literature*. Princeton, NJ: Princeton University Press, 2005.

Brown, Wendy. "Resisting Left Melancholy." In *Loss: The Politics of Mourning*. Ed. David L. Eng and David Kazanjian. Berkeley: University of California Press, 2003.

Budgen, Frank. *James Joyce and the Making of "Ulysses," and Other Writings*. London: Oxford University Press, 1972.

Bulfinch, Thomas. *Bulfinch's Mythology*. New York: Grosset & Dunlap, 1913.

Buruma, Ian. *Year Zero: A History of 1945*. Harmondsworth, UK: Penguin, 2013.

Bush, George W. Address to the United Nations General Assembly. November 10, 2001.

———. Speech at the National Endowment for Democracy. October 6, 2005.

Butler, Judith. *Frames of War: When Is Life Grievable*. London: Verso, 2009.

———. *Precarious Life: The Powers of Mourning and Violence*. London: Verso, 2004.

Buzard, James. "Mass-Observation, Modernism, and Auto-ethnography." *Modernism/modernity* 4.3 (September 1997): 93–122.

Cappelluti, Frank J. "The Life and Thought of Giulio Douhet." PhD diss., Rutgers University, 1967.

Caruth, Cathy. *Literature in the Ashes of History*. Baltimore: Johns Hopkins University Press, 2013.

———. *Unclaimed Experience: Trauma, Narrative, and History*. Baltimore: Johns Hopkins University Press, 1996.

Cascardi, A. J. "Totality and the Novel." *New Literary History* 23.3 (Summer 1992): 607–27.

Caserio, Robert L. "Imperial Romance." In *The Cambridge History of the Novel*. Ed. Robert L. Caserio and Clement Hawes. Cambridge: Cambridge University Press, 2012. 517–32.

Cassell, Richard A., ed. *Critical Essays on Ford Madox Ford*. Boston: G. K. Hall, 1987.

Ceadal, Martin. "Popular Fiction and the Next War, 1918–1939." In *Class Culture and Social Change: A New View of the 1930s*. Ed. Frank Gloversmith. Brighton: Harvester Wheatsheaf, 1980. 161–84.

Chamayou, Grégoire. *A Theory of the Drone*. Trans. Janet Lloyd. New York: New Press, 2014.

Chapelle, Wayne L., Amber Salinas, and Kent McDonald. "Psychological Health Screening of Remotely Piloted Aircraft (RPA) Operators and Supporting Units." Wright-Patterson Air Force Base, OH: Department of Neuropsychiatry, USAF School of Aerospace Medicine, 2012.

Charlton, L. E. O. *Charlton*. London: Faber & Faber, 1931.

——. *Deeds That Held the Empire: By Air*. London: John Murray, 1940.

——. *More Charlton*. London: Longmans, Green and Co., 1940.

——. *Near East Adventure*. London: Thomas Nelson and Sons, [1934].

——. "The New Factor in Warfare." In *The Air Defence of Great Britain*. Ed. L. E. O. Charlton, G. T. Garratt, and R. Fletcher. Harmondsworth, UK: Penguin, 1938.

——. *War from the Air: Past Present Future*. London: Thomas Nelson and Sons, 1935.

——. *War over England*. London: Longmans, Green and Co., 1936.

Chickering, Roger. "Total War: The Use and Abuse of a Concept." In *Anticipating Total War: The German and American Experiences, 1871–1914*. Ed. Manfred F. Boemeke, Roger Chickering, and Stig Förster. Cambridge: Cambridge University Press, 1999. 13–28.

Clark, Kenneth. *Another Part of the Wood: A Self-Portrait*. New York: Harper & Row, 1974.

Clarke, Arthur C. *From the Ocean, From the Stars: An Omnibus Containing the Novels "The Deep Range" and "The City and the Stars" and Twenty-Four Short Stories*. New York: Harcourt, Brace & World, 1961.

Clarke, I. F. *Voices Prophecying War: Future Wars 1763–3749*. Oxford: Oxford University Press, 1992.

Clausewitz, Carl von. *On War*. Ed. and trans. Michael Howard and Peter Paret. Princeton, NJ: Princeton University Press, 1976.

Clayton, Anthony. *The British Empire as a Superpower, 1919–1939*. Athens: University of Georgia Press, 1986.

Clinton, Alan. "Conspiracy of Commodities: Postmodern Encyclopedic Narrative and Crowdedness." *Rhizomes: Cultural Studies Emerging* 5 (2002): n.p.

Cole, Sarah. *At the Violet Hour: Modernism and Violence in England and Ireland*. New York: Oxford University Press, 2012.

Coleman, Alexander, and Charles Simmons, eds. *All There Is to Know: From Abracadabra to Emile Zola . . . Here Is the Highest Monument to Victorian Culture—Readings from the Illustrious 11th Edition of the Encyclopaedia Britannica*. New York: Touchstone, 1994.

Collins, Wilkie. *The Woman in White*. Harmondsworth, UK: Penguin, 1999.

Cordle, Daniel. *States of Suspense: The Nuclear Age, Postmodernism, and United States Fiction and Prose*. Manchester, UK: Manchester University Press, 2008.

Costello, Peter. *The Life of Leopold Bloom: A Novel*. Lanham, MD: Roberts Rinehart, 1992.

Coviello, Peter. "Apocalypse from Now On." In *Queer Frontiers: Millennial Geographies, Genders, and Generations*. Ed. Joseph A. Boone et al. Madison: University of Wisconsin Press, 2000. 39–63.

Crangle, Sara. *Prosaic Desires: Modernist Knowledge, Boredom, Laughter, and Anticipation*. Edinburgh: Edinburgh University Press, 2010.

Creech, James. "'Chasing After Advances': Diderot's Article 'Encyclopedia.'" *Yale French Studies* 63 (1982): 183–97.

Crowley, Ronan. "Fusing the Elements of 'Circe': From Compositional to Textual Repetition." *James Joyce Quarterly* 47.3 (Spring 2010): 341–61.

Crump, Charles. "Records." *Encyclopedia Britannica*, 11th ed. Vol. 22. New York: Encyclopaedia Britannica, 1911. 955–66.

Cunningham, John Christopher. "The American Encyclopedia: The Book of the World in the New World." PhD diss., Duke University, 1996.

Cvetkovich, Ann. *An Archive of Feelings: Trauma, Sexuality, and Lesbian Public Cultures*. Durham, NC: Duke University Press, 2003.

D'Alembert, Jean le Rond. *Preliminary Discourse to the Encyclopedia of Diderot*. Trans. Richard N. Schwab and Walter E. Rex. Indianapolis, IN: Bobbs-Merrill, 1963.

Daly, Nicholas. *Modernism, Romance, and the Fin de Siècle: Popular Fiction and British Culture, 1880–1914*. Cambridge: Cambridge University Press, 1999.

Danto, Arthur C. *Analytical Philosophy of History*. Cambridge: Cambridge University Press, 1965.

Daudet, Léon. *La guerre totale*. Paris: Nouvelle Librairie Nationale, 1918.

———. "Une guerre totale: eux ou nous." *Action Française*, March 11, 1916.

Davies, J. Conway, ed. *Studies Presented to Sir Hilary Jenkinson*. London: Oxford University Press, 1957.

Davis, Mike. *Late Victorian Holocausts: El Niño Famines and the Making of the Third World*. London: Verso, 2001.

Davis, Thomas S. *The Extinct Scene: Late Modernism and Everyday Life*. New York: Columbia University Press, forthcoming.

Dean, David J. *Air Power in Small Wars: The British Air Control Experience*. Maxwell Air Force Base, AL: Air University Press, 1985.

Deer, Patrick. *Culture in Camouflage: War, Empire, and British Literature*. Cambridge: Cambridge University Press, 2009.

Deleuze, Gilles, and Félix Guattari. *Kafka: Toward a Minor Literature*. Trans. Dana Polan. Minneapolis: University of Minnesota Press, 1986.

———. *A Thousand Plateaus: Capitalism and Schizophrenia*. Trans. Brian Massumi. Minneapolis: University of Minnesota Press, 1987.

Deming, Robert H., ed. *James Joyce: The Critical Heritage*. 2 vols. London: Routledge and Kegan Paul, 1970.

Derrida, Jacques. *Archive Fever: A Freudian Impression*. Trans. Eric Prenowitz. Chicago: University of Chicago Press, 1996.

———. "No Apocalypse, Not Now (full speed ahead, seven missiles, seven missives)." Trans. Catherine Porter and Philip Lewis. *diacritics* 14.2 (Summer 1984): 20–31.

Dickens, Charles. *Dombey and Son*. London: Penguin, 2002.

Diderot, Denis. *Diderot: Oeuvres complètes*. Vol. 7: *Encyclopédie* III, Lettres D–L. Ed. John Lough and Jacques Proust. Paris: Hermann, 1976.

———. "Encyclopédie." In *Encyclopédie*. Vol. 5 (1755). Rpt. in *Rameau's Nephew and Other Works*. Trans. Jacques Barzun and Ralph H. Bowen. Indianapolis: Bobbs-Merrill, 1964.

Dimock, Wai Chee. "Weak Theory: Henry James, Colm Tóibín, and W. B. Yeats." *Critical Inquiry* 39.4 (Summer 2013): 732–53.

Dinshaw, Carolyn, Lee Edelman, Roderick A. Ferguson, Carla Freccero, Elizabeth Freeman, Judith Halberstam, Annamarie Jagose, Christopher Nealon, and Nguyen Tan Hoang. "Theorizing Queer Temporalities: A Roundtable Discussion." *GLQ: A Journal of Lesbian and Gay Studies* 13.2–3 (2007): 177–95.

Dinshaw, Carolyn. *Getting Medieval: Sexualities and Communities, Pre- and Postmodern*. Durham, NC: Duke University Press, 1999.

Douhet, Giulio. *The Command of the Air*. Trans. Dino Ferrari. New York: Coward–McCann, 1942.

———. *Il dominio dell'aria: saggio sull'arte della guerra aerea, con una appendice contenente nozioni elementari di aeronoautica*. Rome: Stabilimento Poligrafico per l'Amministrazione della Guerra, 1921.

———. *Le profezie di Cassandra: raccolta di scritti*. Genoa: Lang & Pagano, 1931.

Dudziak, Mary L. *War•Time: An Idea, Its History, Its Consequences*. New York: Oxford University Press, 2012.

Duffy, Enda. "Disappearing Dublin: *Ulysses*, Postcoloniality, and the Politics of Space." In *Semicolonial Joyce*. Ed. Derek Attridge and Marjorie Howes. Cambridge: Cambridge University Press, 2000. 37–57.

———. *The Subaltern Ulysses*. Minneapolis: University of Minnesota Press, 1994.

Edelman, Lee. *No Future: Queer Theory and the Death Drive*. Durham, NC: Duke University Press, 2004.

Edmonds, C. H. K. "Air Strategy." *Journal of the Royal United Services Institution* 70 (1925): 191–210.

Eliot, George. *Middlemarch*. Ed. Bert G. Hornback. New York: Norton, 2000.

Eliot, T. S. *The Complete Poems and Plays: 1909–1950*. Orlando, FL: Harcourt, 1952.

———. "Tradition and the Individual Talent." In *Selected Prose of T. S. Eliot*. Ed. Frank Kermode. Orlando, FL: Harcourt, 1975. 37–44.

Ellmann, Richard. *Four Dubliners: Wilde, Yeats, Joyce, and Beckett*. New York: George Braziller, 1988.

———. *James Joyce*. New York: Oxford University Press, 1959.

———. *James Joyce*. Rev. ed. New York: Oxford University Press, 1983.

Emme, Eugene M. *The Impact of Air Power: National Security and World Politics*. Princeton, NJ: D. Van Nostrand, 1959.

Encyclopaedia Britannica: A Dictionary of Arts, Sciences, Literature, and General Information. 11th edition. 29 vols. Ed. Hugh Chisholm. Cambridge: Cambridge University Press, 1910–11.

Encyclopaedia Britannica International. *Banquet at Guildhall in the City of London, Tuesday 15 October 1968: Celebrating the 200th Anniversary of the Encyclopaedia Britannica and the 25th Anniversary of the Honorable William Benton as Its Chairman and Publisher*. [London]: Encyclopaedia Britannica International, 1968.

Epstein, E. L. "Nestor." In *James Joyce's "Ulysses": Critical Essays*. Ed. Clive Hart and David Hayman. Berkeley: University of California Press, 1974.

Esty, Jed. *A Shrinking Island: Modernism and National Culture in England*. Princeton, NJ: Princeton University Press, 2004.

Fairhall, James. *James Joyce and the Question of History*. Cambridge: Cambridge University Press, 1993.

Favret, Mary. *War at a Distance: Romanticism and the Making of Modern Wartime*. Princeton, NJ: Princeton University Press, 2010.

Felski, Rita. *Doing Time: Feminist Theory and Postmodern Culture*. New York: New York University Press, 2000.

———. "Everyday Life." *New Literary History* 33.4 (Autumn 2002): 607–22.

Fernald, Anne E. "Introduction." In Virginia Woolf. *Mrs. Dalloway*. Ed. Anne E. Fernald. Cambridge: Cambridge University Press, 2014. xxxix–xc.

Ferrer, Daniel. "'Circe,' Regret and Regression." In *Post-Structuralist Joyce: Essays from the French*. Ed. Derek Attridge and Daniel Ferrer. Cambridge: Cambridge University Press, 1988. 127–44.

Fitzgerald, Thomas W. H., ed. *Ireland and Her People: A Library of Irish Biography*. Vol. 4. Chicago: Fitzgerald, 1910.

Flower, C. T. "Manuscripts and the War." *Transactions of the Royal Historical Society* 25 (1943): 15–33.

Ford, Ford Madox. *Great Trade Route*. London: Allen & Unwin, 1937.

———. *It Was The Nightingale*. Philadelphia: J. B. Lippincott Company, 1933.

———. *Letters of Ford Madox Ford*. Ed. Richard M. Ludwig. Princeton, NJ: Princeton University Press, 1965.

———. *A Man Could Stand Up—*. Ed. Sara Haslam. Manchester, UK: Carcanet, 2011.

———. *No More Parades*. Ed. Joseph Wiesenfarth. Manchester, UK: Carcanet, 2011.

———. *Parade's End*. New York: Alfred A. Knopf, 1950.

———. *Return to Yesterday: Reminiscences of James, Conrad, and Crane*. New York: Horace and Liveright, 1932.

———. *Some Do Not . . .* Ed. Max Saunders. Manchester, UK: Carcanet, 2010.

———. *Thus to Revisit: Some Reminiscences*. New York: E. P. Dutton, 1921.

Forster, E. M. *A Passage to India*. San Diego, CA: Harcourt, 1984.

Freccero, Carla. *Queer/Early/Modern*. Durham, NC: Duke University Press, 2006.

Freud, Sigmund. *Beyond the Pleasure Principle*. Trans. James Strachey. New York: Norton, 1961.

———. *Inhibitions, Symptoms, and Anxiety*. Trans. Alix Strachey. New York: Norton, 1959.

Friedman, Susan Stanford. "Definitional Excursions: The Meanings of Modern/Modernity/Modernism." *Modernism/modernity* 8.3 (September 2001): 493–513.

———. "Periodizing Modernism: Postcolonial Modernities and the Space/Time Borders of Modernist Studies." *Modernism/modernity* 13.3 (September 2006): 425–43.

———. "Planetarity: Musing Modernist Studies." *Modernism/modernity* 17.3 (September 2010): 471–99.

Friedrich, Jörg. *The Fire: The Bombing of Germany, 1940–1945*. Trans. Allison Brown. New York: Columbia University Press, 2006.

Froula, Christine. *Virginia Woolf and the Bloomsbury Avant-Garde: War, Civilization, Modernity*. New York: Columbia University Press, 2005.

Furbank, P. N. *Diderot: A Critical Biography*. London: Secker & Warburg, 1992.

Fusillo, Massimo. "Epic, Novel." Trans. Michael F. Moore. In *The Novel*. Vol. 1. Ed. Franco Moretti. Princeton, NJ: Princeton University Press, 2006. 32–63.

Fussell, Paul. *The Great War and Modern Memory*. New York: Oxford University Press, 1975.

Gallagher, Catherine. "George Eliot: Immanent Victorian." *Representations* 90 (Spring 2005): 61–74.

Gat, Azar. *A History of Military Thought from the Enlightenment to the Cold War.* Oxford: Oxford University Press, 2001.

Gibson, Andrew. "Introduction." In *Reading Joyce's "Circe": European Joyce Studies* 3. Ed. Andrew Gibson. Amsterdam: Rodopi, 1994. 3–32.

Gibson, Mary Ellis. *Epic Reinvented: Ezra Pound and the Victorians.* Ithaca, NY: Cornell University Press, 1995.

Gordon, Caroline. "The Story of Ford Madox Ford." *New York Times Book Review,* September 17, 1950: §7, pp. 1, 22.

Graham, J. W. "The Drafts of Virginia Woolf's 'The Searchlight.'" *Twentieth-Century Literature* 22.4 (December 1976): 379–93.

Grausam, Daniel. *On Endings: American Postmodern Fiction and the Cold War.* Charlottesville: University of Virginia Press, 2011.

Grayling, A. C. *Among the Dead Cities: The History and Moral Legacy of the WWII Bombing of Civilians in Germany and Japan.* New York: Walker & Co., 2006.

Grayzel, Susan R. *At Home and Under Fire: Air Raids and Culture in Britain from the Great War to the Blitz.* Cambridge: Cambridge University Press, 2012.

Green, Martin. *Dreams of Adventure, Deeds of Empire.* New York: Basic Books, 1979.

Green, Robert. *Ford Madox Ford: Prose and Politics.* Cambridge: Cambridge University Press, 1981.

Greene, Graham. "Introduction." *The Bodley Head Ford Madox Ford,* Vol. III. London: Bodley Head, 1963.

Groden, Michael. *"Ulysses" in Focus: Genetic, Textual, and Personal Views.* Gainesville: University of Florida Press, 2010.

———. *"Ulysses" in Progress.* Princeton, NJ: Princeton University Press, 1977.

Gross, Oren, and Fionnuala Ní Aoláin. *Law in Times of Crisis: Emergency Powers in Theory and Practice.* Cambridge: Cambridge University Press, 2006.

Groves, P. R. C. *Behind the Smoke Screen.* London: Faber and Faber, 1934.

———. "The New Warfare." *Times* (London), March 21, 1922.

———. *Our Future in the Air: A Survey of the Vital Question of British Air Power.* London: Hutchinson & Co., 1922.

Gunn, Ian, and Mark Wright. "Visualizing Joyce." *Hypermedia Joyce Studies* 6.1 (2006): n.p.

Gunn, Ian, Clive Hart, and Harald Beck. *James Joyce's Dublin: A Topographical Guide to the Dublin of "Ulysses."* London: Thames & Hudson, 2004.

Habermas, Jürgen. "A Review of Gadamer's Truth and Method." In Fred R. Dallymayr and Thomas A. McCarthy, eds. *Understanding and Social Inquiry.* Notre Dame, IN: University of Notre Dame Press, 1977.

Halberstam, Judith. "The Anti-Social Turn in Queer Studies." *Graduate Journal of Social Science* 5.2 (2008): 140–56.

Hall, Hubert. *British Archives and the Sources of the History of the World War.* London: Oxford University Press, 1925.

Hall, Stuart. Interview with David Scott. *BOMB* 90 (Winter 2005): n.p. http://bombsite.com/issues/90/articles/2711.

Hamilton, Cicely. "Bombarded." *North American Review* 208 (October 1918): 574–80.

———. *Life Errant.* London: J. M. Dent & Sons, 1935.

Hamilton, Cicely. *Marriage as a Trade*. London: Women's Press, 1981.

———. *Theodore Savage: A Story of the Past or the Future*. London: Leonard Parsons, 1922.

Hampton, R. G. "'Toft's Cumbersome Whirligig': Hallucinations, Theatricality, and Mnemotechnic in V.A.19 and the First Edition Text of 'Circe.'" *Reading Joyce's "Circe": European Joyce Studies* 3. Ed. Andrew Gibson. Amsterdam: Rodopi, 1994. 143–78.

Harrison, William H. *Mother Shipton Investigated: The Result of Critical Examination in the British Museum Library, of the Literature Related to the Yorkshire Sibyl*. London: W. H. Harrison, 1881.

Hartman, Geoffrey H. "On Traumatic Knowledge and Literary Studies." *New Literary History* 26.3 (Summer 1995): 537–63.

Harvey, David Dow. *Ford Madox Ford 1873–1939: A Bibliography of Works and Criticism*. New York: Gordian Press, 1972.

Haule, James M. "*To the Lighthouse* and the Great War: The Evidence of Virginia Woolf's Revisions of 'Time Passes.'" In *Virginia Woolf and War: Fiction, Reality, and Myth*. Ed. Mark Hussey. Syracuse, NY: Syracuse University Press, 1991. 164–79.

Haule, James M., Virginia Woolf, and Charles Mauron. "'Le Temps passe' and the Original Typescript: An Early Version of the 'Time Passes' Section of *To the Lighthouse*." *Twentieth Century Literature* 29.3 (Autumn 1983): 267–311.

Hayot, Eric. *On Literary Worlds*. New York: Oxford University Press, 2012.

Hegel, Georg Wilhelm Friedrich. *Aesthetics: Lectures on Fine Art*. 2 vols. Trans. T. M. Knox. Oxford: Oxford University Press, 1975.

Herman, Luc, and Petrus van Ewijk. "Gravity's Encyclopedia Revisited: The Illusion of a Totalizing System in *Gravity's Rainbow*." *English Studies* 90 (2009): 167–79.

Hersey, John. *Hiroshima*. New York: Alfred A. Knopf, 1946.

Holland, Thomas Erskine. *The Elements of Jurisprudence*. Oxford: Clarendon Press, 1880.

Holman, Bret. "21st century Charlton?" December 2, 2005, posting on "Airminded: Air Power and British Society." http://airminded.org/2005/12/02/21st-century-charlton/.

Homer. *The Iliad*. Trans. Robert Fagles. New York: Penguin, 1990.

Homer. *The Odyssey*. Trans. Robert Fitzgerald. New York: Farrar, Straus and Giroux, 1998.

Hoyt, Nelly S., and Thomas Cassirer. "Introduction" to *Encyclopedia: Selections by Diderot, d'Alembert, and a Society of Men of Letters*. Trans. Nelly S. Hoyt and Thomas Cassirer. Indianapolis: Bobbs-Merrill, 1965). i–xlv.

Hungerford, Amy. "On the Period Formerly Known as Contemporary." *American Literary History* 20:1–2 (Spring/Summer 2008): 410–19.

Hutcheon, Linda. "Historiographic Metafiction: Parody and the Intertextuality of History." In *Intertextuality and Contemporary American Fiction*. Ed. Patrick O'Donnell and Robert Con Davis. Baltimore: Johns Hopkins University Press, 1989. 3–32.

Hynes, Samuel. *A War Imagined: The First World War and English Culture*. New York: Collier Books, 1990.

Ivy, Marilyn. "Trauma's Two Times: Japanese Wars and Postwars." *positions: east asia cultures critique* 16.1 (Spring 2008): 165–88.

Jaffe, Audrey. *Vanishing Points: Dickens, Narrative, and the Subject of Omniscience*. Berkeley: University of California Press, 1991.

Jaji, Tsitsi. *Africa in Stereo: Modernism, Music, and Pan-African Solidarity*. New York: Oxford University Press, 2014.

James, David, and Urmila Seshagiri. "Metamodernism: Narratives of Continuity and Revolution." *PMLA* 129.1 (January 2014): 87–100.

Jameson, Fredric. "Modernism and Imperialism." In Terry Eagleton, Fredric Jameson, and Edward W. Said. *Nationalism, Colonialism, and Literature*. Minneapolis: University of Minnesota Press, 1990. 43–66.

Jeffery, Keith. *Ireland and the Great War*. Cambridge: Cambridge University Press, 2000.

Jenkinson, Hilary. *A Manual of Archive Administration, Including the Problems of War Archives and Archive Making*. Oxford: Clarendon Press, 1922.

———. "Reflections of an Archivist." *Contemporary Review* 165 (June 1944): 355–61.

———. *Selected Writings of Sir Hilary Jenkinson*. London: Alan Sutton, 1980.

———. *War Service of a Siege Battery, 1916–1918*. Privately printed, 1919.

Johnson, Charles. *The Care of Documents and Management of Archives*. Helps for Students of History, no. 5. London: Society for Promoting Christian Knowledge, 1919.

Joyce, James. *The James Joyce Archive*. 63 vols. Ed. Michael Groden, Hans Walter Gabler, David Hayman, A. Walton Litz, and Danis Rose. New York: Garland, 1977–79.

———. *Joyce's Notes and Early Drafts for "Ulysses": Selections from the Buffalo Collection*. Ed. Phillip F. Herring. Charlottesville: University Press of Virginia, 1977.

———. *Letters of James Joyce*. 3 vols. Ed. Stuart Gilbert and Richard Ellmann. New York: Viking, 1966.

———. *A Portrait of the Artist as a Young Man*. New York: Viking, 1964.

———. *Selected Letters*. Ed. Richard Ellmann. London: Faber and Faber, 1975.

———. *Ulysses: The Corrected Text*. Ed. Hans Walter Gabler with Wolfhard Steppe and Claus Melchior. New York: Vintage Books, 1986.

Kahan, Benjamin. *Celibacies: American Modernism and Sexual Life*. Durham, NC: Duke University Press, 2013.

Kato, Norihiro. "Goodbye Godzilla, Hello Kitty." *The American Interest*, September 1, 2006. http://www.the-american-interest.com/articles/2006/09/01/goodbye-godzilla-hello-kitty/.

———. *Haisengo ron*. Tokyo: Kodansha, 1997.

Keegan, John. *A History of Warfare*. New York: Alfred A. Knopf, 1993.

Kenner, Hugh. "Circe." In *James Joyce's Ulysses*. Ed. Clive Hart and David Hayman. Berkeley: University of California Press, 1974. 341–62.

———. *Joyce's Voices*. Berkeley: University of California Press, 1978.

———. *The Pound Era*. Berkeley: University of California Press, 1971.

———. *Ulysses*. Baltimore: Johns Hopkins University Press, 1987.

Kenworthy, J. M. *Peace or War?* New York: Boni & Liveright, 1927.

Kermode, Frank. *The Sense of an Ending: Studies in the Theory of Fiction*. Oxford: Oxford University Press, 1967.

Kern, Stephen. *The Culture of Time and Space: 1880–1918*. Cambridge, MA: Harvard University Press, 1983.

Knebel, Fletcher, and Charles W. Bailey. *No High Ground*. New York: Harper & Bros., 1960.

Knowlson, James. *Damned to Fame: The Life of Samuel Beckett*. New York: Simon & Schuster, 1996.

Koepp, Cynthia J. "The Alphabetical Order: Work in Diderot's *Encyclopédie*." In *Work in France: Representations, Meaning, Organization, and Practice*. Ed. Steven Laurence Kaplan and Cynthia J. Koepp. Ithaca, NY: Cornell University Press, 1986. 229–57.

Konvitz, Josef W. "Cities as Targets: Conceptions of Strategic Bombing, 1914–1945." Working Paper No. 85. Princeton, NJ: International Security Studies Program, Woodrow Wilson International Center for Scholars, 1987.

Koselleck, Reinhart. *Futures Past: On the Semantics of Historical Time.* Trans. Keith Tribe. Cambridge, MA: MIT Press, 1985.

LaCapra, Dominick. *History in Transit: Experience, Identity, Critical Theory.* Ithaca, NY: Cornell University Press, 2004.

———. "Toward a Critique of Violence." In *The Modernist Imagination: Intellectual History and Critical Theory Essays in Honor of Martin Jay.* Ed. Warren Breckman, Peter E. Gordon, A. Dirk Moses, Samuel Moyn, and Elliott Neaman. New York: Berghahn, 2009. 210–41.

———. *Writing History, Writing Trauma.* Baltimore: Johns Hopkins University Press, 2001.

Le Guin, Ursula K. *The Wind's Twelve Quarters.* New York: Harper & Row, 1975.

Lee, Hermione. *Virginia Woolf.* New York: Knopf, 1997.

Levenback, Karen L. *Virginia Woolf and the Great War.* Syracuse, NY: Syracuse University Press, 1999.

Levenson, Michael. *A Genealogy of Modernism: A Study of English Literary Doctrine 1908–1922.* Cambridge: Cambridge University Press, 1984.

Levin, Harry. "What Was Modernism?" *Massachusetts Review* 1.4 (August 1960): 609–30.

Levine, Caroline. *The Serious Pleasures of Suspense: Victorian Realism and Narrative Doubt.* London and Charlottesville: University of Virginia Press, 2003.

Leys, Ruth. *Trauma: A Genealogy.* Chicago: University of Chicago Press, 2000.

Liddell Hart, Basil Henry. *Paris, or The Future of War.* New York: E. P. Dutton, 1925.

Lifton, Robert J. *Death in Life: Survivors of Hiroshima.* New York: Random House, 1967.

Lifton, Robert J., and Greg Mitchell. *Hiroshima in America: Fifty Years of Denial.* New York: G. P. Putnam's Sons, 1995.

Lindqvist, Sven. *A History of Bombing.* Trans. Linda Haverty Rugg. New York: New Press, 2001.

Lough, John. *The Encyclopédie.* New York: David McKay, 1971.

Love, Heather. *Feeling Backward: Loss and the Politics of Queer History.* Cambridge, MA: Harvard University Press, 2007.

Ludendorff, Erich. *Der totale Krieg.* Munich: Ludendorffs Verlag, 1935.

Lukács, Georg. *The Historical Novel.* Trans. Hannah and Stanley Mitchell. Lincoln: University of Nebraska Press, 1983.

———. *The Theory of the Novel: A Historico-Philosophical Essay on the Forms of Great Epic Literature.* Trans. Anna Bostock. Cambridge, MA: MIT Press, 1971.

MacKay, Marina. *Modernism and World War II.* Cambridge: Cambridge University Press, 2007.

Mackinder, H. J. "The Geographical Pivot in History." *Geographic Journal* 23.4 (April 1904): 421–37.

MacShane, Frank, ed. *Ford Madox Ford: The Critical Heritage.* London: Routledge and Kegan Paul, 1972.

Mahaffey, Vicki. "Sidereal Writing: Male Refractions and Malefactions in 'Ithaca.'" In *"Ulysses"—En-Gendered Perspectives: Eighteen New Essays on the Episodes.* Ed. Kimberly J. Devlin and Marilyn Reizbaum. Columbia: University of South Carolina Press, 1999. 254–66.

Marcus, Laura. "'In the Circle of the Lens': Woolf's 'Telescope' Story, Scene-Making, and Memory." *Journal of the Short Story in English* 50 (Spring 2008): n.p.

Marqusee, Mike. "Imperial Whitewash." *Guardian*, July 31, 2006. http://www.guardian. co.uk/commentisfree/2006/jul/31/whitewashingtheempire.

Marshall, R., and Sandro Galea. "Science for the Community: Mental Health after 9/11." *Journal of Clinical Psychiatry* 65 (2004, Supplement 1): 37–43.

Marx, Joseph L. *Seven Hours to Zero*. New York: Putnam's, 1967.

McDonald, Christie V. *The Dialogue of Writing: Essays in Eighteenth-Century French Literature*. Waterloo, ON: Wilfred Laurier University Press, 1984.

McFee, William. "Tietjens Once More." *New York Herald Tribune Books*. January 15, 1928.

McHale, Brian. "Period, Break, Interregnum," *Twentieth-Century Literature* 57.3–4 (Fall/ Winter 2011): 328–40.

McLoughlin, Kate. *Authoring War: The Literary Representation of War from the Iliad to Iraq*. Cambridge: Cambridge University Press, 2011.

Mellor, Leo. *Reading the Ruins: Modernism, Bombsites and British Culture*. Cambridge: Cambridge University Press, 2011.

Mendelson, Edward. "Encyclopedic Narrative: From Dante to Pynchon." *Modern Language Notes* 91 (1976): 1267–75.

———. "Gravity's Encyclopedia." In *Mindful Pleasures: Essays on Thomas Pynchon*. Ed. George Levine and David Leverenz. Boston: Little, Brown and Company, 1976. 161–95.

Micir, Melanie. "'Living in Two Tenses': The Intimate Archives of Sylvia Townsend Warner." *Journal of Modern Literature* 36.1 (Fall 2012): 119–31.

———. "Public Lives, Intimate Archives: Queer Biographical Practices in British Women's Writing, 1928–1978." PhD diss., University of Pennsylvania, 2012.

Mieszkowski, Jan. "Great War, Cold War, Total War." *Modernism/modernity* 16 (2009): 211–28.

———. *Watching War*. Stanford: Stanford University Press, 2012.

Miller, D. A. *The Novel and the Police*. Berkeley: University of California Press, 1988.

Minkowski, Eugène. *Lived Time: Phenomenological and Psychopathological Studies*. Trans. Nancy Metzel. Evanston: Northwestern University Press, 1970.

Moffat, Wendy. *A Great Unrecorded History: A New Life of E. M. Forster*. New York: Farrar, Straus and Giroux, 2011.

Moore, John Bassett. *International Law and Some Current Illusions and Other Essays*. New York: Macmillan, 1924.

Moretti, Franco. *Modern Epic: The World System from Goethe to García Márquez*. Trans. Quintin Hoare. London: Verso, 1996.

———. *Signs Taken for Wonders: Essays in the Sociology of Literary Forms*. Trans. Susan Fischer, David Forgacs, and David Miller. London: Verso, 1988.

Morris, George C. "The Other Side of the COIN: Low-Technology Aircraft and Little Wars." *Airpower Journal* 5.1 (Spring 1991): 56–70.

Morson, Gary Saul. *Narrative and Freedom: The Shadows of Time*. New Haven: Yale University Press, 1994.

Muller, S., J. A. Feith, and R. Fruin. *Manual for the Arrangement and Description of Archives*. Trans. Arthur H. Leavitt. New York: Wilson, 1940.

Mumford, Lewis. *The Culture of Cities*. New York: Harcourt Brace & Co., 1938.

Musil, Robert. *The Man without Qualities*. 2 vols. Trans. Sophie Wilkins. New York: Vintage, 1995.

Nicholson, Hubert. *Half My Days and Nights: Autobiography of a Reporter*. London: W. Heinemann, 1941.

Norris, Margot. *Virgin and Veteran Readings of "Ulysses."* New York: Palgrave Macmillan, 2011.

———. *Writing War in the Twentieth Century.* Charlottesville: University of Virginia Press, 2000.

North, Michael. *Reading 1922: A Return to the Scene of the Modern.* New York: Oxford University Press, 1999.

Norway, Mary L. *The Sinn Fein Rebellion as I Saw It.* London: Smith, Elder, 1916.

Nossack, Hans Erich. *The End: Hamburg 1943.* Trans. Joel Agee. Chicago: University of Chicago Press, 2004.

O'Brien, Terence. *Civil Defense.* History of the Second World War, United Kingdom Civil Series. London: HMSO, 1955.

O'Driscoll, Michael J. "Derrida, Foucault, and the Archiviolithics of History." In *After Poststructuralism: Writing the Intellectual History of Theory.* Ed. Tilottama Rajan and Michael J. O'Driscoll. Toronto: University of Toronto Press, 2002: 284–309.

Ogura, Toyofumi. *Letters from the End of the World: A Firsthand Account of the Bombing of Hiroshima.* Trans. Kisaburo Murakami and Shigeru Fujii. Tokyo: Kodansha, 1997.

Olson, Liesl. "Everyday Life Studies: A Review." *Modernism/modernity* 18.1 (January 2011): 175–80.

———. *Modernism and the Ordinary.* New York: Oxford University Press, 2009.

Omissi, David E. *Air Power and Colonial Control: The Royal Air Force 1919–1939.* Manchester, UK: Manchester University Press, 1990.

———. "The Hendon Air Pageant, 1920–37." In *Popular Imperialism and the Military, 1850–1950.* Ed. John M. MacKenzie. Manchester, UK: Manchester University Press, 1992: 198–220.

Ouma, Joseph A., Wayne L. Chapelle, and Amber Salinas. "Facets of Occupational Burnout Among U.S. Air Force Active Duty and National Guard/Reserve MQ-1 Predator and MQ-9 Reaper Operators." Wright-Patterson Air Force Base, OH: Air Force Research Laboratory, USAF School of Aerospace Medicine, 2011.

Overy, Richard. *The Bombers and the Bombed: Allied Air War Over Europe 1940–1945.* New York: Viking, 2013.

———. *The Twilight Years: The Paradox of Britain Between the Wars.* New York: Penguin, 2009.

Pacific War Research Society. *The Day Man Lost: Hiroshima, 6 August 1945.* Tokyo: Kodansha, 1972.

Panchasi, Roxanne. *Future Tense: The Culture of Anticipation in France Between the Wars.* Ithaca, NY: Cornell University Press, 2009.

Pape, Robert A. *Bombing to Win: Air Power and Coercion in War.* Ithaca, NY: Cornell University Press, 1996.

Paris, Václav. "Everyday Epic: Evolution, Sexuality, and Modernist Narrative." PhD diss., University of Pennsylvania, 2014.

Parsons, David Willard. "British Air Control: A Model for the Application of Air Power in Low-Intensity Conflict?" *Airpower Journal* 8.2 (Summer 1994): 28–39.

Patterson, Ian. *Guernica and Total War.* Cambridge, MA: Harvard University Press, 2007.

Peake, C. H. *James Joyce: The Citizen and the Artist.* London: Edward Arnold, 1977.

Phillips, Siobhan. *Poetics of the Everyday: Creative Repetition in Modern American Verse.* New York: Columbia University Press, 2009.

Pike, David L. *Metropolis on the Styx: The Underworlds of Modern Urban Culture, 1800–2001.* Ithaca, NY: Cornell University Press, 2007.

Piper, Karen. *Cartographic Fictions: Maps, Race, and Identity*. New Brunswick, NJ: Rutgers University Press, 2002.

Platt, Len. "'Unfallable encyclicing': *Finnegans Wake* and the *Encyclopedia Britannica*." *James Joyce Quarterly* 47.1 (Fall 2009): 107–18.

Primoratz, Igor, ed. *Civilian Immunity in War*. Oxford: Oxford University Press, 2007.

Procter, Margaret. "Life Before Jenkinson: The Development of British Archival Theory and Thought at the Turn of the Twentieth Century." *Archives* 33.119 (October 2008): 136–57.

Puchner, Martin. *Stage Fright: Modernism, Anti-Theatricality, and Drama*. Baltimore: Johns Hopkins University Press, 2002.

Pynchon, Thomas. *Gravity's Rainbow*. New York: Viking, 1973.

Quinn, Patrick J., and Steven Trout, eds. *The Literature of the Great War Reconsidered: Beyond Modern Memory*. New York: Palgrave, 2001.

Raleigh, John Henry. *The Chronicle of Leopold and Molly Bloom: "Ulysses" as Narrative*. Berkeley: University of California Press, 1977.

Raleigh, Walter Alexander, and H. A. Jones. *The War in the Air: Being the Story of the Part Played in the Great War by the Royal Air Force*. 6 vols. Oxford: Clarendon Press, 1922–1937.

Randall, Bryony. *Modernism, Daily Time, and Everyday Life*. Cambridge: Cambridge University Press, 2007.

Redmond, John Edward. "Ireland and the Coronation." In *The World's Famous Orations, Vol. VI: Ireland, 1775–1902*. Ed. William Jennings Bryan. New York: Funk & Wagnalls, 1906.

Reichman, Ravit. *The Affective Life of Law: Legal Modernism and the Literary Imagination*. Stanford: Stanford University Press, 2009.

Reizbaum, Marilyn. *James Joyce's Judaic Other*. Stanford: Stanford University Press, 1999.

Repington, Charles à Court. *After the War: London-Paris-Rome-Athens-Prague-Vienna-Budapest-Bucharest-Berlin-Sofia-Coblenz-New York-Washington; A Diary*. Boston: Houghton Mifflin, 1922.

Report of the General Board of the Navy, presented by Rear Admiral W. L. Rodgers, Chairman. *Proceedings of the Conference on the Limitation of Armament, 1921–1922*. Washington, DC: Government Printing Office, 1923.

Resnick, H., Sandro Galea, D. G. Kilpatrick, and D. Vlahov. "Epidemiology of Post-Traumatic Stress Disorder in the General Population after September 11 Attacks." *PTSD Research Quarterly* 15.1 (2004): 1–7.

Ricoeur, Paul. *Amour et justice*. Tübingen: J. C. B. Nohr, 1990.

Robinson, Douglas H. *The Zeppelin in Combat: A History of the German Naval Airship Division, 1912–1918*. London: G. T. Foulis, 1962.

Rodgers, William L. "The Laws of War Concerning Aviation and Radio." *American Journal of International Law* 17.4 (October 1923): 629–40.

Rodstein, Susan de Sola. "Back to 1904: Joyce, Ireland, and Nationalism." In *Joyce: Feminism/Post/Colonialism: European Joyce Studies* 8. Ed. Ellen Carol Jones. Amsterdam: Rodopi, 1998: 145–85.

Rogers, Gayle. *Modernism and the New Spain: Britain, Cosmopolitan Europe, and Literary History*. New York: Oxford University Press, 2012.

Roper, Michael. *The Records of the War Office and Related Departments, 1660–1964*. Kew, UK: Public Record Office, 1998.

Rougeron, Camille. "La guerre totale et l'aviation." *L'Illustration 4619* (September 12, 1931): 30–32.

Rubenstein, Michael. *Public Works: Infrastructure, Irish Modernism, and the Postcolonial.* Notre Dame, IN: Notre Dame University Press, 2010.

Ruotolo, Lucio. *The Interrupted Moment: A View of Virginia Woolf's Novels.* Stanford: Stanford University Press, 1986.

Rushdie, Salman. *Midnight's Children.* Harmondsworth, UK: Penguin, 1980.

Ruthven, Ken. *Nuclear Criticism.* Melbourne: Melbourne University Press, 1993.

Saint-Amour, Paul K. "Air War Prophecy and Interwar Modernism." *Comparative Literature Studies* 42.2 (Spring 2005): 130–61.

——. "Bombing and the Symptom: Traumatic Earliness and the Nuclear Uncanny." *diacritics* 30.4 (Winter 2000): 59–82.

——. "Over Assemblage: *Ulysses* and the *Boîte-en-valise* from Above." In *Cultural Studies of James Joyce: European Joyce Studies* 15. Ed. R. Brandon Kershner. Amsterdam: Rodopi, 2003. 21–58.

——. "Queer Temporalities of the Nuclear Condition." In *Silence of Fallout: Nuclear Criticism in a Post-Cold War World.* Ed. Michael Blouin, Morgan Shipley, and Jack Taylor. Newcastle-upon-Tyne, UK: Cambridge Scholars, 2013. 59–80.

Satia, Priya. *Spies in Arabia: The Great War and the Cultural Foundations of Britain's Covert Empire in the Middle East.* New York: Oxford University Press, 2008.

Saunders, Max. *Ford Madox Ford: A Dual Life.* 2 vols. Oxford: Oxford University Press, 1996.

Scarry, Elaine. *Rule of Law, Misrule of Men.* Cambridge, MA: MIT Press, 2010.

Schell, Jonathan. *The Fate of the Earth: and The Abolition.* Stanford: Stanford University Press, 2000.

Schelling, Thomas C. *Arms and Influence.* New Haven: Yale University Press, 1966.

Scheppele, Kim Lane. "Law in a Time of Emergency: States of Exception and the Temptations of 9/11." *University of Pennsylvania Journal of Constitutional Law* 6 (2004): 1001–83.

Schmitt, Carl. "Total Enemy, Total War, and Total State." Rpt. in *Four Articles, 1931–1938.* Trans. Simona Draghici. Washington, DC: Plutarch Press, 1999. 28–36.

Schwenger, Peter. *Letter Bomb: Nuclear Holocaust and the Exploding Word.* Baltimore: Johns Hopkins University Press, 1992.

Scott, David. *Conscripts of Modernity: The Tragedy of Colonial Enlightenment.* Durham, NC: Duke University Press, 2004.

Sebald, W. G. *On the Natural History of Destruction.* Trans. Anthea Bell. New York: Random House, 2003.

Sedgwick, Eve Kosofsky. *Touching Feeling: Affect, Pedagogy, Performativity.* Durham, NC: Duke University Press, 2003.

Sherman, Stuart. "Vanity Fair in 1924." *New York Herald Tribune*, November 16, 1924: 1–2.

Sherry, Vincent. *The Great War and the Language of Modernism.* New York: Oxford University Press, 2003.

Slote, Sam. "The Thomistic Representation of Dublin in *Ulysses*." In *Making Space in the Works of James Joyce.* Ed. Valérie Bénéjam and John Bishop. London: Routledge, 2012. 191–202.

Smith, Jane F. "Theodore R. Schellenberg: Americanizer and Popularizer." *American Archivist* 44 (Fall 1981): 313–26.

Solomon, J. Fisher. *Discourse and Reference in the Nuclear Age*. Norman: University of Oklahoma Press, 1988.

Sontag, Susan. "The Imagination of Disaster." In *Against Interpretation*. New York: Farrar, Straus, and Giroux, 1966. 209–25.

Spaight, J. M. *Air Power and War Rights*. London: Longmans, Green, 1924.

Spoo, Robert. "'Nestor' and the Nightmare: The Presence of the Great War in *Ulysses*." *Twentieth Century Literature* 32 (1986): 137–54.

Stalnaker, Joanna. *The Unfinished Enlightenment: Description in the Age of the Encyclopedia*. Ithaca, NY: Cornell University Press, 2010.

Stead, Alistair. "Great War *Ulysses*." *James Joyce Broadsheet* 71 (2005): 4.

Steiner, George. *In Bluebeard's Castle: Some Notes Toward the Redefinition of Culture*. New Haven: Yale University Press, 1971.

———. *Language and Silence: Essays on Language, Literature, and the Inhuman*. New York: Macmillan, 1967.

Strachan, Hew, and Andreas Herberg-Rothe, eds. *Clausewitz in the Twenty-First Century*. Oxford: Oxford University Press, 2007.

Strecker, Trey. "Ecologies of Knowledge: The Encyclopedic Narratives of Richard Powers and His Contemporaries." *Review of Contemporary Fiction* 18 (1998): 67–71.

Sueter, Murray F. *Airmen or Noahs: Fair Play for our Airmen; the Great "Neon" Air Myth Exposed*. London: Sir Isaac Pitman & Sons, 1928.

Swift, Jonathan. *The Drapier's Letters, and Other Works, 1724–1725*. Ed. Herbert Davis. Oxford: Basil Blackwell, 1959.

Sykes, F. H. *Aviation in Peace and War*. London: Edward Arnold, 1922.

Theoharis, Theoharis C. "Unveiling Joyce's Portrait: Stephen Dedalus and the *Encyclopaedia Britannica*." *Southern Review* 20.2 (April 1984): 286–99.

Thomas, Gillian. *A Position to Command Respect: Women and the Eleventh "Britannica."* Metutchen, NJ: Scarecrow Press, 1992.

Tomkins, Sylvan. *Affect Imagery Consciousness*. Vol. 2, *The Negative Affects*. New York: Springer, 1963.

Townshend, Charles. "Civilization and 'Frightfulness': Air Control in the Middle East Between the Wars." In *Warfare, Diplomacy, and Politics: Essays in Honour of A. J. P. Taylor*. Ed. Chris Wrigley. London: Hamish Hamilton, 1986. 142–62.

Tucker, Herbert F. *Epic: Britain's Heroic Muse, 1790–1910*. New York: Oxford University Press, 2008.

United States Department of Defense. "Total Military Personnel and Dependent End Strength by Service, Regional Area, and Country." March 31, 2014. https://www.dmdc.osd.mil/appj/dwp/getfile.do?fileNm=SIAD_309_Report_P1403.xlsx&filePathNm=milRegionCountry.

Unsigned. *Dublin and the 'Sinn Fein Rising.'* Dublin: Brunswick Press, 1916.

———. "The Eighth RAF Display." *Flight International* 19 (Summer 1927): 460.

———. "Mr. Baldwin on Aerial Warfare—A Fear for the Future." *Times* (London), November 11, 1932: 7b.

———. "A Psycho-Analytical Autobiography." *Flight International* 23 (Autumn 1931): 1116.

———. "The R.A.F. Aerial Pageant." *Flight International* 14 (June 1922): 368–73.

———. "Results of Air Raids on Germany Carried out by the 8th Brigade and Independent Force." Air Publication (A.P.) 1225, 3rd ed. Air Ministry, London, January 1920.

———. "Royal Air Force Notes." *Journal of the Royal United Service Institution* 67 (May 1922): 392–94.

———. "Sky-Writing by Aircraft: Wide Scope in War and Peace." *Times* (London), August 18, 1922: 5d.

———. "Zeppelins Kill Four in London; Riots Renewed." *New York Times*, June 2, 1915.

Uppsala Conflict Data Program. http://www.pcr.uu.se/research/ucdp/.

Uppsala Universitet. "Two out of Five War Fatalities Occurred in Syria." Press release, June 12, 2014.

Vattimo, Gianni. *The End of Modernity*. Trans. Jon R. Snyder. Baltimore: Johns Hopkins University Press, 1988.

Vattimo, Gianni, and Santiago Zabala. "'Weak Thought' and the Reduction of Violence: A Dialogue with Gianni Vattimo." Trans. Yaakov Mascetti. *Common Knowledge* 8.3 (Fall 2002): 452–63.

Végső, Roland. *The Naked Communist: Cold War Modernism and the Politics of Popular Culture*. New York: Fordham University Press, 2013.

Vizenor, Gerald. *Fugitive Poses: Native American Scenes of Absence and Presence*. Lincoln: University of Nebraska Press, 1998.

Walkowitz, Rebecca L. *Cosmopolitan Style: Modernism Beyond the Nation*. New York: Columbia University Press, 2006.

Weale, Adrian, ed. *Eye-Witness Hiroshima*. New York: Carroll & Graf, 1995.

Weisenburger, Steven C. *A "Gravity's Rainbow" Companion: Sources and Contexts for Pynchon's Novel*. Athens: University of Georgia Press, 2006.

Wells, H. G. *Anticipations of the Reaction of Mechanical and Scientific Progress Upon Human Life and Thought*. Mineola, NY: Dover Publications, 1999.

———. *The War in the Air*. Lincoln and London: University of Nebraska Press, 2002.

———. *Washington and the Riddle of Peace*. New York: Macmillan, 1922.

Westinghouse Electric Corporation. "1965 Commemorative Brochure."

———. "Time Capsule II Deposited for 5,000 Years at World's Fair." Press release, October 16, 1965.

———. *Book of Record of the Time Capsule of Cupaloy: Deemed Capable of Resisting the Effects of Time for Five Thousand Years, Preserving an Account of Universal Achievements, Embedded in the Grounds of the New York World's Fair, 1939*. Utica, NY: G. Leonard Gold, 1938.

White House. "Remarks by the President at the National Defense University." Press release, May 23, 2013. http://www.whitehouse.gov/the-press-office/2013/05/23/remarks-president-national-defense-university.

Whitelaw, Lis. *The Life & Rebellious Times of Cicely Hamilton, Actress, Writer, Suffragist*. London: Women's Press, 1990.

Wicke, Jennifer. "Coterie Consumption: Bloomsbury, Keynes, and Modernism as Marketing." In *Marketing Modernisms: Self-Promotion, Canonization, Rereading*. Ed. Kevin J. H. Dettmar and Stephen Watts. Ann Arbor: University of Michigan Press, 1996. 109–32.

Wilder, Gary. "Untimely Vision: Aimé Césaire, Decolonization, Utopia." *Public Culture* 21.1 (Winter 2009): 101–40.

Williams, Paul Whitcomb. "Legitimate Targets in Aërial Bombardment." *American Journal of International Law* 23.3 (July 1929): 570–81.

Williams, T. Harry. *Lincoln and His Generals.* New York: Knopf, 1952.

Wittkower, E., and J. P. Spillane. "A Survey of the Literature of Neurosis in War." In *The Neuroses in War.* Ed. E. Miller. New York: Macmillan, 1940. 1–32.

Wollaeger, Mark A. "Reading *Ulysses*: Agency, Ideology, and the Novel." In *Joyce and the Subject of History.* Ed. Mark A. Wollaeger, Victor Luftig, and Robert Spoo. Ann Arbor: University of Michigan Press, 1996. 83–104.

Wood, Gillen D'Arcy. *Tambora: The Eruption That Changed the World.* Princeton: Princeton University Press, 2014.

Wood, Michael. *The Road to Delphi: The Life and Afterlife of Oracles.* New York: Picador, 2003.

Woodall, James. *Borges: A Life.* New York: Basic, 1996.

Woolf, Virginia. *The Complete Shorter Fiction of Virginia Woolf,* 2nd ed. Ed. Susan Dick. San Diego: Harcourt Brace Jovanovich, 1989.

——. *The Diary of Virginia Woolf.* 5 vols. Ed. Anne Olivier Bell with Andrew McNeillie. New York: Harcourt Brace Jovanovich, 1977–84.

——. *The Essays of Virginia Woolf.* 6 vols. Ed. Andrew McNeillie and Stuart N. Clarke. London: Hogarth Press, 1994–2011.

——. *Jacob's Room.* Orlando, FL: Harcourt, 2008.

——. *The Letters of Virginia Woolf.* 6 vols. Ed. Nigel Nicolson and Joanne Trautmann. New York: Harcourt Brace Jovanovich, 1975–80.

——. *Moments of Being.* Ed. Jeanne Schulkind. San Diego, CA: Harcourt Brace Jovanovich, 1985.

——. *Mrs. Dalloway.* Orlando, FL: Harcourt, 2005.

——. *Three Guineas.* San Diego, CA: Harcourt Brace Jovanovich, 1938.

——. *The Years.* San Diego, CA: Harcourt Brace Jovanovich, 1937.

Yeo, Richard. *Encyclopaedic Visions: Scientific Dictionaries and Enlightenment Culture.* Cambridge: Cambridge University Press, 2001.

Zaleski, Carol. "The Great EB." *The Christian Century,* March 24, 2011. http://www.christiancentury.org/article/2011-03/great-eb.

Žižek, Slavoj. *The Sublime Object of Ideology.* London: Verso, 1989.

Zwerdling, Alex. *Virginia Woolf and the Real World.* Berkeley: University of California Press, 1986.

INDEX

Numbers in boldface type refer to illustrations.